PRINCETON SERIES ON THE MIDDLE EAST

Bernard Lewis and András Hámori, Editors

KABUL UNDER SIEGE

For Constance

KABUL UNDER SIEGE:

Fayz Muhammad's Account of the 1929 Uprising

Translated, abridged, re-worked, and annotated by

R.D. McCHESNEY

Markus Wiener Publishers
Princeton

For information write to: Markus Wiener Publishers
231 Nassau Street, Princeton, NJ 08542

Library of Congress Cataloging-in-Publication Data

Muḥammad, Fayz, d. 1931.
[Kitāb-i taẕakkur-i inqilāb. English]
Kabul under siege: Fayz Muhammad's account of the 1929 Uprising/translated, abridged, re-worked, and annotated by R.D. McChesney.
(Princeton series on the Middle East)
Includes bibliographical references and index.
ISBN 1-55876-154-3 hardcover
ISBN 1-55876-155-1 paper
1. Afghanistan—History I. McChesney, R.D., 1944– .
II. Title. III. Series.
DS369.M8513 1998
958.1—dc21
98-29652
CIP

Markus Wiener Publishers books are printed in the United States of America on acid-free paper, and meet the guidelines for permanence and durability of the committee on production guidelines for book longevity of the council on library resources.

Contents

Maps

Illustrations

Fayz Muhammad "Katib" Hazarah

Preface, Acknowledgments, and Note on Transliteration

For the past two decades, Afghanistan has been known to the rest of the world as a country in the process of meltdown. A decade-long defensive war against a foreign occupier, the Soviet Union, ended in 1989 and immediately transformed itself into a civil war that has been raging ever since. The combatants in this struggle represent themselves, or are represented, as groups with a specific tribal, ethnic, or religious exclusiveness, identities that evoke primordial loyalties. Contextualizing this struggle and trying to understand its roots and motivations is not easy. Though there is a long history underlying the antagonisms and violence of the present, that history (in contrast to the developmental history of the country) has not been very accessible, either because the worldview of the historiographer of Afghanistan does not encompass that history or because the evidence of it has been largely hidden from view.

One such attempt to record a moment in the history of civil violence in Afghanistan is the present work, an unfinished, partially revised memoir of a nine-month period in 1929 at the beginning of which the Afghan government was overthrown by a band of outlaws and throughout which those subalterns and their supporters struggled, ultimately in vain, to consolidate their power against a disparate and uncoordinated resistance. That period presages, in a condensed and technologically somewhat less destructive form, the civil condition of Afghanistan in the 1990s. This memoir, or more accurately the partially completed revision of it, in both its subject matter and tone, stands in sharp contrast to the available triumphalist narratives of that period. The latter view the rise and downfall of the Tajik outlaw who led the uprising as an aberration or rupture in the rightful order of things and a usurpation of the legitimate place of the Pushtuns, the Afghans proper, at the apex of the hierarchy of power. But the author of the memoir, Fayz Muhammad, presents the nine-month period in far starker and, at least today, more recognizable terms. His field of view sweeps over a plain of ethnic, religious, and gender violence and across an amalgam of isolated micro-societies themselves marked by gender, class, and sectarian fault lines.

He depicts a larger "society" in which the motives for, and rhetoric of, civil violence are at the forefront of its history, unobscured by heroic tales of kings and kingly victories and little dampened by overarching structures of law and government. For the 1990s it is a sobering and realistic context for viewing the social condition of the territory marked on modern maps as "Afghanistan."

* * * * * * *

For help on this project, I must particularly acknowledge and thank a true expert on the period, May Schinasi. The information she generously gave helped resolve a number of problems and she often steered me toward sources of which I was otherwise unaware. Because Fayz Muhammad's memoir, unfinished as it is, comes to us only through a Russian translation, the opportunities for introducing or compounding error in the English translation and commentary were innumerable, and her guidance has helped me avoid some of the more egregious. In addition, her own collection of period photographs was put at my disposal to help illustrate this book. I am also indebted to Sayed Askar Mousavi, as knowledgable a person as there is on the Hazarahs, the group to which Fayz Muhammmad belonged, for careful reading of the manuscript and invaluable suggestions and corrections. Over the years Amin Tarzi and Helena Malekyar have encouraged my interest in Fayz Muhammad. In reading various versions of the present work they have frequently emended my misconstruings of Afghan terminology and helped identify people and places, and to them too I am ever grateful. Needless to say, I alone am responsible for errors that do survive here.

Note on Transliteration

On the general principle that full transliteration with diacritics of names and terms (e.g. the family name Muṣāḥibān) originating in the Arabo-Persian alphabet may be more distracting than useful to the readers of this book, I have restricted full transliteration to the notes, glossary, index, and to Persian book titles that appear in the text. Non-English terms are italicized and transliterated only on first occurrence. Otherwise, names and terms are rendered without diacritics (e.g. Musahiban).

The proper names and terminology that appear here have first passed through the filter of the Cyrillic alphabet, and this introduces a layer of complexity to the English form. In all cases (except those few where a Russian name is involved), I have transliterated not the Cyrillicized form (e.g. the term *khazret*) but the Arabo-Persian form (*ḥażrat*), in accordance with the transliteration system of the *International Journal of Middle East Studies*, with two small modifications. The Arabic letter "thā'" I render s̲ rather than just s. The same goes for the Arabic letter "d̲h̲āl "which I transliterate as z̲ rather than z. Where the spelling of a word has wide acceptance in English (Herat instead of Harāt, for example) I have followed common usage. Webster's Ninth New Collegiate Dictionary is the authority for foreign words and place names. Where the Arabo-Persian form of place names could only be guessed at from the Cyrillic, I have followed the Arabo-Persian spellings used in *Qāmūs-i jughrāfiyāʾī Afghānistān* by Muhammad Hakim Nahiz.

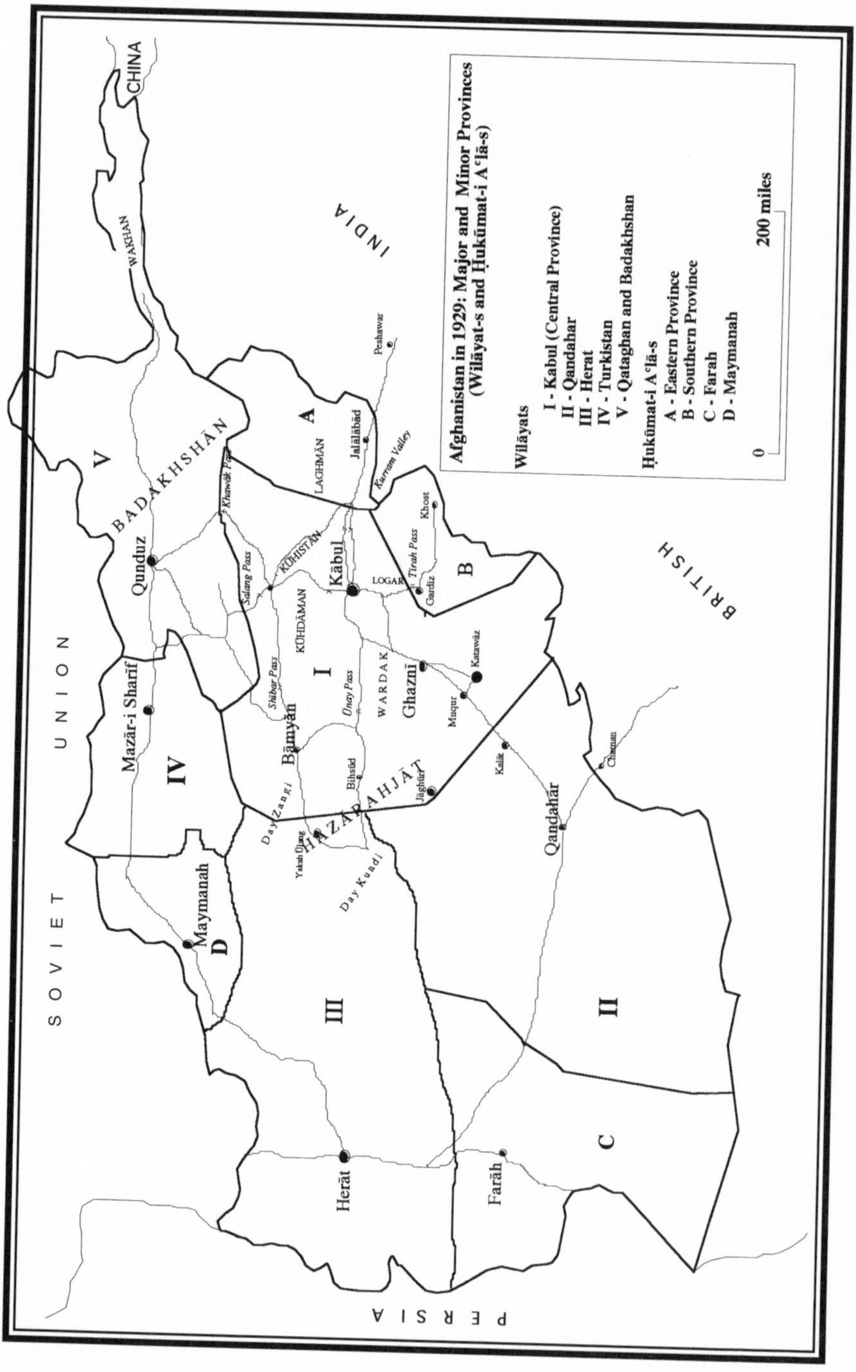

Afghanistan in 1929: Major and Minor Provinces
(Wilāyat-s and Ḥukūmat-i Aʿlā-s)
Wilāyats
I - Kabul (Central Province)
II - Qandahar
III - Herat
IV - Turkistan
V - Qataghan and Badakhshan
Ḥukūmat-i Aʿlā-s
A - Eastern Province
B - Southern Province
C - Farah
D - Maymanah
0
200 miles
SOVIET UNION
CHINA
WAKHAN
INDIA
BRITISH
PERSIA
BADAKHSHAN
Qunduz
Mazār-i Sharīf
Maymanah
Herāt
Farāh
Qandahār
Kābul
Ghaznī
Bāmyān
Jalālābād
Peshawar
LAGHMĀN
KŪHISTĀN
KŪHDĀMAN
LOGAR
WARDAK
HAZĀRAHJĀT
Khawāk Pass
Salang Pass
Shibar Pass
Unay Pass
Tīrah Pass
Kurram Valley
Khost
Gardiz
Katawāz
Muqur
Kalāt
Chaman
Jāghūrī
Bihsūd
Yakah Ūlang
Day Zangī
Day Kundī

Introduction

On January 18, 1929, a Tajik villager from north of the Afghan capital entered the Arg in Kabul, the long-time seat of Afghan rulers, accepted oaths of loyalty from various tribal and urban leaders and so claimed the throne of the Amirate of Afghanistan. His name was Habib Allah and he hailed from Kalakan, a hamlet just east of the main road connecting the capital with the northern part of the country and some twenty miles from the city. In the 1920s those few miles represented a considerable gulf separating Kalakan from a relatively cosmopolitan center with better communications to the outside world than to its own rural regions. The rise of this rural Tajik, an ex-soldier turned highwayman, a "mulberry-eater" as our writer contemptuously refers to him, a man who had spent most of his forty-odd years struggling to make ends meet and provide food for his family, was extraordinary, given the history of the region and the political domination of the Persianized Pushtuns in it. Before his amirate, no non-Pushtun had held the throne at Kabul since the days of the country's birth in the mid-18th century.

Amir Habib Allah
"Bachcha-i Saqqa"

Habib Allah Kalakani was known to his enemies and detractors as "the watercarrier's boy" because his father had been employed in that humble occupation during a stint in the army.[1] Habib Allah seized the throne after a short and surprisingly easy rebellion against the Muhammadzai amir, Aman Allah Khan. Habib Allah's reign lasted only nine months (from January 18 to October 13, 1929), but because of his origins and because his reign was a transition from one dynastic family to another, his short regime has been a subject of considerable interest and debate. Long maligned by the guardians of Muhammadzai history, among whom we must count our author Fayz Muhammad, as a bloodthirsty tyrant whose reign set Afghanistan back "a hundred years," in more recent times the figure of Habib Allah has been given a somewhat different gloss, as a representative of the underclasses in Afghanistan struggling against the oppression of Pushtun domination. His success, however fleeting, has been interpreted as a blow struck for the socioeconomic rights of the historically disadvantaged, rural villagers and peasants.[2]

Although many accounts of Kalakani's nine-month reign have been written, the only known eyewitness account from inside Kabul for most of the period was compiled by a Hazarah historian and minor government official, Fayz Muhammad, known as "Katib" (The Writer).[3] There are a handful of memoirs from the period by individuals in Afghanistan but none have the immediacy of Fayz Muhammad's. Only one other author, Muhyi al-Din Anis, spent any time in Kabul during 1929. His memoir, *Buḥrān wa nijāt* (*Crisis and salvation*), was published after the downfall of the "watercarrier's boy" and was heavily colored by the success of the "savior," Muhammad Nadir Khan, who assumed the throne and the Iranian royal style of "shah" in October 1929. Anis was in Kabul for only the first two months of the siege and by the time he wrote had a broader view of events in the rest of the country.

As an inside account, Fayz Muhammad's narrative provides a rather different perspective on Habib Allah's reign. Part of the value of Fayz Muhammad's work is the narrow and limited view it has of events. His account shows us a very small world limited to the confines of Kabul and its immediate vicinity. Much of the action occurs within a forty or fifty mile radius, close enough so that much of the time the amir and his supporters could commute to the front, wherever it happened to be. At the level of daily routine and the intensely personal, we get a very real sense of the uncertainty that residents of Kabul felt during this time as fighting waxed and waned in the vicinity of the capital and one group after another rose in opposition and then disappeared from view. The reader feels the effects of the siege, the unpredictability of its outcome, and the mood swings created by every bit of news that filtered through: rumor and the inferences drawn from official proclamations, by carefully reading the official newspaper of the new regime, the *Ḥabīb al-Islām*, from the sight of trucks depositing wounded at hospitals in Kabul, or from the sound of distant gunfire. In reading the account one feels the cycles of elation and depression, hope and despair, that many people in the city must have experienced, whether supporters or enemies of the new regime. Fayz

Muhammad knew very little of what the deposed amir, Aman Allah, was up to during the four months in which he attempted to mount a campaign from Qandahar to reclaim his amirate. He said nothing at all about distant Herat.

Fayz Muhammad's narrative makes a major contribution to history in its coverage, however partisan, of the activities of the Hazarah people during the first seven months of Kalakani's reign. The detail that he provides is found nowhere else. Anis, for example, gives the Hazarahs credit for resisting Habib Allah but says very little about them otherwise.[4]

In Fayz Muhammad's account we hear the constant drumbeat of ethnic and sectarian loyalties and conflicts and the ways in which ethnicity and sectarianism shaped worldviews and assumptions, inspired the public rhetoric, and determined policy. Economic grievances or calls to loyalties transcending tribe, sect, or family seem to have played no role whatsoever. One finds little hint of common interests that might be presumed to derive from living in a unified territory in a nominal nation-state. Kabul, rather than representing the interests of the country as a whole, seems mostly to have stood in people's minds as the key to power and, through power, wealth for their own group. Besides being the center for the taxation and customs departments that channeled the surplus wealth of the countryside to the city, and therefore a place of bureaucratic expertise, after 1919 Kabul was also the site of foreign embassies which were a potent symbol of, and potential channel for, the wealth of the outside world. Within the memory of all parties to the struggle, the British Legation had been the source of a large cash subsidy that lasted for many decades, supporting the royals and their retainers and helping them pay the military which kept them in power. In exchange, the Afghan government allowed the British to manage their relations with the rest of the world. With full independence in 1919, other embassies opened, each representing possible sources of income whether in the form of public works projects, military equipment, or outright cash grants. Control of the city then, as today, not only sanctioned claims to political supremacy, it was also understood to be the sine qua non of international recognition. And international recognition had meant, at least since the days of ᶜAbd al-Rahman Khan (r. 1880–1901), the influx of foreign money.

In 1929 Kabul was the capital of a country that lacked much evidence

Amir ᶜAbd al-Rahman with Habib Allah

of national integration. There was virtually no infrastructure of communications and transportation. There was no industrial base in the manufacturing, financial, or extractive sectors. Agriculture was small-scale and unmechanized. Granted, Afghanistan's main cities—Kabul, Qandahar, Herat, and Mazar-i Sharif—and some of its larger towns—Jalalabad, Maymanah, Qunduz, Ghazni, and Khost—were knit together by a centralized officialdom and by telegraph wires, if not by all-weather roads. But the vast expanse of the country, nearly the size of Texas, was isolated from those urban points and generally resistant (more so in the east than the west) to efforts by Kabul to assert its jurisdiction. The demarcated territory known as Afghanistan (or more commonly known within the country as "Afghanistan and Afghan Turkistan"), a landlocked region in the heart of Asia, is defined not by topographic features—no seas, deserts, or mountains give it natural boundaries—nor by ethnic, communal, economic, or social bonds. Afghanistan as it existed in 1929 and as it exists today is the product of the strategic imagination of one superpower, Great Britain, with the compliance and cooperation, if not always willing, of another, Russia (later the Soviet Union).

Afghanistan's international borders were drawn during the last three decades of the 19th century, at the initiative of and generally in accordance with the concern of Britain for the security of its colonial possessions in South Asia. A nation of nations was thereby created, a grab bag of ethnic groups with little in common historically, speaking three distinct languages—Pashto, Persian, and Turkish (not to mention hundreds of dialects)—and with identities so local that in the middle of the twentieth century people in Qandahar thought of Kabulis as just as foreign as someone from Germany or China. The larger communities to which the Pushtuns, Uzbeks, Turkmens, Tajiks, and Hazarahs of Afghanistan still belong are trans-national. The larger Pushtun community lies on both sides of the eastern boundary of the country, the notorious Durand Line. The Uzbeks and Turkmens look to the north for their communities, the Tajiks to a larger Persian cultural world to the north and west and the Hazarahs to Iran, the home of their fellow Twelver Shi^{c}ites. When Fayz Muhammad, not just a writer but also one of the leaders of the Hazarah community in Afghanistan, sought political mediation with his own government officials, he turned not to his representatives in the National Assembly but to the Iranian Embassy. Before claiming authority over the cultural and ethnic amalgam that was Afghanistan, any would-be wielder of power had to reckon with the ways in which the people he governed were linked to communities across borders.

Within the territory itself, history produces little evidence of a national sense of belonging or loyalty extending much beyond family, clan, and village. Instances of apparent unity in the face of outside aggression—the First Afghan War of 1839–42, the second conflict with the British spanning 1878–80, and the War of Independence in 1919—have all been local affairs, involving small segments of the population operating in limited areas. When the conflict with the outsider has involved the entire country territorially, as in the case of the recent ten-year jihad against the Soviet Union and its aftermath, the response has also been decidedly local, organized on tribal, clan, family, ethnic, or sectarian lines and focused not on national but on local objectives.

In the decade of the 1920s, the internal political situation was inflamed by the state-building efforts of an ambitious and politically naive head of state, Amir Aman Allah. The preceding twenty years or so of laissez-faire rule from Kabul by his father, Habib Allah Khan (r. 1901ā1919), the son of the great political consolidator, ^{c}Abd al-Rahman, had been relatively calm. Aman Allah seemed captivated by what was happening in the rest of the world and by what he imagined his place in history was going to be. It was an age of political and social upheaval, of nations claiming the

Amir Habib Allah Khan,
son of ᶜAbd al-Rahman Khan

Amir Aman Allah Khan

right of self-determination, and of colonial power collapsing everywhere. For the Russian, Austro-Hungarian, and Ottoman Empires, the Great War in Europe had been the end of the road. Their collapse had profound psychological and material repercussions on emerging nations around the world. The postwar world seemed made for a new breed of politician, a Lenin, an Ataturk, a Riza Khan, reformers who would stamp out the legacy of the past, seize hold of the future, and revive and restore their lands to glory. Aman Allah seems to have caught this mood, encouraged by the "Young Afghans," an indigenous group of reform-minded people whose ideas had been allowed to develop more or less unhindered in the decade and a half before he came to power in 1919. But these men were for the most part Kabulis, people who seemed unaware that Afghanistan was not Iran, Russia, Turkey, or Japan but a place with a markedly different past, one in which the signs of national sentiment for, or a sense of belonging to, a territory or nation called Afghanistan were conspicuous by their absence.

In Fayz Muhammad's time, Afghanistan had what might be called five distinctive "cultural zones." First, there was an urban zone comprising the four major cities and the tenuous links provided by the technology of the time that held them together—in the 1920s, the telegraph and the motor car. These cities were home to a rentier and merchant class that set the political and cultural agenda. Among the landlords, traders, shopkeepers, government officials, and soldiers, the urbanized Pushtun dominated, and among the Pushtuns the Muhammadzai royal clan was paramount.

Second was the tribal zone that covered what was called in 1929 the Eastern and Southern Provinces (comparable today to the provinces of Nangarhar and Paktiya respectively). This region was and still is the homeland of the Pushtun (Pathan, Pashtun) tribes, the Shinwari, Mohmand, Kakar, Mangal, Khugyani, Jaji, Ahmadzai, Ghilzai, Safi, and many others. Here politics has always been local in the extreme, centering on village and clan, and governed by senior tribesmen (*maliks*, *khan*s) and *jirgah*s (tribal councils). The tribal zone provided the military resources of the urban zone but on a militia, or plunder-as-you-go, basis. Tribal volunteers were always available because war was an opportunity to make money or acquire weapons, which amounted in the end to the same thing. But calling out tribal militias was a double-edged sword and could be as disastrous as it might be useful. Fayz Muhammad's account of Habib Allah Kalakani's reign gives a good picture of the fluidity of political alliances and the mutability of promises and oaths, as well as giving a bureaucrat's-eye view of the frustrations felt within the urban zone when dealing with the Pushtun tribes.

The third zone was the mountainous region in the center and northeast corner of the country, the former area known as the Hazarahjat and the latter as Badakhshan. The Hazarahjat is a web of mountain valleys in the Kuh-i Baba Range protected intermittently by difficult and easily defended passes. The Unay Pass played a major role in the 1929 events as a prime battleground between the Tajik government and the Hazarahs of the region, and the Shibar and Salang Passes were points of conflict both in 1929 between Tajik and Hazarah and again, in 1997, between the Pushtun Taliban and local Hazarah militias. Badakhshan played no role at all during the regime of Habib Allah Kalakani, or at least Fayz Muhammad had nothing to say about it.

The Hazarahjat is the homeland of the Hazarahs, a distinctive people probably formed over a long period from the intermingling of an aboriginal mountain people with waves of Turkish, Mongol, and Iranian invaders. What sets the Hazarahs apart is their almost universal devotion to Twelver or Imami Shiᶜism in the midst of profoundly Sunni populations. Hazarah villages are distinguished by *ḥusayniyah*s, community centers where the Shiᶜi holidays are celebrated, especially the mourning period for the Imam Husayn during the first ten days of Muharram (the first month of the Muslim calendar). Sectarian differences especially between Hazarah and Pushtun have been the flashpoint of recurrent antagonism over the years, as today, and at one particular time they led to a genocidal campaign conducted against the Hazarahs by ᶜAbd al-Rahman in the 1890s. That campaign has been characterized by pro-Muhammadzai historians as suppression of a "rebellion." But it was only a particularly dramatic evocation of the hostility that the Sunni populations of Afghanistan, especially of the tribal groups of the east, have displayed toward the Shiᶜite Hazarahs. The vicious fight for control of the Shibar Pass in the spring of 1997 between Hazarahs and the predominantly Pushtun (and therefore Sunni) Taliban forces and the slaughter of Taliban in their abortive attempt to take Mazar-i Sharif in May 1997 are but the latest manifestations of this deeply-rooted antipathy.[5] A dominant theme in Fayz Muhammad's account of the reign of Habib Allah Kalakani is the ethnic and sectarian antagonism between Pushtun and Hazarah.

The fourth zone was the western highland plain with the oasis and city of Herat at the center, a region with a long and proud history of ties not to the Afghan east but to the Iranian west. Herat was the center of its region, long known as Khurasan, under the Safavid state in the sixteenth and seventeenth centuries. In the mid-eighteenth century it came under the control of the newly formed empire of Ahmad Shah Abdali, himself from this cultural zone. But as his dynasty became "Afghanized" in the course of the second half of the 18th century, and found its support among the Afghan tribes of the east, Herat became a distant appanage as far as the Afghan capital was concerned. In the eighteenth and early nineteenth centuries, Herat developed its cultural and economic ties with the Zand and Qajar states of Iran. Well into the nineteenth century those who governed Herat, nominally on behalf of their relatives in Kabul, actually paid tribute to the Qajar governor of Mashhad. In 1837–38 the Qajar ruler of

Persia, Muhammad Shah, conducted a long but ultimately unsuccessful siege of Herat in an attempt to restore it to Iran. He was thwarted not by Kabul's intervention but by the British, who feared its capture by the Iranians would benefit Russia. British warships were sent to Kharg Island in the Persian Gulf and threatened war unless the shah withdrew from Herat. This decided the outcome and kept Herat firmly within Afghan borders. Twenty years later, in October 1856, the army of another Qajar shah, Nasir al-Din, actually occupied Herat but was forced to relinquish it the following spring, again under intense British pressure. In an ironic twist, in the aftermath of the Second Afghan War of 1880, the British government of India actually proposed to cede Herat and Sistan to Iran, but the negotiations came to nothing. Despite the fact that Herat has remained within the borders of Afghanistan ever since, Iran's influence and interest in its culture, economy, and political affairs have remained strong.

The fifth zone was the Turkish north, or "Afghan Turkistan" as it was referred to by the Afghan government itself in the 1920s and before. Outside the urban center of Mazar-i Sharif, Afghan Turkistan was and still is demographically dominated by "Turks"—i.e. Uzbeks, Turkmens, and a smattering of Qirghiz (Kyrgyz)—despite the efforts to relocate Pushtuns and Hazarahs there during and after ᶜAbd al-Rahman's time. From time immemorial this region, separated from the Pushtun lands by the Hindu Kush and Kuh-i Baba ranges, was culturally and politically oriented northward to the oases of Bukhara and Samarqand. It was only with the final conquest of the region by the Afghans in the mid-nineteenth century that control over the region was completely surrendered by Bukhara and transferred to Kabul. Yet topography (in winter the Shibar, Salang, and Khawak Passes could be closed by snow for several months, requiring communications from the capital to go the very roundabout route through Herat), lack of an Afghan infrastructure (roads, railways, or telecommunications), and cultural and ethnic heritage continue to tie the region to the lands, now countries, north of the Oxus (Amu) River. The Soviet period created something of an artificial hiatus in those ties but they have now been resumed.

Each of these zones makes its own particular demands on any effort at political centralization or state building. Even after the most intense era of political consolidation experienced in the region—the twenty-one years of ʿAbd al-Raḥman Khan's regime from 1880 to 1901—when exile, mass repression, and summary and exemplary uses of capital punishment were all employed on behalf of an emerging state, these zones maintained their cultural and political distinctiveness.

All the zones share a religio-political vernacular that is still in use. This is a language with many facets, simultaneously expressing a heritage of common purpose and a history marked by conflict and division. The focal point of the discourse is the Shariʿah, a term often translated "Islamic law" but really more appropriately, and literally, translated as the "Islamic Way" since Shariʿah in theory touches on all aspects of the believer's life.

Fayz Muhammad's work is laced with, one might almost say founded on, this language and what it invokes. When individuals whose ethnic, class, or occupational identities otherwise differ address each other and want to stress commonality and solidarity, it is not as Afghans or Kabulis, or as fellow human beings, but as "Muslims" or "Believers," citizens not of a territory called Afghanistan but of a larger non-territorially based entity known as "the community of Islam," which could be as extensive as circumstances warranted. The "Islamic kingdom" could coincide with the territory of the demarcated Afghanistan or it could extend well beyond those boundaries.

When used to express separateness and antipathy, the language invoking Shariʿah favors the charge of the violation of the Shariʿah, of acting contrary to the Islamic Way and of an individual's being, therefore, godless, irreligious, an unbeliever (*kafir*). The Islamic idiom, in both its appeals to a common heritage and in its accusations of irreligion and unbelief, was the lingua franca of politics in 1929 and, apparently, today as well, a language common to all parties but only at its most general (and least influential), a language of community. In 1929, the basis for accusing an individual or group of unbelief (*kufr*) seems to have been nothing more than simple political opposition. When differences seemed irreconcilable, the heavy language guns were rolled out and the opposition bombarded with accusations of unbelief. The terms of the discourse are uncompromising and unambiguous. One's opponent violates the Shariʿah, destroys the religion of God and His prophet, and thus becomes a kafir and deserves death. Fayz Muhammad's work is replete with such formulations of positional rigidity. The attraction of the "violation of

Shari^cah" charge is its consummate clarity. The speaker seizes the moral high ground and consigns his opponent to a well-deserved Hell. Afghanistan's political leaders needed and still need to master and manipulate this language and somehow adapt their own actions to it. Popular opposition is a consequence of failure to use and control the Islamic idiom. For example, Aman Allah's failure to take account of the operative rhetoric of his political arena (while trying to use the language of modernization and progress with its implicit secularism) and to defuse it or co-opt its practitioners in some fashion was in large part responsible for his inability to achieve changes comparable to what his contemporaries in other regions of the world were managing.

In this rhetorical field, Aman Allah's activist social policies seem particularly ill-advised. He began his career with enormous psychological advantages, given the historical tendency of the territory over which he reigned toward localism and separatism. He played to the hilt his role as holy warrior (*ghāzī*) against Christendom in the short war with Great Britain in 1919 that cost Afghanistan its British subsidy but won it full control over its foreign relations. Initially, in sharp contrast to his later initiatives, his actions in the social sphere were those of a Muslim conservative and seem to have been geared to winning the approval of the mulla networks. He appears to have tried to rein in some of the tendency toward European dress of his father's age and what it represented to the conservative clerics of an official policy encouraging greater public freedom for women. He is reported to have forbidden women to appear without veils in public or to wear European dress.[6] Only much later would he reverse course on this issue. He was also aware of the favorable way in which he was viewed by Muslims in India after he had gained full independence from the British. Indian Muslims had long been an influential force in Afghanistan as educators, bureaucrats, and merchants and were an important line of communication between the highlands of Afghanistan and the northern Indian plain. By the early 1920s, there was some support among Indian Muslims for Aman Allah to accept the position of Caliph of Islam, a post vacant since the collapse of the Ottoman Empire and the secularist policy of the new ruler of its now-shrunken territories, Kemal Ataturk. This vision probably inclined Aman Allah to a more Islamist public posture. Besides pulling the British lion's tail with overtures to the Muslims under British rule, Aman Allah also allowed his international ambitions to wander northward where backers of the new Soviet government in Russia were struggling against nationalist and Islamist resistance forces in what was formerly the tsarist governorate-general of Turkestan and the amirate of Bukhara. Until the middle of 1922, at least, Aman Allah gave material support and refuge to the resistance forces fighting north of the Amu Darya. But under pressure from the Soviet Government his active involvement in Transoxiana ceased. After 1922 he appears to have largely abandoned whatever dreams he may have had of world status as preeminent pan-Islamic figure and instead turned his energies to his own land.

In the social, political, economic, and legal realms of his country, Aman Allah's activities are embodied in the laws promulgated by him. They were first offered for ratification to a grand assembly (*loya jirgah*) of delegates sent to Kabul from all over the country in 1923. These laws were contained in a series of publications called *niẓām-nāmah*s, each dealing with a specific subject—taxation, marriage, the building of a governmental complex (Dar al-Aman), a constitution, prisons, official titles and offices, and the budget, among many others. Although he asserted the underlying authority of the Shari^{c}ah for this legislation, the ordinances

Dar al-Aman (Dar al-Habib), Chihil Sutun palace, background

presented in this legislation were seen by many as actually contravening the spirit of the Shari[c]ah and removing much legal authority from the hands of Muslim judges, the *qāẓīs*. Particularly troublesome to the delegates were the rules governing marriage. Polygamy was discouraged by taxing second, third, and fourth wives. Marriages had to be registered, child marriages were forbidden, and proposals were made to regulate the payment of bride price.[7] The regulation of the place of women in society proved to be the most explosive issue of Aman Allah's reign and the one most easily exploited by opponents of greater central government control of the countryside.

On the economic front, the ending of the British subsidy was partly offset by Soviet aid. But the expenses of Aman Allah's government, establishing and maintaining foreign embassies, purchasing military hardware and the equipment needed for domestic development (cement, pipe, and telegraph poles, for example) were comparatively large. To economize he cut back on tribal subsidies and government salaries, himself setting a personal model for thrift. But the cuts in tribal subsidies were not appreciated outside Kabul and the cuts in officials' salaries must have been in part responsible for the rise in corruption that is a central theme of Fayz Muhammad's condemnation of Aman Allah's regime. Furthermore, to help him develop and implement his policies, Aman Allah had invited a number of Turkish technicians, military and legal advisors, and other foreigners whose presence and high salaries were an affront to Afghans.

In 1924, the Mangal tribe from Khost in the Southern Province rebelled. There were several motives behind the uprising. One source says that the nizam-namah on passports that would have restricted passage for the eastern tribes across the Durand Line (the eastern border of the country) was a major factor in the rebellion.[8] But other social issues seem to have been at least as much to blame. Fayz Muhammad has an interesting passage giving a local perspective on the rebellion which is worth quoting in full here:

> In 1303, equivalent to 1924 in the Christian calendar, a manual on public punishments translated from Turkish[9] was published with corrections and addenda. It was prepared by a great military officer from Turkey,

> Jamal,[10] was approved by the Consultative Assembly (*hayʾat-i shūrā*), and a group of ulama, the Chief Justice, ᶜAbd al-Shukur Khan, Mulla ᶜAbd al-Wasiᶜ Kakari, Qazi ᶜAbd al-Rahman Begtuti, and other scholars of the Hanafite [Sunni legal] school, and so took effect. Some of its provisions were very controversial among pseudo-mullas who lacked any knowledge of the Shariᶜah. These included the prohibition of polygamy and child marriage, the imposition of property taxes, and other regulations aimed at ending strife and violence between obstinate and benighted people who, out of baseness and an absence of any sense of honor, consider a fine of five rupees as more shameful than anything else. The mullas used these provisions to incite general discontent and rebellion. As a consequence of the insolent, brazen, and deceitful actions of the district chiefs (*ᶜalāqahdār*s), governors (*ḥākim*s), and military officers, the bribery of ministers, judges and clerks, the ignoring of the pleas of the needy, the increases in the land tax and customs duties, the military draft, and many other things, discontent toward the government sprang up among the citizenry.
>
> At this time a man from the Mangal tribe laid claim to a woman to whom he said he was betrothed, declaring that he had been engaged to her in childhood. But some enemies of his went to the governor, ᶜAmr al-Din Khan, and the qazi-magistrate, Mulla ᶜAbd Allah, and challenged his claim. With the consent of the fiancée, ᶜAmr al-Din rejected the man's claim. But the magistrate had taken a bribe to see that the girl was betrothed to the plaintiff and so was unhappy with the way this dispute was settled. He sent the governor a letter of protest, asserting that the Shariᶜah had been violated. The governor paid no attention to him and so Mulla ᶜAbd Allah made up his mind to instigate a rebellion. By inciting the plaintiff and appealing to the Pushtun honor of the tribal elders, he was able to ignite the flames of hatred and discord. With appeals, incitements, and promises of Paradise for true-believing Muslims, Mulla ᶜAbd Allah, the "Lame," succeeded in raising all the tribes of the Southern Province against the government. The war lasted for a year and two months. Fourteen thousand people perished and the cost to the government was 30 million rupees. Moreover, Islamic society suffered great material and spiritual loss. Thanks to this war, what comes to mind when the names of Amir Aman Allah Khan and Mulla ᶜAbd Allah are mentioned are the Monument of Knowledge and Ignorance (*Manār-i ᶜilm wa jahl*), with the list of dead soldiers carved on it, and the Victory Arch (*ṭāq-i ẓafar*) at Paghman.[11]

The rebellion lasted most of the year and was suppressed only at great human, political, and economic cost. The concessions that had to be made to win support from other tribes against the Mangal proved to be at the expense of Aman Allah's social reforms. But what eventually precipitated his downfall was the unwise decision to make a grand tour of European capitals in 1928, a costly undertaking that produced little benefit for Afghanistan internationally and alienated the powerful at home. Photographs of Aman Allah's wife, Queen Soraya, bare-faced and bare-shouldered, sitting with men not related to her, circulated widely in the tribal zone and inflamed Islamist sensibilities.

Queen Soraya, wife of Aman Allah

By late June 1928 Aman Allah had returned home. He convened another consultative assembly to review proposed new reforms inspired by his European experiences. Had they been implemented, the reforms would have led to a round of new taxes and would have required the Muslim clergy, the mullas, to take government examinations in order to teach Islamic subjects. Popular discontent grew, and in mid-November 1928 the Shinwari, a notoriously uncooperative tribe, attacked government posts around Jalalabad, cut the telegraph wires, and blocked the road to the capital. They drafted a manifesto of ten grievances, five of which related to what they saw as Aman Allah's insupportable meddling with the status of women. The stage was now set for the emergence of the Tajik outlaw from Kalakan.

Fayz Muhammad: His Life and Works

We need now to situate our author, Fayz Muhammad, in the Afghan context. Fayz Muhammad was a Hazarah and his career, given the expectations most Hazarahs would probably have had at the time, was quite remarkable. Outside their homeland in the Hazarahjat, the Hazarahs have long been limited to the most menial of professions, and it is an indication of Fayz Muhammad's unusual talents and willingness to endure lifelong discrimination that he was able to carve out a respectable and respected career in the capital in service to two successive rulers, Amir Habib Allah and his son, Aman Allah.

He was born and spent his early years in the village of Zard Sang in the Qarabagh district, some thirty miles southwest of the city of Ghazni, itself about ninety miles southwest of Kabul. His father, Sa^{c}id Muhammad, and his grandfather, Khudaydad, belonged to the Muhammad Khwajah clan (*qawm*) of the Hazarahs. It is uncertain when Fayz Muhammad was born. Some believe his birth should be dated to 1279 Hijri (1862–63) while others prefer a date ten years later, 1289 Hijri (1872).[12] The date and place of his death are undisputed. He died in Kabul on March 3, 1931.

In Qarabagh, he studied Arabic and the Koran under the guidance of Twelver Shi^{c}i mullas. Then in 1880 he moved to the district of Nawar, northwest of Ghazni, and later the same year to Qandahar, apparently because of sectarian strife in Nawar. In 1887, he left Qandahar for a year's travel that took him to Lahore and Peshawar, where he spent some time studying English and Urdu. We do not know what drew him to the Punjab and then back to Afghanistan. The biographical material available about him is slight and largely secondhand, based on occasional information he himself provides in his works and on stories told by his children and students.

In the *Sirāj al-tawārīkh*, his most famous work, he writes, "This humble writer who had gone from Qandahar to Lahore as a student and from there had come to Jalalabad [while the court was spending the winter there] by way of Peshawar was befriended by a courtier (*pīshkhidmat*), Ja^{c}far Ali Khan, the son of Baz Ali Khan Jaghuri [a fellow Hazarah]."[13] In this way, he managed to attach himself to the court. The amir, ^{c}Abd al-Rahman, returned to Kabul on April 23, 1888, and when he did Fayz Muhammad was a member of the royal party. Later, the amir assigned him to the entourage of the heir-apparent, Habib Allah, as a secretary. It was from this occupation that his nickname *Kātib*, "The Writer," was derived and by which he is generally known among Hazarahs today.

We know that Fayz Muhammad accompanied Habib Allah in late 1893 from Kabul to the winter palace in Jalalabad, for there is a manuscript of 230 folios, a copy of a collection of decrees of the late seventeenth-century Moghul ruler of India, Awrangzib, the son of Shah Jahan, that he copied and dated 29 Rajab 1311 (February 5, 1894), which places him in Jalalabad.[14] He seems to have been a favorite of the prince's and to have grown in his esteem as time passed. There is no sign of how the vicious genocidal war against the Hazarahs, fought by his patron's father from the spring of 1891 to the fall of 1893, affected their relations. Habib Allah seems to have retained confidence in his secretary, though the evidence is not particularly overwhelming. About the only thing we know of him during these years is that when the crown prince's younger brother, Nasr Allah, toured England on a state visit in 1895, Habib Allah assigned Fayz Muhammad to copy the detailed letters sent back by his brother and post them in the main market in Kabul so that "noble and commoner alike would be apprised of the honor and respect that the English were according him."[15]

Sometime after Habib Allah came to the throne in October 1901, Fayz Muhammad became involved with the Young Afghan and Constitutionalist movements. An Afghan historian, ᶜAbd al-Hayy Habibi, has written that he was one of the first constitutionalists in the country.[16] Around 1909–10 he was jailed briefly for his activities but went back to working for the amir on his release. He also is said to have been associated with the publication of the reformist journal, *Sirāj al-Akhbār*, and three other newspapers, *Anīs*, *Ḥayy ᶜalaʾl-falāḥ*, and *Āʾīnah-i ᶜirfān*. He continued his practice as a copyist, and some six thousand pages of manuscript copied by him are said to survive.

But he was also commissioned to write compositions of his own. One of them was a detailed history of Afghanistan for Habib Allah Khan, a three-volume work entitled *Tuḥfat al-Ḥabīb* (*Habib's Gift*). The first volume was finished in 1902. A. I. Shkirando, the Russian translator of Fayz Muhammad's memoir of the 1929 events, was struck when examining the manuscript of *Tuḥfat* in the Afghan National Archives by the degree to which the manuscript had been red-penciled, probably by Habib Allah himself.[17] For whatever reason, the work was never published, although the manuscript did survive, at least into the 1980s.[18]

Despite his unhappiness with the *Tuḥfat al-Ḥabib*, the amir did not lose confidence in his Hazarah scribe and he ordered him to begin again. Fayz Muhammad was able to incorporate much of the presumably corrected material from the *Tuḥfat* into what would be his great legacy as a historian, the massive, multi-volumed work entitled *Sirāj al-tawārīkh* (*The Lamp of Histories*—an allusion to the amir's royal style "The Lamp of the Nation and Religion," *Sirāj al-millah wa'l-dīn*). The work was to cover the history of the country from the time of Aḥmad Shah down through the reign of Habib Allah Khan. But it too had publishing problems, being withdrawn from the press partway through the printing of the third volume.[19] According to an Afghan historian, Muhammad Ghubar, publication of the third volume, which was supposed to cover ᶜAbd al-Raḥman Khan's entire reign, was halted in mid-sentence at page 1240 for unspecified reasons, but he notes that, although orders were given for the destruction of the printed volumes, many made their way into private hands.[20]

According to a Soviet historian and Afghan specialist, V. A. Romodin, the process of publishing the third volume lasted several years. Although the title page bears the date 1333 H. (1914–15), publication ground to a halt only after Habib Allah's death in 1919.[21] It is difficult to say when the presses were stopped, but Romodin's view that it was during Aman Allah's reign (1919–29) would seem to be correct. Habib Allah himself insisted on reading over the manuscript before it went to the press and his notes are found in the margins of the manuscript of volume one, which was kept in the Foreign Ministry in Kabul. The *Sirāj al-akhbār*, the reformist journal edited by Mahmud Tarzi and published in Kabul, carried advertisements for the *Sirāj al-tawārīkh* from early 1916 until at least as late as mid-1917. These advertisements describe volumes one and two (up to the reign of ᶜAbd al-Rahman) as available and volumes three (ᶜAbd al-Rahman's reign) and four (Habib Allah's) as "in press."[22] Unless this editorial process broke down and pages slipped by the amir's vigilant eye, there is little reason to think objectionable material would have gotten as far as the Government Press before anyone noticed, at least during Habib Allah's lifetime.

After securing the throne in the late winter of 1919, Aman Allah at first showed interest in this project of chronicling the history of the Afghan state. In mid-1920, typesetting for the third volume resumed and it probably went on for at least a year. A *farmān* issued by the amir on May 5, 1920 (16 S̲awr 1299) announced that Fayz Muhammad had been ordered to complete the *Sirāj* and then begin work on a chronicle of the reign of Aman Allah himself, to be named *Tārīkh-i ᶜaṣr-i Amānīyah.*[23] There is some reason to believe that he did indeed carry out these commissions, although nothing more was ever published and the manuscripts of volume four and the *Tārīkh-i ᶜaṣr-i Amānīyah* have not turned up.[24]

The reason it took so long (from 1915 to 1920) for the third volume to be printed may have been Fayz Muhammad's method of work under Habib Allah, apparently bringing batches of manuscript for approval and then shipping the approved text to the press. Aman Allah, on the other hand, may have adopted a different technique of reviewing the work, perhaps checking pages as they were printed rather than in manuscript. Sometime after the May 1920 farman was issued he apparently read and was angered by sections from the third volume dealing with Anglo-Afghan relations, for he did an about-face and ordered the presses stopped and all the printed but still incomplete copies of the third volume seized and burned.[25] Luckily, "people of good literary taste" (*ashkhāṣ bā-z̲awq*), in Ghubar's words, managed to make off with several of the 860-page volumes before the order could be carried out.[26] The unpublished remainder of the third volume, some 416 folios of manuscript, was eventually turned over to the National Archives by Fayz Muhammad's son, ᶜAli Muhammad.[27]

The *Sirāj al-tawārīkh*, especially the surviving part of the third volume, has earned Fayz Muhammad the accolade, "a modern-day Bayhaqi"—comparing him to the great twelfth century historian of eastern Iran.[28] The whole printed work is 1,240 quarto pages, approximately 800,000 words, and covers the history and geography of Afghanistan from 1747 to 1896. The early history (down through the mid-nineteenth century) is based on chronicle sources, which the author lists at the beginning. The last part of this massive work—all of volume three (which is two-thirds of the whole)—is derived from documentary and eyewitness accounts. In it Fayz Muhammad reproduces document after document—decrees, entire administrative manuals, treaties, and letters—organizing them into a chronological format. The work remains largely unused by historians of Afghanistan, partly because the third volume is hard to find, and partly because of its size. One of the ironic aspects of the current struggle in Afghanistan today is the heightened interest in Iran in Fayz Muhammad as a representative of the beleaguered Twelver Shiᶜite communities in Afghanistan. As a consequence, efforts are ongoing in Iran to publish his work and study his life.[29]

After Habib Allah Khan's assassination in February 1919, Fayz Muhammad's regular job was at the Ministry of Education, where he worked on textbook revision. Sometime later, he was appointed to a teaching position at the Habibiyah Lycée in Kabul. How important a figure he may have been within the Afghan government is difficult to gauge. As already mentioned he continued his work on the chronicle at least through 1919. In late December 1919, a Soviet mission headed by Yakov Z. Suritz[30] reached Kabul. One of its members, I. M. Reisner, remembered the presence at the amir's court of Fayz Muhammad, who attended all the audiences and receptions but stayed at the back and kept himself out of the limelight.[31] It is clear then that as long as Aman Allah's interest in the chronicle project continued, Fayz Muhammad had access to the court.

Besides the Soviet record of his activities in Kabul during Aman Allah's reign, two Iranians, Hajji Mirza ᶜAbd al-Muhammad Muᵓaddib al-Sultan and Sayyid Mahdi Farrukh have published information about Fayz Muhammad. In 1927, toward the end of Aman Allah's reign, Farrukh, who was the Iranian ambassador in Kabul, compiled a "who's who" of contemporary Afghan leaders.[32] One of the worthies he includes is Fayz Muhammad, describing him as a devout Shiᶜite who was a leader among his own people, the Hazarahs, and was also highly regarded by the Shiᶜite Qizilbash community of Kabul. He also notes that Fayz Muhammad was an important source of information for the Iranian mission about what was going on in the capital.[33] Certainly Fayz Muhammad was helpful to Sayyid Mahdi not only as an informant but also as a contributor, wittingly or otherwise, to the ex-ambassador's book *Tārīkh-i siyāsī-yi Afghānistān.*[34]

Mirza ᶜAbd al-Muhammad, a resident of Cairo and editor of the Persian-language weekly paper there, *Chihrah-namā*, undertook an ambitious project, a seven-volume compilation called *Amān al-tawārīkh*, a work first proposed to Habib Allah Khan through Mahmud Tarzi and eventually dedicated to Aman Allah but not, to the author's disappointment, ever properly rewarded by the amir. ᶜAbd al-Muhammad visited Afghanistan in 1922 at the invitation of Tarzi, then Foreign Minister. In the course of his two-month stay he met Fayz Muhammad and became acquainted with his work. (Mirza ᶜAbd al-Muhammad also solicited a blurb from Fayz Muhammad that appears in the seventh volume of the *Amān al-tawārīkh*.)

There also exists a single document, a *tamlīk-nāmah* (a transfer of ownership) which Fayz Muhammad drafted in favor of his sons and their mother in 1344 (1925–26). It gives us some information about his wife and about a courtyard house (*yak darband-i ḥawīlī*) of unspecified location that he owned. In the document he conveys ownership of the house to his sons, ᶜAli Muhammad, Wali Muhammad, and Muhammad Mahdi, and their mother, "the daughter of Mirza Khan Baba Khan and granddaughter of Mirza Ahmad ᶜAli."[35]

During the nine months of the Kalakani or Saqqawist regime, Fayz Muhammad spent almost the entire period inside the city, keeping a journal of events for at least the first seven months of the occupation. We have no idea how he lived, for he gives no indication that he still had a salaried position with the government. From June 7 to 29, he was, in his own words, a reluctant, though paid, participant in a delegation sent to negotiate with Hazarah groups opposing the Tajik leader. According to his own account, he managed to subvert the amir's plans and cause the mission to fail. But he and the delegation's leader, Nur al-Din Agha Jawanshir, a Qizilbash Shiᶜite from Kabul, paid a heavy price, both being severely beaten. The Iranian mission in Kabul, under a directive from Riza Shah to do what it could to aid the Shiᶜites of Kabul, sent medicine to Fayz Muhammad's house. He eventually recovered enough to travel the following year to Tehran for more medical care. After somewhat less than a year he returned to Kabul where he died on 6 Shawwal 1349 (March 3, 1931), probably at the age of 68 or 69. His death may or may not have been a result of the beating. He had complained of pain and swelling in his neck on the eve of the delegation's departure for the Hazarahjat and was sick at least twice during the three weeks he was away from the capital. Certainly the beating could have contributed to hastening the progress of something more insidious.

Fayz Muhammad authored many books but only a few have been published.[36] Besides the *Sirāj al-tawārīkh,* only one other work was published in his lifetime. This was a book on prophets and sages of antiquity "from Adam's fall to the appearance of Jesus," published by the Ministry of Education in 1923.[37] Recently, Iranian interest in him has led to the re-publication of parts of the *Sirāj al-tawārīkh* and the issuing of a very important work, his ethnography of Afghanistan entitled *Nizhād-nāmah-i Afghān.*[38] Information from that work had already been used by both ᶜAbd al-Muhammad and Sayyid Mahdi in their own books. ᶜAbd al-Muhammad had been shown both *Sirāj al-tawārīkh* and the ethnography, which was in manuscript and which he calls *Nasab-nāmah-i ṭawā'if-i Afāghinah wa taᶜaddud-i nufūs-i īshān* (*A Genealogy and Census of the Afghan Tribes*) and which he appears to have reproduced in volume five of his work, giving due credit there to Fayz Muhammad.[39] Farrukh used some of it in his *Tārīkh-i siyāsī-yi Afghānistān* along with sections from an unpublished work of Fayz Muhammad called *Fayż-i fuyūżāt*.

Fayz Muhammad's Journal/Narrative of the 1929 Putsch

The present work, which he himself calls *Kitāb-i tazakkur-i* (or *tazkirah-i*) *inqilāb* (*Memoir of the Coup*), has an even more unusual history. As already mentioned, Fayz Muhammad kept a journal during the nine-month reign of Kalakani, but if that has survived, either it is among the papers turned over to the National Archives by his son in 1979 or its whereabouts are unknown. What we have instead of the journal itself is a preliminary reworking of that journal by Fayz Muhammad into a connected narrative. On at least three occasions, in the entries for July 30, August 6, and August 15, he refers to his journal as a separate work, or he uses the phrase "as we will see" a clear sign of the narrative, rather than journalistic, mode of the present work.[40] He must have started the revision either during the Kalakani period or shortly thereafter, probably before leaving for Tehran. He modeled it on the format of the *Sirāj al-tawārikh* and it bears two of the distinctive stylistic hallmarks of that work, the phrases "as we have already mentioned" followed by a brief summary of a preceding discussion and "as we will soon see" followed by a brief outline of something which would happen at a later date and be described more fully when he reached that chronological point. It is clear from the state of the composition as it has reached us that this reworking was never completed. What has come down to us instead appears to be a very early draft, but not the first one, for the author has added marginal notations and corrections in several places and has frequently crossed out words and phrases. The work is also in all probability incomplete. Although all evidence is that Fayz Muhammad remained in Kabul through the entire Kalakani era (January–October 1929) except for the three weeks in June spent in the Hazarahjat, the work that we have breaks off abruptly on August 28.

Besides being incomplete, the work is also quite unpolished and far from the standard Fayz Muhammad set in *Sirāj al-tawārīkh* and *Nizhād-nāmah-i Afghān.* He repeats stories with slight variations as if he had not told them before. The story of the sayyid from Kunar who raises Aman Allah's flag in Kabul is one of many such examples.[41] He confuses names (ᶜAli Aḥmad Khan and Aḥmad ᶜAli Khan, for example). He also makes mistakes in correlating his dates. The work keeps dates in three formats (lunar Muslim, solar Afghan/Muslim, and Christian) and this caused the author problems. He failed to notice that he had two July 10s and so from that point on, the Christian date is one day off. (Here I have dispensed with the two Muslim systems and corrected his error at July 11.) There are numerous inconsistencies that one would have expected the author to correct before publication. On April 14 he says the wives of the Musahiban men (Nadir Khan and his brothers Shah Wali and Shah Mahmud) were arrested and held at the house of Fath Muhammad Khan then the next day he has them being brought to the Arg from the house of the "hazrats" (the Mujaddidis). When he refers to the proclamation in which Habib Allah posts a reward for the capture or killing of Nadir and his brothers, he first says the amount promised by Habib Allah was thirty thousand rupees for any one of them (April 12). Then, in reproducing the proclamation of April 15, he has the reward as forty thousand rupees for Nadir if brought in alive or thirty thousand if dead, and ten thousand for any of his brothers dead or alive. Similarly Mahmud Khan Yawar (an aide-de-camp to Aman Allah) first manages to redeem his life from a death sentence by paying a thirty-five thousand rupee bribe (April 7) but on April 21 is said to have paid a hundred thousand rupees. And in describing Sayyid Husayn's routes and advance towards Mazar-i Sharif, the information diverges considerably over the five-day period May 7 to May 11.

On occasion he says, "as I have already mentioned" when he hasn't (e.g. the story of the Hazarahs of Sar Chashmah sending on a message from the Behsud Hazarahs on April 17). And over and over again, he repeats rote condemnations of Habib Allah and his government that would have had more impact had there been fewer of them and had he altered the wording. One that he particularly liked was to cite Habib Allah's adopted style, "Servant of the Religion of the Prophet of God," and then say that rather than being the servant of the religion, he was its destroyer.

He also introduces a peculiar and inexplicable precision into the work with his frequent notations of the hour of the day. Things happen at "one o'clock" or "five o'clock" or "five-thirty," but how he would have known these precise times or what mention of them is meant to signify is not at all clear. One gets the sense that this is simply a rhetorical device to lend a kind of scientific authority to the writing.

He makes no attempt to hide his feelings and strong prejudices. He has nothing but contempt for the Tajik occupiers of the capital. They are "mulberry-eaters who wear rags for clothing" or "people who have never tasted wheat bread in their lives" and individuals who "yesterday were roaming mountain and steppe and today rule the country." To him they are thieving, vicious, and depraved and Habib Allah is the "king of the thieves" and the "chief debaucher." Sayyid Husayn Charikari, Habib Allah's partner and virtual equal in matters of government, is a "brutal man who has killed hundreds of people." Of all the members of Habib Allah's administration only two are treated with a measure of respect, the Mayor of Kabul, Taj al-Din, and the Minister of Court, Shayr Jan.

Fayz Muhammad tells of numerous sexual offenses on the part of the Tajiks and others supporting them including allegations that the Tajiks, on taking Kabul, used the registration lists from the Masturat Girls School to distribute girls to the soldiers; the efforts of Habib Allah to force his attentions on reluctant women; and tales of the molestation of young boys by the amir's Tajik supporters. He condemns the Tajiks of Kuhistan and

Sayyid Husayn Charikari

Shayr Jan, Minister of Court

Kuhdaman for molesting "women, young girls, and boys" but this formulaic charge is repeated so often that it loses much of its force in the course of the book. (In this abridgement and reworking of his book, I have omitted much of the repetitiveness while trying to preserve what I believe is the force of his accusations.)

His contempt is by no means limited to the Tajiks from the north. He has an extremely low regard for certain Pushtun tribes, especially the Shinwari, Mangal, and Khugyani. Over and over, he condemns them as thieves and looters and as flagrant violators of their oaths and solemn promises. On the other hand, his own people, the Hazarahs, appear as invariably courageous and faithful to their word. When Hazarah leaders act contrary to what he believes to be right, he condemns them as misguided individuals. But his condemnations of the Pushtuns are blanket ones. His feelings about Nadir, the eventual victor in the struggle for Kabul, are mixed. On the one hand, he is continually optimistic that Nadir will come and save Kabul from Habib Allah, although by August there is little indication that the head of the Musahiban family is meeting with much success in his efforts to unite the tribes of the Eastern and Southern

Muhammad Nadir Khan (c. 1920)

Provinces against the Tajik regime. On the other, Fayz Muhammad is severely critical of Nadir when he appears to make a deal with Habib Allah, even though the latter has, in Fayz Muhammad's eyes, dishonored the wives of Nadir and his brothers.

Perhaps his greatest contempt is reserved for the Sunni "pseudo-mullas,"[42] who are responsible in his eyes for encouraging Habib Allah to attack Kabul, but most culpable for their anti-Shi^{c}ism, which culminates in the fatwa issued against the Hazarahs accusing them of being infidels, thereby legalizing attacks against them and the appropriation of their property. Although, for the most part, he does not name these "pseudo-mullas," they almost certainly include leading members of the Mujaddidi family, the "Hazrat of Shor Bazar," Gul Aqa, and his brother, Shayr Aqa.[43] To Fayz Muhammad, religious war is never far from the surface in the struggles between the Hazarahs and other parties involved in the events of 1929.

At this point in his life at least, Fayz Muhammad was also a confirmed Anglophobe. To him most of the tribal disturbances in the east and south, not to mention the instability of the political situation in the country generally, could be blamed on the British. He also believed that the British were anti-Shi^{c}ite, citing as proof their role in a pogrom carried out against the Qizilbash of Qandahar early in ^{c}Abd al-Rahman's reign by Khushdil Khan Luynab, the father of ^{c}Ali Ahmad, a man who figures prominently in the events of 1929. When Fayz Muhammad wrote the *Nizhād-nāmah*, he introduced the controversial figure of T. E. Lawrence, identifying him as the British agent responsible for inciting the Shinwari in the revolt that led indirectly to Aman Allah's abdication.[44] He says nothing in the present work, however, about Lawrence.

One of the more intriguing aspects of the work and what gives it a distinctive flavor is Fayz Muhammad's description of his own activities during the period. On the one hand he portrays himself as an implacable opponent of the Tajik government. But on the other, he did serve, under duress he asserts, as a member of a delegation of Shiᶜites (mainly Qizilbash) sent to the Hazarahjat to try to convince the local leaders to reach agreement with Habib Allah. That he was sentenced to a beating on his return, a beating which he survived but which may well have been a contributing factor in his death less than two years later, tends to support his view of himself as committed to subverting the purpose of the mission. It is not surprising that Fayz Muhammad would have wanted to justify himself in the eyes of posterity by depicting himself as a saboteur of the amir's goals. But his self-portrait is not entirely convincing and one is left with the sense that had he had more time to edit his work, some of the self-justification would have turned out less blatant and therefore perhaps more persuasive.

Beyond the detailed picture of Hazarah politics that Fayz Muhammad's memoir provides, the whole account underscores the primary importance of ethnic and religio-ethnic politics in Afghanistan's turbulent history. Absent from the account are any appeals to a citizenship broader than that of ethnic or sectarian affiliation. Political calculations seem always to have been made in terms of the tribal or religious loyalties of the parties involved. This is important in understanding the history of the country in 1929 and, not less, the dynamics of the struggle as it is being played out today.

* * * * * * *

Presenting this work to an English readership is not an easy task. Over and above the fact that the Persian was still in a very unfinished state when Fayz Muhammad died, the work comes to us today only through a Russian translation. The Persian original, according to the Russian translator, A. I. Shkirando, was acquired by the National Archives in Kabul from Fayz Muhammad's son ᶜAli Muhammad in 1980, and Shkirando worked from a microfilm of it.[45] Conditions in Afghanistan between 1980 and the present have made research in the archives virtually impossible and I have therefore had to rely on the Russian translation.

In the present version of Fayz Muhammad's work, I have made substantial changes to the Russian version. Most of what seemed unnecessarily repetitive has been eliminated. For example, in the Russian (probably following the Persian), proper names are almost invariably given in their full form with honorifics and titles regardless of how many times the name has already appeared. Here I follow the convention of English, rendering names in abbreviated form when there is no doubt about identity, i.e. Nadir Khan or simply Nadir for Muhammad Nadir Khan or Habib Allah for His Highness, Amir Habib Allah Khan. As a rule the suffixed title "khan" is dropped after its first use. All names are given in their full form in the index.

The author despised the main object of his narrative, the Tajik outlaw-turned-king, Habib Allah Kalakānī, and rarely refers to him by any other name than the pejorative "watercarrier's boy." Since he does on occasion accord him, perhaps sarcastically, the full style of office, "His Highness Amir Habib Allah Khan, Servant of the Religion of the Prophet of God," I have throughout called him by his own name, Habib Allah, or referred to him by title ("the amir") rather than by the nickname "Bacha-i Saqao" used in most English writing. Using the Tajik amir's proper name does give rise to possible confusion with his earlier namesake, Habib Allah, the father of Aman Allah. Fayz Muhammad himself usually identifies the earlier Habib Allah as "martyred" or "murdered" and that generally eliminates any ambiguity.

Fayz Muhammad's introduction, in which he denounces, in very general terms, the venality of Aman Allah's ministers, has been omitted. It is bombastic and lacking in specifics and the interested reader can refer to the Russian translation. As noted above, Fayz Muhammad had started reworking his journal into a coherent narrative but never finished. He had carried his major restructuring of the work only as far as April 1, at which point the text, as it has come to us, reverts to the journalistic format. Even after that point he made numeorus corrections and revisions, evident in the microfilm, according to Shkirando, from his crossing out words and phrases and adding marginal notes.

With the aim of creating a more coherent narrative flow and eliminating unnecessary repetition, I have tried to carry on what I think was his intent for the whole work by reorganizing it into discrete sections based on certain topics—the different fronts on which Habib Allah had to fight, the situation in Kabul itself, and—what constitutes the real focus of the work—Habib Allah's efforts to persuade the Hazarahs to accept his government. To provide the necessary background for the general reader, I have added a considerable amount of information in italics, making use of a number of reference sources, including two important works edited by Ludwig Adamec and Nahiz's four volume gazetteer mentioned in the preface.[46]

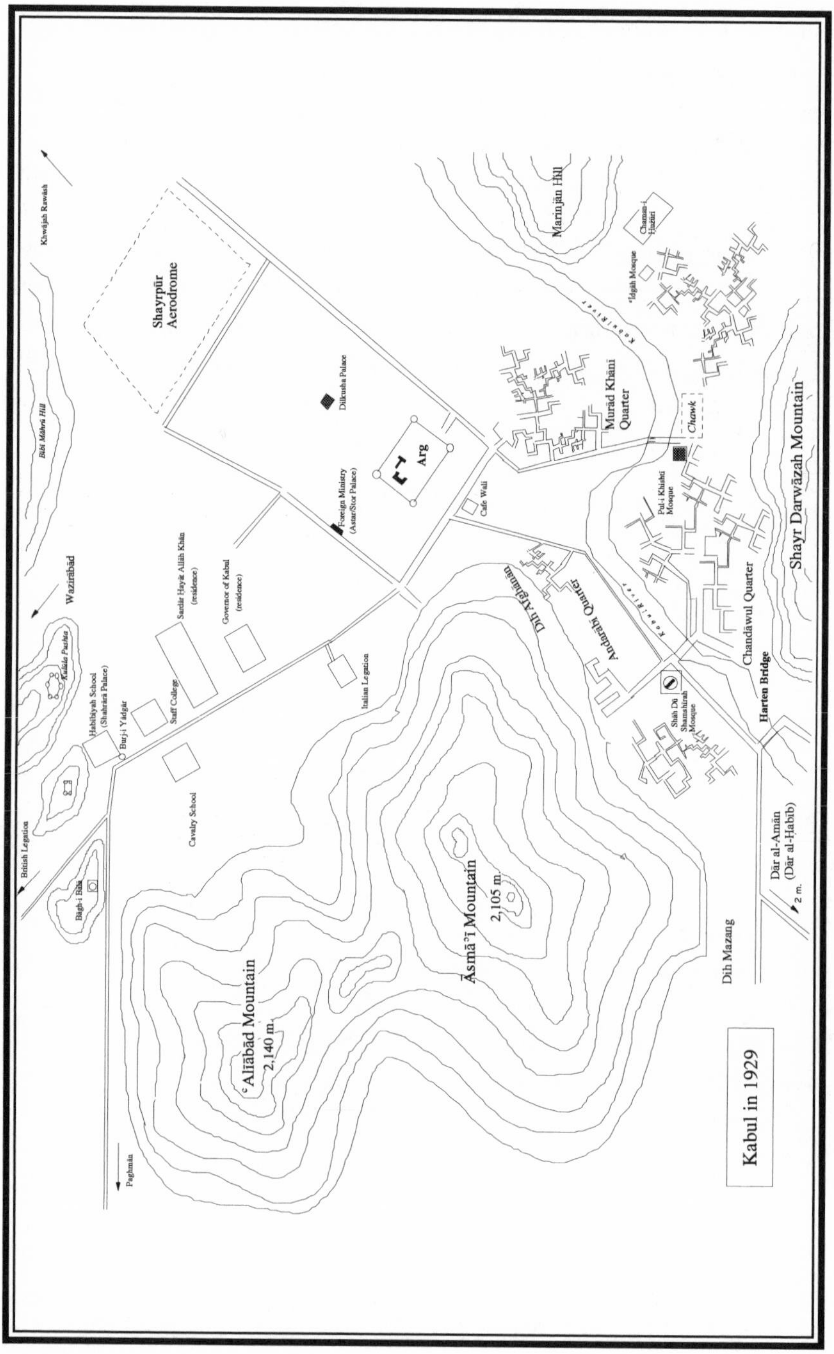
Kabul in 1929
Shayrpūr Aerodrome
Khwājah Rawāsh
Bībī Mahrū Hill
Wazīrābād
Dilkusha Palace
Arg
Foreign Ministry
(Astar/Stor Palace)
Sardār Ḥayāt Allāh Khān
(residence)
Governor of Kabul
(residence)
Cafe Wali
Marinjān Hill
ᶜĪdgāh Mosque
Chaman-i Ḥużūrī
Murād Khānī Quarter
Chawk
Kabul River
Pul-i Khishtī Mosque
Shayr Darwāzah Mountain
Chandāwul Quarter
Harteu Bridge
Dih Afghānān
Āndarābī Quarter
Shāh Dū Shamshīrah Mosque
Italian Legation
Staff College
Ḥabībīyah School
(Shahrārā Palace)
Burj-i Yādgār
Kulūla Pushta
Cavalry School
British Legation
Bāgh-i Bābā
ᶜAlīābād Mountain
2,140 m.
Āsmā'ī Mountain
2,105 m.
Dih Mazang
Dār al-Amān
(Dār al-Ḥabīb)
2 m.
Paghmān

PART ONE

The Tajiks Take Kabul

On July 1, 1928, Aman Allah Khan, the amir of Afghanistan, returned to Kabul from a nearly seven-month grand tour of Europe. The reasons for the long and expensive trip were economic and educational. The king was to "[obtain] better means for the life and well-being of his country,"[47] presumably by signing contracts for economic development, soliciting direct grants of aid, or negotiating loans from at least some of the countries he visited—Egypt, Italy, France, Belgium, Switzerland, Germany, England, Poland, the Soviet Union, Turkey, and Iran. But the trip produced little in the way of tangible commitments and within six months of his return, the amir would be unceremoniously ousted from his capital. Five months after that, he would be driven from the country forever.

Aman Allah was the ninth in the line of Afghan Muhammadzai kings, a family from the Barakzai tribe, itself reckoned a part of the larger Durrani confederation of the Pushtun people. His father and grandfather, Habib Allah and ᶜAbd al-Rahman, had each ruled for about twenty years and he obviously believed that the crown sat securely on his own head.

But he had pressed various reforms in the legal, educational, social, and political spheres that had already led to one major rebellion, the 1924 Mangal uprising. He had suppressed that only with great difficulty and the revolt had been followed by a weakening of the amir's reformist zeal. His long absence from the country in 1928 further eroded his government's position. Much of the official corruption that Fayz Muhammad complains of was undoubtedly exacerbated by the amir's absence. But the trip revitalized him and his ideas about what had to be done. He returned from Europe more convinced than ever that Afghanistan, an economically self-sufficient, if relatively poor, country had to make drastic reforms in order to move into the modern world. Through a loya jirgah of a thousand tribal and community leaders that met in the summer of 1928, he succeeded in having a whole series of new administrative, educational, legal, and social reforms adopted, although a few of his proposals, such as a law setting the marriage age at twenty-one for men and eighteen for women, were rejected as un-Islamic.

*Meanwhile the religious leadership of the country, especially the Mujaddidi family, who derived enormous influence from their position as head of the Naqshbandi Sufi organization in Afghanistan, was agitating against the government's reforms and finding a receptive audience among the Pushtun tribes of the Eastern and Southern Provinces. In September, shortly after the close of the loya jirgah, they circulated a proclamation labeling Aman Allah's reforms as contrary to Islamic law (the Shari*ᶜ*ah). In November, their agitation prompted attacks by Shinwari tribal forces on government posts, the severing of telegraph lines, and the stopping of traffic on the Kabul-Jalalabad road. Now the rhetorical heat was turned up. Aman Allah was accused of defaming the Prophet at the loya jirgah and was labeled a kafir, thus legitimizing the use of violence against him.*

But Aman Allah's troubles in the east were about to pale in comparison with a problem developing closer to home. Less than an hour's drive north of Kabul is a region known as Kuhdaman, literally the "skirts of the mountain," where the Kabul plain ends and the formidable peaks and remote valleys of the Hindu Kush range begin. There, in the village of Kalakan, which lies just to the east of the main road connecting Kabul with the north, a Tajik ex-soldier, Habib Allah, son of Amir Allah,[48] *had begun to establish a considerable following. Like his father before him, he had seen military service, but not as a watercarrier. He had served in the "Model Battalion" (*Qaṭᶜah-yi Namūnah*) that was organized and trained by the Turk, Jamal Pasha. Habib Allah had fought with the battalion in the 1924 rebellion of the Mangal tribe. He was demobilized after the uprising ended, according to Fayz Muhammad, but British records say that he deserted the "Model Battalion" at some unspecified time and after working in Peshawar moved to Parachinar (on the Afghan border) where he was arrested and sentenced to eleven months imprisonment. Other sources have him arrested in Peshawar in January 1928, then sentenced to three years' imprisonment because he was unable to post bond. But this information seems problematic since by August 1928, he was in Paghman, just west of Kabul, and soon after in Kuhdaman where we pick up Fayz Muhammad's account of him.*[49]

The Background of Habib Allah, "the Watercarrier's Boy"

Habib Allah returned from the army to his home in the village of Kalakan in Kuhdaman. He had no means of providing for himself and his family and considered the occupations common among Kuhdamanis, like viticulture and selling firewood, to be beneath him, reasoning that these could hardly ever provide wheat bread for his table. So instead he began to rob caravans and nearby villages. He was joined by men of a similar mind, men like Sayyid Husayn from Charikar, Malik Muhsin from Saray Khwajah, and others, twenty-four in all, and they spent their time robbing and killing Muslims. For three years [1924–27?] they lived in mountain caves, venturing out during the day to rob and hiding out at night, all the time fearful of government retaliation. Sometime later, Habib Allah fled to Peshawar where he was a tea seller and petty thief. After British police arrested and jailed an accomplice of his, A^{c}zam from Maydan, Habib Allah fled Peshawar for Tal-i Tutga [Tutgai] where he stayed awhile, supporting himself by petty theft. When his notoriety made life difficult, he headed back to Kalakan. Afraid he might be arrested, he did not return to his own home but began preying on the defenseless with a group of accomplices.

Malik Muhsin,
Governor of Kabul
or Central Province

During the months before his move against Kabul, Habib Allah built local support by judicious use of the protection money paid him by merchants whose caravans from Turkistan, loaded with carpets, karakul wool, and Russian goods, had to traverse Kuhdaman. Some of this money went to recruit followers; much of it was paid directly to local officials to turn a blind eye to his activities. One of the most important recipients of his money, according to Fayz Muhammad, was Muhammad Wali Khan, the amir's legal representative (wakīl), *who was in Kuhdaman. Muhammad Wali sold Habib Allah a written guarantee of personal safety* (amān-i jān) *which he was able to use to avoid arrest. But the news of his freebooting ways and the protection he enjoyed in high circles proved too much for the amir to ignore for long. Though tied down with the*

Shinwari uprising in Jalalabad, Aman Allah sent Ahmad ᶜAli Khan Lodi, one of his more trusted courtiers, with instructions to dispose of Habib Allah in some fashion, or at worst, buy him off. The prestige and dignity of the government required that the legend that was growing up around Habib Allah's name be suppressed. But Ahmad ᶜAli may not have been the best choice.

Habib Allah's incorrigible desperados had murdered the governor of Charikar, Ghulam Ghaws Khan, and a district headman (*ᶜalāqahdār*). When the government sent a force of cavalry and infantry with artillery to arrest them, the bandits went into hiding in the mountains and the government force accomplished nothing. Aman Allah now sent Ahmad ᶜAli, the son of ᶜAbd al-Wahid Lodi, to capture the bandit. Ahmad ᶜAli had once been governor (*ḥākim*) of Kuhdaman and was notorious there for his tyrannical rule. Later he had been sent as ambassador to Germany and upon returning home was appointed mayor (*raʾīs al-baladīyah*) of Kabul. As mayor, he had tried to force everyone to wear the clothing decreed by the government, including European-style hats.

Immediately after arriving at the citadel of Jabal al-Siraj, Ahmad ᶜAli sent for Habib Allah and Sayyid Husayn, both of whom he knew from his days as governor. He gave them guarantees of personal safety, confirmed by oaths on the Koran, promised them appointments as lieutenant generals (*nāʾib sālār*), and presented each of them with three thousand rupees in cash and seven-shot rifles, with ammunition, for each of the rebels who marauded alongside them.

When Aman Allah dispatched the promised money and weapons along with a signed decree naming the two men lieutenant-generals, they declared that they would go to Kabul to assure themselves of his sincerity. They left Jabal al-Siraj for Charikar, which lies some 36 miles north of Kabul, found a telephone operator there and rang up the amir. Habib Allah, pretending to be Ahmad ᶜAli, said, "I've reached agreement with the watercarrier's boy and have him in custody. What do you want me to do with him?" Aman Allah replied, "Kill him." Habib Allah then asked the amir, "But I've given him a guarantee of safe conduct. How can I kill him?" Aman Allah heard him out and said, "True, he made an agreement with you, but not with me. Do not let him live!" Convinced now of the amir's duplicity, Habib Allah did not immediately hang up but instead told the amir who he really was, then cursed him, and vowed that he would shortly attack Kabul and make the amir pay. This brazen threat, not to mention the various understandings which the amir's own *wakil* (attorney), Muhammad Wali Khan, and other ministers and influential people of Kabul, had reached with Habib Allah, infuriated Aman Allah. He ended the conversation by hurling the telephone down on the table.

Meanwhile, in Jalalabad things were not going at all well for the amir. The two representatives he had sent to suppress the Shinwari uprising, his foreign minister, Ghulam Siddiq Khan, and Shayr Ahmad Khan, who was head of the National Council, had had a falling out in late November and, according to Fayz Muhammad, were negotiating separately with the tribes. Ghulam Siddiq is said to have incited some of the Shinwari to attack Shayr Ahmad Khan, the main consequence of which was that the Shinwari burned the amir's winter palace in Jalalabad to the ground.

The situation around Jalalabad appeared so perilous that the amir turned to his brother-in-law, ʿAli Ahmad Khan Luynab, former governor of the Kabul region and High Commissioner (raʾis-i aʿla) *of the Southern and Eastern provinces, to deal with the problem and sent him off on the third of December 1928 with regular troops, militia levies, and a sizable treasury with which to conciliate the tribal leaders. Ghulam Siddiq and Shayr Ahmad were ordered back to Kabul.*

ʿAli Ahmad Khan Luynab

In the meantime, calls had gone out for tribal levies to assist the regular army in dealing with the Shinwari uprising and armed tribesmen from the east, south, and west—the Mangal (only recently themselves at war with Aman

Allah's government), Waziri, Wardak, Ghilzai and Tajiks—were trickling into the capital. These men had no particular loyalty to the government and saw the situation simply as an opportunity for enrichment. As it turned out, there was no need to send them on to Jalalabad. ᶜAli Ahmad managed to conciliate the Shinwari leaders and put an end to the uprising, but as it took a while for this news to spread through the countryside, the armed tribesmen continued to arrive in the capital.

The First Tajik Assault on Kabul

Aman Allah, we assume, welcomed the news of the Jalalabad settlement. But any feeling of relief would have been very temporary. Habib Allah and his Tajik supporters were about to descend on the capital from the north. It is not entirely clear what their aim was, besides revenge for Aman Allah's attempt to have Habib Allah killed. Perhaps the two Tajik leaders wanted to extract more money or other concessions from the amir. It is difficult to imagine that they would have seriously contemplated actually seizing control of the government. They lacked any credible claim to the amirate themselves, nor do they appear to have had a legitimate Muhammadzai candidate to put forward. If Fayz Muhammad's picture is at all accurate, they may have been encouraged by various influential people in Kabul, including Gul Aqa (Muhammad Sadiq) Mujaddidi, the "Hazrat of Shor Bazar." The tentativeness of the first assault on Kabul and the quick retreat suggest no real purpose at that point other than the usual one of looting.

After reaching agreement with Ahmad ᶜAli Lodi and after the telephone conversation with the amir, Habib Allah returned to Jabal al-Siraj from Charikar with Sayyid Husayn and the bandits who always accompanied them and there besieged Ahmad ᶜAli. After 18 days [from late November to December 11 or 12, 1928], Ahmad ᶜAli and the squads of cavalry and infantry from the amir's personal guard agreed to surrender the citadel of Jabal al-Siraj peacefully. With a guarantee of safe passage, they handed over to the bandits all the government funds in the town along with eighteen machine guns, an unspecified number of heavy weapons, and some of their rifles, and then they escaped back to Kabul.

The insurgents were much emboldened and began preparations for an attack on Kabul itself, assembling tribal contingents under the pretext of responding to the call for tribal levies for Jalalabad.

Several influential Kabuli figures urged Habib Allah on and even told him the best time to attack. On Friday, December 14, 1928, some two thousand men, only two hundred of whom actually had rifles, the rest armed only with sticks and axes, entered the Murad Beg Fort [Qal^cah-i Murad Beg] on the northern slopes of the Kuh-i Kutal, not far from the village of Khirs Khanah. This latter village had been renamed Khayr Khanah by the late Amir Habib Allah Khan. This second name [Abode of Good] is something of a misnomer because you meet only thieves and pseudo-mullas there, wolves in sheep's clothing who harbor nothing but evil in their hearts.

Here the insurgents declared that without an amir an attack on Kabul would not be legal according to the laws of the Shari^cah and if anyone were killed his blood would be considered shed in vain. So they offered up the Friday prayer and homily (*khuṭbah*) in the name of Habib Allah Khan, thereby proclaiming him amir, and then embarked on their chosen path. With shouts of "*yā chahār yār*"[50] they passed through the village of Dih-i Kupak at 3:00 p.m. and around 3:15 reached Bagh-i Bala Park and the British Embassy.[51] They occupied the Bagh-i Bala palace, formerly the summer residence of Amir ^cAbd al-Rahman and at this time a military hospital for the Amir's personal guard and the residence of the Turkish physician, Bahjet Beg. After disarming and dismissing the watchmen who guarded the palace and the Embassy, they stationed their own guards, reassuring the employees of the embassy that they were guests of the nation and as such no harm would come to them.

At the behest of traitorous ministers and influential Kabulis like the Hazrat of Shor Bazar [Gul Aqa Mujaddidi], Sardar Muhammad ^cUsman Khan,[52] Muhammad Wali [Aman Allah's wakil], and others who had advised Habib Allah as to the best time of attack and offered the insurgents their support, the mutineers entered the house of the late prime minister, ^cAbd al-Quddus Khan, as easily as a son-in-law entering the home of his father-in-law.[53] At this time it housed the War College (*madrasah-i ḥarbiyah*) where instruction was under the supervision of Isma^cil Khaka-Beg and other Turkish officers. The insurgents also managed to gain entry into the house and fortress tower of Shahr Ara, the site of the Habibiyah School [or Lycée], whose headmaster was another Turk, Shawkat Beg.

A son of Muhammad Akbar Khan, known as Mir Bachchah, commanding a small force, put up some resistance as far as the reservoir in Dih-i Afghanan where water from Paghman is stored. And a group of cavalry officers, whose barracks were in a building in the park of the late Amir Shayr ᶜAli Khan located southeast of the Habibiyah School, rose in defense and prevented the insurgents from entering the old city.

The whole city was filled with the thunder of artillery and gunfire. But only the cavalry of the Amir's personal guard and a few other soldiers actually put up a fight. The rest of the army was in a mutinous mood because their officers had been appropriating the soldiers' rations. Holding their commanders rather than the rebels to blame for the trouble, when ordered to shoot, the soldiers simply fired their weapons into the air.

Tumult and confusion were now widespread. The amir was incensed when he heard of the treachery of his officials and ordered that weapons be distributed to the residents of Kabul and to the tribesmen who had come into the city but had not yet left for Jalalabad to fight the Shinwari. At this point, Her Highness, Aman Allah's mother,[54] was in the palace arsenal where Kabulis were grabbing up weapons. Overcoming her terror in the face of the masses clamoring around her, she called them her sons and tried to inspire them to take up the defense of the city.

But the distribution of fifty thousand rifles and a huge quantity of cartridges from the arsenal to the residents of the capital and of Chardihi[55] and to various tribal groups had no effect, largely due to the universal loathing felt for the amir's venal ministers and officials. Even worse, some of the Waziri, Mangal, and Ahmadzai tribesmen who had come to join in the fight against the Shinwari took up positions on Asmaᵓi Hill in the center of Kabul and began to fire on the amir's own troops.

Ghulam Ghaws, the son of Malik Jahandad Ahmadzai (the latter had rebelled against the late Amir Habib Allah and been put to death) made off with more than 300 rifles, returned to Khost, armed his people there and rose up against the government. Other tribes acted similarly because there was no control over the distribution of weapons.

Convinced that the residents of Kabul and Chardihi—his last hope and support—had also turned their backs on him, Aman Allah grew frightened. Four days after Habib Allah and Sayyid Husayn's assault on Kabul began, he sent his mother, wife, sister, and small children by plane to Qandahar along with much of the treasury.

The fighting dragged on for twelve days and eleven nights without letup. Weapons stores in Kulula Pushta and Bagh-i Bala fell into the hands of the Kuhdamanis, Kuhistanis, and other rebels. The bulk of the weaponry stockpiled since ᶜAbd al-Rahman's time and meant for use by the leadership of the country in repelling outside aggressors was irretrievably lost.

During the fighting, Habib Allah was wounded in the shoulder by fragments from an aerial bomb and he immediately retreated to Kuhdaman.

The Second Tajik Assault, the Abdication of Aman Allah, and the Three-Day Amirate of ᶜInayat Allah Khan

The fighting at this point, around December 25 or so, had been exceedingly haphazard. Habib Allah's shoulder wound, treated, so one story goes, in the infirmary of the British Embassy, took him for the moment out of the fight. He withdrew with his followers to the Murad Beg Fort, some twenty kilometers north of Kabul, to recover. This gave Aman Allah a chance to regroup his forces and try to disperse the Kuhdamanis. Fayz Muhammad says the amir's troops shelled and bombed the fort where Habib Allah was camped from late in December until mid-January but to no apparent effect. Equally unavailing was a government decree that put a price of forty thousand rupees on Habib Allah's head.[56]

The fighting went on day and night until Sunday, January 13. Aman Allah was apprehensive about the lack of support from the regular army and tribal contingents and from the residents of Kabul and Chardihi who were unhappy with the government. It was also very disquieting to him that thousands of rifles and cannons had been handed out to no avail and that his pilots seemed unable to deliver decisive strikes on the enemy's main positions. The amir now lost faith in his ability to win and so created the conditions for Habib Allah's victory.

During the early morning hours of Monday, January 14, Aman Allah abdicated and turned the reins of government over to his elder brother,

Sardars ^{c}Inayat Allah Khan (l) and Hayat Allah Khan (r)

Mahmud Tarzi (1919)

^{c}Inayat Allah Khan. At nine o'clock in the morning, taking ten million rupees worth of gold in Russian and British coin, Aman Allah hurriedly left for Qandahar with Mahmud Tarzi;[57] the foreign minister, Ghulam Siddiq; the minister of court, Muhammad Ya^{c}qub; the deputy minister of internal affairs, ^{c}Abd al-Ahad Khan;[58] and six bodyguards in a convoy of five vehicles.

Aman Allah's decision to abdicate is one of the great mysteries of modern Afghan political history. Although most Western sources attribute the abdication to Habib Allah's second attack on the city and the lack of support the amir received from those he thought he could rely on, Fayz Muhammad tells a different story. According to him, fighting was still going on at the Khayr Khanah (Khirskhanah) Pass seven miles north of Kabul when Aman Allah turned the reins of government over to his older brother, ^{c}Inayat Allah Khan. Nothing had yet been decided when the amir threw in the towel. In retrospect, it seems like the kind of impetuous, heedless action for which the amir was noted. His attempts at social reforms in imitation of Ataturk in Turkey, his dabbling in the Khilafat movement of India, his support and then withdrawal of support for the Muslims fighting against Soviet hegemony in Central Asia, his decision to make a grand tour of Europe at a particularly inappropriate time, his allowing his wife to be photographed during the tour with shoulders and face uncovered (tantamount to the Queen of England's being photographed in *full Islamic dress), and his ministerial appointments all seem to have been based on an absence of policy and a lack of deliberation. His reign is marked by a constant shifting with the political winds and what appears, with the benefit of hindsight, to have been an utter misunderstanding of the nature of the country over which he ruled. But Fayz Muhammad's treatment of him is interesting. Exasperated by his tolerance of official incompetence and corruption, appalled by the way in which the government arsenal was thrown open to plundering tribesmen, and then later alternately buoyed and depressed by news first of Aman Allah's advances against Habib Allah and then what seemed his inexplicable retreats, Fayz Muhammad remained, almost to the end, loyal to the ex-amir and hopeful that he would succeed in regaining the throne. Much of his attitude and loyalty has to do with his detailed knowledge of the tragedy of Hazarah history under Afghan domination and his gratitude to Aman Allah for the steps he had taken to provide Hazarahs with protection from enslavement and the routine abuse and injustice which they had long endured in Afghan society. Aman Allah's abdication was a great blow to Fayz Muhammad and he laid primary responsibility for it at the feet of his favorite* bêtes noires, *Gul Aqa Mujaddidi (the Hazrat of Shor Bazar), and Sardar Muhammad ᶜUsman and Muhammad Wali, two of Aman Allah's most trusted advisors.*

At one o'clock in the afternoon while battles were raging around the Khayr Khanah Pass, ᶜInayat Allah invited some residents of Kabul and representatives of the army and the tribal militias to the Dilkusha Palace to receive their oaths of allegiance. But these people had not gathered to fight for him but only to get money and weapons. The ceremony lasted about two hours. Oaths were given and received and Aman Allah's abdication decree was read out. Afterwards, ᶜInayat Allah sent off that scoundrel, the Hazrat of Shor Bazar, Muhammad ᶜUsman, and two or three of the pseudo-mullas who were themselves instigators of insurrection to meet with those inveterate thieves and desperados, Habib Allah and Sayyid Husayn. They were supposed to deliver the following message:

> Now that Aman Allah, whom you accused of unbelief (*kufr*), is no longer around and all the residents of Kabul, whether ordinary people or well-to-do, strong or weak, military or civilian, have come to the city and

> sworn oaths of allegiance to me and set me on the amirid throne and since you also consider me a true Muslim, therefore the reasons for bloodshed should now be banished. If you truly fought and shed blood in the name of truth and not for the sake of enmity between Muslims, then it is necessary to set aside all discord and recognize the authority of the Afghan amir.

On the way to meet with Habib Allah and Sayyid Husayn these men notified military units and tribal groups who were manning strongpoints along the way that Aman Allah had left for Qandahar and transferred authority to ᶜInayat Allah. They called on the soldiers to suspend all military activity, informing them that they were on their way to see Habib Allah and Sayyid Husayn. "If Sayyid Husayn and Habib Allah accept our conditions," they said, "then we will escort them to Amir ᶜInayat Allah and end the war and the bloodshed. You also should stop fighting and observe the truce." At this, many of the soldiers simply abandoned their positions and headed for the city while only a very small number held on until they could get a clearer idea of what was going on.

Having reached Habib Allah and Sayyid Husayn, the envoys delivered the contents of ᶜInayat Allah's message and then stated "in light of the fact that Habib Allah ascended the throne on the first of Rajab [December 14, 1928][59] while ᶜInayat Allah's accession corresponds to the second of Shaᶜban [January 14, 1929], therefore you, not ᶜInayat Allah, are the rightful occupant of the throne. If ᶜInayat Allah does not declare his allegiance to you then, according to the Shariᶜah, his actions may be considered illicit."

Habib Allah and Sayyid Husayn rejoiced when they heard this coming from emissaries of ᶜInayat Allah and thereupon ordered their colleagues to prepare to go to Kabul. En route, they collected rifles, cannons, and munitions abandoned at the deserted positions and toward sunset on that same day—Friday—twenty-eight armed men accompanied by a group of unarmed Kuhdamanis dressed in rags passed through the village of Dih-i Afghanan and burst into the capital shouting "ya chahar yar" and firing rifles and machine guns into the air, as if they were at a wedding. Alienated by the abuse of power of Aman Allah's ministers and provoked by the actions of the mayor, Ahmad ᶜAli Lodi, on matters of dress, the residents of the city were already inclined against Aman Allah. They refused to make use of the huge quantity of weapons which had been distributed to them and so the partisans of Habib Allah and Sayyid Husayn easily established control over the city.

Habib Allah, along with ᶜInayat Allah Khan's envoys—now his honored guests—entered the Bagh-i Bala palace. Sayyid Husayn, meantime, had set out to reconnoiter the city. Finding the situation calm, he joined Habib Allah at the Bagh-i Bala that evening. On the evening of the very first day of his reign, ᶜInayat Allah was forced to barricade himself in the Arg with several of his ministers. For the next twenty-four hours there was continuous firing on all sides.

On Tuesday, January 15, the population of Chardihi and many of the residents of Kabul including the princes, Sardar Hayat Allah Khan and Muhammad Kabir Khan, both sons of the late Amir Habib Allah, and other sardars[60] who only the day before had vowed allegiance to ᶜInayat Allah Khan, now headed in small groups to Bagh-i Bala with gifts for [the new] Amir Habib Allah. After assuring him of their devotion and congratulating him on his accession to the throne, they returned to their homes.

That same evening, after all matters in the city had become subject to the will and wishes of Habib Allah, the Hazrat of Shor Bazar, Sardar Muhammad ᶜUsman, and other traitorous ministers and their minions went to ᶜInayat Allah to tell him their impressions of Habib Allah and Sayyid Husayn. In so doing, they frightened him and shook his resolve to defend the throne.

On Wednesday the 16th, while the amir's forces and the Kuhdamanis were still exchanging fire, and 80 Hazarahs from Bihsud were defending the Qalᶜah-i Buland fortress and the arsenal at Kulula Pushta, some city leaders declared their allegiance to Habib Allah. These included the head of the National Council, Shayr Ahmad; the minister of education, Fayz Muhammad Khan; a former minister of trade, ᶜAbd al-Hadi Khan; the minister of finance, Mir Hashim; Sardar Amin Allah Khan and Muhammad ᶜUmar Khan, sons of Amir ᶜAbd al-Rahman; and a number of deputy ministers and heads of state bureaus.

That evening, Sayyid Husayn went to the home of Nur al-Din Khan, the son of Qazi Qutb al-Din Jawanshiri of the Qizilbash. He accepted Nur al-Din's gracious offer of tea and then pressured him to order that the gates of the Qalᶜah-i Chandawul [the heart of the old city and a quarter heavily populated by Qizilbash Shi^{c}ites] be opened to the Kuhistanis. At sunset the town crier announced that all shops were to open the next day and anyone caught looting would be shot. However, the Kuhistanis themselves freely looted the homes of Kabulis and raped women and young girls. These outrages continued until the middle of March.

On the same day [January 16], out of fear of the Kuhistanis, Qizilbash leaders went to Bagh-i Bala and offered their allegiance to Amir Habib Allah.

The skirmishes soon died down; the Hazrat of Shor Bazar along with Sardar Muhammad ^{c}Usman and several ministers tried to persuade ^{c}Inayat Allah to relinquish power quickly and leave the palace. Only the commandant of the Arg (*qal^{c}ah-begī*), Ghulam Dastagir Khan son of ^{c}Abd al-Rashid Khan Muhammadzai, and the minister of defense, ^{c}Abd al-^{c}Aziz Khan[61] son of Muhammad Allah Khan Barakzai, refused to participate in this contemptible plot against the authority of Aman Allah and ^{c}Inayat Allah, the only rightful heirs to the amirid authority established by Amir ^{c}Abd al-Rahman.

Habib Allah Takes Full Possession of the Capital

The absence of Kabuli support, combined with the treasonous activity of the Hazrat of Shor Bazar, Muhammad ^{c}Usman, Muhammad Wali, and other influential people who were ready to betray him, unnerved ^{c}Inayat Allah and hastened his abdication. The Hazrat, playing the role of intermediary between ^{c}Inayat Allah and Habib Allah and Sayyid Husayn, advised ^{c}Inayat Allah to abandon the Arg, which was full of money and firearms that had been accumulated over generations. ^{c}Inayat Allah wanted to take his family and three hundred thousand rupees and go to Qandahar via Peshawar and the Punjab. Habib Allah agreed to those conditions and the two sides signed such an agreement, ratifying it with oaths sworn on the Koran.

On Wednesday, Habib Allah sent the Hazrat of Shor Bazar to ^{c}Inayat Allah with a farman guaranteeing him and his retainers safe passage. With tears in his eyes, ^{c}Inayat Allah said goodbye to the wives of his late father and to his brothers and sisters who were still in the Arg. To each of them, he gave some twenty-five pounds sterling to help them survive the difficult days ahead. He also distributed money to the soldiers of the royal guard and other defenders of the Arg.

Thursday eve[62] ᶜInayat Allah signed the abdication agreement. It read:

> My brother, Habib Allah! It is known to all that I have no wish to be padishah. After the death of my father, I never harbored any desire for the throne. I was compelled to accept it only at the insistence of the leaders (*arbābs*) who linked my accession to the throne with the prosperity of the people and the strengthening of Islam. But now, as I see the blood of Muslims being shed, I have decided to relinquish my claim to the Afghan amirate and give you my oath of allegiance like other true-believing Muslims. Today with me in the Arg, the following distinguished people have pledged their allegiance to you: Muhammad Wali Khan, ᶜAbd al-ᶜAziz Khan, Muhammad Sarwar Khan, Ghulam Haydar Khan, Ahmad ᶜAli Khan, Ghulam Dastagir Khan, ᶜAbd al-Ghiyas Khan, ᶜAta al-Haqq Khan, Muhammad Aman Khan, Muhammad Amin Khan, Muhammad Ishaq Khan, Sayyid Qasim Khan, ᶜAbd al-Wahhab Khan, ᶜAbd al-Tawwab Khan, Shah Mahmud Khan, Sayyid ᶜAbd Allah Khan, Sultan Muhammad Khan, Sayyid Ahmad Khan, Mir ᶜAli Ahmad Khan, and Muhammad Akram Khan.
>
> This oath of allegiance is tendered on observance of the following conditions:
>
> First, safety must be guaranteed for me, my immediate family and other members of my extended family, the above-named persons, and all officers and soldiers here in the Arg. Their personal belongings should not be touched.
>
> Second, my family and I are going either to Qandahar or abroad. I ask that an airplane be put at my disposal for my trip to Qandahar.
>
> Third, I ask that Muhammad Wali Khan, ᶜAbd al-ᶜAziz Khan, and Ahmad ᶜAli Khan be allowed to come with me.
>
> Fourth, not later than a month from today, permission should be granted to any high-ranking figures who wish to go abroad with their families.
>
> Fifth, until such time as an airplane is ready for my departure, I will be in the Arg. You may occupy the palace once I have boarded the aircraft and it has taken off.
>
> Thursday eve. 5 Shaᶜban 1347 A.H. [January 17, 1929][63] ᶜInayat Allah

When this agreement had been drafted and delivered, artillery and small arms fire throughout the city ceased.

On Friday eve,[64] the minister of defense, ᶜAbd al-ᶜAziz; ᶜAbd al-Habib

Khan; the amir's wakil, Muhammad Wali; and the Kabul mayor, Ahmad ^{c}Ali Shah, all swore oaths of allegiance on the Koran and sent the text of these oaths to Habib Allah via the hand of that troublemaker and schemer, the Hazrat of Shor Bazar:

> We, the undersigned, ^{c}Abd al-^{c}Aziz, ^{c}Abd al-Habib, Muhammad Wali, and Ahmad ^{c}Ali, swear to Habib Allah Khan on the Koran that we will never act against him and his authority as Amir and we will live, like all citizens of Afghanistan, under the good offices of the Islamic government. Friday eve, 6 Sha^{c}ban 1347 A.H. [January 18, 1929][65] ^{c}Abd al-^{c}Aziz, Ahmad ^{c}Ali, ^{c}Abd al-Habib, Muhammad Wali.

At eleven o'clock Friday morning, at Habib Allah's request, two British planes landed at Kabul. At 1:00 p.m. ^{c}Inayat Allah Khan, with his immediate family and two of his relatives, ^{c}Abd al-^{c}Aziz Khan and Ahmad ^{c}Ali Khan, took off for Peshawar. The planes did not have room for ^{c}Abd al-Wahhab and ^{c}Abd al-Tawwab, sons of Mahmud Tarzi, nor for several of ^{c}Inayat Allah's own children, who had to wait another day.

That evening, Habib Allah sent Sayyid Husayn to take possession of the Arg while he himself went to the Bagh-i Aqa palace where the provincial law court and finance administration were housed. His ignorant followers, who were looting the belongings of the Hazarahs, Wardaks, Waziris, Mangal, the cavalrymen of the royal guard, and Kabulis in the Park-i Nizam wa Kumandan, fired their guns and rifles in celebration, terrifying the residents of the capital, who were not used to such violent fusillades and wild carryings-on.

Sayyid Husayn ordered the men under his command to stop the shooting. When they refused to obey, he fired his own rifle into the chest of one of them, killing the man on the spot. The rest, witnessing this brutal act of a man who had already killed hundreds of people, now went along quietly to the Arg. But despite the oaths taken on the Koran, these ignorant people tortured, stripped, and killed anyone they came across there. Among their victims were Mulla Zaman, the qal^{c}ah begi [Ghulam Dastagir], and others. Some of the dead they dragged out of the Arg. They also tortured four guardsmen who were coming from the bazaar and then shot them on the Chawk.

Despite all their claims of devotion to Islam, these marauders perpetrated horrors the likes of which are completely alien to the religion. I have invoked God's condemnation on these self-styled Muslims a thousand times and I pray to God to send them all straight to Hell. When I think about the activities of this gang of rebels and thieves the only thing that comes to mind are curses. The pseudo-mullas who call these bandits and thieves "fighters for the faith" (*mujāhidīn*) and refer to their ringleader as a "holy warrior" (*ghāzī*) incited them against the true Muslims who perform the prayer five times a day. These people shed the blood of hundreds of people and retarded the development of an Islamic society by a hundred years. They plundered and destroyed all the resources of the government, which were intended for the defense of the national honor, the country's independence, and the religion.

On Saturday January 19, the sons of Mahmud Tarzi and the rest of the children and relatives of ᶜInayat Allah arrived in Peshawar on a British plane and from there, accompanied by ᶜInayat Allah and his immediate family, left by train for Chaman.[66] Then by car they rejoined Aman Allah Khan in Qandahar.

The transfer of power was now complete.[67] *Those who could had left. Kabul was soon to become a city under siege, pressed on all sides by enemies of the new amir.*

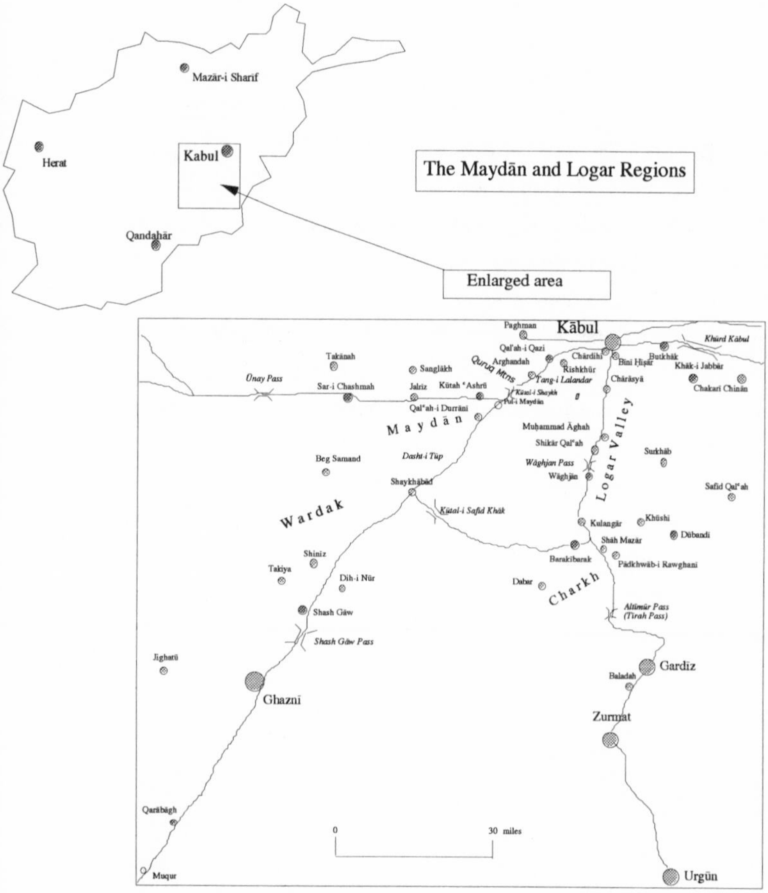

Mazār-i Sharīf
Herat
Kabul
Qandahār
The Maydān and Logar Regions
Enlarged area
Paghman
Kābul
Khūrd Kābul
Qal'ah-i Qazi
Takānah
Sanglākh
Arghandah
Chārdihi
Butkhāk
Bini Ḥiṣār
Khāk-i Jabbār
Quruq Mtns
Rishkhūr
Ūnay Pass
Sar-i Chashmah
Jalriz
Kūtah ʿAshrū
Tang-i Lalandar
Chārāsyā
Chakari Chinān
Kūtal-i Shaykh
Pul-i Maydān
Qalʿah-i Durrāni
Maydān
Muḥammad Āghah
Logar Valley
Shikār Qalʿah
Beg Samand
Dasht-i Tūp
Surkhāb
Wāghjan Pass
Wāghjān
Shaykhābād
Safid Qalʿah
Wardak
Kūtal-i Safid Khāk
Kulangār
Khūshi
Dūbandi
Shāh Mazār
Shiniz
Barakibarak
Pādkhwāb-i Rawghani
Takiya
Dih-i Nūr
Dabar
Charkh
Shash Gāw
Altimūr Pass
(Tirah Pass)
Shash Gāw Pass
Jighatū
Gardīz
Baladah
Ghazni
Zurmat
Qarābāgh
0
30 miles
Muqur
Urgūn

PART TWO

The Tajiks Consolidate and Resistance Grows

Kabul was now empty of Muhammadzai royals and the new amir took possession of the Arg, the fortified residence of the king in the center of the city, on Friday, January 18. Fayz Muhammad speaks with contempt of Habib Allah and his colleagues and relates the following story as evidence of the uncouth and unschooled character of the Tajik mountain man. On his first night in the Arg, Habib Allah invited his father to join him for dinner. In Fayz Muhammad's characterization, Amir Allah "was much more comfortable roaming the mountains wearing nothing but rags" than he was in the civilized setting of the royal palace. Mistaking a water closet for the dining room, the two men seated themselves, according to Fayz Muhammad, and began with soup which they spooned from a white china pitcher, Aman Allah's chamber pot. The story sums up the disdain which Fayz Muhammad consistently displays in his work for the Tajik government. He repeatedly refers to Habib Allah as the "watercarrier's boy" or "chief of the bandits" and after derisively using Habib Allah's self-awarded title "Servant of the Religion of the Prophet of God" or his brother Hamid Allah's "Support of the State" he cannot resist adding "while in reality they were the destroyers of the religion and the state" or words to that effect.

As for Fayz Muhammad's characterization of the situation in Kabul after the takeover, the weight of evidence is that for a time the supporters of the new rulers did run amok in the city. The suspicion that people were hiding weapons and ammunition was sufficient pretext for searching and looting a house and molesting its inhabitants, according to Fayz Muhammad. (But this was not out of the ordinary. When the Musahiban, Shah Wali, entered the city in October, his men were granted a three-day period in which they were free to loot at will. What made the Taliban cap-

ture of Kabul in September 1996 memorable was the fact that the victors seem to have refrained from the customary period of looting.)

Despite the agreement with ᶜInayat Allah to safeguard the lives and property of people remaining in the Arg, the new amir arrested the twenty who had not left and confiscated their belongings. Concerned about a counterattack from Aman Allah loyalists, he also began to move what was left in the treasury north to Kuhdaman. But when it became clear that there was no imminent danger, he halted the transfer.

ᶜAli Ahmad Khan Luynab's Amirate in the East

The first concerted opposition to Habib Allah's seizure of power came from a member of the Luynab family, ᶜAli Ahmad Khan. The Luynabs were also from the Barakzai branch of the Durranis. They rose to prominence under Amir Shayr ᶜAli Khan and then were exiled, along with many other prominent Kabul families, at the beginning of the reign of ᶜAbd al-Rahman in 1880. ᶜAli Ahmad was born about 1883 in Mashhad, Iran. His family was moved to India at the request of the Afghan amir and then was allowed to return to Afghanistan when ᶜAbd al-Rahman's son, Habib Allah, came to power. ᶜAli Ahmad's father, Khushdil Khan Luynab, then was appointed to a series of governorships and ᶜAli Ahmad himself began his own rise at court. Fayz Muhammad despised the Luynabs. To him they were among the more aggressively Pushtun chauvinist families in Afghanistan and in his eyes Khushdil Khan was responsible for a genocidal campaign against the Shiᶜite Qizilbash of Qandahar just before Aman Allah came to the throne.

ᶜAli Ahmad was a colorful figure in Afghan politics. He had a somewhat checkered career, first under Amir Habib Allah Khan and then under Amir Aman Allah Khan. In the early 1920s he played a leading and controversial role in the convoluted negotiations that finally ended the British-Afghan war of 1919, generally known outside Afghanistan as the Third Anglo-Afghan war and inside as the War of Independence.[68] *To Fayz Muhammad, ᶜAli Ahmad was a very suspect figure on account of the anti-Shiᶜite activities of his father, Khushdil. In retaliation for the sword that ᶜAli Ahmad's father had wielded against Fayz Muhammad's coreligion-*

ists in Qandahar, the author brings the considerable venom of his pen to bear on the son, relating for perpetuity a scandalous story of ᶜAli Ahmad's illicit love affair with Aman Allah's eldest sister.

After Amir Habib Allah's assassination, ᶜAli Ahmad's father incited an attack by the Pushtun of Qandahar and its environs on the Qizilbash who lived in the region and had fought alongside the British at Chaman and Kadni [during the 1919 War of Independence]. As a consequence of his instigating the Pushtun, a monstrous tragedy occurred. Sardar ᶜAbd al-Quddus, the prime minister, who was sent to Qandahar to direct military action against the English, managed to settle the conflict. Khushdil was then recalled to Kabul where he remained at home for the rest of his life.

They say that the groundwork for the annihilation of the Qizilbash of Qandahar was laid by the English, who paid Khushdil Luynab a huge sum of money to perform these horrific deeds. It is also said that every political provocation which has occurred and still occurs inside Afghanistan, on its eastern and northern borders, is not connected so much with the ignorance and savagery of the people or the corruption and oppression of the government, as it is with the subversive activities of the English government. Because of its rivalry with Russia, England gives the Pushtuns significant aid and support, for it sees in them an iron shield to repel any attack on Afghanistan by her rival. If these rumors correspond in any way to reality, then, despite Pushtun assurances of their devotion to Islam, one must consider even their leaders to be godless ignorant people. If they truly believed in the Shariᶜah of the Prophet or if they had spent any time reading the Koran or listening to mullas recite the verse which says: "O believers! Take not Jews and Christians as friends; they are friends of each other. Whoso of you makes them his friends is one of them. God guides not the people of the evildoers!"[69] then they would never submit to the provocations of England, which professes Christianity.

ᶜAli Ahmad negotiated with the English and concluded a temporary truce with them by which the independence of Afghanistan was declared. However, some articles of the agreement contravened the interests of the Afghan government and enemies of his brought this to Amir Aman Allah's attention, accusing ᶜAli Ahmad of siding with the English and taking bribes from them. Moreover, they accused him of having an affair with Aman Allah's elder sister. When the amir heard this, he ordered that ᶜAli Ahmad be put to death. However, at the petition of Her Highness [ᶜUlya Hazrat Sarwat al-Saltana]—the mother of the princess—the amir pardoned him but kept him under house arrest, warning him that if he left the house, he would be shot. ᶜAli Ahmad also agreed to marry the princess.[70]

Although Fayz Muhammad does not say when this incident occurred, he places it prior to the Mangal rebellion at Khost of 1924 for which ᶜAli Ahmad was freed and sent to the east to rally the tribes, especially the Khugyani and Shinwari, against the Mangal. Fluent in Pushtu as well as Persian, Urdu, and English, he made alliances at this point which he tried to revive later on in support of his claim to the amirate. In 1928, he accompanied Aman Allah on the tour of European capitals but again managed to offend him during the trip. In a meeting with the German Foreign Secretary, Carl von Schubert, ᶜAli Ahmad expressed republican sentiments and decried the special consideration that had to be accorded Aman Allah's views as king.[71] *It was probably for this that he was stripped of office and title when the party returned to Kabul.*

ᶜAli Ahmad was expecting to be granted a promised pension when the Shinwari and other tribes of the Eastern Province rose up against Aman Allah Khan. An army led by Mahmud Khan Yawar;[72] the president of the national assembly, Shayr Ahmad Khan; and the foreign minister, Ghulam Siddiq, was sent to put down the rebellion. But because of the double-dealing of Ghulam Siddiq, who faked capture by the rebels but in reality went over to their camp voluntarily and incited them to attack Jalalabad, success eluded the force.

ᶜAli Ahmad was then appointed High Commissioner (*raʾīs-i aᶜlā wa mukhtār-i muṭlaq*)[73] of the Eastern and Southern Provinces and ordered to suppress the revolt. A week before the first attack by the "watercarrier's boy" on Kabul, in late December, ᶜAli Ahmad left for Jalalabad at the head of a large force equipped with mountain guns, siege weapons, and armored cars. There he managed to pacify the rebels, winning over the savage Shinwaris to obedience to the amir with cash and other gifts.

After ᶜInayat Allah's abdication and the capture of Kabul by Habib Allah's forces, the people of the Jalalabad region proclaimed ᶜAli Ahmad amir. However, being a man of foresight, he refused to accept the amirate at first and agreed only after concluding pacts with the heads of the tribes.

He then put together a force to attack Kabul and overthrow Habib Allah. It was made up of both the regular army troops who had been sent to Jalalabad to pacify the Shinwari, as well as contingents from the Shinwari itself and from the Khugyani. He ordered some of them to march to Samuchha-i Mulla ᶜUmar and take up positions there and others to go to Tangi Khurd Kabul and Chinari.[74] He also let it be known that he would lead the campaign force against Kabul himself. Then at the head of two thousand regular army and tribal militia, ᶜAli Ahmad marched to Jagdalak,[75] where he waited for a force of Mohmands who had promised to join him. Over the course of seven days, from January 23 to 29, 1929, he sent out farmans proclaiming his amirate to tribal elders in Kabul, Logar, the Hazarahjat, the Southern Province, and elsewhere, and called on people to join him and render their obedience.

When ᶜAli Ahmad and his force arrived in Jagdalak to await the arrival of the Mohmands, rumors circulated in Kabul that his attack on the city would begin in a day or two. Driven to despair by the tyranny of the mountain marauders, the inhabitants of Kabul patiently waited for ᶜAli Ahmad's attack so that they could avenge themselves on Habib Allah, Sayyid Husayn, and the other felons.

However, during this time of hopeful anticipation, Malik Qays of the Khugyani tribe, who had at first allied himself with ᶜAli Ahmad, now annulled his agreement on the grounds that ᶜAli Ahmad had insulted the Khugyani and had bastinadoed him. With a few of his followers, Malik Qays came to Habib Allah and, in return for the sum of seventeen thousand rupees and the rank of lieutenant general, promised to capture ᶜAli Ahmad and deliver him to Kabul in chains. Two or three days before Malik Qays' arrival, Habib Allah had sent emissaries to ᶜAli Ahmad—Muhammad Musa Khan Muhammadzai and ᶜAli Ahmad's uncle, Muhammad ᶜAli Khan, whose home the amir had looted and whom he had arrested and then released. He sent a farman with these men which called on ᶜAli Ahmad to renounce the amirate, declare his obedience to Habib Allah, and voluntarily come to Kabul. Otherwise both of his wives, one of whom was Amir Aman Allah's sister and the other the sister of Gul Muhammad Khan and daughter of Taj Muhammad Khan,[76] as well as other close relatives of his—the aunt of the minister of education Fayz Muhammad and the mother of Ghulam Muhammad Khan and Nur

Ahmad Khan—would be dishonored and then killed.

The two men reached ᶜAli Ahmad and delivered the farman. They had yet to receive an answer from him when the godless Malik Qays departed Kabul and arrived in Tangi Khurd Kabul where ᶜAli Ahmad's new headquarters were then situated. Malik Qays called on the Khugyani tribals and the regular troops who were manning the region to lay down their weapons. After some minor skirmishes he managed to put ᶜAli Ahmad's troops out of action and they straggled into Kabul, demoralized and stripped of their weapons. Consequently, the forces supporting ᶜAli Ahmad that were in Chinari and Samuchha-i Mulla ᶜUmar awaiting orders to attack Kabul were neutralized. They abandoned their field guns and rifles and headed for Kabul to declare their obedience to Habib Allah. For two days they camped on the parade ground (*chaman-i ḥużūrī*) where they were serenaded by the military band. Later they went to see the Amir in the Arg. Festivities went on for three nights after which the amir issued an order that the tribal irregulars who had come to Kabul were to enroll in his army.

The news of the Khugyani tribe's treachery aroused feelings of envy in the deluded hearts of the two thousand Shinwaris stationed at Chang Pass[77] and still loyal to ᶜAli Ahmad. When they had first arrived in Jagdalak, ᶜAli Ahmad had ordered them to share some cows that he gave them for food. But being accustomed to getting whatever they wanted by force, they refused the cows on the grounds that they were too old and scrawny and instead they attacked the transport, disarmed the regular soldiers, tore down ᶜAli Ahmad's tent, and scattered his gear on the ground. ᶜAbd al-Rahman Khan[78]—the son of ᶜIsmat Allah Khan Ghilzai—who for some time had nurtured a feeling of hatred for the government, seized approximately three hundred thousand rupees from ᶜAli Ahmad. A small group of maliks from Laghman then managed to spirit away ᶜAli Ahmad, two of his sons, and the son of Mirza Aqa Jan Khan, his clerk, and deliver them to the safekeeping of the man who had proclaimed ᶜAli Ahmad's amirate.

This man, a *naqīb*,[79] was well aware of the whole situation and what the Khugyani and Shinwari were up to and himself decided to depart for India with his family. Although the Khugyanis and Shinwaris were preoccupied at this time with plundering and fighting over weapons and ammunition, nevertheless, as soon as they learned of his plans, they came to him, apologized for their actions, and begged him not to go. The naqib agreed on condition that they again offer ᶜAli Ahmad their support. But ᶜAli Ahmad, who realized that the Shinwari and the other border tribes simply could not be trusted to uphold their agreements, concluded that there would be no point in a new pact and so only negotiated with them to extricate himself from their clutches. Later, complaining of his treatment at the hands of the tribal sardars and the pseudo-mullas who supported them, he recalled the verses of Amir ᶜAbd al-Rahman Khan which the latter had translated into Persian from a Pushtu verse and recorded in his own journal:

> You may try gently for hundreds of years to make friends,
> But it is impossible to make scorpions, snakes and Shinwari, friends.[80]

The Tajik Administration in Kabul

With Ahmad ᶜAli's claim to the amirate now shown to be without much substance, Fayz Muhammad continues the saga of Habib Allah's regime, stressing the hardships it placed on the residents of Kabul and, in particular, on his own people, the Hazarahs. He begins with a report of administrative edicts and reorganizations but quickly lapses into recounting the depredations of the "northerners." He accuses them of committing assaults, break-ins, and theft. He especially highlights sexual assaults on women and children. Over and over he characterizes the Kuhistanis and Kuhdamanis as uncivilized people, "wanderers in the desert and roamers in mountain wastes, thieves, brigands, and mulberry-eaters," the latter perhaps intended as the worst slur of all.

Two days after ᶜInayat Allah Khan's abdication, Habib Allah and Sayyid Husayn along with a group of Kuhistani and Kuhdamani know-nothings and miscreants, bestowed high ranks on themselves and took up the reins of government.

First of all, they issued an edict on the status of all government employees. But almost immediately another decree superseded the first.[81] The ministry of trade, which oversaw the import and export of goods and controlled public expenditure for imported goods, thereby protecting the wealth of the country and maintaining a steady flow of the necessities of life such as food and clothing, was abolished. The ministries of health, education, and justice were also abolished. The employees of several other government ministries were dismissed and salaries were cut for those who remained.

In departments and bureaus they reverted to the old system employed under the amirs ᶜAbd al-Rahman and Habib Allah. They threw out the *handasah* system of numbers and re-introduced the *siyāq* system of symbols in place of numbers.

All judicial processes were now transferred back to the *qażi*-courts. The regulations on public punishments,[82] which are a deterrent to irrational animosity and a defense against immorality, were committed to the flames, with the exception of two or three articles. This, despite the fact that all the discarded articles were in conformity with the Hanafi-Sunni Shariᶜah.[83] Regarding judicial procedure, it was decreed that the qazi-judge, as in the time of Amir Aman Allah Khan, did not have the right to hear a case if no documentary evidence were presented. However, the new qazi of Kabul, conscious of the fact that he would not be able to take bribes if this were the case, began to process cases without such evidence, finding his authority in the Koranic, "O Believers, when you contract a debt one upon another for a stated term, write it down and let a writer write it down between you justly."[84] Because of this, people began to file frivolous lawsuits against one other. This pushed society toward the abyss: plaintiffs were compelled to bribe the judge and students to bribe officials. As a result, no one had money left even for food.[85]

Amirid decrees were affirmed at sessions of the National Council (*majlis-i shūrā*) and the Islamic Regulatory Commission (*Hayʾat-i Tanẓīmīyah Islāmīyah*). This was staffed by other infidels from Kuhistan and Kuhdaman. But not one of these edicts, which were posted in places where people congregate, was ever carried out.

In late Jady [mid-January], Habib Allah issued a farman to pay a monthly salary to Afghan teachers who taught writing and the fundamentals of the Shariᶜah in the madrasahs. The teachers went to Malik Muhsin, the governor-general of Kabul, to get him to implement this for them. But he accused them of unbelief and ordered them beaten. Some were struck on the head, neck, and abdomen with rifle butts. Others were attacked with rocks and sticks.

I do not know how it is possible to correlate these acts with their assurances of devotion to the religion. To the contrary, it is impossible to call them anything but enemies and destroyers of religion, state and the Islamic people. There are no other words to describe their barbarism. All the farmans and decrees signed and circulated by the Amir and all their assurances of religious devotion are simply a fraud on the people. They appropriated all the wealth of the government that was intended for the defense of the country and the honor of its people. In addition, people are forced to serve in the army of Habib Allah without pay. This army is in reality an army of Satans, destroying buildings and plundering homes. Nonetheless, the corrupt ministers, hazrats, false mullas, and other godless people regard this tragic situation, for which they are guilty, as quite normal. Well, we will see how Almighty God will deal with them!

^{c}Ata al-Haqq, Foreign Minister

Anyway, Shayr Jan, who had commanded a squadron of the Royal Cavalry during the late Amir Habib Allah's reign, was named minister of court and his brother ^{c}Ata al-Haqq was appointed foreign minister. ^{c}Abd al-Ghafur Khan, the son of Muhammad Shah Tarabi [*sic*—Tagabi][86] of the Safi tribe, became minister of the interior; Malik Muhsin of Saray Khwajah was named governor-general of the Central Province [Kabul]; Sayyid Husayn, minister of defense (*wazīr-i jang*); and Purdil Khan and ^{c}Abd al-Wakil Khan, field marshals (*sipāhsālār*s) of the army. Hamid Allah, the "second son of the water-carrier," was given the title "Sardar-i ^{c}Ali" [life or honorary sardar]. And the rest of these criminals were given high military rank—such as general, brigadier-general, lieutenant-general, and colonel.

*Burhan al-Din Kushkaki, writing soon after the collapse of the Saqqawist regime, adds to Fayz Muhammad's list of central government appointments Sayyid Muhammad as commander of the Arg (*qal^{c}ah-begi*);*[87] *Mirza Mujtaba Khan as minister of finance (*wakīl-i wizārat-i māliyah*) and (Muhammad) Mahfuz as war minister (*wakīl-i wizārat-i ḥarbiyah*), an office presumably distinct from minister of defense.*[88]

Hamid Allah, brother of Habib Allah

Muhammad Mahfuz,
Deputy Minister of War

We know other appointments were also made at this time and must assume that the normal requirements of rewarding his supporters would have compelled the new amir to fill every available post with his own people. One of the more important and soon beleaguered officials was Kaka Muhsin, a Qizilbash of the Kacharlu clan. Kaka Muhsin was appointed governor of the Hazarahjat and tried to take up his post in Bihsud but, as will be seen, was unable to do so. Elsewhere, Muhammad Karim Khan was sent as governor to Ghazni; Khwajah Mir ᶜAlam was named governor of Mazar-i Sharif; Ghulam Muhammad Khan was given the governorship of Tagab; Chighil Khan was sent as governor to Charikar; a Jaghuri Hazarah, Nadir ᶜAli, was named governor of Jaghuri and Malistan, but like Kaka Muhsin was unable to take up his post because of local resistance; and Mir Baba Sahib Charikari was sent to Qataghan. There were, no doubt, many other appointments at this time as well.

The very early days of Habib Allah's regime are not well represented in Fayz Muhammad's work and his silence about what was happening in the second half of January and all of February is difficult to explain. Perhaps he did not actually begin to keep a journal until March when opposition to Habib Allah reached a certain intensity. Or perhaps the takeover was first greeted with hope that the corruption of the Aman Allah regime would be replaced with administrative probity. The Hazarah historian may have felt an initial sympathy for the Tajik leader. Like the Hazarahs, the Tajiks were a minority in Afghanistan and like the Hazarahs subject to the caprices of the Afghan majority. The Tajik takeover may have seemed like a good thing at first. But the honeymoon, if there was one, lasted no longer than the requisite month.

After the brief record of initial administrative appointments, Fayz Muhammad reverts to a narrative condemning the new regime for a variety of sins.

During the first few days of his regime, Habib Allah promised to give those sardars and notables who voluntarily came to wait upon him a sum of money equal to half the salary of a *mu*ᶜ*īn*.[89] In their stupidity they believed his promises and rejoiced. But of course they were simply arrested and their belongings confiscated. After that, Habib Allah and his followers began to extort large sums of money from merchants and community leaders (arbabs).[90]

Then they started on the women. They forced the daughter of the late "Naᵓib al-saltanah" (Vice-Regent) Sardar Nasr Allah Khan [the second son of Amir ᶜAbd al-Rahman] to marry her uncle, Prince Amin Allah Khan, another son of ᶜAbd al-Rahman. They found the registration list containing the names of the girls attending the Masturat School[91] and ordered that each of these girls be given to a Kuhistani or Kuhdamani brigand, men who ate mulberries and wore rags for clothing.

People who had never laid eyes on wheat bread in their lives were now issuing orders to remove from the Arg the treasury and arsenal which had been accumulated over the course of fifty years through the toil and sweat of the common people. By day and by night they trucked this wealth away to Charikar and Jabal al-Siraj. The Arg, once a symbol of purity, was transformed by these thieves into a latrine. Hiding behind Islamic slogans, they wrought a disaster impossible for the human mind to comprehend.

Each day the voice of the town crier could be heard: "Shops must open and anyone caught looting will be shot." But this gang of thieves would never pay for goods but would stuff them in the sacks that they always carried. There was a proclamation that if a weapon was found in anyone's home, the owner of the house would be shot and his property confiscated. So, on the pretext of searching for weapons, these bandits would break into homes and seize money and household belongings. Many people suffered grievous losses as a result. These looters even stopped Waziri, Mangal, Wardak, and Hazarah militiamen and stole their weapons and money. And if anyone resisted, he was shot.

One day a group of Hazarahs who had fallen into difficult straits and turned to Habib Allah for help received permission to return to their homes. The group, which numbered some fifteen hundred men, had reached the Mashin Khanah Bridge,[92] which connects with the Qal^{c}ah-i Hazarah, when suddenly one of Habib Allah's gang confronted them and ordered one of the Hazarahs to remove his shoes and hand them over. But the Hazarah, knowing how difficult it would be to go barefoot in the middle of January, appealed to him, "O brother! You say you are a Muslim and a fighter for the faith. We too are Muslims. So I beg you to excuse me and let me keep these old shoes. Truly, they don't belong to the government but to me." But without even letting the Hazarah finish what he was saying, this infidel clubbed him to death with his gun and yanked off his shoes. People who witnessed this incident then seized the godless one and brought him to Habib Allah. The amir, eager to show that he was a zealous follower of the Shari^{c}ah, declared, "We must exact vengeance on this sepoy." However, there was a colonel present named Ghulam Nabi who was himself of Hazarah origin and had worked hard to reach his high rank. Not knowing the laws of the Shari^{c}ah, he turned to Habib Allah and his courtiers, inveterate miscreants all, and said in an obsequious way, "One of our brothers has already perished. We do not want another one to perish as well. Therefore we will not demand revenge." The mullas and others present at the assembly nodded their heads in approval, applauding his declaration with cries of "well done!" although he had no kinship tie whatever with the murdered man.

So they freed the murderer and gave not a thought to the relatives of the victim—his wife, son and daughter—who were his legal heirs. They ignored the verse of the Koran which says, "And the thief, male and female: cut off the hands of both, as a recompense for what they have earned and a punishment exemplary from God."[93]

Evacuation of Foreigners

During the turmoil, the ambassadors of Italy, France, Germany, Turkey, and Iran, concerned about the fate and the property of their citizens who worked in Kabul under contract with the Afghan government and others employed in trade and tourism, appealed to the Great Power—England—and requested she evacuate their countrymen from Afghanistan. Britain agreed to do so. First women then men were taken by plane from Kabul to Peshawar. The evacuation of all foreign citizens from Kabul began on January 24 and lasted until the evening of February 21. After everyone had been evacuated, the English minister plenipotentiary, Francis Humphrys, along with the envoys of Italy, France, and Germany, flew to Peshawar.[94]

At the French Embassy, one interpreter remained, a Kabul resident. At the Italian legation there was only a caretaker. The German Embassy was manned by an acting chargé d'affaires who was supposed to negotiate the discontinuance of trade ties. All foreign citizens received compensation for their contracts as well as a month's salary and were sent home in a contented state of mind.[95]

Demonstrations of Support for Aman Allah in Kabul

Local opposition to the new regime in Kabul itself was somewhat muted. Fayz Muhammad records only two instances of public protest, one of them involving a dream about the First Shi[c]*ite Imam (and fourth Sunni caliph),* [c]*Ali b. Abi Talib.*

On February 21, Muhammad Aslam Baluch, who had once been a British subject and then fled and settled in Kabul, wrote an appeal to the people of the capital and posted it at the Chawk where people always gather. "O people," he wrote, "any of you who do not yet have rifles, get them! The new government will give you cartridges so that you can defend yourself and your property from the tribes which have risen against Amir Aman Allah." He was arrested by Habib Allah's people and fined two thousand rupees, but then because of a lack of evidence they released him from prison.

On March 4, ^{c}Abd al-Razzaq, a *sayyid* [descendant of the Prophet Muhammad] from a line of Kunar sayyids, broke into the house of an Iranian citizen named Ziya Humayun who was one of those evacuated to Peshawar. Ziya had locked his house and sent the key to the Iranian consulate. The sayyid broke into the house and raised a flag on it bearing the logo of Aman Allah's government. He then declared that his forebear, ^{c}Ali Murtaza [the son-in-law of the Prophet], had appeared to him in a dream and told him to raise the flag. When the story spread through the city, people came in small groups to have a look at the flag.

Habib Allah's men ordered the sayyid to take it down. But he refused saying, "I raised it as ordered by my revered ancestor and I therefore cannot take it down. If you think you can, you take it down." But try as they might, the men were unable to. In the aftermath of this incident, a rumor spread that Habib Allah had sent the sayyid two thousand rupees to take down the flag, which he refused. Then he was promised ten or twenty thousand rupees if he would lower the flag but still he refused. Finally, on March 14, the new governor-general, Malik Muhsin, ordered the flag be lowered and the sayyid hoisted instead. His men then tore down the flag, hung the sayyid up by his heels and attached the flag to his side. He hung there until Sayyid Husayn, a rival of the governor-general's, saved him. Sayyid Husayn also confiscated several leaflets from him which had been circulating throughout the city and which called for people to support Amir Aman Allah Khan. Some of those leaflets, which were distributed in Kuhdaman, bore the date 24 Ramazan 1347 [March 7, 1929].

Sayyid ^{c}Abd al-Razzaq, spared by Sayyid Husayn who respected him as a fellow sayyid, was soon in trouble again. He and 400 other Kabulis signed a declaration of loyalty to Aman Allah and put their thumbprints on the document in black ink. For this, Habib Allah had him hanged in the Chawk on March 23 along with Muhammad ^{c}Isa, the son of Muhammad Ishaq Khan Popalzaʾi. Muhammad ^{c}Isa had been a supervisor (*nāẓir*)[96] during ^{c}Ali Ahmad's governorate-general in Kabul and later had incited the people of Logar against Habib Allah on behalf of ^{c}Ali Ahmad in the latter's abortive campaign for the amirate. Habib Allah ordered their bodies to be left hanging for three days.

Habib Allah's Struggle to Extend His Control and Defend Kabul

It was one thing to seize control of the capital, oust the Muhammadzai royals, and appoint new officials. It was quite another to extend the authority represented by the capital to other parts of the country. On the one hand, Habib Allah was now master of the Kabul region, but on the other he was effectively surrounded and besieged. For the next several months he would fight opponents on a number of fronts. Although opposition emerged in many parts of the country, there were five main areas in which Fayz Muhammad reports that armed resistance was concentrated. These areas, not coincidentally, also happened to be the homes of ethnic groups opposed for one reason or another to a Tajik takeover of the government. They were, first, the mainly Pushtun regions known as the Eastern Province and the Southern Province; second, the southern part of the Central, or Kabul, Province, now Logar and Maydan (also known as Wardak); third, the Hazarahjat west of the Kabul-Ghazni road; fourth, the Ghurband Valley to the north, through which communications ran to Mazar-i Sharif and Afghan Turkistan; and fifth, Tagab to the northeast, which was an important accessway to the Laghman Valley and lay along one route to the Panjshir (or Panjshayr) Valley, which in turn provided access to the northeastern part of the country. If one imagines Kabul as the hub of a wheel and the roads connecting Kabul to the rest of the country as the wheel's very irregular spokes, each of these spokes would become a battleground. It would not be until mid-August that some sort of equilibrium would be reached, with Habib Allah having either negotiated or won by contest control of those spokes and the villages and towns that lay along them.

Much of Fayz Muhammad's narrative is taken up with these contests and negotiations, but because the narrative is arranged in a fairly strictly controlled journalistic format, it is difficult for the reader to follow events in any one of the regions. On occasion it appears that it was difficult for the author himself. To make it easier to follow what was happening in the country, I have rearranged the material according to the regions where the fighting took place rather than follow his strictly day-by-day method of narrating the events.

The Kabul-Qandahar Routes

One of the most difficult tasks for the amir was securing control of the main road between Kabul and Qandahar, the country's two largest cities. Qandahar (Kandahar) lies about 320 miles southwest of Kabul. From Qandahar the road runs northeast to Ghazni, 220 miles away. From there two more or less parallel routes continue on to Kabul, the more easterly one via the Logar Valley and the other via the region known as Maydan or Wardak (this latter route about ten miles longer). Some of the stiffest resistance faced by the new amir came along the Maydan/Wardak branch of the route between Ghazni and Kabul where loyalty to the ousted amir, Aman Allah, remained particularly strong.

About twenty miles southwest of Kabul are two junctions, not far apart, linking the Maydan/Wardak road with the mountainous heart of the country known as the Hazarahjat. One road heads due west through the heart of the Maydan region to the towns of Kut-i Ashru, Jalriz (Jaliz), and Sar-i Chashmah, and then on to the Unay Pass, which marked the beginning of Hazarah territory. The junction farther to the south leads to Narkh, then over another pass, the Khirs Khanah Pass, to the town of Day Mirdad and then on to the Bihsud region. These roads allowed Wardak and Hazarah forces to link up, when they were of a mind to do so, and bring their combined forces to bear on the Kabul-Ghazni road, where fighting was heavy in March and April.

There was a good deal of fighting in the Logar Valley as well, the parallel route running south from Kabul through the Altamur or Tirah Pass to Gardiz. Here pro–Aman Allah forces were less in evidence than were backers of one of Aman Allah's generals, Field Marshal Muhammad Nadir Khan. Combined with the discussion of the Logar Valley theater of operations is the account of what was taking place along the road from Kabul that follows the Kabul River east to Jalalabad. This road skirts the northern end of the road up through the Logar Valley to the capital. The activities of opposition groups along this route were generally closely related to opposition fighting in the Logar Valley.

The first of the major battles fought along the Maydan branch of the Kabul-Ghazni road, according to Fayz Muhammad, did not occur until early March, sometime before the 13th, although Fayz Muhammad uncharacteristically provides no exact date. It took place at Shaykhabad, 46 miles from Kabul, or halfway to Ghazni. Here the Wardak people, whom the British in the nineteenth century understood to be "a tribe of Saiyids,"[97] *that is, descendants of the Prophet Muhammad, controlled a long stretch of the route and had given their name to the region in the process. Fayz Muhammad provides a relatively detailed account of this battle, compared to his other more laconic reports on instances of fighting.*[98]

Karim Khan Wardak, who had refused to pledge allegiance to Habib Allah, set up defenses at Shaykhabad and the region of Zarani [Zarnay] and dug tunnels under the snow. A 3,000-man force left Kabul for Ghazni and Qandahar under the command of ᶜAbd al-Wakil Khan, a field marshal. When it reached Qalᶜah-i Durrani [thirty miles from Kabul] and the village of Bini Badam, the army halted there to deal with Karim Khan's forces and only then to proceed. But Karim Khan, along with the Wazir and Hazarah leaders who had gathered at Shaykhabad in support of Aman Allah, sent a joint message to the field marshal that said,

> We, the peoples of the region of Wardak, consider ourselves subjects of Amir Habib Allah. However, since we have yet to send him our oaths of allegiance, we fear that if his army should come it might be to attack us and plunder our property. But if he shows forgiveness and agrees to these four conditions, we will not stand in the way of your victorious army. Our conditions are the following:
>
> First: the fortress of ᶜAbd al-Ahad Khan who left for Qandahar with Amir Aman Allah must be protected against looting and his people from punishment.
>
> Second: The rifles distributed to us by Amir Aman Allah must be left in our possession.
>
> Third: All of us, the people of Wardak, living on the territory up to Ghazni, must not be subject to looting nor violence even though we have not yet sent oaths of allegiance.
>
> Fourth: When your army passes through our territory during its two day march, all forage and provisions must be procured for cash at market prices and not taken without payment or in the form of a requisition (*sūrsāt*).
>
> Once your army has passed through, we promise to go to Kabul and offer our oath of allegiance to the Amir with sincere hearts.

The inexperienced ᶜAbd al-Wakil accepted this message at face value and ordered the Model Battalion, which numbered eighteen hundred men and was stationed at Qalᶜah-yi Durrani, to march to Shaykhabad along with four hundred of the Royal Cavalry and eight hundred Kuhistani and Kuhdamani infantry militia who had halted near the village of Bini Badam. The road over which they marched was hemmed in on both sides by snow-covered hills so that the men had to walk in close formation and were forced to drag their baggage, artillery, and pack animals along with them. The march utterly exhausted them. As the vanguard passed the fort at Zarani, which stands at the edge of the Dasht-i Tup waste land, and the rest of the force was approaching the hills that lay nearby, one of the soldiers shot at a bird. The Wardak, waiting in ambush, heard the shot, thought that their positions had been discovered, and opened fire.

From both sides of the road and from the hilltops a mighty fusillade came thundering down. Men and horses dropped like flies. During the attack, the Wardak shouted to the Model Battalion soldiers and the men from Chardihi to save themselves and get away from the Kuhistanis. But because the units of the army were all intermingled they could not do this. Those who could escape fled toward Logar to the east with the Wardak in pursuit. Many more of the amir's men were killed at the pass leading to the Logar Valley and their weapons fell into the hands of the Wardak braves and their allies. The people of Logar then robbed and shot the rest. A number managed to survive and get back home where Habib Allah had them arrested and beaten. Of the entire force only twenty of the four hundred cavalrymen survived.

Over the course of the next two weeks Habib Allah's forces seem to have made little progress. Bottled up in the Maydan region about thirty miles from Kabul, they had to be concerned about the possibility of forces loyal to Aman Allah marching on Kabul. But the disparate groups that remained loyal to Aman Allah had their own problems. Unable to coordinate their activities, they did not succeed in mounting a sustained offensive against Kabul along this route. They fought well against efforts by Habib Allah to dislodge them but were never able to move from the defensive to the offensive. As in the struggle against the Soviets and then the successive governments of Najib Allah, Rabbani, and the Taliban in the 1980s and 1990s, village localism prevailed over regional cooperation and fighters fought best, or often would only fight, on their own turf.

Although Fayz Muhammad identifies the Wardak and the Hazarahs of the region as loyal to Aman Allah, each ethnic force or collection of forces seems to have been waiting for one of the others to take the initiative. Habib Allah on the other hand was willing to force the issue at every opportunity. Fayz Muhammad sees the amir's forces defeated and thwarted at every turn and only grudgingly refers to their successes but Habib Allah, in stark contrast to Aman Allah, seems to have understood that he would have to take the fight to his opponents, if he were to prevail. And he did so.

The people of Maydan, Jalriz, and Sanglakh[99] refused to offer allegiance to Habib Allah and instead came out in support of Aman Allah Khan. They formed an alliance with the Wardak and attacked Habib Allah's army in Maydan and Qal^{c}ah-i Durrani. The troops in Maydan were surrounded and the detachment in Qal^{c}ah-i Durrani overrun. Some of the latter escaped to Arghandah [14 miles west of Kabul]. The smaller units stationed in Arghandah were also unable to resist and scattered toward Qal^{c}ah-i Qazi, Chardihi, and Kuhdaman [i.e. into Kabul itself and north to Tajik territory].

The defeat of his own forces combined with the discontent of the people of Kabul who were praying for a quick end to him heightened the amir's worries, and he and a group of his devoted miscreants drove out of Kabul on Friday, March 22 at 5:30 heading for Arghandah. There he managed to bolster the spirits of his soldiers who had fled from Maydan and they now turned around and attacked Aman Allah Khan's supporters who were at Kutal-i Shaykh [a low pass near the intersection with the road west to the Unay Pass]. Habib Allah himself took part in the fighting, drove Aman Allah's backers from Kutal-i Shaykh, and then marched into Maydan.

The battle lasted until evening. While Habib Allah's soldiers were along this side of the [Kabul] river, not far from the Maydan Bridge, he returned to Arghandah and there berated the family and relatives of Muhammad Akbar Khan, Sar Buland Khan's[100] son, for the fact that Akbar had supported Aman Allah and refused provisions to the amir's soldiers. The night before, the amir had ordered the confiscation of Muhammad Akbar's house in Kabul. Muhammad Akbar himself was now arrested and taken back to Kabul. His brother was also arrested and the property of four relatives was confiscated. The amir claimed that he had marched as far as Shaykhabad, routed the Wardak, and seized their women.

At 8:30 in the morning on March 23, Habib Allah ordered that five hundred militiamen from Najrab be brought back to Kabul from Maydan where he had sent them several days before. [Najrab lies some forty miles northeast of Kabul and is the next town north of Tagab, where there was active resistance to Habib Allah at this time.] The Najrabis were barracked in a fort that had once belonged to Sardar Wali Muhammad Khan, a son of Amir Dust Muhammad Khan [d. 1863]. The late Amir Habib Allah renamed it Qal^{c}ah-i Mahtab Bagh after building a royal palace and garden there. Habib Allah decided to recall these militiamen because the fighting with the Tagabis had already lasted for too long and he was worried that the militiamen might go over to them. They were disarmed and sent back to Kabul.

Over the course of the next few days, fighting waxed and waned around Habib Allah's positions on the Maydan Road. On the 24th, 26th, and 28th the fighting was relatively intense, according to the news that was reaching Fayz Muhammad, and in his recording of news, the fortunes of the amir appear to swing back and forth.

At eight in the evening on Sunday, the 24th, the amir ordered some Kuhdamanis, Kuhistanis, and people from the villages of Dih-i Nur, Maydan, and Arghandah to cover the army rear which was then at Qal^{c}ah-i Durrani and Pul-i Maydan and so deny those awaiting its defeat the chance to march on Chardihi and Kuhdaman. With reinforcements, Field Marshal Purdil Khan, who had since been named minister of defense (*wazir-i jang*),[101] was now sure of victory and today he shelled and destroyed several forts in Maydan. Because of these barbaric acts, the people of Maydan, Arghandah, and Sanglakh were all the more committed to fighting Habib Allah. They even won to their cause the Tajiks living in Takana and Jalriz. So, the war goes on. But despite the capture of Maydan, Habib Allah's army is not able to advance toward Wardak and Ghazni, for the Wardaks are holding fast.

On the 26th more fighting broke out in Maydan. Habib Allah's forces were defeated and fled to Arghandah and Qal^{c}ah [-i Qazi?] but could not find a safe haven.

At this time, Aman Allah was supposedly leaving Qandahar with a tribal army (lashkar) *made up of Durrani, Khattak, Ghilzai, and Hazarah fighters. Fayz Muhammad would not know this until two weeks later, when he heard a report broadcast from Bombay.*

On March 27, Habib Allah ordered his brother, Hamid Allah, to lead a force of Panjshiris [i.e. Tajiks] and a detachment of the amir's personal guard, backed by fourteen siege guns, to Maydan. Soldiers were not to use their rifles but only the siege guns, which they were supposed to emplace on hilltops with the aid of elephants and then use to bombard the forts until they surrendered. At Kutal-i Shaykh, this force scattered the defenders with artillery fire and then marched into Maydan. There they destroyed several forts, taking prisoner twenty-five men whom they delivered to Kabul.

On the 28th, brave Jadrani, Waziri, and Wardak warriors who held positions in the hills overlooking Maydan, Qal^{c}ah-i Durrani,[102] and Dasht-i Tup made a night attack on the amir's army, killed and wounded a thousand men, captured their field guns and rifles, and withdrew into the hills. Before sunrise, survivors of the attack sent to Kabul twenty-eight men who lived in Lalandar and Maydan, had not expressed their obedience to Habib Allah, and were taken prisoner during the fighting. At noon on the 28th, their faces smeared with filth, they were led through the bazaars to the accompaniment of music played by the military band. This sowed much anxiety in the hearts of the people who, depressed and driven to despair by the violence of the Kuhistanis and Kuhdamanis, have been impatiently awaiting the return of Aman Allah Khan.

But Fayz Muhammad continued to interpret the rumors coming from Maydan in as favorable a light as possible, blaming Habib Allah's supporters for spreading false rumors that Aman Allah, whom Fayz Muhammad believed was actually in the Maydan region, had now fled back to Qandahar. His depiction of the fighting relied heavily on his own observations of trucks bringing the wounded back to Kabul and on rumors filtered through his own conviction that Aman Allah would return and rescue Kabul from the "watercarrier's boy." From the very end of March until the middle of April, the amir's troops seem to have had a difficult time advancing along the road, or at least to consolidate their positions. Qal^{c}ah-i Durrani, a fort some thirty miles from Kabul, was crucial *to their efforts to move against the disparate forces in the Maydan-Wardak region and it is the one place their opponents never managed to seize.*

March 30:[103] At dawn today, men from the Wazir, Jadran, and Wardak tribes,[104] along with residents of Maydan and other partisans of Aman Allah, attacked Habib Allah's army at Maydan and Qal^c^ah-i Durrani. They surrounded some detachments in the fortress known as Qal^c^ah-i ^c^Abd al-Ghani Khan Beg Samandi[105] and routed others, driving them into the mountains of Kuh-i Quruq. A large part of the defeated army escaped to Arghandah and Qal^c^ah-i Qazi. Habib Allah dispatched reinforcements from Kabul that reached the battlefield toward evening.

The next day, at two in the afternoon, Karim Khan, the leader of the Wardaks who lived in Tangi, was brought to Kabul in a car escorted by forty-two guards riding in three trucks and shouting "ya chahar yar." Recently, backed by ^c^Abd Allah Khan the son of Qazi Ghulam of Shaykhabad, some nomads from the Waziri tribe, and a group of the Wardak, Karim had attacked Habib Allah's force that was headed for Ghazni and Qandahar. A young man who had led an advance party of Karim's force was also brought in. Once in the city, they were paraded through the streets and bazaars. There is a rumor, however, that the person they brought in was not Karim Khan but another Wardak named ^c^Abd al-Karim. This proved to be true and so the next day the amir ordered ^c^Abd al-Karim's release.[106]

For several days, the Wardak-Maydan front was relatively quiet, or at least little news was making its way to Fayz Muhammad. He reported that the amir went to Maydan on the 31st and returned in the evening claiming progress for his forces, a claim Fayz Muhammad would dismiss, though he doesn't say how he knew it to be false. He also reports the news reaching him of prisoners being brought from the Wardak region. On the 31st eight Wardak men were brought to a prison near the Harten Bridge (Pul-i Artan)[107] *and the following day another seventy. Because of his pointed dislike of the amir, one has to assume that Fayz Muhammad was downplaying the amir's successes and exaggerating his setbacks. It seems clear that Habib Allah was making progress toward Ghazni because Fayz Muhammad, having up to now told of battles about thirty to forty miles from Kabul, suddenly has Wardaks attacking Habib Allah's army as it approached Shash Gaw, a village near the pass of the same name, just thirteen miles north of Ghazni. This meant that rather than being bottled up near Qal*[c]*ah-i Durrani some thirty miles from Kabul and sixty from Ghazni, the Tajik amir's men had almost reached Ghazni itself. But there was also information that Aman Allah had actually made his way to Ghazni.*

April 2: At 5:30 the radio reported that Aman Allah had entered Ghazni and is going to move on Kabul. But we do not know how likely this is.

April 3: This evening, the Wardaks, lying in wait in the mountains, attacked Habib Allah's army as it approached the village of Shash Gaw. They killed or wounded seven hundred men, capturing their rifles and pieces of field artillery. Five hundred men from Najrab who were in the amir's army are unaccounted for. They say that Aman Allah's older brother, [c]Inayat Allah, led the attackers.

But the fighting went on for another three weeks or so before the backers of Aman Allah gave up and made their separate deals with the Tajik amir. One skirmish on April 7 at Shiniz, another village near Ghazni, was serious enough to prompt the amir to divert a thousand-man force he was planning to send to the Hazarahjat toward Wardak, or so Fayz Muhammad says. There must have been another serious clash about the same time northwest of Ghazni at Jaghatu, well to the west of the Kabul-Ghazni road, because Fayz Muhammad tells us that on the 9th, a hundred Wardak prisoners taken there were paraded around the bazaars of Kabul to show its citizens that Habib Allah now had control of the whole Ghazni region. That same day, the second Battle of Shaykhabad was fought, more or less the last major offensive of the anti-government forces.

April 9: A fierce battle was fought today in the village of Shaykhabad, on Wardak territory. Habib Allah's army realized that Aman Allah's supporters were far stronger than they were and had telephoned Kabul the day before for reinforcements. At one o'clock in the afternoon, the amir left for the battlefield together with his brother Hamid Allah, Sayyid Husayn Charikari, his Field Marshal and Minister of Defense Purdil Khan, and other battle-hardened veterans. They traveled in seven vehicles.

Fayz Muhammad does not relate the outcome if he knew it. But two

A group of "Northerners," Hamid Allah front row, center

days later he is reporting (probably false) news of a major defeat for Habib Allah's forces at some unspecified place near Ghazni.

April 11: There are rumors today among the partisans of Aman Allah that the troops of Habib Allah have suffered a crushing defeat near Ghazni (on the 9th). Two men, a brigadier general and a colonel, nephews of Malik Zayn al-ᶜAbidin (an official in the Central Customs Department), were severely wounded and taken prisoner; many others were also killed or captured; the survivors reportedly fled to Qalᶜah-i Durrani. The two wounded nephews of the above-mentioned Zayn al-ᶜAbidin were transported to Kabul. One died the first night but the other survived.

April 12: In response to the rumor that Aman Allah had surrounded Ghazni, Purdil telephoned for more ammunition and Habib Allah sent him a wagon train with a huge supply.

April 13: Rumor has it that Habib Allah received a letter today from Aman Allah in which the latter demanded that he stop the bloodshed, rebellion, and destruction and step down from the throne. Otherwise, in a few days Aman Allah would launch a major offensive against him. And victory will go to the one whom God helps.

On the 14th of the month there were reports of wounded government soldiers being brought to Kabul hospitals from Wardak and Ghazni and two days later there were more reports that indicated that Aman Allah was winning out against Habib Allah's supporters.

April 16: Today, three planes made two sorties each to Ghazni and Logar, where fighting rages. They dropped bombs and a proclamation that denounced Muhammad Nadir Khan and his brothers as infidels[108] as well as others that said that Aman Allah was under arrest and being brought to Kabul by plane.

Also today, Hazarahs of the Bul Hasan clan of Bihsud and ᶜAla al-Din of Jaghuri[109] attacked Purdil Khan at Shash Gaw. Purdil, one of the amir's field marshals, had abandoned Ghazni to Aman Allah and then halted in Shash Gaw and requested reinforcements, armaments, and artillery for a counterattack on Ghazni. He and thirteen other men were surrounded but then managed to escape.

Mountain guns, 36-pound guns, and a huge quantity of arms have been sent from Kabul to Ghazni. Rumor has it that Aman Allah Khan took Ghazni, made his headquarters at the fortress called Qalᶜah-i ᶜAbd al-Ahmad Khan, then routed the Sulayman Khayl tribe and reached Shaykh Amir by way of the Majid Pass, where he has defeated detachments loyal to Habib Allah.[110]

On the 19th, after describing the situation as worsening for the amir in Kabul, Fayz Muhammad has him sending Hamid Allah, his brother, to Ghazni with a thousand men. Two days later Fayz Muhammad writes that 385 of the amir's personal guard had been taken prisoner by Aman Allah's forces and that two three-hundred-man battalions had surrendered to the former amir. By the 20th, rumors placed Aman Allah's forces on the doorstep of Paghman, just west of the capital. Moreover, Hazarah forces were rumored to have crossed the Unay Pass and were heading east to attack Kabul.

April 20: Rumors spread that Aman Allah Khan's army had entered Wardak and units of Habib Allah Khan's forces, who had been holding positions on the slopes of the Chihil Tan Mountain, which lies to the north of Qalᶜah-i Qazi, had retreated to the heights of Kuh-i Asmaʾi[111] where they have guns set up.

Word also came today that six thousand Hazarahs from Bihsud have crossed over the Unay Pass on their way to Ghurband and that another force of some one thousand Hazarahs has occupied positions at the pass in order to block Habib Allah's army on its way to the Hazarahjat. Hamid Allah, sent to rally the forces dispatched to Ghazni and the Hazarahjat, gave them their instructions and then returned to Kabul. The force sent to Ghazni retreated back to Shiniz-i Wardak.

April 21: Seven trucks loaded with soldiers left for Ghazni tonight. The situation there is very difficult for the amir's men. Three hundred and eighty-five of his personal guard have been taken prisoner by Aman Allah's forces; fifteen cavalrymen managed to escape, and one made his way to Kabul, where he reported that two three-hundred-man battalions (*fawj*) had laid down their arms and surrendered to Aman Allah.

Toward evening, part of Habib Allah's defeated army arrived in Kabul. Though military leaders had been requesting help by telephone, no soldiers were left in Kabul. Unable to send more forces, the amir ordered his troops to return to the Qal^{c}ah-i Durrani fort and to prevent the units of Aman Allah's army from advancing past it.

The situation was clearly not so dire for the Tajik amir as Fayz Muhammad was painting it. Although rumor had anti-government forces on the doorstep of the capital, within three days the amir was reported driving all the way to Shash Gaw, just north of Ghazni. Fayz Muhammad may have been a reliable reporter of rumor but the rumors were not reliable indicators of the actual military situation. Over the next few days, piecing the rumors into a coherent picture became increasingly difficult.

April 24: In conjunction with the worsening situation in Ghazni, Habib Allah drove with his accomplices tonight in ten cars almost as far as Shash Gaw [thirteen miles northwest of Ghazni]. One of the cars, travelling a long way ahead of the others, was captured by a scouting party loyal to Aman Allah. Habib Allah now posted a 160,000-rupee reward for the assassination of Aman Allah and ordered that leaflets with this announcement be scattered by air.

April 28: Today word came by telephone that Aman Allah's army has been routed at Ghazni and that the victors will bring to Kabul a hundred sixty prisoners, forty automobiles, and four hundred cans of gasoline captured in the fighting.

April 29: Just as lies are of short duration, so is today a contrast to yesterday, when they said that 160 men and forty automobiles had been captured. The rumor is now circulating that Field Marshal Purdil Khan supposedly informed the amir yesterday by telephone that he had not captured any automobiles but rather two armoured cars, twenty-five cans of gasoline, and a hundred fifty people.

Another report says that forty-five vehicles had been seized from Aman Allah and four hundred cans of gasoline, that he himself had fled and his turban had fallen into the hands of one of Habib Allah's soldiers. The amir ordered drivers to bring in the captured vehicles. They also said that of the one hundred fifty men, a hundred were shot—those who were Hazarahs—and the rest were in captivity. But this all turned out to be untrue. They actually brought in only about twenty prisoners from Aman Allah's army, among whom were three Hazarahs. Ten automobiles also arrived carrying government wounded.

From Fayz Muhammad's standpoint, prospects were improving for Aman Allah, and he continues to report the arrival of wounded to Kabul, which he interprets as signs of Habib Allah's weakening position.

During the night [April 30–May 1], sixty-three wounded were brought to Kabul from Ghazni, where a fierce battle had taken place on Tuesday [April 30]. Units of the amir's, occupying positions in Shaykhabad, Takiya, and Shash Gaw—all of which are in the district of Shiniz—have been defeated by Aman Allah Khan's forces and retreated to Dasht-i Tup and Shaykhabad. During the day, four large vehicles arrived in Kabul, in each of which there were twenty to twenty-five wounded men. The people of Chardihi were advised to go to the battlefield and collect their dead.

On May 1 there was another major fight at Dasht-i Tup and Shaykhabad. Again, Fayz Muhammad preferred to interpret the reports as a sign that Aman Allah's forces had the new amir's on the run.

During the fighting Wednesday [May 1] in Dasht-i Tup, several of Habib Allah's men were killed, wounded, or taken prisoner. Aman Allah's men cut off the noses and ears of the prisoners and sent them to Kabul. They released those who paid a ransom of one pound sterling in gold or thirty-five rupees. These actions by Aman Allah's supporters are a response to the brutality, which contravenes the norms of Islam, of those close to Habib Allah. Notwithstanding the precepts of the Prophet and the Shari^cah, the northerners burn the dead, hack the living to pieces, impale them on stakes, nail them by the ears to trees, hang them, and blacken their faces with filth and parade them around the bazaar. They ought to know that a man is a human being, not an animal. The Kuhistanis and Kuhdamanis, on the other hand, are neither humans nor Muslims, but only animals, thieves, and vampires. Therefore, the principle of "a tongue for a tongue and condign punishment for any injury" should be upheld when dealing with them.

May 2: Tonight some 220 wounded who had fought at Shaykhabad, Dasht-i Tup, and Qal^cah-yi Durrani were brought to the city under cover of darkness. Hamid Allah, after setting off for the battlefield four days ago and after the subsequent rout of his force, fled to save himself and returned to the city, where he reported the defeat.

At 7:30 this morning, the two brothers again headed for the battlefield with a gang of brigands and aides in five vehicles.

On the 4th Fayz Muhammad reports conflicting news about Aman Allah and the progress of the struggle on the Kabul-Maydan-Ghazni road.

May 4: Today the mayor of Kabul, Khwajah Taj al-Din, posted notices in some of the busiest areas of the city, announcing the flight of Aman Allah after the defeat of the Sulayman Khayl, Andar, and several other tribes, and the victorious return of the amir's forces. The purpose of posting this notice was to show that the amir's forces had not fled the battlefield in defeat but, on the contrary, had carried the day and then simply dispersed to their homes. They say that such lies and deceit can be learned only from the devil, but in their duplicity and machinations these people far surpass the devil himself.

At this point, Aman Allah sent a message to the people of Kabul that read, "I am fully aware of the difficulties, hardships, unbearable conditions, violence, and robbery being inflicted on the oppressed populace of Kabul. God willing, in a short time I will march into the city and with the help of the All-High rid you of these bloodthirsty brigands." He sent it by the hand of one of his sepoys, who was dressed in civilian clothing. En route the soldier was stopped and searched. He threw the pouch with the letter in it on the ground and ran away. The inspectors delivered the pouch to Habib Allah, who had the two policemen and a colonel arrested for letting Aman Allah's messenger escape.

Also on the evening of the 4th, several vehicles with a large number of wounded again arrived from Shaykhabad. The amir's troops, routed there, have been surreptitiously returning throughout the day in small groups to the city and to Chardihi. Defeated Kuhistanis and Kuhdamanis have also been going home via Begtut and Paghman.

Sometime before May 7, Fayz Muhammad writes that Habib Allah, his back—or so the author believes—against the wall, made an overture to Aman Allah about a possible truce.

May 7: Tonight, forcibly conscripted units were sent to Mahtab Qal^c^ah and Arghandah to set up defenses there. At ten o'clock in the morning an airplane returned. It had delivered a message regarding a possible truce and brought back Aman Allah Khan's answer.

He never does provide, however, a precis of either Habib Allah's message or Aman Allah's response, if indeed there was one. Between May 7 and May 20 he depicts a distraught and desperate Habib Allah.

These days, Habib Allah is depressed because of the defeat of his forces, the loss of dead and prisoners, the escape of survivors back to Kuhdaman and Kuhistan via Paghman and Begtut, and also because of the return to Chardihi of the units routed at Shaykh Yasin, Bambi, and Dasht-i Tup. On May 7, under cover of night, he moved all his women, with the exception of the daughter of Amir Muhammad Khan Muhammadzai who, as was already mentioned, had been forcibly brought to him for his amusement, to the residence of the late prime minister ^c^Abd al-Quddus Khan, which adjoins the northern part of the Burj-i Yadgar[45] and the Shahr Ara palace.

May 8: Five officers who were at Qal^c^ah-yi Durrani were recalled to Kabul because they had threatened Sayyid Muhammad Khan, the brother of the governor-general, Malik Muhsin, at gunpoint. Sayyid Muhammad was aide-de-camp (*yāwar*) to Habib Allah and held the title of qal^c^ah-begi. [In an unrelated case] General ^c^Umar Khan, the son of an official in Central Customs, Zayn al-^c^Abidin Da^o^udza^o^i, was sentenced to a caning and then imprisoned along with a brigadier general (*gundmishr*), the son of Sa^c^id Shah, and ten of his supporters.

Fayz Muhammad later gives the reason for the imprisonment of General ^c^Umar on May 8. The general was recalled to Kabul from

Ghazni and punished when he refused to execute his fellow tribesman, Qazi ᶜAbd al-Rahman Khan.[113] *According to Fayz Muhammad, he had been ordered to draw and quarter the qazi while he was still alive and this he refused to do. Fayz Muhammad also says he was accused of secret correspondence with Aman Allah. The consequence of the arrest was the alienation of the Daᵓudzai tribe, who now allied themselves with Aman Allah. This in turn led Habib Allah to take retribution against the general. He ordered him crucified on May 14. His father, Zayn al-Din, was simultaneously dismissed from his position as head of the Central Customs.*

Purdil Khan, Habib Allah's Field Marshal (sipahsalar)

Purdil Khan departed today (May 8) for Charikar. Also today, two large trucks carrying wounded arrived in Kabul from Dasht-i Tup and Bini Badam where fighting is raging. The casualties were admitted to the Qalᶜah-i Baqir Khan hospital.

Wounded also arrived on the 9th and the 14th, and news of the capture of one of Habib Allah's generals, General Muhammad ᶜUmar Khan, known as "Janrāl-i Sūr" *in Wardak, came on the 14th.*

May 14: Tonight, General Muhammad ᶜUmar and his unit were taken prisoner by troops of Aman Allah Khan who were at Shaykh Yasin in Wardak. Muhammad ᶜUmar, better known as "General Sur," was the son of Lieutenant-General (*naᵓib salar*) Ghulam Nabi Khan, who was from the Nasir tribe and a landowner in Kuhdaman. Muhammad ᶜUmar laid claim to the land of his father but was denied his inheritance and on the day the partisans of Habib Allah attacked and conquered Kabul, he committed an act of treachery, abandoning his position at Khayr Khanah Pass and surrendering his unit's weapons to Hamid Allah, whose force numbered only thirty-three men. Muhammad ^{c}Umar himself fled into the city. After the rebels took the city, he was arrested but was released on account of his services. In the end, he was reinstated to the rank of general and sent to the front with a force of a thousand men.

May 15: Many soldiers from the amir's units have arrived in Chardihi (southwest section of Kabul) after being defeated in Ghazni and Wardak. They were hungry and broke into shops in Unchi, Baghbanha, Dih Buri, and Dih Mazang, and made off with everything edible including mulberries, peas, and raisins. They then headed to Kuhdaman on the road through the Shah Mardan Pass and ^{c}Aliabad. As they had notified the government about the defeat by telephone from Qal^{c}ah-i Durrani, Habib Allah, fearful that Aman Allah's army would enter the city in pursuit of the vanquished, raised several units and sent them to the heights of Kuh-i Asma$^{\circ}$i and Shayr Darwazah, where they awaited the enemy attack until morning.

Fayz Muhammad's hope for the restoration of Aman Allah's rule must have reached its apogee on or about the 15th. But he was apparently misled by inaccurate information about Aman Allah's whereabouts. The ex-amir had marched on and laid siege to Ghazni but without success. According to at least one historian, Aman Allah disregarded the advice of his supporters to bypass Ghazni and head straight for Kabul.[114] *Instead, on April 26, he gave the rather inexplicable order to retreat back to Qandahar. Rather than being at the very gates of Kabul, in mid-May, as Fayz Muhammad's reporting suggests, he had already retreated to Kalat, some eighty miles north of Qandahar and nearly two hundred fifty miles from Kabul. Fayz Muhammad found it hard to believe this news and reports on May 19, a mere four days after having Aman Allah's forces at Kabul's doorstep, that there was talk that Aman Allah was under siege at Kalat, a rumor which he dismisses.*

May 19: Subsequently, the northerners have spread rumors that Habib Allah's men had surrounded Aman Allah in the fort at Kalat, which is situated five stages (*manzil*) north of Qandahar. The fortress is now just about to fall and Aman Allah will be captured or killed. The amir sent five iron cages by truck so that if they take the former amir alive, they can bring him and his top advisors back to Kabul in the cages and set them out for viewing as a lesson to others. The rumor is completely unfounded.

But it was not unfounded. Four days later, on May 23, Aman Allah crossed over into India at the border post at Chaman, having abandoned Afghanistan forever. It would take a few days for this news to reach Fayz Muhammad. However, two actions taken by Habib Allah and reported by Fayz Muhammad suggest that he knew that the Tajik ruler had control of the whole Ghazni region.

May 23: Today the amir ordered the release of some two hundred Wardak tribesmen who had been taken captive and held in prison in Kabul. The rest he wanted kept as hostages so that the Wardaks would provide him with two thousand soldiers. Habib Allah believed that the people of Kabul and its environs supported him, a thief, only because they were unhappy with the former corrupt government of Aman Allah. But as soon as he became padishah and the violence, looting, and rape began again, the people had turned away from him too and were praying to God to destroy him.

Elders from the Ghazni Tajiks, who had declared against Aman Allah and in support of Habib Allah, had, until the arrival of Aman Allah's army, billeted the amir's troops and the governor, Muhammad Karim Khan, around the city and nearby villages and in their own homes. They supplied forage and expelled Aman Allah's governor, Jan Baz Khan, from the city. But notwithstanding this local support, Habib Allah's governor and his troops plundered their hosts, who came to Kabul and complained. Each was awarded ten rupees and promised compensation for losses.

From this point on, Fayz Muhammad has little more to say about Aman Allah, how he came to escape Kalat, for example, or why, if his forces were making such good progress against the northerners, he had decided to throw in his hand and flee the country. Two minor notices are given, one in late May, the other in early June: the first signals the author's lost hope for Aman Allah and the second the fate of Qandahar after his departure.

May 26: A special bulletin was broadcast on the radio today announcing that Aman Allah Khan and his family had left Qandahar for Bombay. This information had a depressing effect on the residents of Kabul, especially on Aman Allah Khan's supporters.

The Capture of Qandahar and Its Aftermath

At this point, although Qandahar was yet to surrender, the road south of Ghazni was open and for Habib Allah it was just a matter of negotiating agreements and oaths of allegiance with the former supporters of the ex-amir. Within two weeks, Qandahar would be handed over to Purdil Khan, Habib Allah's field marshal. Fayz Muhammad, in recording the fate of Qandahar, aims a blast at the Pushtun tribes and singles out for particular vituperation Ahmad ᶜAli Khan Lodi. Ahmad ᶜAli was an experienced and well-traveled bureaucrat-administrator in the Afghan government who had served in the two preceding administrations. He had been involved in Aman Allah's earlier attempts at negotiation with Habib Allah and was mayor of Kabul when the city fell.[115] *British records have him accompanying Aman Allah to Qandahar and then going into exile with him in India, and later accompanying ᶜInayat Allah to Iran. He would return after the Saqqawist period ended to continue his career in the Afghan bureaucracy.*[116] *Fayz Muhammad blames him for easing the way for the Saqqawist takeover.*

Fayz Muhammad's account also indicates that when Aman Allah left Afghanistan for good, he once again abdicated. When he arrived in Qandahar in January he announced his re-assumption of the amirate from his brother ᶜInayat Allah and had proclamations sent out to this effect. When he departed Qandahar he seems to have left his brother in charge again, although there is little evidence that ᶜInayat Allah was particularly eager for the remnants of the crown being left him.

June 1: After Aman Allah gave up any hope of support from the savage Pushtun tribes who are true neither to their alliances, nor to their oaths, nor to the faith, he left Afghanistan with his family and circle of courtiers. From Bombay he left for France, and on that day Ahmad ᶜAli, the son of ᶜAbd al-Wahid and grandson of Muhammad Rafiq of the Lodi tribe, committed an act of treason in Qandahar. By this time, Ahmad ᶜAli ought to have been hanged for all the evil he had done. Though he came from a poor family, he had risen to the post of minister plenipotentiary (*wazīr-i mukhtār*)[117] and other high positions. But in the end, instead of showing gratitude, he betrayed his benefactor. Earlier, he had sent money and weapons to Habib Allah and Sayyid Husayn in Jabal al-Siraj by which he helped them when they first attacked Kabul.[118] But this was not enough for him. Now he approached Prince ᶜInayat Allah in Qandahar and offered him his allegiance. But this was simply a diabolical scheme on his part. As soon as Aman Allah left Qandahar, he summoned elders from the five branches of the Durrani tribe[119] to the city and announced to them "now we must place on the throne a person as worthy as Ahmad Shah, who was elected padishah after the assassination of Nadir Shah [in 1747] by the Durrani tribe." Because of this provocative overture to the tribal elders, pro–Aman Allah forces that had been sent to Kabul and had made gains as far as Qarabagh of Ghazni, now abandoned their positions.

Ahmad ᶜAli secretly sent a message to Habib Allah's field marshal, Purdil Khan, which said, "I have done what I can on your behalf. The rest is up to you. March on Qandahar as soon as possible and take the city." By this time, Purdil Khan had already captured Kalat. Since the Durrani tribal leadership had gathered in Qandahar and was busy consulting on the election of a padishah, Purdil left Kalat and marched to Qandahar without encountering any opposition. The Qandaharis, only now realizing that they had placed themselves in mortal danger, shut the city gates and prayed to God to save them. They sought a seven-day truce at the end of which they would submit, swear an oath of allegiance, and thereby obtain guarantees of safety. Purdil agreed, camped at Manzil Bagh and notified Habib Allah of Ahmad ᶜAli Khan's treachery. This gave the amir great satisfaction.

It would now only be a matter of time before Qandahar, too, came under Habib Allah's control, giving him two of the four urban centers of the country. Qandahar's fall would also mark the end of the checkered career of ᶜAli Ahmad Luynab.

June 2: Today at 10 a.m. the airplane that yesterday took off for Qandahar returned to Kabul. It brought oaths of allegiance from the disloyal and hypocritical population of Qandahar and also news about the transfer of ᶜAli Ahmad [Luynab], now the mayor, to the custody of Purdil Khan. The town crier spread this unwelcome news around Kabul and at the time of the evening prayer, a 101-gun salute was fired to mark the victory.

June 3: When the city of Ahmad Shah [Qandahar] was captured by Habib Allah's forces, ᶜAli Ahmad Luynab was found in the home of a

Hazarah and arrested. [As mentioned above] he had declared himself amir in Jalalabad, been ousted, and fled with his sons Ghulam Ahmad and Nur Ahmad to Aman Allah in Qandahar. Nur Ahmad was now killed by Purdil Khan while ^{c}Ali Ahmad was sent to Kabul with the Chief Justice (*Qazi al-quzat*) ^{c}Abd al-Shukur Khan the son of Chief Justice Sa^{c}d al-Din Khan, ^{c}Abd al-Wasi^{c}, and another mufti. Today at eleven o'clock they arrived in the city. They were stripped naked and paraded around the bazaars. For ^{c}Ali Ahmad this was just reward for his betrayal of Aman Allah, who had named him to the post of high commissioner (*raʾis-i a^{c}la*) of the Eastern and Southern Provinces and sent him to Jalalabad to put down the rebellion of the savage Shinwari and other tribes.[120] But, dreaming of taking the amirid throne at that point, he deceived Aman Allah by sending him a letter which reported that 23,000 Shinwari and other tribesmen had set out for Kabul. The letter frightened Aman Allah, who believed that his corrupt ministers would support the Tajik bandit, Habib Allah. People say that Aman Allah abdicated mostly because of this letter from ^{c}Ali Ahmad Luynab. Well, now ^{c}Ali Ahmad himself is forced to sit in shackles and endure punishment for his misdeeds.

In Qandahar, Ahmad ^{c}Ali Lodi, who had helped Habib Allah at the very outset and also later, at the taking of Qandahar, thus betraying the government and the people, was also arrested. But he has yet to suffer any punishment.

^{c}Ali Ahmad, accompanied by Chief Justice ^{c}Abd al-Shukur and Mulla ^{c}Abd al-Wasi^{c}, was brought before His Highness Habib Allah, who asked him, "Why didn't you come to me from Jagdalak? If you had come I would have received you with honor." ^{c}Ali Ahmad replied, "There is no questioning fate." Mulla ^{c}Abd al-Wasi^{c}, in reply to the amir's question "Why do you accuse me of irreligion?" said, "I do not call and have never called any Muslim an unbeliever (*kafir*). If I called you a kafir then that is what you are." The amir ordered all four imprisoned.

When the residents of Kabul as well as the Hazarahs and Afghans, all of whom—with the exception of the savage Shinwari, Khugyani, Sulayman Khayl, Andar, and Taraki tribes—had nurtured hope of salvation from the oppression and tyranny of the northern plunderers and had supposed that a happy day would soon dawn for them, learned of the arrest of these four men and of the capture of Qandahar and the flight of

Aman Allah, they fell into deepest despair. The arrest of ᶜAli Ahmad particularly affected them.

June 4: Today Ahmad ᶜAli Lodi, who had been chained, paraded in disgrace around the bazaars, and then held under house arrest, was released. For his services to the Kuhistani and Kuhdamani brigands, his house in Murad Khani was returned to him. As governor-general he had frequently spared and released from prison those who had committed crimes against the government of Aman Allah Khan. Today these same men hold high ranks like field marshal, minister of court, and commandant. Those for whom he had once interceded now came to his defense and asked that he be pardoned and released from jail. Field Marshal Purdil Khan wrote from Qandahar requesting a pardon for Ahmad ᶜAli, and Commandant Sayyid Agha Khan begged the amir on his knees to spare him. Some of the hazrats who had incited the brigands and thieves, destroyed the government and the religion, and sowed dissension among the people also spoke up in his defense.

Today the governor-general, Malik Muhsin, and Na'ib al-Saltanah Hamid Allah left for Qandahar by car to restore order to the city whose population had only just surrendered and sworn an oath of loyalty.

The Final Chapter for ᶜAli Ahmad Luynab

For more than a month ᶜAli Ahmad was kept imprisoned. For reasons that Fayz Muhammad either did not know or did not wish to explain, Habib Allah finally decided to put him to death.

July 11:[121] As we mentioned earlier, ᶜAli Ahmad, the son of Khushdil Khan Luynab, was arrested in Qandahar. It was at the home of a Hazarah migrant named Samad ᶜAli, a notorious libertine who had even committed incest with his sister and aunt. Today ᶜAli Ahmad, Qazi ᶜAbd al-Shukur, and Mulla ᶜAbd al-Wasiᶜ were paraded around the bazaars barefoot and bareheaded. ᶜAli Ahmad was extremely thirsty and appealed to the Kuhistanis as fellow Muslims to give him a drink. But instead of a drink of water these infidels struck him on the back with their rifle butts and cursed him. Then they strapped him and ᶜAbd al-Wasiᶜ to the muzzle of a cannon and blew them to bits.[122] When Habib Allah issued the order to tie him to the cannon, Aman Allah's sister [Sahirah], her head bare, prostrated herself before the tyrant and laid her small child at his feet. She begged for permission to see her husband for one last time. But neither she nor any other relative was permitted to approach the gun. However, Zayfah, their son's nurse, ignoring insults and blows from rifle butts, made her way to the slain man and retrieved his head for his wife who wept a sea of tears. Some time later, she left Afghanistan in the company of her uncle, Prince Amin Allah, and her brother, Muhammad Kabir, to join her other brother, Aman Allah, and her mother [the ᶜUlya Hazrat].

The Logar Valley

More or less simultaneous with the fighting taking place along the Kabul-Ghazni-Qandahar road were skirmishes and pitched battles in the Logar (Lahugar) Valley, which runs south from Kabul. The Logar Valley is a breadbasket for the city as well as the main road to Gardiz, a large town about seventy-five miles due south of Kabul. Gardiz, an ancient town, commands the route to India through the Kurram Valley, which was long a route for armies invading India from the Afghan highlands. The Logar Valley also provides an alternate route to Ghazni. About halfway to Gardiz, the road to Ghazni veers off to the southwest. One of the more important regions on this branch is Charkh, home of a leading Pushtun family, the Charkhis, one of whom, Ghulam Nabi, figures prominently in the events of the time. Between Kabul and Gardiz the road passes through the Altamur Pass at 9,600 feet, about fourteen miles north of Gardiz, and a narrow defile, the Waghjan (Wahjan, Ahujan, Agujan) Gorge, some 7,000 feet high and about twenty-five miles south of Kabul between Muhammad Aghah and Kulangar, two major localities along the way.

The resistance to Habib Allah in the Logar Valley would at first be local and Fayẓ Muhammad names some of the Logari leaders.

On March 16, Habib Allah sent 129 of his bandits in trucks to Logar on a reconnaissance mission. There the populace has risen against Habib Allah, blockaded the road and stopped the flow of provisions to Kabul. They are led by a native Logari, Mirza Nawruz, who was construction manager of the Dar al-Aman project, and Muhammad Ṭahir Khan, a cousin of Muhammad Ayyub Khan, minister of court under Amir Aman Allah.[123]

At Waghjan Gorge, between Khushi in Kulangar and Shikar Qal^cah, they were fired on by the Logaris, who had taken up positions on two nearby hills. The Logaris drove the bandits, who suffered many casualties, back to the garrison at Rishkhur on the southern outskirts of Kabul. The dead and wounded were not brought back to Kabul lest people find out what had happened. But rumors began to spread that either that day or the next the Logaris would rise against Habib Allah and attack Kabul. But the Logaris were depending on the Wardaks for a coordinated attack on Kabul along the road through Maydan, Tangi Lalandar, Charasya, Musaʾi, and Bini Hisar. The Wardakis had at first intended to attack Habib Allah's forces from two sides, but now suspended their plan because the people of Ghazni, the Hazarahs, and residents of the Southern Province had not come to help as expected. Just before this, Habib Allah reinforced his army and sent them out in two directions—along the route to Maydan through Qalʿah-i Mahtab Bagh, Qalʿah-i Durrani, Qalʿah-i Qazi, and Arghandah, and via Charasya and Musaʾi to Logar.

On the same day, and related to the emergence of resistance in the Logar Valley, Habib Allah delivered a speech in which he called for the disarming of the citizens of Kabul.

On Tuesday March 16, Habib Allah summoned the heads (*kalāntar*s) of the city quarters and other urban worthies to the Astar [Stor] Palace, where the ministry of foreign affairs is now located. Concerned by rumors of an impending attack on Kabul by people from Khust, Wardak, Ghazni, and Logar, aided by people from Chardihi and Kabul itself, and by reports of the barbaric behavior of his men toward the people of Kabul and its environs, he began to commend the people of Kabul for their goodwill and steadfastness. At the end he revealed the real reason for his speech. He said, "If anyone has government-issue rifles with ammunition at home or even just ammunition, these should be handed over to government officials. Anyone who surrenders a rifle should hand over ammunition as well. If not, my officials will interrogate and punish them. Persons from whom rifles and cartridges have been stolen will not be held responsible. Persons who hand over their personal weapons will be compensated for their value in cash. This order will remain in effect for the next twenty days. At the end of that time, anyone who is found to have a rifle in his possession will be subject to the confiscation of his property and personal belongings, severe punishment, and a fine of five hundred rupees."

The Arrival of Nadir Khan in the Logar Valley

By the end of March a second major opposition figure planning to use the Logar Valley to approach the capital had appeared on the scene. After Aman Allah, the second most important threat to the position of Habib Allah was posed by this hero of the 1919 War of Independence, Field Marshal Muhammad Nadir Khan of the Musahiban family. Nadir could trace his lineage to both the Muhammadzai and Saduzai clans of the Durrani and thus had as potent and legitimate a claim as Aman Allah. Moreover, in contrast to Aman Allah, he was an accomplished military man, having distinguished himself on campaigns during the reign of Aman Allah's father, Amir Habib Allah. For his services, he had been promoted to the top military rank of field marshal (sipahsālār) *in 1914. In the early twenties, he had something of a falling-out with Aman Allah because of his criticism of the haste with which the amir was implementing his modernization policy. Nadir was consequently named ambassador to France in early 1924, ambassadorships being a genteel form of exile in Afghan politics. In 1926 he became ill and resigned the post but stayed in France. What prompted him in late January 1929*[124] *to leave his sickbed in Grasse, France (Mohammed Ali, one of his champions, has him carried aboard ship on a stretcher) and return to Afghanistan has been variously interpreted. Patriotic accounts attribute his motive to the selfless desire to save the country from the "oppression" of the watercarrier's boy. But the watercarrier's boy had come to power only on January 18, a mere week before Mohammed Ali, for example, has the marshal boarding ship to return home. This does not leave much time for Habib Allah to establish a reputation as an oppressor, for that information to reach Nadir Khan in France, and for him to make the decision and the arrangements to leave by ship from Nice (or Marseilles). Fayz Muhammad has a somewhat different interpretation of Nadir Khan's motives for returning and suggests Habib Allah himself made overtures to the exile. But it seems clear that the decision to return was made before Habib Allah's representative reached him. It may, in fact have been made even before Aman Allah's abdication, and been reached not for any particularly patriotic reasons but simply because political opportunity was created by the uprising of the Shinwari and the weakness of Aman Allah's position after returning from his European tour and attempting to reinvigorate his social reforms. Fayz Muhammad's account is interesting for the emphasis it places on Habib Allah's role in encouraging Nadir Khan's return.*

Habib Allah named Sultan Ahmad, the son of Col. Shayr Ahmad, a cartographer, as ambassador to Tehran to replace ᶜAbd al-ᶜAziz Khan.[125] On the advice of several people, including Sardar Muhammad ᶜUsman, Hazrat Shayr Aqa Mujaddidi and his brother [Gul Aqa], and a number of foreigners, the amir then sent ᶜAbd al-ᶜAziz Khan to Paris to persuade Muhammad Nadir and his brothers—Shah Wali and Muhammad Hashim—to return to Afghanistan.[126] Nadir's nephew—Ahmad Shah—was sent along with ᶜAbd al-ᶜAziz. They flew on an English plane. When Nadir arrived in Bombay, Habib Allah gave his brother—Shah Mahmud—a thousand pounds sterling for travel expenses and sent him to bring Nadir Khan back to Kabul.

Rumors now spread that Nadir had come to Peshawar via Lahore, and that he had continued to Khust, to the Southern Province, thence to Jalalabad and the Eastern Province, to Qandahar, and back into the Southern Province. In Jalalabad, rumor had it that he was rallying the tribes of both provinces to attack Habib Allah and the Kuhistanis. Such stories, which were making the rounds day and night, gave rise to widespread excitement. Since Habib Allah did not know for certain that Nadir and his brothers had reached Afghan soil, he summoned a son of the late Amir Habib Allah—Asad Allah, whose mother was Nadir's sister—to give him reliable information about Nadir Khan's arrival. But Asad Allah said that he knew nothing.

In mid-March, Nadir and his brother Hashim arrived in Jalalabad, [briefly] joined forces with ᶜAli Ahmad, and sent Habib Allah a letter over Nadir's name that read,

> I have no doubt of your courage and I admire the fact that you have succeeded in driving Amir Aman Allah Khan from Kabul and occupying the throne yourself. What concerns me is Afghan honor and so I have arrived

on this soil to put out the flames of rebellion. The thought of occupying the throne or any other high post has never occurred to me. Due to the youthfulness, arrogance, and inexperience of Amir Aman Allah and his haste to implement policies without the most basic support behind them, thoughtful people have been put in a very difficult position. As a consequence, I declined the post of prime minister (*ṣadr-i aᶜẓam*) and instead settled in Paris. I have no wish to live in Afghanistan with its savage and ignorant people where presently there is nothing but killing and destruction of property. As for now, O victorious brother, I express only feelings of goodwill, but do not depend on these lasting. I advise you to end the bloodshed among Muslims and the destruction of Afghanistan. The government and the people have suffered enormously and the wealth of the country has been plundered. It is time to cease and desist and permit no further destruction of our country, government, and people. This calamity has thrust Afghanistan back a hundred years, sapped its strength, and given rise to utter misery. We will not allow such sedition to continue and will see to it that the holy principles of Shariᶜah are not further violated. God forbid that these disturbances should develop into war between the peoples of the East and the West, for if they do, the country will turn into a battleground for foreigners. The people of the northern province, you, our brother, and all the tribes and peoples of Afghanistan will be annihilated. Those who survive will have only a miserable existence. Repentance will not avail them. They will only say "It would be better if we were turned to dust." When the losses are tallied, the illustrious Pushtun tribes—the Sarban, Ghurghusht, Batan, Ghilzai, Karran,[127] and others, whose numbers total several hundred thousand courageous fighters—will not leave the reins of government in the hands of our brother. We propose therefore that he leave the throne to someone who enjoys influence among the Pushtun. If our brother wishes to continue to have some power then I would guarantee him the post of caravan leader (*kāfilah*) and will do my best to help him achieve success.

After receiving this letter, Habib Allah invited to court a number of people who were calling for an end to the uprising and they advised him to write Nadir [the following]: "After the arrival in Kabul of your advice and suggestions regarding the administration of the country, if your advice is correct and corresponds to all the norms of the Shariᶜah and the will of the All-High, it will be carried out and I will relinquish this fraught business of governing the country."

But Sardar Muhammad ᶜUsman and the two hazrats [Gul Aqa and

Shayr Aqa Mujaddidi?] who had ignited the flames of revolution, along with some of the corrupt ministers and high-ranking officials, read over the rough draft of this letter, which is now in my hands, and persuaded him not to renounce the throne. They summoned relatives of Nadir and forced them to address a letter to him which read, "We, so-and-so, both men and women, know the respect that Amir Habib Allah Khan feels for you. We enjoy full health and peace of mind now, but if you refuse the honor of being received by him then we face destruction."

Habib Allah entrusted this letter to the two hazrats and told them to deliver it to Nadir. He also instructed them to call on the people living along the route to render obedience to the amir and to denounce Nadir at every opportunity. The hazrats took more than three hundred thousand rupees from the treasury for the trip, but because of the uprising in Logar, they were forced to postpone their departure.

After the letter was written, an inventory of Nadir's household belongings was drawn up on the night of March 14 and his house was locked and sealed. Should he refuse to come voluntarily, all of his property will be confiscated and his wife and the wives of Shah Wali and ᶜAli Ahmad will be dishonored. All are sisters of Amir Aman Allah and the daughters of Her Highness [ᶜUlya Hazrat]. At this time, they languish in the house of a certain hazrat known for his lechery.

Meanwhile, the amir was doing his best to suppress the Logar opposition, while dealing with the problem of advancing along the Maydan road toward Ghazni. On March 23 he had withdrawn a group of five hundred irregulars from the fighting on that front. These men were from Najrab, a town northeast of Kabul and the next town north of Tagab, a place where heavy fighting against Habib Allah's regime was also in progress. The amir's fear, according to Fayz Muhammad, was that they would mutiny because of the news coming from Tagab, and so he had disarmed them. Fayz Muhammad mentions that things began to go well for the amir in Tagab and he had restored the Najrabi's weapons that he had taken away only a day or two before. This was probably the same group he now sent down the Logar Valley to deal with Mirza Nawruz and other local opponents of his regime.

The five hundred men whom Habib Allah impressed into service arrived in Charasya[128] with four field guns and two eight-pound siege guns along with a group of the amir's partisans. Their leader was Panin Beg Khan, a Chitrali *ghulam.*[129] During the late Amir Habib Allah's reign he had risen to the rank of colonel but under Aman Allah had been stripped of rank, position, and status, and for this he felt great resentment against that regime. The members of this force had no wish to advance beyond Charasya or to establish defensive positions against a Tagabi attack.[130] When they heard that Nadir had arrived in the Charkh district with a tribal force from the Southern Province backed by the forces that were permanently garrisoned in that region, the soldiers abandoned their positions at Charasya and marched south to Muhammad Aghah and from there on the 24th of March set off for Kulangar. But the Logaris ambushed them and many were killed or wounded.

Fayz Muhammad's treatment of what had been happening meanwhile in the east is sketchy and abrupt and probably accurately reflects the partial information available to him. Nadir and his brothers, Hashim and Shah Wali, landed in Bombay on February 22, travelled to Peshawar, and crossed into Afghanistan on or about March 8 just east of Matun in the Kurram Valley.[131] *The jirgah (assembly) of tribes to which Fayz Muhammad now refers without any preliminaries is probably the gathering organized by Mir Ghaws̱ al-Din Khan son of Jandad Khan Ahmadzai.*[132] *It is not clear when it was held, but sometime around March 20 seems likely. By Fayz Muhammad's account, Nadir was not present at the jirgah, for he has the tribal leaders addressing Hashim. The story Mohammed Ali tells, assuming he is referring to the same jirgah (which he dates March 22), has Nadir not only present but more or less presiding and then rejecting the tribal leaders' offer of the throne.*[133]

On March 27, some of the Shinwari and Khugyani men who had been responsible for the looting and destruction of government buildings in Jalalabad, and moreover had violated their oaths and so feared for their lives at the hands of irate Pushtun tribesmen, especially from the the tribes of the Eastern Province, arrived in Kabul on the pretext of delivering oaths of obedience to Amir Habib Allah but in reality seeking a safe haven. After their arrival, forty proclamations were sent to the elders of Jalalabad who had in the meantime gathered for a jirgah with Nadir's brother, Hashim, to discuss the overthrow of Habib Allah. These proclamations called for an end to the fighting and for oaths of allegiance to be given to Habib Allah.

When the jirgah met, all the leaders and elders of the tribes of the Eastern Province attacked the regime of Aman Allah. And to show that they no longer recognized the ex-amir's authority, they told Hashim,

Sardar Nasr Allah Khan,
son of amir ᶜAbd al-Rahman

On the day the late Amir Habib Allah Khan was killed [February 19, 1919], all the people of the Eastern Province, whether civilians or soldiers, elders of the tribes, sardars and princes, proposed that the "Vice-Regent" (Naᵓib al-Saltanah) Nasr Allah Khan [Amir ᶜAbd al-Rahman's second son], who knew the Koran by heart and was a true Muslim, succeed to the throne and they swore oaths of allegiance to him. However, Aman Allah Khan, who had no right at all to the throne, seized power. Being a person of belief, Nasr Allah decided not to be the cause of bloodshed and civil war and so let the reins of government pass to Aman Allah, who then summoned Nasr Allah to Kabul by cunning and refused to let him go into exile. Nasr Allah was sincere in his feelings for Aman Allah and when relations were strained between Aman Allah and his father he had spoken up for him and for Her Highness, Aman Allah's mother. Nasr Allah had protected them from the heavy-handedness of Amir Habib Allah Khan and looked upon Aman Allah as a friend and a son. Therefore he came to Kabul in an easy frame of mind, escorted by bodyguards and thinking, "I have always thought well of Aman Allah. His choosing his own servants as bodyguards for me is only an expression of his high regard. There is no reason at all for me to come to harm. When I get to Kabul, things will be fine."

However, contrary to his expectations, Aman Allah came out to Butkhak and ordered his arrest. A little more than a year later, on a Friday night, May 9, 1920,[134] after a heavy bout of drinking, Aman Allah ordered him put to death and then began to adopt policies which went directly counter to Muslim traditions. He changed the day of rest from Friday, abolished the veil, and introduced a number of other laws that were contrary to the Shariᶜah and so greatly offended the ulama. In imitation of the Turks, he forced people to study both the Latin alphabet and the Arabic one in which

> Qur'anic commentaries, the Qur'an itself, and religious books and treatises are all written. And we should recognize as amir a godless person like this who advocates violating the fundamental principles of Islam?

In reply to the elders, Hashim Khan asserted that the repentance of Aman Allah, who had never once spoken the truth, was all merely a trick to deceive believing Muslims and that the elders were right to refuse to recognize him as amir. Then he began to speak of ᶜInayat Allah, describing his piety and high moral standards. However, those attending the jirgah also rejected ᶜInayat Allah's candidacy for the throne, recalling his and the chamberlain (*īshīk agāsī*) ᶜAbd al-Habib's bad behavior when ᶜInayat Allah was still prince. Then they spoke of ᶜAbd al-Rahman, whose despotic rule also did not conform to the Shariᶜah, although many mosques were constructed by him. Eventually, they concluded that no member of this family had the right to be amir and they resolved as well to be rid of the godless, bloodshedding, debauched ignoramus, Habib Allah [Kalakani]. Once that was achieved, they would consult with representatives of all the people of Afghanistan and would unanimously elect a person amir who was recognizably sincere about religion, pure of heart, able to provide peace and tranquillity to the nation, govern the country in conformity with the guidance of God and the Prophet, and prove popular with all its citizens. Having ended their discussion at this point, they agreed to choose a number of men to send as a delegation to Habib Allah. Through persuasion and counsel based on the Shariᶜah, this delegation was supposed to convince him that it was of fundamental importance to end the fighting, sedition, bloodshed, and looting between brethren in the True Faith and to relinquish the throne. The jirgah adopted the following resolution:

> The strength of Islamic society is sapped, it has been plunged into civil war and blood has been shed. It is now time to put an end to the looting, the degradation of both the common people and sincere adherents of the religion, and the plundering of the resources of the government and the Islamic nation, which have taken fifty years to accumulate. It is time to put an end to all evil acts. As for Habib Allah, Sayyid Husayn, and their accomplices, they should assume the obligation to fulfill their duty and to assure peace and well-being. If they accept these conditions, well and good. Otherwise there will be war with the valiant Pushtun tribes like the

> Durrani, Ghilzai, and others. May God grant us His support. Let success be our companion and injustice be wiped from the face of the earth!

A delegation from the jirgah approached Kabul on March 30. Habib Allah sent his brother, Hamid Allah, the "Support of the State" (Muᶜin al-Saltanah), to Butkhak with an escort of eighty-four men to welcome it. But bad news from the Maydan front caused Hamid Allah to turn around on March 31 and head off toward Maydan before meeting it. Fayz Muhammad tells us that the delegation was eventually greeted by an honor guard and escorted into the city. Its entrance was the occasion for an indiscriminate firing of guns into the air which in turn gave rise to the unfounded rumor that the amir's troops had won a great victory at Tagab. After this Fayz Muhammad provides no clue as to what became of the delegation and any proposals it might have brought. Instead he devotes considerable space to a counterattempt by the Shinwari, in very bad odor with the other tribes of the Eastern Province because of their looting and burning of government buildings at Jalalabad, to neutralize the effect of the arrival of the jirgah representatives.

In the east, the tribes of the Eastern Province had excluded the Shinwari and Khugyani from their alliance and the jirgah of tribes. They wanted to punish them for having broken their agreement by destroying government buildings, pillaging Jalalabad, and confiscating pack animals and handing them over to Habib Allah's army. So when Malik Muhammad ᶜAlam Shinwari heard of the arrival in Kabul of the delegation from the Eastern Province, he set off for Kabul to offer his allegiance, taking with him some two to three hundred Shinwaris. Malik Muhammad ᶜAlam himself was lodged in the Arg as an honored guest and his companions were put up at the War College. Each Shinwari was given money for expenses. ᶜAlam Khan was personally fed from the amir's kitchens and he was awarded the title "lieutenant general of the army and the nation" (*nāʾib sālār-i lashkarī wa kishwarī*).

Malik Muhammad ᶜAlam's hope was that he and his men would be given arms and ammunition to defend themselves and to fight the other tribes of the Eastern Province. However, directly contrary to their wishes, the government demanded they give up their weapons. They refused to surrender them, however, but stayed for a time in Kabul.

The Shinwari presence became as much of a threat to the security of Habib Allah's regime in Kabul as it was an opportunity to undercut the Eastern Province tribal support for Nadir Khan. By the end of the first week in April, the number of Shinwari in the city had grown to two thousand, according to Fayz Muhammad, and when three hundred government soldiers were deployed to the top of Maranjan Hill in the eastern part of the city, no one was sure whether it was to defend Kabul against those hostile to the regime or against the Shinwari, nominally allied now with the Tajik ruler. On April 9 some of the Shinwari left Kabul for home, though Malik Muhammad and his followers stayed on a while longer and for good reason.

Today [April 7] three hundred armed men were ordered to occupy positions on the heights of Maranjan Hill in the eastern part of Kabul. People knew that occupying these positions was either because an attack on Kabul by Hashim Khan and the tribes of the Eastern Province was expected or because of the steady and significant increase of Shinwaris in Kabul. On the first day they numbered only four hundred or so, but in the course of the third, fourth, fifth, and succeeding days their numbers have increased to two thousand and still they come. These defensive positions were therefore readied so that if the Shinwari harbored evil intentions toward the populace of the city it might be possible to prevent them from penetrating into the heart of the city.

By April 11, a majority of the Shinwari had left Kabul. And on that date the few remaining also planned to depart. Malik Muhammad ᶜAlam and his companions were given fifteen thousand rupees and the malik himself, who had already received the rank of "lieutenant general of the army and the country," was given a farman appointing him governor of Jalalabad. But now in order to re-establish their good name among the tribes of the Eastern Province, other Shinwari attacked the fortress of Malik Muhammad ᶜAlam, the mastermind of all the misery and misfortune of the Eastern Province, looting and destroying it. When he heard this, the Shinwari leader, fearing for his life, decided to remain in Kabul.

But the volatile element that the Shinwari always represented had not yet been defused either for Nadir or for Habib Allah. While the Shinwari were complicating matters for the amir, Nadir was slowly making his way into the Logar Valley. Shortly after the jirgah, on March 23, a six-thou-

sand-man tribal army from the Mangal joined him at Matun in Khust. Four days later, with his combined forces, he left Khust marching west toward Urgun, which he reached, according to Mohammed Ali, on April 5. From there he turned north toward Gardiz on the road through Sar-i Rawzah and Zurmat. But there was now increasing resistance to his march from the Sulayman Khayl and tribal groups in Zurmat who had little use for the Kabul government and its officials. Only through repeated assurances that he had no designs on the throne did Nadir Khan make his way without incident to Baladah, three miles south of Gardiz, where he was welcomed by the Ahmadzai, whose town it was. Gardiz was just then in the hands of Muhammad Siddiq Khan, in Fayz Muhammad's book a loyal backer of Habib Allah. The presence of Nadir Khan just outside Gardiz prompted some of Muhammad Siddiq's erstwhile supporters to reassess their loyalties and compel him to negotiate with Nadir. Muhammad Siddiq went out to meet with Nadir and, in a murky shooting incident in which there were some casualties, was arrested by Nadir Khan. On April 15 Nadir took control of Gardiz.[135]

His advance clearly was not going unnoticed by the amir. On April 6 Habib Allah had sent a thousand men down the Logar Valley road to counter any offensive by Nadir Khan. The group may have been led by Malik Muhsin, governor-general of the Central (Kabul) Province. This force reached the regions of Khushi and Kulangar, took hostages there, then returned to Kabul when it seemed that the threat of Nadir Khan was not so immediate as rumor would have it.

April 11: The amir received three hundred residents of Logar, to the accompaniment of the military orchestra playing in the background. These were the same people whom Malik Muhsin had taken hostage two or three days earlier near Khushi and Kulangar, when he found himself besieged in the fortress. Yesterday, he was freed and driven to Kabul by Habib Allah himself.

Two planes took off today in the direction of Ghazni and Logar to reconnoiter. From the information they brought back it is clear that the rumors of Nadir's force being in Khushi and Aman Allah's army being at the manzil of Takiyah Wardak are just propaganda spread by supporters of Aman Allah.

On April 15, the same day that Nadir was taking Gardiz, Habib Allah ordered the arrest of the wives of Nadir and his brothers, Shah Mahmud and Shah Wali, and at the same time announced a reward for the arrest or assassination of any of them.

On April 11, Habib Allah dispatched twenty-six criminal types to assassinate Nadir. He promised thirty thousand rupees to anyone who brought back Nadir's head or the heads of any of his brothers. Who knows whether they will succeed or not? Two of them are thieves from Chardihi.

On Sunday, the 14th, all the members of Nadir's extended family were arrested. As was mentioned earlier, the former ambassador of Afghanistan to Tehran, ᶜAbd al-ᶜAziz, had delivered a hundred fifty thousand rupees to Nadir in Paris and an invitation to return to Afghanistan sent by Habib Allah. But Nadir did not accede to Habib Allah's wishes and rejected the post he was offered. After writing Habib Allah and renouncing any desire for power, Nadir appealed to the honor of the Pushtuns and urged them to oppose the watercarrier's boy, at the same time warning them against supporting Aman Allah. Now he has gathered an army and decided to attack Kabul. Hence the arrest of his family.

Through the night, the arresting soldiers taunted the family and, when day broke, confiscated their homes, took the women into custody, and escorted them to the home of Fath Muhammad Khan. At the same time Prince Asad Allah Khan, son of the late Amir Habib Allah Khan, was taken to the Arg along with some other detainees.

On the evening of the 15th, Habib Allah Khan ordered that the wives of Shah Wali, Shah Mahmud, and Nadir be brought to the Arg from the house of the hazrats [the Mujaddidis].[136] The first was a full sister of Aman Allah; the second, a half-sister; the third, the sister of Sulayman Khan the son of Sardar Muhammad Asif Khan.[137] It is not known how the amir spent his time in seclusion with them.

Then during the day, airplanes leafletted the tribes of the Eastern and Southern Provinces. The leaflets, prepared yesterday by a committee of mullas and printed by order of Habib Allah, declared that Nadir Khan and his brothers were infidels. No one knows what effect these pamphlets will have. Here is the decree:

> In the name of God, the Merciful, the Compassionate! A government proclamation. May it be known to brother Muslims in the Eastern and Southern Provinces!

Information about the cowardly and treacherous activity of Field Marshal Nadir proves that he has shown himself to be an infidel acting contrary to the holy religion of Islam and a rebel against the Islamic government and that he is trying to divide Muslim from Muslim. Under the protection of God, I am obliged to tell you about the character of this rebel, who continually exerts himself in treasonous behavior, and about his great sin. This is the same Nadir who was field marshal during the reign of the murdered amir [Habib Allah Khan] and his brothers were lieutenant generals. His father and his uncle were close confidants of the [late] amir and were on duty around his tent at Qal^{c}ah-i Gush.[138] All of Afghanistan knows what these traitors did to His Highness, the late amir, and you know best of all. Afterwards, they supported Aman Allah Khan. For all their perfidy, it is obligatory to wipe their names and their services from the memory of our compatriots as soon as possible. As for Nadir, he betrayed the Muslim world and moved to France. But let's leave that aside. Your servant, who merits, according to the will of God, the title "Servant of the Religion of the Prophet of God," on the one hand, has never been able to rest easy knowing their treachery and, on the other, has proposed they be annihilated. But since they are Muslims, so—glory be to God!—in an ever-stronger Muslim state they should have been given the opportunity to serve in its administration and return to their own land from abroad. Therefore, I bestowed the title of *ra$^{\circ}$īs* on [Nadir's] brother Shah Mahmud. He swore loyalty to me and was given a large sum from the treasury for service to Islam. I also invited Nadir himself to return home with honor. But he behaved like a kafir while in Europe and ate a lot of pork, which has blackened his bones and marrow. In response to my generosity and sincerity, he refused obedience to Islam. He himself is spreading lies in the Southern Province while his brothers do the same in the Eastern. But thanks to the grace of God, these devils will not be able to lead the faithful into error but will only corrupt themselves. Because of his and his brothers' treachery, His Highness brings to your attention, O true Muslims, the fact that the blood of these traitors is lawful according to the Shari^{c}ah. The one who wipes them out will be acknowledged as a warrior for the faith (*ghazi*) and a defender of Islam and will also be entitled to the following from the court of the Islamic government:

1. Anyone who brings Nadir in alive will be paid forty thousand rupees. Thirty thousand rupees, a rifle, and ammunition will go to anyone who brings in his head.

2. Whoever brings [his] three brothers in alive will get for each of them ten thousand rupees or thirty thousand for all three. Whoever brings in only one alive or brings in his head will receive ten thousand rupees and a rifle with ammunition.

> Thus His Highness's order regarding Nadir and his brothers. With the goal of preventing discord and eliminating strife, you, as true Muslims, having gained the approval of the Almighty, his Prophets, the Servant of Religion, and the Supporter of Islam, are hereby obliged to give this due regard.
>
> Kabul, the Government Press.

Similar kinds of proclamations accusing Aman Allah of unbelief were also frequently printed. But if the ulama turn to the Koran where it says "If you should quarrel on anything, refer it to God and the Messenger, if you believe in God and the Last Day; that is better and fairer in the issue"[139] and to the Prophetic reports (*hadith*s) and the opinions (*fatwa*s) of the religious authorities (*mujtahid*s) then they will recognize all this as lies.

Habib Allah also contracted with a director of the Afghan-German Trading Company [Deutsche-Afghanische Companie], Muhammad Musa Khan Qandahari, and seven other Qandaharis, to assassinate Aman Allah, promising them a large reward if they did so.

On the 16th, at nine o'clock in the morning, two planes took off on a reconnaissance flight over the Southern Province, which had already been leafletted with pamphlets accusing Nadir of unbelief, to find out how many people had joined his cause. At the same time, the wives of Nadir and his brothers, who had been taken to the Arg and spent one whole night there, were allowed to leave and were lodged again at the house of the hazrats. They had been told that if they handed over their belongings and valuables, then nothing improper would be asked of them, and they agreed to do so.

On April 20, Fayz Muhammad reports that Panin Beg, the Chitrali colonel who had led a force into the Logar for Habib Allah, approached Nadir ostensibly to offer his support but in reality, says our author, lured by the reward money and hoping to seize him. But instead he himself was arrested and his men disarmed.

Gardiz had been taken by the Musahiban family on April 15. According to the sequence provided by Mohammed Ali, Nadir Khan sent his forces from Gardiz northwest on the main road toward Kabul while he himself followed shortly behind. He spent April 23 in Safid Qal^{c}ah at the southern entrance to the Altamur (or Tirah) Pass. The next day he continued through the pass to Charkh. There he was confronted by a force *sent by Habib Allah and by the untimely defection of one of his early backers, Mir Ghaws al-Din Ahmadzai. The rest of the tribal forces backing Nadir Khan also began to drift away and after some initially successful attacks on Habib Allah's forces in the village of Dabar in Charkh, the momentum swung against Nadir Khan and on the 27th he was forced to retreat to Sijinak east of Gardiz.*[140]

Fayz Muhammad's scenario differs considerably from this. The reports he received about the movements of Nadir Khan's forces and the countermoves of Habib Allah were fragmentary. He does seem to have been aware of Nadir's defeat at Charkh, but for whatever reasons preferred not to describe it.

April 22: Today some soldiers who had been torn away from their work in the fields, or in other occupations by which they provided subsistence for their families, and been conscripted into Habib Allah's army, were sent to Logar to defend it against Nadir. His advance force, led by his first cousin, Ahmad Shah, and his brother, Shah Mahmud, reached Dubandi and the village of Khushi. Habib Allah's army, having decided that it could not put up a defense, retreated to Kabul. The amir was outraged and when the force arrived in the city he ordered the soldiers punished and their weapons taken away. In their stead, another 1,350 conscripts were quickly sent off around sunset toward Logar.

April 23: At 6:25 this morning two planes took off for Logar on a reconnaissance and bombing mission. They returned at nine. On this same day, because of rumors about the defeat of Habib Allah's army and its retreat to Qal^{c}ah-i Durrani on the Maydan-Ghazni road, the amir himself, with a group of devoted followers, set out in five automobiles for the battlefield to bolster the morale of his troops. He returned to the city at night. Then, in response to rumors that Hashim Khan was approaching the city under cover of darkness with militia from the Mohmand, Afridi, and other tribes of the Eastern Province, the amir sent those same seven pieces of ordnance that he had earlier sent to reinforce positions in Ghazni and then brought back to Kabul to Butkhak and Maranjan Hill. Troops led by Nadir Khan now reached the Waghjan Gorge.

April 24: At one p.m. today word spread that Nadir's force had entered the village of Tangi Waghjan [Aghujan] in Logar about twenty-two miles south of Kabul. This news was deeply disturbing to Habib Allah, Sayyid

Husayn, and their colleagues. Sayyid Husayn quickly set off for Logar to ascertain the situation. After gathering information about Nadir's army and deploying his own troops to repel any attack, Sayyid Husayn returned to the capital. The sepoys had just begun to drive horses and pack animals that they had forcibly requisitioned after Sayyid Husayn when he reappeared and with a gesture of his hand directed the sepoys who were moving along the road riding on the backs of the pack animals to turn around. They all returned to Kabul about sunset.

April 25: Sent by Nadir, a militia unit of the Mangal tribe arrived in Hisarak today in Logar where it routed the amir's troops. Many government soldiers were killed, four hundred were taken prisoner, and the rest were scattered. A unit of Nadir's own army now also reached Hisarak in Khurd Kabul and planned to attack the amir's troops at Butkhak. But it withdrew without taking any action.

In conjunction with the arrival of Nadir's units in Khurd Kabul and Chakari Chinan, this evening all units forcibly recruited from Maydan and other villages were hastily dispatched to Butkhak before they had even had time for a meal. But when Nadir's units pulled back, Habib Allah's partisans breathed easier.

April 26: On the eve of the 26th, Muhammad Siddiq arrived in Kabul and went to see Habib Allah. During Aman Allah's reign he had been a brigadier general (*ghundmishr*)[141] and since the [1924] Mangal uprising he and his forces had been stationed in Khost. There he had been captured by Nadir but escaped. On the basis of what he recounted, Ghulam ᶜAli, the aide and adjutant of Sayyid Husayn, and other partisans of Habib Allah circulated the story that on Tuesday, April 25,[142] a battle had taken place at Tirah Pass in which Nadir's force was routed and all his military equipment, tents, and rations were plundered by Pushtuns such as the Shinwaris and Khugyanis who had been unfaithful to the tribal alliance and disloyal to ᶜAli Ahmad [Luynab]. It was said Nadir himself had fled to the protection of the Jadran tribe.

April 28: Today the amir named Major General Muhammad Siddiq military high commissioner (*raʾis-i tanzimiyah*) for the Southern Province. People say he is Nadir Khan's man because he was supposed to have said to Habib Allah: "The Pushtuns and Hazarahs will not give you the opportunity to rule. It would be better if, as a sincere Muslim and one who has adopted the title 'Servant of the Prophet of God,' you put an end to the bloodshed, torment, and humiliation and prohibit your northerners from the thievery they are engaged in."

Though fighting continued between Nadir's and Habib Allah's backers for a few more weeks, Nadir was unable to make any progress toward the capital. But Fayz Muhammad continues to hear generally encouraging, though largely inaccurate, news from that front.

May 1: Fighting involving the units of the Southern Province under the leadership of Nadir has already lasted three days. Last night six hundred men from Habib Allah's vanquished army arrived in Kabul, bringing in fifty wounded. Also today the heads of two dead fighters from units under Nadir were hung up on the Chawk after being burned black, as a lesson to onlookers. The forces of Nadir that had been engaged in desultory fighting for two days have now pulled back.

The Kuhdamanis, quoting an official in the Central Customs, Malik Zayn al-ᶜAbidin and his family, spread word through the city that Ghulam Ghaws, the son of Jandad Ahmadzai, seeking the reward announced by Habib Allah, has captured Nadir and will bring him to Kabul tomorrow.

May 2: Today a large truck filled with wounded arrived from Logar where there is fighting with Nadir's units.

May 3: Having returned in the evening, the amir, at six o'clock this morning, headed for Qalᶜahcha-i Khumdan and Bini Hisar, reportedly just on an outing. They say that he is studying the situation in Surkhab in Logar, where Nadir's forces under the command of Ahmad Shah have fortified several places from which they have been harassing the amir and preventing his units from advancing into the Southern Province. The amir returned to the city after learning the facts of the situation and giving instructions for defensive measures.

Also today the amir's forces attacked and plundered Charkh, despite the fact that the people of Charkh have broken their alliance with the people of the Southern Province, provided support for the amir's forces, and recruited soldiers for his army from among their own residents. In the attack, forts and houses were burned.

May 5: It has been three days now since there has been any information from Nadir. No one knows where he is. The people of Shah Mazar having heard the announcement that whoever captures him will get a reward of forty thousand rupees, invited him to come to them. They said he would be their guest. But aware of their cunning, he has gone to either Gardiz or Khost with five hundred men who had arrived in Shah Mazar. Frustrated by the ignorance, stupidity, and irreligion of the Pushtuns of those regions, he [reportedly] went to Ghazni. People say that he made peace there between Aman Allah and the Sulayman Khayl [tribe] and then returned to Gardiz.

May 6: Over the course of the past three or four days, including today, units of new conscripts from the Logar districts of Charkh, Khushi, Kulangar, and Surkhab along with units exhausted from the fighting in the Southern Province, have been summoned to Kabul with and without weapons, and then sent north to Charikar. The units that were defeated at Ghazni and in the western regions are returning home in small groups and going into hiding.

Fayz Muhammad's next bulletin on Nadir's activities seems to have been mostly wishful thinking.

May 11: Today rumors are flying that Nadir with his own troops as well as militia from the tribes of the Southern Province has arrived in Charkh, in Logar. Tribal elders from Logar have secretly allied with him and declared that they will smash Habib Allah's army by any means at hand and so save the Logar region from his oppression. Nadir Khan then prepared for battle and waited for the approach of Habib Allah, who had ordered the residents of the Logar to supply provisions to his army while he was advancing with his forces. As his army neared the ambush laid by Nadir's units the residents of Logar closed in from the rear. Those lying in ambush opened fire. Most of the amir's soldiers were killed; some were taken prisoner; and all of their weapons and artillery were captured. The rest of Habib Allah's soldiers cut and ran. After Nadir's troops had retired to their positions and the Logaris who had prepared provisions for them had dispersed, Habib Allah's units managed to collect their wounded from the battlefield and send them back to Kabul.

Where this report came from is not at all clear. The Charkh battle he refers to would seem to be the one that occurred two weeks before and rather than a victory for Nadir was an utter defeat, according to Mohammed Ali, who, as a stout advocate for Nadir, tried to paint the incident in the most favorable terms possible. Perhaps this represents the first word Fayz Muhammad had of the battle. Later, when he reports events of May 8, he refers to a "defeat at Charkh." It is also possible that Habib Allah's troops had had another fight in Charkh after the one at the end of April. But Nadir himself seems to have been ensconced at Sijinak, north-east of Gardiz, at this point while Hashim, his brother, was in the Eastern Province struggling to rebuild tribal support for the Musahiban family during the first week of May. Fayz Muhammad reports, with some skepticism, that Hashim was successful in his recruiting but there is insufficient evidence that his information was at all accurate and certainly nothing came of this evanescent rallying of the notoriously fickle Pushtun tribes.

May 8: Earlier this month, following the defeat at Charkh, Hashim, appealing to Afghan honor and making effective use of propaganda, persuaded the Pushtun tribes of the Eastern Province to unite against Habib Allah. They agreed to raise forty thousand fighters who would advance in three formations along the road through Tagab, Tangi Gharu, Chakari, and Lataband and attack Kuhdaman, Kuhistan, and Kabul. To supply the men with provisions, the tribes hurriedly harvested their crops and sent their men off. Today, they reached the region of Pul-i Hashim Khayl in Gandamak and at Tagab made plans to continue farther along the road.

Tribes of the Southern Province under the command of Nadir and the tribes of the Western Province,[143] under the leadership of Aman Allah, followed the example of the tribes of the Eastern Province. They agreed that sooner or later they would attack the northern region from four sides, that is from Maydan, Charasya, Butkhak, Tangi Gharu, Tagab, Ghurband, Kutal-i Safidkhak, from the mountains of Paghman, Farza, Shakar Darra, and from Istalif. Perhaps they will be successful.

Another important element in the opposition of the Pushtun tribes to Habib Allah's government, according to Fayz Muhammad, was the activity of a member of the Mujaddidi family, Hazrat Fazl ᶜUmar, also known as Shayr Aqa. The Mujaddidis, in the author's view, bore no small responsibility for Habib Allah's taking Kabul in the first place. Opposed to Aman Allah because of their distaste for his social and religious policies, they had by this point lost faith in the new regime, perhaps because of conditions in Kabul, and were working for its overthrow. In dealing with the activities of Shayr Aqa, Fayz Muhammad also sheds considerable light on what people believed about the hand of the British government in

India in the uprising. It is clearly his conviction that the British wanted Aman Allah ousted and supported the government of Habib Allah and that they had people planted at the highest levels of the Afghan government to do their bidding. Fayz Muhammad does not go so far as to name names, however.

May 8: There are stories going around that Hazrat Fazl ᶜUmar, better known as Shayr Aqa, had arrived in Katawaz and Zurmat. Fearing persecution at the hands of Aman Allah, he settled in India two years ago, after returning from Mecca, and announced that he would never return to Kabul again. People say that he now came to Katawaz and Zurmat at the behest of the English, who hoped to get the Sulayman Khayl, Andar, Taraki, and ᶜAli Khayl tribes, which had stopped fighting Aman Allah, to rise again. There were also rumors going around that his brothers, who live in Kabul and have been responsible from the outset of the uprising for a good deal of bloodshed, would end the carnage after this. Russians and Turks living in Kabul, whenever they meet their countrymen in the bazaars, all say that this hazrat has come to Katawaz and Zurmat at the behest of the English in order to prolong the uprising and force Aman Allah to leave the country.

But people who are interested in contemporary politics and are supporters of the faith reject this notion. Wherever people gather, two views are usually expressed. One is that the English, who fear Russia, are trying to use Afghanistan as a buffer between India and Russia to protect English control of India from attack by the latter and prevent her interference in Indian affairs. The other view is that the ulama and tribal maliks would not be able to act under English instruction against their own government on the pretext of strengthening the religion and spreading Islamic principles since the English are Christians and their teachings are alien to Islam. They believe it is clear that the instigators of the uprising are not the English, but the ignorant pseudo-mullas and maliks who are neither adherents of the religion nor followers of the Prophet.

Therefore, their opposition, their violation of oaths and agreements, and their killing and plundering confirm the fact that Hazrat Shayr Aqa came to Katawaz and Zurmat at the request of the Muslims of Peshawar and other regions to persuade the Sulayman Khayl, Andar, and other tribes of the absolute necessity of supporting Aman Allah, overthrowing

Habib Allah, and putting an end to the uprising. The Russians, Turks, and others disquieted by his emergence are undoubtedly mistaken in asserting that he came to Katawaz and Zurmat at the behest of the English. In point of fact, he is raising the people against Habib Allah. And because of this, once word came about his arrival in those regions, Habib Allah has had the brothers of the hazrat watched and has forbidden them from leaving their homes on pain of death.

Tribal forces from the Eastern Province began to move on Kabul, only to be blocked by fighting provoked by those tireless troublemakers, the Shinwari.

May 11: Groups of Eastern Province tribes neared the city today. The Shinwaris who have been escorting merchants from Kabul to Peshawar have postponed their departure until Tuesday. Along the road to Kabul, bands of Shinwari thieves have been attacking Surkhrud and Chaparhar.[144] Since the people of Surkhrud have ammunition captured from government forces as well as a large number of rifles, they were able to rout the Shinwaris, killing or wounding about 120 of them. The Surkhrudis themselves sustained twelve casualties.

Because of this fighting, the Eastern Province tribes stopped advancing toward Kabul and a Shinwari caravan was forced to return to the city. The people of Surkhrud refuse to allow any Mohmands to cross their territory en route to the capital. They say that the efforts of Nadir's brother, Hashim, have been fruitless and so the attack on Kabul by Eastern Province tribesmen has been delayed.

And rumors continued to circulate that Nadir was advancing up the Logar Valley toward Kabul.

May 12: Because eighty wounded men were brought to Kabul yesterday, rumors flew today that Nadir had crushed Habib Allah's force at the village of Bidak. This was the force that the amir had sent to Logar.

Three days later Fayz Muhammad has Nadir's forces again crossing the Tirah Pass (Altamur Pass) in an incursion into the Logar Valley—although if the previous information about his success was accurate, why the Musahiban leader would still have been on the far side of the pass at this point is not clear.

May 15: Nadir's army crossed the Tirah Pass today, giving notice of its arrival in Logar with cannon volleys. The Logaris, tired of the tyranny of Habib Allah's soldiers who killed, stole, assaulted five-year old girls, chopped off the heads of small boys, forced every family to pay a land tax of 120 rupees, and sent every male without exception off to war, now declared for Nadir.

May 16: The fighting that began yesterday in Logar continues. At sunrise a large group of soldiers returned to Kabul. They had been sent to Logar and the Southern Province but had been defeated by Nadir, whose army pursued them as far as Kulangar, Kutub Khayl [Kutti Khayl], and Muhammad Aghah. At 1:00 p.m. the amir received two letters, one from Sayyid Husayn in Charikar [at this point battling for control of the Ghurband Valley] and the other from the commander of the unit in Butkhak. From the latter he learned that a six-thousand-man force supporting Nadir Khan had arrived in Khak-i Jabbar via the road through Hisarak. Straight away, Habib Allah set off by car for Butkhak to organize its defenses. However, a story from people close to him says that he broke down and cried after reading the letter from Sayyid Husayn and had gone not to Butkhak but to Charikar. The populace of the city, having prayed to God day and night to deliver them from Sayyid Husayn, believe the rumors that Sayyid Husayn has been fatally wounded in the battle at Burj-i Guljan and that Habib Allah has gone there to see him for the last time as well as to assess the situation.

The story of Sayyid Husayn's demise was also wishful thinking, as were the continued rumors of Nadir's imminent assault on Kabul. While the situation in Logar remained unsettled, with Habib Allah in more or less secure control of the region north of the Altamur Pass and Nadir dominant south of it, Habib Allah attempted to negotiate a settlement. His chief negotiator was Mawlawi ᶜAbd al-Latif, a controversial figure in the accounts of the time. Mohammed Ali characterizes Mawlawi ᶜAbd al-Latif as "a treacherous fortune-hunter" who "meddled" in Afghan politics. Fayz Muhammad is hardly more generous in his views. Mawlawi ᶜAbd al-Latif was born in India and settled in Afghanistan, according to Mohammed Ali as a direct consequence of the Hijrat movement under which Aman Allah, entranced by the idea of himself as successor to the Ottoman sultans in the role of leader of the world Muslim community, opened the borders to any Indian Muslims who wished to "make hijrat *(emigrate) from the 'Abode of War' of India to the 'Abode of Peace' of*

Afghanistan."

During these cataclysmic events, Habib Allah decided to write a letter to Nadir and his brothers, Shah Wali and Shah Mahmud, about a truce. He was advised to do so by an Indian emigrant, Mawlawi ᶜAbd al-Latif, who, when it came to deception, cunning and conspiracy, was a schemer second to none. Everyone considers him a servant and spy for the English as well as an evil man. On Saturday, May 11, Habib Allah Khan wrote them a letter in which he promised to send Nadir Khan money and invited him to share in the administration of the state. He also wrote,

> Although you did not come to Kabul, but opposed my government and began a war, the road to peace is still open. But in order for this to happen you must end the bloodshed and killing of Muslims and, as I originally suggested, come to Kabul. If not, all the blood that is shed, and all the property and wealth that is plundered, will be on your head. If something happens to your families, you will also be to blame, not I. You may assure yourself of the sincerity of this offer through Mawlawi ᶜAbd al-Latif, who is my fully empowered representative, with whom you may conclude any agreement or understanding and on whom you may rely.

The mawlawi, who had orchestrated this affair at English bidding, set off on May 17 to see Nadir and his brothers, after receiving the message signed by the Minister of Court, Shayr Jan, and bearing Habib Allah's seal. God willing, his returning empty-handed will be recounted below.

After Mawlawi ᶜAbd al-Latif delivered the amir's letter, Nadir called a truce until the Feast of the Sacrifice [*ᶜĪd-i Qurban*, the 10th of Dhu'l-Hijjah, which fell this year on May 20] was over.

It was learned today [May 18] that Hazrat Shayr Aqa [Mujaddidi] had arrived in Zurmat and Katawaz, supposedly at the request of the Muslims of India, and was staying with the Sulayman Khayl and Andar tribes in order to aid in suppressing the rebellion that the Pushtuns had raised against Aman Allah. In fact, he was carrying out the instructions of the English, who did not want Aman Allah to return as amir.

It should be noted here that this interpretation of Hazrat Shayr Aqa Mujaddidi's motives in stirring up the Eastern Province Pushtuns differs from what Fayz Muhammad gave earlier.[145] *There, he concluded that the hazrat had come to those tribes to rally support for Aman Allah and over-*

throw Habib Allah. Here he presents precisely the opposite view. Fayz Muhammad seems to be saying that this member of the Mujaddidi family, all of whose members he clearly despised, had been urged by Muslims in India to agitate in favor of Aman Allah but, in accordance with British wishes, he exerted himself not on behalf of the ex-amir, but for Nadir.

The hazrat, after meeting with the Sulayman Khayl and Andar elders and setting them against Aman Allah, left to join the tribes of the Southern Province who had concluded an agreement with Nadir. They had resolved that after the capture of Kabul and banishment of Habib Allah and following consultation with representatives of all the people, they would put on the throne a man worthy of the honor of governing the country. He could be from either the Durrani, Ghilzaʾi, Hazarah, Tajik, or Uzbek tribes and they would give him their allegiance. But it would have to be someone who would not harm the government and would allow everyone the opportunity to earn a living. It had also been decided that the Pushtun tribes of the Southern Province, who did not want Aman Allah to be amir because of the treachery and corruption of his ministers, would support Nadir if he agreed to be amir of Afghanistan. But being a judicious and pious man, he thought that this would provoke the English, who could cause harm to the Afghan nation. But Shayr Aqa persuaded the Southern Province Pushtuns to unite behind the resolution and then called on them to rise up and overthrow Habib Allah. Then, in conformity with British policy, he used cunning and deception to persuade Nadir to accept the amirate. But since Aman Allah has many supporters in Russia, in Turkey, and among the Muslims of India, the Durrani Pushtun tribes, and the Hazarahs, it is most likely that as a result of this shortsighted policy of Shayr Aqa, the rebellion will continue.

May 19: There is another rumor making the rounds and that is that Nadir Khan has been proclaimed amir and the time for the assault on Kabul by his and Aman Allah's troops has been fixed for three days after the holiday [that is, on May 23].

May 20: There is word today that Nadir reportedly accepted the proposal, delivered by Mawlawi ᶜAbd al-Latif, to end the bloodshed. Having successfully completed his mission, ᶜAbd al-Latif was given leave by Nadir. Then, either from Barakibarak or Muhammad Aghah, he telephoned the amir to tell him that he had fulfilled his charge. The amir then ordered the release of all Nadir's family members from custody and the return of their confiscated property, and he let float a rumor that Nadir had sent his oath of allegiance and recognized him as amir.

The residents of Kabul, brought to the brink of despair by the oppression, humiliations, and violence perpetrated by Habib Allah and his partisans, heard this news and began to curse Nadir, whom they had considered a person unparalleled in their time and devoted to the religion, a man in whom the best qualities of a son of the Afghan people were combined. To themselves they said that if he had in fact sent such an oath to the amir then he had neither pride, nor faith, nor honor, nor feelings of shame. The amir had brought his wife and the wives of his brothers to the Arg, women who were daughters of [the late] Amir Habib Allah, had held them there for a time, and had committed adultery with them. Nadir knew all about this but because of a lack of pride he had put it out of his mind and so had trampled on the honor of the Afghans and his own name, which up until now had been unblemished. The residents of the city finally calmed each other by saying these agreements were all a lie and that Nadir's patience is limitless. Yesterday [May 19], in fact, more than twenty thousand men who recognized him as amir heard the *khutbah*, and performed the daily prayers, in his name.[146] Had he been so thoughtless and impetuous as to accede to the wishes of Habib Allah, then the very mention of his name would blacken the pages of history.

May 22: Partisans of Habib Allah rejoiced today at news of Nadir's letter which, as was already mentioned, he sent via Mawlawi ᶜAbd al-Latif. At the beginning of the letter Nadir expresses his views about coming to Kabul,

> In inviting me to Kabul, you wrote that the Russians have bombed Mazar-i Sharif and that therefore we ought to end the civil war; further, when I return to Kabul you expect me to occupy myself with getting government affairs back into order and that you will begin to fight the Russians and cleanse our land of their encroachments. Very good. Having read and understood your wishes, I will come to Kabul.[147]

But after reading the end of the letter, where Nadir says, "I will arrive in Kabul with a six-thousand-man force and so an adequate quantity of fodder and provisions should be readied," the partisans of Habib Allah grew anxious and regretted that they had spread the rumor that Nadir Khan had supposedly given an oath of allegiance and recognized Habib Allah as amir.

May 23: Today there were rumors of a meeting in Logar between Nadir and Habib Allah through the mediation of Mawlawi ᶜAbd al-Latif. The two men were reportedly reconciled and agreed that Habib Allah would be ruler of the north and Nadir would sit on the throne as amir but would not oppress the people of the northern regions. In connection with this, they freed Nadir's nephew, ᶜAli Shah,[148] from custody and sent him to his uncle accompanied by several mullas.

However, this same day, a force of three hundred men with eighteen pieces of artillery was sent to Logar. But immediately after, there was talk that since Habib Allah has sent this force at the very moment when truce negotiations are going on, he is obviously plotting against Nadir and still aiming to strike a decisive blow.

May 24: Meantime, as was recounted, Nadir, through Mawlawi ᶜAbd al-Latif, had persuaded Habib Allah to accept a truce and now sent a messenger to Kabul in which he set forth the conditions for his arrival in the capital. They were the following: as evidence of good faith on Habib Allah's part he was to send his brother, Hamid Allah, as a hostage to Nadir. He in his turn would send his brother, Shah Mahmud, with a *lashkar* [tribal army] of six thousand men to Kabul. The force would occupy the Arg and take control of the government arsenals. Habib Allah would himself head north and become ruler there. After that, Nadir would come to Kabul with a lashkar of forty thousand men.

Habib Allah accepted Nadir's written offer and sent his brother and Mawlawi ᶜAbd al-Latif back by car today to join Nadir. It was the amir's intent now to launch a jihad against the Russians, something which the English had put him up to. First, Hazrat Shayr Aqa appeared among the savage tribes of the frontier, and then Nadir proclaimed himself amir. It is clear that the English, who raised the specter of a wider war in Central Asia, are involved in all of this. We will see what time brings. As for now the glorious name of Nadir lies trampled in the mud.

May 26: Rumors are circulating ever more feverishly about the imminent arrival of Nadir in Kabul and his intention of taking the throne and also about the commencement of a jihad against the Russians under the leadership of Habib Allah.

May 28: The amir continues to spread the rumor of the proclamation of Nadir's amirate and that the latter had expressed his allegiance to him. With the help of similar rumors and talk about a truce, he has tried to deceive Nadir, who has neither a treasury nor arms, and to build up his own strength in order to destroy him.

But we have little evidence that the rumor had any truth to it. Did Hamid Allah actually go to Nadir as a guarantee that this rumored agreement would be carried out? Was there even an agreement about Nadir's receiving Kabul and the division of the country between north and south? If one thinks of the transnational issues, for example, where Pushtun support lay and where the Tajik connections were, there was a certain rationale to such a division, as present events have shown. But Fayz Muhammad provides no strong evidence of such an agreement, nor is there any follow-up in his work to this story. I have not been able to find that Anis or Kushkaki refer to it, though that is not surprising given the time in which they wrote.

June 6: Fighting is now beginning in the Southern province against Nadir. In reply to Habib Allah's offer[149] Nadir sent this reply: "In exchange for my property which you have confiscated, send me a hundred thousand rupees and also the members of my family so that I may go abroad and leave these savage Pushtuns behind. The throne will then be yours."

Fayz Muhammad at this moment seems to have lost hope that Nadir was the answer to the problem of Habib Allah. His conclusion would be strengthened by Nadir's loss of Gardiz, which was retaken by the man who had first surrendered it, Muhammad Siddiq. Gardiz would remain in Nadir's control for another month or so, though it is clear from Fayz Muhammad's growing silence on the activities of the Musahiban clan that Nadir was receding as a serious threat to take Kabul. On the 4th of Saratan (June 26) according to Anis,[150] *Gardiz finally fell to Muhammad Siddiq. Tribal support, on which Nadir depended, once again proved unreliable. At this point, late in June, largely deserted by his Mangal and Ahmadza'i supporters, Nadir was taken in by the Jaji tribe whose lands lay near the Indian border at the head of the Kurram Valley. There he remained more or less* hors de combat *at least through much of June.*

Nadir's name would dominate later historical reflections on the period because of his success in eventually ousting Habib Allah from Kabul. But as is clear from Fayz Muhammad's condemnation of Nadir's behavior, at this point (that is, in late May), he appeared to have no chance of taking Kabul. But after the Hazarah mission of June ended (see Part Three) and Fayz Muhammad returned to Kabul, the activities of Nadir are revived in Fayz Muhammad's writing, at least for his coverage of the events of early July, after which the figure of Nadir again recedes into the background.

The Tagab Front

A third major source of resistance to the Kabul regime was the Tagab-Najrab (Tagao-Najrao) region northeast of Kabul. The neighboring valleys of Tagab and Najrab are connected by the broad plain of the Panjshir River on its way to join the Kabul River just north of Sarubi (Sarobi), an important ford on the Kabul River. To the east of Tagab lies the Laghman (Lamkan) Valley. Legend has it that Noah's ark came to rest in the mountains of the Laghman Valley and that the valley's name derives from his father, Lamech, known locally as Mihtar (Elder) Lam. According to legend, Lamech drove the infidels from the valley. The town of Mihtarlam in the southern part of the valley commemorates the Biblical figure and is the site of an ancient pilgrimage shrine said to have been founded by Sultan Mahmud of Ghazni in the late 10th century C.E. *in honor of Lamech.*

Tagab, somewhat distant from Kabul, was a place from which resistance campaigns could be launched south to cut the main road from Kabul to Jalalabad and west toward the Ghurband Valley, the main route from Kabul to Mazar-i Sharif and Afghan Turkistan. Tagab was inhabited by the Safi Pushtun tribe and by the Ghilzai. Fayz Muhammad sees the Tagab resistance to the new Kabul regime stemming not so much from ancient ethnic enmity as from personal grudges.

Pir Muhammad, the brother of Field Marshal Amir Muhammad Khan and first cousin of the mother of the "Mu^{c}in al-Saltanah" ^{c}Inayat Allah, harbored an enduring hatred for his nephew, Ghulam Muhammad, whom

Habib Allah had appointed governor of Tagab. He therefore incited the residents of the Laghman Valley against the amir. One of Habib Allah's deputies had taken a force of one thousand infantrymen and two cannons and gone to Sarubi, Habib Allah's headquarters during his bandit days.[151] Ghulam Muhammad was in Tagab to defend Kabul from attack by the Laghmanis. But he now renounced his obedience and called on the Tagabis first to attack Sarubi and Gugamandan [just north of Sarubi], rout this thousand-man force, and then attack Jabal al-Siraj and Kuhistan [to the northwest]. Because Habib Allah's main forces were in and around Kabul, there was a good chance of victory.

So the Tagabis launched a surprise attack on Sarubi and Gugamandan, as Ghulam Muhammad had urged. The soldiers there were taken by surprise and the Tagabis captured two cannons, weaponry and other military supplies, and all the soldiers' personal effects. They then returned to Bandar-i Salang. On Sunday, March 17 they prepared themselves for an assault [northward] on Jamal Agha [in Kuhistan], and on the 18th they attacked, defeating Habib Allah's forces, capturing six field pieces and sixty thousand rupees. Crossing the Ghurband River, they ransacked the homes of some well-to-do people in Riza Kuhistan and occupied Jamal Agha. They then decided to try to take the citadel at Jabal al-Siraj.

Sayyid Husayn and Habib Allah's brother, Hamid Allah (both of whom had recently conferred on themselves a number of high positions and lofty titles including wazir-i jang, sardar-i ᶜali and, by resolution of the Islamic Regulatory Commission, the titles naᵓib al-saltanah and muᶜin al-saltanah respectively), had been preoccupied debauching women and children. When they learned about the uprising of the Tagabis, they panicked and drove out that night with a group of their confederates to set up defenses. They quickly reached Sehab and from there requested reinforcements from Kabul.

On Tuesday, March 19, Habib Allah sent two aircraft and three thousand Kuhistani villains to Tagab. While in Kabul, these people have ransacked homes, destroyed government buildings and parks, burned scientific books, and assaulted women, girls, and young boys. But despite aerial bombing and the best efforts of Habib Allah's soldiers, success eluded them. The fighting lasted three or four days and was still raging when Habib Allah took the advice of Sardar Muhammad ᶜUsman and Hazrat

Shayr Aqa and sent ᶜAbd al-Ghafur the son of Muhammad Shah of Tagab to negotiate a truce and put an end to the uprising. During Aman Allah's reign ᶜAbd al-Ghafur was a member of the National Council and at this time was serving as minister of the interior. His brother, who had declared for Habib Allah, was killed during Aman Allah's last days. Habib Allah gave him thirty thousand rupees with which he was supposed to bribe the mullas and maliks supporting the uprising. On Wednesday, March 20 he sent a convoy toward Tagab and himself departed Kabul on the 21st. On the night of the 22nd Hamid Allah (who had meantime returned to Kabul) asked Muhammad Khan Qarabaghi, assigned by Habib Allah to guard the motor pool, for gasoline and said he would take it on his own account. Later that evening, when Habib Allah found this out, he ordered the motor pool guard killed and his body buried in a pit.

On March 23 in the evening, rumors began to circulate that the people of Durnama, Sujnan, and Bulaghin, had attacked the Tagabis, defeated them, and occupied their positions. They then returned to the Najrab militiamen who were their allies the weapons that had been taken from them.

On the 26th, two Tagabis were brought to the Chawk.[152] One of them was an old man, the other a youth. After an announcement that these two were the ringleaders of the Tagabi uprising, they were hanged and next to them a sign was posted that read, "This fate awaits anyone who dares rebel against the government."

April 1: Today, more prisoners were brought in from Tagab, above and beyond the forty men already mentioned.[153] Habib Allah felt sorry for them and released them.

The Tagab resistance seems to have been brought under control by Kabul by the end of March. Fayz Muhammad's silence on the subject is the most eloquent testimony that Habib Allah was no longer seriously threatened there. The hideous execution on April 30 of a qazi who supported Aman Allah and was captured in Tagab is another sign.

April 30: Today Qazi ᶜAbd al-Rahman was publicly executed.[154] From the very outset of the uprising he had opposed Habib Allah and Sayyid Husayn and vowed to Aman Allah that someday he would arrest the bandits and deal with them. But they murdered his brother and looted the house he owned in Kuhdaman and the enmity between them grew. When Habib Allah and Sayyid Husayn captured the capital, Qazi ᶜAbd al-

Rahman fled his home there and joined forces in Kuhdaman and Kuhistan with ᶜAta Muhammad, the son of Malik Muhammad. There with the residents of Tagab he fought against Habib Allah until captured in Dih Sabz[155] where he was hiding. By order of Habib Allah he was drawn and quartered on the Chawk while he was still alive. This monstrous infliction of the death penalty, bestial in its cruelty, finally convinced those who witnessed it or heard about it of the utter barbarism of the northerners.

May 5: Information was received today that armed tribesmen of the Eastern Province, having heard about the barbaric acts of Habib Allah and his soldiers toward the people of Kabul—drawing and quartering living people, raping women, young girls, and young boys, charging people who had never committed even the smallest misdeed with crimes, hanging innocent people and sayyids and shedding blood illegally—arrived in Tagab where they joined forces with the Hazarahs, who had seen nothing from Habib Allah but oppression and violence.

The author's reference here to Hazarahs is to the Hazarahs in general, especially those of the Hazarahjat region, whose threat to the Kabul government was taken very seriously by Habib Allah at this time. There were no Hazarahs in Tagab at this time as far as we know.

The Ghurband Front

Outside of Kabul, the road north linking the capital with the vast region beyond the Hindu Kush and south of the Oxus River—the area known since the mid-19th century as "Afghan Turkistan"—first passes through Kuhistan and Kuhdaman, homeland of the Tajiks who had taken the capital. This area was, and still is, known as "The North" (Shamal) *and its people as "northerners"* (shamaliyan). *Habib Allah's native village, Kalakan, lies a few miles off the road and about twenty miles or so north of the capital, and Charikar, Sayyid Husayn's home, another sixteen or so beyond that. But six miles beyond Charikar, the road divides into three segments and the ethnic and political landscape changes dramatically.*

One road, heading west into the Ghurband Valley, leads to the 9,240-foot Shibar Pass about sixty miles to the west. The pass is approached by

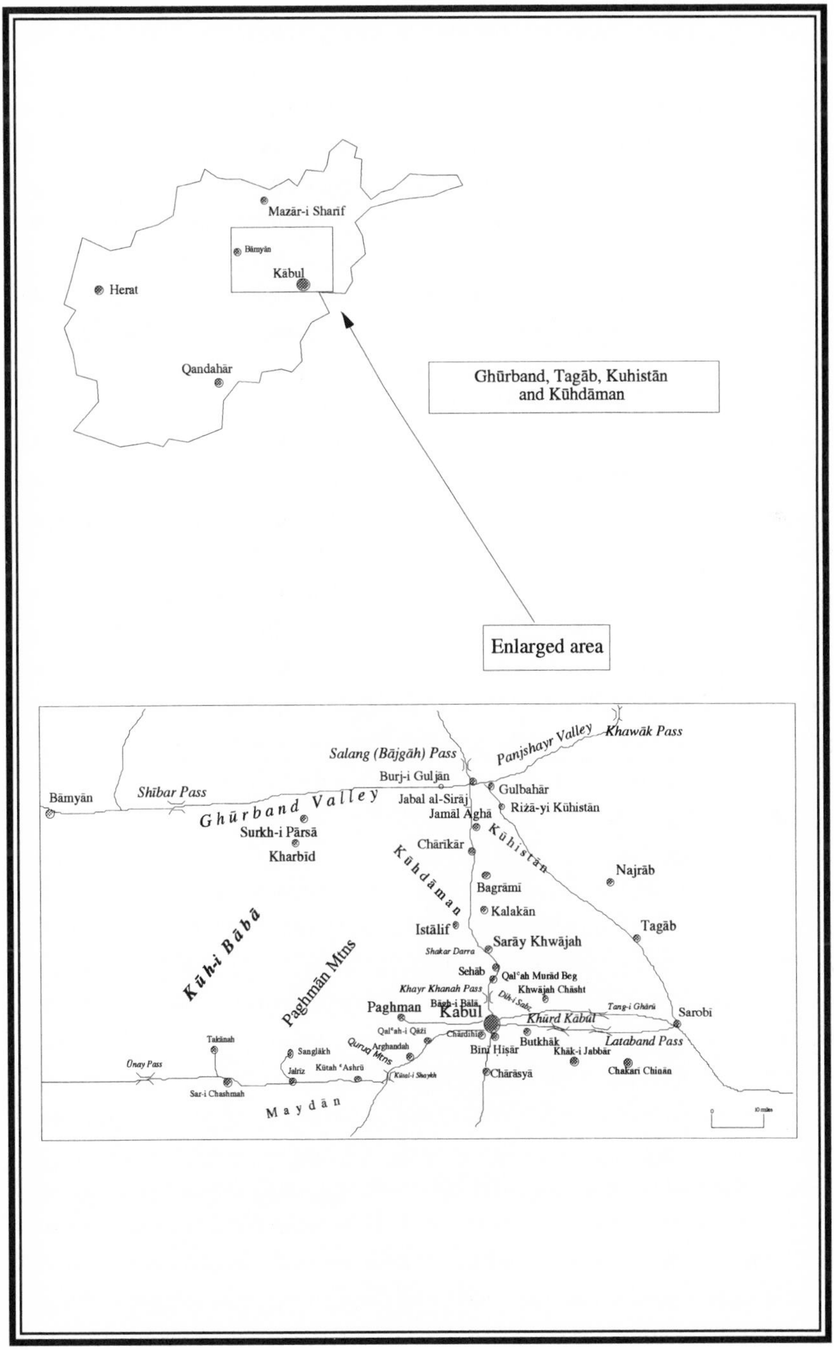

Mazār-i Sharīf
Bāmyān
Kābul
Herat
Qandahār
Ghūrband, Tagāb, Kuhistān and Kūhdāman
Enlarged area
Salang (Bājgāh) Pass
Panjshayr Valley
Khawāk Pass
Bāmyān
Shībar Pass
Burj-i Gul jān
Gulbahār
Ghūrband Valley
Jabal al-Sirāj
Jamāl Aghā
Rizā-yi Kūhistān
Surkh-i Pārsā
Kharbīd
Chārīkār
Kūhistān
Kūhdāman
Najrāb
Bagrāmī
Kalakān
Kūh-i Bābā
Istālif
Tagāb
Paghmān Mtns
Shakar Darra
Sarāy Khwājah
Sehāb
Qalᶜah Murād Beg
Khayr Khanah Pass
Khwājah Chāsht
Dih-i Sabz
Paghman
Bāgh-i Bālā
Kabul
Tang-i Ghārū
Sarobī
Khūrd Kābul
Qalᶜah-i Qāzī
Chārdihi
Takānah
Sanglākh
Quruq Mtns
Arghandah
Butkhāk
Lataband Pass
Bini Ḥiṣār
Khāk-i Jabbār
Ūnay Pass
Jalrīz
Kūtah ᶜAshrū
Kūtal-i Shaykh
Chārāsyā
Chakari Chinān
Sar-i Chashmah
Maydān
0
10 miles

a fairly gradual ascent and until the building of the Salang Tunnel it was the principal route through the Hindu Kush for travelers between Afghan Turkistan and Kabul. Some thirty miles beyond the pass is the valley of Bamyan. In 1929, the region around the pass was dominated by Hazarahs, as it is today. About halfway between the Shibar Pass and Bamyan the route north to Baghlan, Samangan, Qunduz, and Mazar-i Sharif branches off.

*The second road junction just north of Charikar bends off to the north-east and runs up the Panjshayr (Panjshir, Panjsher) Valley, "the Valley of the Five Lions." About fifty miles or so up the valley and about a hundred fifteen miles from Kabul is the 11,650-foot-high Khawak Pass, another major cut through the Hindu Kush linking Afghan Turkistan and Badakhshan with the rest of the country. Today control of the valley and the pass is in the hands of another Tajik warlord, Ahmad Shah Mas*ᶜ*ud, the "Lion of the Panjshayr."*

The third road, not as important in the 1920s as it is today, leads from Charikar north to Jabal al-Siraj at the beginning of the ascent to the Salang (or Bajgah "customs post") Pass, at around 12,000 feet. Like the Khawak and Shibar Passes, it was a seasonal route for caravans going to Afghan Turkistan. Until the Soviets constructed a tunnel that was opened in 1964 beneath the pass, the Salang route was only open to camel caravans and was closed for a good part of the year by snow.

Beyond Charikar, resistance to Habib Allah's regime developed quickly, particularly in the Ghurband Valley, the most important line of communication with Afghan Turkistan. Securing the Ghurband fell largely to Habib Allah's principal colleague in the takeover, Sayyid Husayn, himself a native of Charikar. Sayyid Husayn's chief opponents in the Ghurband appear to have been Hazarahs, or so the ethnically loyal Fayz Muhammad presents the case. Their homes and lands lay back in the valleys that opened into the Ghurband along the entire route from its beginning at the village of Pul-i Matak north of Charikar to the heights of the Shibar Pass. (This road and the Hazarah resistance all along it stymied the Taliban in the spring and summer of 1997 as well and was a large factor in their failure to take control of the north.) The most important valleys in Fayz Muhammad's account are those of the region which he calls "Surkh Parsa and Turkman." Today Surkh Parsa (alternately "Surkh-i

Parsa" or "Surkh and Parsa,"[156]*) is the mountainous region along the southern side of the road leading to the Shibar Pass from the east. It includes several large valleys extending southward from the Charikar-Bamyan road, and these have branch valleys extending back into the fastness of the Kuh-i Baba Range, the western end of the Hindu Kush.*

Fayz Muhammad puts heavy emphasis on the crucial role of the Hazarahs in all the planning for a coordinated attack on the Kabul regime. In a frequently repeated scenario, he has the Hazarahs of the Hazarahjat and the Hazarahs of the Ghurband region attacking Kabul from the west and northwest, Nadir and the tribes of the Southern Province attacking from the south, Aman Allah's supporters driving up from the southwest and the tribes of the Eastern Province under Hashim, Nadir's brother, attacking from the east. But structural factors—ethnic, sectarian, and political differences—were as antithetical to stable political coalitions in 1929 as they are today and continual talk of coordinated attacks was, at least in retrospect, wishful thinking on our author's part.

Although Fayz Muhammad presents his fellow Hazarahs as a fairly unified force, the fact is that the Hazarahs were no more free of the kinds of local, particularist loyalties that hampered the formation of interregional coalitions than were their Afghan, Tajik, Turkmen, and Uzbek counterparts. Fayz Muhammad clearly would have liked the Hazarahs to have shown more unity as a group, and obviously believed their interests lay in ethnic solidarity, but it is equally clear from his account that local interests often took precedence over any sense of a larger community.

In general, the areas of military operations tend to separate the Hazarahs into two groups, those fighting in the Ghurband region (the Hazarahs of Surkh-i Parsa, Shaykh ᶜAli, Bamyan, Balkhab, Turkman, etc.) and those of the Hazarahjat (Bihsud in the central Hazarahjat, Day Zangi and Day Kundi west of Bihsud, and Day Mirdad north of Ghazni). In addition, there were numbers of Hazarahs around Mazar-i Sharif, resettled there by either ᶜAbd al-Rahman or his son, Habib Allah. Fayz Muhammad refers to these as the emigré or "transported" Hazarahs.

It is not entirely clear when armed opposition to the new regime broke out in the Ghurband region, but the fact that it had was signaled by Sayyid Husayn Charikari's move back to his hometown to make it his base for fighting the opponents of the new government. His move may have been connected with the news coming from Afghan Turkistan.

April 1: The Hazarahs of Shaykh ᶜAli, Bamyan, Turkman, Surkh-i Parsa, Day Zangi, Balkhab, Bihsud, and a number of other places refused to render obedience to Habib Allah and came out in support of Aman Allah. People from Shaykh ᶜAli, Surkh-i Parsa, Turkman, and Bamyan prepared to attack Kuhistan and Kuhdaman via Ghurband while the Hazarahs of Bihsud assembled at Unay Pass, planning to attack Kabul from there. The governor of Ghurband and the Hazarahjat, Kaka Muhsin, informed Habib Allah what was happening so he sent a force of a thousand men to the Hazarahjat via the Ghurband road.[157]

When Muhammad Naᶜim Khan of Day Zangi, Nadir ᶜAli Khan Jaghuri, Ghulam Nabi Khan, Suhrab Khan, and Muhammad Ishaq Khan of Bihsud, all of whom were in Kabul, learned of this, they promised that they would secure an oath of loyalty from the Hazarahs so that there would be no confrontation between the Hazarahjat forces and those of the amir. But as of today they had yet to receive a reply from the amir.

April 2: There is talk today that armed groups of Hazarahs, accompanied by a force of Ishaqzaᵓi tribesmen, have occupied positions around Balkh while other Hazarahs, who had been forcibly transplanted to the north, accompanied by residents from Turkman, marched on Aqchah, Andkhuy, Maymanah, and Mazar-i Sharif. They captured allies of Habib Allah, like Mirza Muhammad Khan[158] and others who in their turn had arrested the civilian and military officials who backed Aman Allah, and sent them to Kabul in a convoy. Along the way the Hazarahs [managed to take custody and] won the confidence of these men, including ᶜAbd al-ᶜAziz Khan, son of the late field marshal, Ghulam Haydar Khan Charkhi, and Brigadier General Muhammad Iklil Khan, the son of Muhammad Afzal Khan Darwazah. They agreed on a joint coordinated attack on Kuhistan and Kuhdaman and won over the local population in Ghurband. When he heard about this, Sayyid Husayn set off for Charikar.

April 5: Today, at the invitation of Sayyid Husayn, the amir, along with some cronies, arrived in Khwajah Sayyaran[159] for the festival of "the redbud blossom" (*shukūfah-i arghawān*). The story is that Habib Allah has gone to Kuhistan and Kuhdaman on holiday while at the same time inspecting the numerous positions which have been set up there because of the feared attack by the Hazarahs of Shaykh ^{c}Ali, Bamyan, Surkh-i Parsa, and Turkman.

April 7: Hazarah militia forces from Surkh-i Parsa, Turkman, Shaykh ^{c}Ali, Bamyan, and Balkhab arrived in Siyahgird in Ghurband.

April 9: One thousand conscripts were dispatched from Kabul to Ghurband today to fight off the Hazarahs of Surkh-i Parsa, Turkman, Shaykh ^{c}Ali, Bamyan, and Yakah Ulang who, rumor has it, plan to attack Kuhistan and Kuhdaman.

April 12: Sayyid Husayn went to Jabal al-Siraj, set up defenses on the bridge over which the road to Ghurband passes, and then returned to Kabul on Saturday, April 13.

Sayyid Husayn stayed in Kabul from the 13th to the 18th at his residence, the Astar (Stor) Palace, which had housed the foreign ministry during Aman Allah's time. On the 17th Fayz Muhammad reports Hazarah units had closed the road in the Ghurband Valley leading to Kuhistan and Kuhdaman. Sayyid Husayn returned to Charikar on the 18th after hearing that a combined Ishaqza$^{\circ}$i-Hazarah force had entered the Ghurband.

Sayyid Husayn Charikari

April 18: There are rumors today that Ghulam Rasul Khan, the son of Sayf Akhundzadah Ishaqza$^{\circ}$i, with men from his tribe and also some Hazarahs—settlers from Mazar-i Sharif—had appeared in Ghurband. Sayyid Husayn consequently left for Charikar to repel their attack and counter the offensive of the Hazarahs from Shaykh ^{c}Ali, Bamyan, Balkhab, Yakah Ulang, Surkh-i Parsa, Turkman, and Darghan.

But on the 19th he was called back to Kabul after a phone call from the amir who wanted to discuss the situation in Ghazni, Logar, and Khust. He left for Charikar that same day on word that local partisans of Aman Allah (Fayz Muhammad names only ᶜAta Muhammad, the son of Malik Muhammad Istalifi Kuhdamani) had attacked Charikar. But it was more than politics that drove Sayyid Husayn in this case, if Fayz Muhammad is to be believed.

April 20: Sayyid Husayn left for Charikar to set up a defense against those units that had arrived in Ghurband. There he deputized a group of trusted men to murder ᶜAta Muhammad, whose fiancée he had taken as a wife. For this ᶜAta Muhammad had vowed to kill him. ᶜAta Muhammad had been commandant of the Arg in Kabul prior to Habib Allah's coming to power and Sayyid Husayn had ordered him imprisoned. But he escaped to Kuhdaman and there assembled two to three hundred fighters. Sayyid Husayn's men set up an ambush near the gates of ᶜAta Muhammad's fortress residence. By this morning, word had gone around that ᶜAta Muhammad was as good as dead. Unsuspecting, he walked out the gate of the fort and straight into the ambush. He was shot in the stomach, chest, and forearm and died. Sayyid Husayn, who had been afraid of him, now stopped worrying and returned to Kabul. ᶜAta Muhammad's corpse was transported to the capital and hung on the Chawk as a warning to others.

Sayyid Husayn spent the next week or so in Kabul, returning to Charikar on the 25th again at the news that the Hazarah threat to the Saqqawist's main base of support was growing. An artillery battery was sent from Kabul to support him. As is the case in much of Fayz Muhammad's memoir, the Hazarahs are assigned a leading, often crucial, role.

In Charikar Sayyid Husayn tried to persuade the residents of Kuhistan and Kuhdaman not only to rally to the defense of that region, but also to send troops to Wardak and Logar, where the amir was then fighting the supporters of both Aman Allah and Nadir. Fayz Muhammad suggests his pleas were not well received.

April 26: Hazarah units have reached Katan Mountain.[160] When word spread that they had attacked from there and captured the Kuhdamani villages of Shakar Darra, Farza, Ghaza, Saray Khwajah, and Charikar, followers of Sayyid Husayn along with the soldier-rebels who were in Kabul headed for Kuhdaman, some even running, to defend their homes, families, and children. By evening they had all left the city.

April 27: Today Hazarah militia forces, numbered by some at nine thousand and by others at thirty thousand men, attacked Farza, Shakar Darra, and Istalif [towns in Kuhdaman] and burned two forts. In response to rumors that they had captured territory as far as Charikar and Saray Khwajah, Hamid Allah was sent off to Shakar Darra. Before his arrival, Sayyid Husayn had already set up its defenses. The Hazarahs, after displaying their power and throwing fear into the Kuhdamanis, pulled back. Hamid Allah Khan returned to Kabul, bringing word that there was no longer any threat from the Hazarahs.

When they heard this, those people who at Hamid Allah's order had been sent back from Kabul to Kuhdaman to defend their families and homes, returned to the capital. Simultaneously, the Hazarahs crossed back over the mountain from Shakar Darra and arrived in Ghurband, again creating anxiety among the Kuhistanis and Kuhdamanis.

Sayyid Husayn has compelled all remaining inhabitants of the north [i.e. Kuhistan and Kuhdaman] to assemble and head for the western and southern regions to fend off the attacks of Aman Allah's and Nadir's forces. But the northerners feared the strength of the Hazarahs and refused to obey Sayyid Husayn, telling him: "You forcibly dragged us into war with the government, tore us from our trades and our fields, and led us into misery and destitution. Because of your vile deeds, all the people of Afghanistan, including the Hazarahs, have risen against us and are bent on destroying and annihilating us, our families, and our children. Now that the Hazarahs have occupied positions in the mountains and are preparing to attack, we cannot leave our families and children to the mercy of fate and go off to fight the forces of Aman Allah and Nadir." This answer had a depressing effect on Sayyid Husayn.

Fayz Muhammad's account suggests that the situation was growing somewhat more critical in the north or that the situation in the Logar and Maydan theaters was easing for the amir. A week after Sayyid Husayn's return to Charikar, the amir withdrew men and munitions from the Logar and Wardak fronts and sent them north.

May 2: Tonight Sayyid Husayn returned to Kabul after eight days in Charikar, rounding up the rest of its inhabitants for the army. He has come to report to Habib Allah on the situation in Ghurband and to relay the news that the people of the northern regions do not want to provide recruits for the army because there would be no-one to feed their families. All the young and strong have already left to fight and their families and children are now vulnerable to raids and plundering by the Hazarahs. Having reported this, he again returned to Charikar.

May 3: This evening, approximately four hundred men, ethnic Tajiks from the villages of the Charkh region of Logar, were sent to Kuhistan and Ghurband together with some of the amir's own units. Boxes of ammunition were also shipped there in eighteen wagons. Twenty additional wagonloads of ammunition also left today for Ghurband.

For Fayz Muhammad, May 4 marked something of a low point. From all sides, the news reaching him was depressing. He heard Aman Allah had withdrawn from Wardak and there was no news at all from Nadir after the disaster at Charkh. In the Ghurband, it appeared as if Sayyid Husayn had made a breakthrough and overcome the resistance that faced him. On the 5th, word came to Kabul that he was on his way to Mazar-i Sharif via the road through Qunduz, for he asked that five hundred pack animals be sent. On the 8th he was able to spare some of his forces and send them to Kabul. But on the 10th, new information arrived that he had yet to move from Charikar and that considerable resistance to the Kabul regime was developing to the north of him, on the other side of the Hindu Kush.

May 8: Several days earlier Sayyid Husayn departed for Charikar and there, through intimidation, gathered under his flag what was left of the population of Kuhistan, Kuhdaman, Sujnan, Durnama, Bulaghayn, Ghurband, and Panjshayr. He then had sent this force to Kabul as a display of military might. Every day these people, some of whom were armed and some not, march through the bazaars to the sound of a military band, shouting "ya chahar yar" to inspire terror in the hearts of the people of the city.

Because Ghulam Nabi Khan seized power in Mazar-i Sharif and Turkistan, Sayyid Husayn made plans to attack Mazar-i Sharif by the route [over the Khawak Pass] through Khanabad and Andarab. Daily he requests arms and supplies for his force from Kabul, and daily his chief secretary, Mirza Ghulam Qadir Khan, who had stayed behind in Kabul, sends off arms and materiel to Charikar for him.

They say Sayyid Husayn drives up to Bamyan every day. On the road to the Shibar Pass he raids the Shaykh ᶜAli Hazarahs and plunders and burns their homes. He has sent soldiers against the Hazarahs of Surkh-i Parsa and Turkman, who are under the jurisidiction of the chief governor of the north, and is collecting recruits there by force. These Hazarahs, who are supporters of Aman Allah, have cut the road over which the amir's army has to march. But eventually they were done in by the fact that the Shaykh ᶜAli Hazarahs, being Sunni, had volunteered for Habib Allah's army. Thus, Sayyid Husayn Khan has been able to impose his will on them and demand they provide conscripts for his force.

May 10: Today Sayyid Husayn let it be known that he was going to Mazar-i Sharif. Word had come that Ghulam Jalani Khan had occupied Andarab and Khanabad in Qataghan and the governor (*nāʾib al-ḥukūmah*) of that regions, Mir Baba Sahib Charikari [a Saqqawist] had been killed. Other contributing factors were the outbreak of fighting in Tagab, the advance of the tribes of the Eastern Provinces toward Kabul, Nadir's re-appearance in Logar, and the taking of Ghazni by forces loyal to Aman Allah. Moreover, in the northeast, Lieutenant-General ᶜAbd al-Wakil Khan, a Nuristani convert to Islam, and his tribesmen had begun to fight [against Habib Allah] in Burj-i Guljan and Riza-yi Kuhistan. But, on the road through Bamyan, Sayyid Husayn changed his mind and decided to attack the Hazarahjat in concert with the Pushtun tribes who nomadize in the Hazarahjat.

Today, too, one thousand forced conscripts from Chardihi and other regions were sent to Charikar and four truckloads carrying wounded from Dasht-i Tup [on the Wardak front] arrived in Kabul. Among them was a general.

A day later the news seemed to get better. Sometime around May 9 or 10, Sayyid Husayn received a severe setback at the Shibar Pass, not unlike what the Taliban would experience at the hands of the Hazarahs sixty-eight years later. But it clearly pained Fayz Muhammad that some of his fellow Hazarahs, the Shaykh ᶜAlis, many of whom were Sunni, were siding with the government.

May 11: Two or three days ago, Sayyid Husayn, at the head of a force of twelve thousand men—five thousand from Kuhistan, five thousand

Sunni Hazarahs from Surkh-i Parsa, who, blinded by religious fanaticism, had severed their ties with the Shi^cite Hazarahs and joined forces with Sayyid Husayn, and two thousand from Ghurband—decided to attack the mountaintop fortifications of the Hazarahs of Turkman. Marching to the Shibar Pass, home of the Shaykh ᶜAli Hazarahs, he burned some 120 forts and drove more than fifteen thousand sheep, donkeys, and cattle from their pastures before pulling back. Hazarah militias from Yakah Ulang, Bamyan, Shaykh ᶜAli, and Balkhab, vowing revenge, attacked him in the Ghurband and routed his force. Consequently, Sayyid Husayn has now decided against campaigns to either Mazar-i Sharif or the Hazarahjat and remains in Charikar.

May 12: Today, the following rumors circulated: Sayyid Husayn's forces are surrounded in Kuhistan and he himself has been wounded; an amirid force has arrived in Jabal al-Siraj after being defeated in Qataghan at Khanabad and Andarab when attacked by Muhammad Rahim Khan, son of Sardar Muhammad ᶜUmar Khan and grandson of Amir ᶜAbd al-Rahman Khan; Lieutenant General ᶜAbd al-Wakil Khan has captured Fayzabad in Badakhshan and with units of his tribe has reached Farjaghan [at the head of the Alishang Valley near Tagab and Najrab]; in Kuhistan, in the region of Pul-i Matak [the junction of the road to Ghurband], fighting is just starting; and tribal contingents from the Eastern Province, who as mentioned earlier had marched to Tagab, have crushed the amir's forces that were there. These stories worried the northerners and bolstered the spirits of the Kabulis.

May 13: Today we hear there is fighting in Ghurband and that Sayyid Husayn, after burning the homes of the Hazarahs of Turkman and driving off their livestock, had sent to the Hazarahs ᶜAbd al-Rahman, the son of Malik Dad Muhammad Kuhistani, the single most fanatical instigator of the people of the northern regions [against the Shiᶜite Hazarahs]; Sayyid Talib Shah Khan Ghurbandi, a Shiᶜite from a noble family; and also one other person to persuade them to recognize the government of Habib Allah. He sent a message with the delegation that said,

> Beginning with [the reign of] ᶜAbd al-Rahman down to the day of Aman Allah's abdication from the throne, Pushtuns have oppressed Hazarahs. They have robbed, murdered, arrested, enslaved, immolated, and dispossessed you. Nonetheless, those rulers not only did not punish the

Pushtuns, on the contrary, they incited them to murder, plunder, and enslave you. These same rulers also forcibly exiled Hazarahs to other countries. By your failure to recognize the authority of Amir Habib Allah, you condemn yourselves to death. You should submit, put an end to the bloodshed, and save yourselves.

In reply, the Hazarahs declared,

By the will of God and the Prophet and as is it is written in the Koran, "And the thief, male and female: cut off the hands of both, as a recompense for what they have earned and a punishment exemplary from God."[161] "And whoso slays a believer wilfully, his recompense is Gehenna, therein dwelling forever, and God will be wroth with him, and will curse him, and prepare for him a mighty chastisement."[162] According to the Shari^{c}ah, therefore, we cannot acknowledge the authority of, nor submit to, a man who sheds blood, plunders Muslims, assaults women and children, hacks living Muslims to pieces, scorches the heads of victims with fire or hangs them in the bazaar, and blackens the faces of other Muslims with filth and then parades them around to the music of a military band. How many people has he hanged and shot? He has looted the government treasury, which was designated for the defense of the state and the honor of Muslims, and has shown absolutely no fear of the Almighty. At the same time, the pseudo-mullahs who have gone astray, in order to support the watercarrier's son recite the verse: "O believers, obey God, and obey the Messenger and those in authority among you."[163] And to justify him, they also recite, "O my people who have been prodigal against yourselves, do not despair of God's mercy; surely, God forgives sins altogether; surely He is the All-forgiving, the All-compassionate."[164] They claim that this verse does not, however, apply to Aman Allah. Is it really possible that this verse only pertains to thieves and not all people? The All-High does not recognize him as worthy of the throne and so we are obliged to defend ourselves and our property. Whether we kill or are killed, we will not consider ourselves blameworthy. As long as we live, we will defend ourselves. As for ^{c}Abd al-Rahman, who is now our hostage, we will free him when the leader of the Hazarahs, the chief equerry Ahmad ^{c}Ali, is released from prison in Kabul and sent to us.

But since Ahmad ^{c}Ali had already been hanged, the issue of ^{c}Abd al-Rahman remained unresolved.[165]

It was reported in Kabul that nine hundred men from Habib Allah's army, along with artillery and armaments, were captured in Ghurband by supporters of Aman Allah.

May 14: There is talk today that two thousand crack troops under the command of Sayyid Husayn were defeated and captured during the night by contingents of Hazarahs and Pushtuns who support Aman Allah. Weapons, materiel, and artillery were also seized.

Meanwhile the situation in the far north (Afghan Turkistan) was adding further complexity to Habib Allah's efforts to consolidate his political position. There, the leading member of the Charkhi family, Ghulam Nabi, had returned from his appointment as ambassador to Moscow to organize a northern front on behalf of Aman Allah. When Habib Allah took Kabul in January, Kuhistani and Kuhdamani forces stationed in Mazar-i Sharif mutinied against Aman Allah's officials there, arrested some of them and sent them to Kabul. It may have been at this time that Mirza Muhammad Qasim Uzbek was appointed military high commissioner to Afghan Turkistan and Khwajah Mir ᶜAlam as governor of Mazar-i Sharif. Aman Allah's people, including ᶜAbd al-ᶜAziz Charkhi, the governor, had in turn been rescued by Hazarahs in the Shibar region, while being transported to Kabul.[166] *In late April, Ghulam Nabi with some one thousand men recruited in Soviet territory crossed the border and on the 30th recaptured Mazar-i Sharif in the name of Aman Allah. According to Fayz Muhammad, the loss of the capital of Afghan Turkistan to a supporter of Aman Allah was the reason why Sayyid Husayn returned to Charikar and launched a campaign from there across the Hindu Kush to regain control of the region. The Soviet Union's direct role in this was unclear to Fayz Muhammad but he reports that the amir, at least, believed that the Soviets were behind Ghulam Nabi's return as retaliation for Afghanistan's having sheltered anti-Soviet forces. Early in May, two leaders of the Turkistan Liberation Organization (called "Basmachi" by its enemies), Fayz Allah and Ibrahim Beg, made raids from Afghanistan into Soviet territory. The Soviets believed the raids were instigated by the British acting through Habib Allah.*[167] *Certainly the Soviets, like the British, had an interest in the outcome of the civil war in Afghanistan and while they believed, with good reason, that Delhi and Kabul together were supporting the resistance in Russian Turkistan, the British government in India and the government of Habib Allah had equal reasons to wonder about Soviet activities.*[168] *As far as Fayz Muhammad is concerned, what was happening in the north was mostly an Afghan affair, although later on he puts a geopolitical gloss on events in the far north.*[169]

Some time before the uprising began, the son of the late Field Marshal Ghulam Haydar Khan Charkhi—Ghulam Nabi Khan, formerly the ambassador to Paris—was appointed ambassador to Moscow. When the uprising began, he had come from Moscow to Afghan Turkistan after learning that forces made up of Kuhistanis and Kuhdamanis had rebelled and by order of an Uzbek, Mirza Muhammad Qasim, whom Habib Allah had named military high commissioner, had begun to plunder Aman Allah's officials. The governor-general, ᶜAbd al-ᶜAziz, Brigadier General Muhammad Iklil, and other officers had been arrested and sent to Kabul. Backed by a unit of the Ishaqzaᵓi led by Ghulam Rasul, the son of Sayf Akhundzadah, and also with Hazarah and Turkmen nomad help, Ghulam Nabi captured Mazar-i Sharif. He banished the traitor Mirza Muhammad Qasim to Mawarannahr, arrested and imprisoned the governor-general, the chief finance officer (*mustawfi*), and other officials working for Habib Allah, and restored Aman Allah's officials to their posts. Ghulam Nabi himself then set off for Bamyan where he took command of the Shaykh ᶜAli, Balkhab, Turkman, Surkh-i Parsa, and Yakah Ulang Hazarah forces that had risen against Habib Allah and advanced as far as Ghurband but then withdrawn. It was in conjunction with these events that Sayyid Husayn Khan first headed for Charikar and then set off for Mazar-i Sharif.

May 15: Because of rumors that Ghulam Nabi had attacked and captured Mazar-i Sharif with a contingent of Russian Cossacks disguised as Turkmen, Habib Allah went to the Russian embassy with two of his closest confidants to get information about the Russian government's intentions. The Russian ambassador denied the story of Russian interference in Afghan Turkistan and the amir was satisfied. Today, the northerners spread rumors that when Mazar-i Sharif was captured by Ghulam Nabi, one of Habib Allah's brigadier generals, ᶜAbd al-Rahim Khan, reportedly fled with sixty riders to Herat and captured it, and the Russian and Iranian embassies officially congratulated him on his victory. These lies disheartened supporters of Aman Allah and raised the spirits of the rebel northerners.[170]

Sayyid Husayn, despite the setback a few days earlier in his drive along the road through the Shibar Pass, had not given up and now tried to break through to the north by marching northeast up the Panjshayr Valley and over the Khawak Pass to Andarab and Khinjan. But the pass proved as difficult as the Shibar, according to Fayz Muhammad.

May 16: Tonight a detachment under the command of Captain ᶜAbd Allah Panjshayri along with Hazarahs from Bamyan, Yakah Ulang, Turkman, Shaykh ᶜAli, and other regions, barricaded the road to the Khawak Pass and prevented Sayyid Husayn from passing through on his way to Qataghan and Mazar-i Sharif. Sayyid Husayn and his detachment of cavalry destroyed a small fort in Gul Bahar and then returned to Charikar where he telephoned Habib Allah Khan asking for reinforcements. At four in the morning Habib Allah ordered a thousand men sent. These men were rounded up from the populace of Chardihi and were housed in Shahr Ara, the building which earlier had been the Habibiyah School.

On May 21, the amir had news that a force of Aman Allah's supporters had crossed through the Khawak Pass and was moving down the Panjshayr Valley against Kuhistan. About five days earlier a rumor that Sayyid Husayn had died of wounds suffered in battle had also begun to circulate in Kabul. Fayz Muhammad tried to corroborate it by piecing together bits of information he had about the amir's movements but he seems to have been skeptical about its accuracy.

May 19: There is a rumor today that Sayyid Husayn, wounded in the back in fighting at Burj-i Guljan, has died. Aman Allah's partisans, after their victory there, marched on Charikar, surrounded Sayyid Husayn's force, and routed it. This news brought joy to the hearts of the people of Kabul.

May 21: Today news of the advance of Aman Allah's supporters through the Khawak Pass and Ghurband toward Kuhistan greatly disturbed Habib Allah, as did news of the plans of the Safi tribe to begin fighting in the Tagab region. He sent out detachments to Charikar and Riza Kuhistan in eighteen vehicles and he himself, accompanied by his brother Hamid Allah, the governor-general Malik Muhsin, and armed troops headed for Ghazni at five in the morning in nine touring cars in order to get the latest information about Aman Allah. Two days ago, we heard that Sayyid Husayn had died. Habib Allah, instead of going to Ghazni via the Dih Buri road, set off instead for Charikar. En route to the funeral, he drove through Gardan-i Bagh-i Bala and Qariyah-i Afshar and returned to Kabul in the evening by the same route. They say that he then disguised himself as a Jaji tribesman before leaving for Ghazni. The automobile in which he was riding and five other automobiles carrying his supporters drove straight into an ambush laid by one of Aman Allah's units. By some trickery, the amir managed to get into another car and save himself. Of the nine cars that had set off, only three were seen in the region of the Harten Bridge and those were headed back toward the Arg. No other vehicles than these were seen. This is probably true. There is more and more talk about the death of Sayyid Husayn. These stories began two or three days ago. People so look forward to his death that they actually dream that he has died. Perhaps he has.

May 26: Today a thousand soldiers were sent from Kabul to Qataghan. Also today there was word that Sayyid Husayn, who had been thought dead from his wounds, had arrived in Khanabad and begun to gather conscripts there to oppose Ghulam Nabi Charkhi.

Not only was Sayyid Husayn very much alive, but the news of the advances of Aman Allah's allies down the Panshayr Valley proved to be highly exaggerated if not completely false. If Sayyid Husayn were now in Khanabad, he must have somehow made his way over either the Khawak or Salang Passes and moved without much resistance the hundred or so miles north to Khanabad in a very few days. By the beginning of June, the routes via the Ghurband Valley and the Salang and Khawak Passes appear to have been as securely in the hands of the Kabul government as could be expected given the general state of affairs in the area and the level of technology available. On May 29, the amir was able to spare another twenty-three hundred men to be sent north to reinforce his troops in the Ghurband Valley and forestall Hazarah attacks on Kuhistan and Kuhdaman, his homeland and that of his main supporters.

Fayz Muhammad relays one or two more bits of information about anti-government raids and skirmishes but it seems clear that once he has Sayyid Husayn in Khanabad he sees little hope from that quarter of a serious challenge to Habib Allah's regime. This moment coincides with two other depressing, for him, facts: Aman Allah's abandoning the fight entirely and fleeing to India and the lack of news coming from Nadir. Fayz Muhammad now decides to leave the country himself but is forestalled from doing so by a lack of funds and by paternal responsibilities.

May 27: During this time, I had decided to flee the country with my son, relying on God's mercy and good luck, and managed to scrape together a thousand rupees for the trip. However, before our departure, I wanted to betroth him to his fiancée so that he might then set off with an easy mind. This evening the entire sum I had saved was spent on the betrothal ceremony, for which I had to borrow a small additional sum as well. I thank God for His help in seeing this matter successfully concluded, though. And I hope that His mercy is limitless and I will yet manage to make arrangements to leave.

Still there were bits of news from the north that would bolster his spirits for a while.

May 31: There is news today that Habib Allah's army, which had advanced as far as Bamyan en route to Mazar-i Sharif, had clashed with Hazarah units, been routed, and retreated to Jabal al-Siraj. An army under Sayyid Husayn and numbering more than ten thousand men had tried to push through to Mazar-i Sharif and had come under bombardment at Dasht-i Qipchaq. A large part of that force was killed or wounded. The rest fled to Kuhistan and Kabul in disarray. Habib Allah, upset by the news, telephoned his brother at 9:00 a.m. to send an automobile for Khwajah Mir ᶜAlam, who had been appointed governor of Afghan Turkistan. He and six officers from the force that had retreated from Bamyan to Jabal al-Siraj had begun terrorizing the residents of the north [Kuhistan and Kuhdaman]. They were delivered to Kabul and imprisoned in the Arg.

June 1: Fighting flared up anew today in Burj-i Guljan and Gulbahar. Also today an airplane flew to Qandahar in order to retrieve another plane that a pilot, Muhammad ᶜUmar, had flown from Kabul to bomb Aman Allah's army. The second airplane was delayed there until nightfall.

Also on this day, Habib Allah and his brother took custody of a colonel named Dur Muhammad, drove him to Jabal al-Siraj, and ordered him shot in front of the forces that had retreated there, as a lesson to the rest not to abandon the battlefield again but to fight to the death. This colonel, a recent convert to Islam, had been defeated and, with the governor-designate of Afghan Turkistan, Khwajah Mir ᶜAlam, and other officers, had fled to Charikar. The others were summoned to Kabul and imprisoned but the colonel, who had arrived in Charikar before the others, was arrested by the local governor, Chighil Khan, and sent to Kabul separately.

The Situation in Kabul to the Beginning of June

*Besides the fighting in Wardak, Logar, the Ghurband, and Tagab and the Laghman Valley, Habib Allah was continually anxious about the sentiments and loyalties of the people living in Kabul itself. If Fayz Muhammad's attitude is indicative of more than his own strong prejudices, then the Kabulis in general had little love for the Tajiks from the north. Fayz Muhammad's reports of what was going on in Kabul in the first seven months of Habib Allah's rule shed a good deal of light on many aspects of daily life, including the administration of the city, the economic policies and practices of the new administration, and living conditions generally. Kabul life as portrayed here is dominated by arrests and summary (and grisly) executions, assassination plots, anti-Shi*ᶜ*ite purges, random assaults, and house burglaries committed by the "northerners." Fayz Muhammad laces the narrative with stories of sexual assaults on women and young boys, forced marriages, economic deprivation, and the barrage of propaganda aimed at Aman Allah.*

Confiscations, Requisitions, and Price Controls

Given the level of official corruption that people believed existed and the fact that the new powers had no ties to the old, it is not surprising that seizure of the property of representatives of the former regime should have soon begun. It was a way for the new regime to recover assets that arguably belonged to the nation and, more importantly, to compensate its own supporters. Perhaps more surprising were the apparent efforts, no matter how nominal in Fayz Muhammad's eyes, the new amir made to punish his own officials who took advantage of the confiscations to line their own pockets. He needed the money to pay his troops and make up for the tax revenues lost either because he lacked the authority to collect or because he had already forgiven them by decree.

March 23: Habib Allah went to the home of the former chamberlain Muhammad Sarwar Khan Baba with his brother, Hamid Allah, and the governor-general of Kabul, Malik Muhsin. Habib Allah had summoned Muhammad Sarwar during Ramazan [the month of the fast, February 11–March 12, 1929], planning to arrest him, but because he was seriously ill and not long for the world, the amir did not force the issue. At that time Muhammad Sarwar had given Habib Allah's henchmen three thousand rupees and twenty-five pounds sterling and told them that he did not have another penny to his name. He then went home and two or three days later he died.

Now, entering his home, they broke into his trunks, but found nothing, aside from fifteen hundred rupees and a few rugs and dishes. Habib Allah and his brother castigated Muhammad Ibrahim Khan,[171] the son of Muhammad Sarwar and the governor-general of Herat Province, and his steward as "unbelievers." They were convinced that these two had taken the millions of rupees in gold that they expected to find. Rumors are circulating in Herat that Habib Allah's people then killed Muhammad Ibrahim. Habib Allah gave Muhammad Sarwar's house to Khwajah Ban Jan Khan.

Fayz Muhammad gives little credit to Habib Allah for his efforts to control the rapacity of his officials. Malik Muhsin, as governor-general of the Central or Kabul province, was the official usually conducting the confiscations in Kabul. Fayz Muhammad asserts that he was skimming from the property for his own pocket and that he was twice penalized and forced to reimburse the state treasury for money allegedly stolen.

May 9: Hamid Allah Khan punished Malik Muhsin today because he stole forty thousand rupees at the time of the confiscation of the home of the late chamberlain Muhammad Sarwar and also appropriated valuables from the homes of [Aman Allah's] minister of foreign affairs, Ghulam Siddiq;[172] the minister of court, Muhammad Ya^{c}qub;[173] the minister of defense, ^{c}Abd al-^{c}Aziz;[174] Mahmud Khan Yawar;[175] Hayat Allah Khan, the "^{c}Azud al-Dawlah";[176] and some two hundred other persons. He had hidden these goods in his own house. It is said that Hamid Allah severely caned him and ordered him to repay the forty thousand rupees.

May 24: Today at 11 in the morning, Governor-general Malik Muhsin went to the house of the former governor-general of Kabul, Mir Zaman al-Din, son of "Prince"[177] Hasan Badakhshani. Four years ago Mir Zaman al-Din had been appointed governor of Herat and there he suddenly died. While his widow and two sons slept, Malik Muhsin broke into their house and stole all their valuables, although they had committed no crime. He put even the household utensils under lock and key and warned them that he would come the next day and make an inventory of all movable property.

May 31: On orders from his brother the amir, Hamid Allah collected two hundred thousand rupees from the governor-general [Malik Muhsin], the commandant of Kabul, the minister of court [Shayr Jan], and other thieves for property they had seized illegally.

June 2: Mir Zaman al-Din's distraught widow wrote a letter of complaint to the "Servant of the Religion of the Prophet," Habib Allah, apropos of Malik Muhsin's above-mentioned break-in and theft of twenty-five thousand rupees, some carpets, women's jewelry, and two rifles. In response, the amir assigned the thieving governor-general himself to investigate, although on the very night of the break-in the governor-general had brought Habib Allah some women's jewelry [taken from the widow]. The governor-general threatened the woman with reprisals and she wrote another letter which she and her sons signed that satisfied him. It said that aside from two carpets, nothing else was taken from the house. From this government of thieves you can hardly expect better.

For immediate military needs—rations, transport, weaponry—another traditional source for the government was sūrsāt, *a requisition in kind. Fayz Muhammad mentions the use of compulsory requisitions when Nadir's force was approaching Khushi in the Logar Valley.*

April 11: Because of Nadir's arrival at Khushi in Logar with a large force, the Ministry of Defense began to forcibly requisition pack animals. Their owners had been keeping a low profile because no one paid them for their use. The requisitions were based on registration records kept in the municipality (*riyāsat-i baladīyah*). Ordered to turn their animals over to the detachments that were heading out to relieve Habib Allah's beleaguered forces, the angry owners shouted: "When animals were in demand and hard to find, Aman Allah would pay around thirty rupees per day per animal and ten rupees when demand was low. Now no one pays at all. If they would pay just a few rupees, the sepoys could have their pick of animals whenever they want."

Besides paying for transport animals, the problem of paying even the troops—other than through the freedom to plunder Kabul—was ever-present. In late April, Fayz Muhammad records an edict that promised soldiers a doubling of their pay, or as he puts it, "two month's pay for one month's service." He gives no indication that this translated into actual disbursements, however.

Fayz Muhammad's portrayal of the economic situation inside the beleaguered city is a bleak one from the outset. The amir seems to have faced a limited but challenging degree of non-cooperation from shopkeepers. One unfortunate store owner was accused of having called for a general strike in support of Aman Allah. He was hanged by his heels on the Chawk on April 14. There were other forms of non-cooperation, some forced on retailers by economic necessity.

April 22: Sayyid Husayn had six butchers caned today. From mid-January until now they have been selling one *pāw* [one pao=96 *mis̱qāl*] of lamb and one and a half pao[178] [120 misqal] of beef with bone at a price of one Afghani.[179] But the actual weight of the lamb meat amounted to only 32 misqal and the beef, 40 misqal. Thus two-thirds of the weight was bone. Sayyid Husayn ordered that prices be fixed for one-half of a *chāryak* [i.e. two pao] of lamb and for three pao of beef. He nailed all six butchers by their ears to stakes in three bustling areas of the city so that passers-by would get the message.

He also set the price for *rawghan*-shortening (clarified butter). Shopkeepers have been selling one *sīr* [seer—about sixteen pounds] of shortening for thirty rupees. He ordered them to buy from the dealers at twenty-five rupees per seer and sell at twenty-six. As a result, for every seer sold, the shopkeeper loses four rupees and the dealers lose five. They wrote the amir and petitioned him to allow the dealers to sell at twenty-eight rupees a seer and the shopkeepers at thirty. Otherwise they would all lose money. At the same time, they hoarded the shortening in the bazaar and claimed that there was no more available.

On May 9, apparently as part of an effort to increase security in the city, Habib Allah decreed that permits were required for all persons traveling out of or into Kabul beyond a radius of two kurūh, *approximately four miles. The report of this decree sheds more light on the economic conditions in the city.*

May 9: Notices were printed and posted today in all the places where people congregate. They decree that residents or newcomers going beyond a two *kurūh* radius from the city must get permission from the police chief (*kūmandān-i kūtwāl'*) or from the military commander (*manṣabdārā-i niẓām'*). Anyone arriving in the city must get a permit from the commander of one the regiments stationed in Bandar-i Arghandah, Charasya, Bini Hisar, Butkhak, Kutal-i Pay Manar, Kutal-i Khayr Khanah, or other locations near the city. Anyone who does not have an exit or entrance permit will be arrested. Because of this order, the people of Kabul may not leave even to go to Maydan, Jalriz, Logar, Khurd Kabul, Butkhak, Tangi Gharu, or Dih Sabz, that is, even those regions under the control of the present government. This measure has evoked much fear and confusion in the hearts of the populace. Out of work and unpaid, having consumed all their savings and awaiting with impatience the end of this uprising, people see themselves on the verge of destruction. Violence flourishes in place of justice. Officials of the former government are unemployed, their money and food will be used up within a year, and people have nowhere else to go. Moreover, they are unable to sell their possessions—carpets or china, for example—for even half or a third of their value. And if they do manage to sell, the money doesn't last any length of time because the price of food has soared so much.

May 10: The decree published yesterday also stated that all persons entering and leaving Kabul should be subject to search and interrogation. If any letters are found they are to be handed over to the chief of the Kabul police, Sayyid Aqa Khan. Every letter is to be read to make sure that it contains no anti-government propaganda. The effect of such a decree is to curtail the spread of both lies and well-founded rumors that might interfere with the administration of government. So we will know neither the good nor the ill.

Below is the text of the decree. It was obtained from the Press Administration of the Ministry of Court and was intended for distribution to other departments.

> This decree regarding the movement of travelers through control points proposed by Major General Amir Muhammad and confirmed by His Highness has been prepared for your departments. This is the resolution of

the ministry:

1. Regarding those who travel beyond the city limits of Kabul:
   a) Military and civilian officials have the right to pass through control points with permission from the "Amir Sahib Ghazi" [i.e. Habib Allah], the "Na'ib al-Saltanah Ghazi" [Sayyid Husayn], or the devoted and staunch supporter of the religion and the government, the Mu'in al-Saltanah [Hamid Allah]. Civilians have the same right, with permission from the minister of court, the chamberlain, the aide-de-camp to His Highness, the governor-general of Kabul, or the chief of police.
   b) Servicemen may pass by order of a field marshal, lieutenant general, major general, or general.
2. Regarding individuals coming into Kabul from surrounding regions:
   a) Those civilian officials who have permission from the governor or military high commissioner of the relevant provinces may pass through the checkpoints.
   b) Servicemen may pass through control points with permission from a high-ranking officer.
3. People who have a document corresponding to these terms will be able to pass through the checkpoints freely. But anyone entering or leaving the city without a permit will be arrested by the checkpoint commander (*bandardar*) and turned over to the major general, who must send an investigation report to His Highness.
4. Anyone who tries to pass through a checkpoint without permission will be arrested forthwith and handed over to the major general for interrogation. He will forward a report to His Highness.

This is the amir's decree regarding the resolution of the ministry:

The terms of this resolution concerning transiting checkpoints are affirmed by His Highness and you must adhere to them. Documents, obtained by travelers from officials, must be checked. If it is found that they have a proper permit, then they may pass. It is absolutely essential to examine the documents of suspicious persons. For all people either engaged in or sent on government service, special identity papers should be printed up permitting them passage into and out of the city. These papers should be distributed to the relevant departments and, with the proper seals affixed to them, should be considered proper documentation for civilians passing through checkpoints.

Copies of this decree should be printed and distributed.

After the promulgation of this decree, Major General Amir Muhammad; the minister of court, Shayr Jan; and the amir himself have all been praised [for their parts in drafting and publishing the decree] because it is aimed at the arrest of spies and saboteurs. However, the amir seems not to be aware that the people of the city, worn down by high prices, hunger, and oppression, are on the brink of death because rice dealers and sellers must first get a permit from the governor or military commissoner to pass through the checkpoints and transport essential goods and foodstuffs like wheat, lamb, oil, firewood, charcoal, and clothing into the city. It is only possible to get such a permit after paying a bribe and spending several days getting permission. What is more, even after obtaining the permit it is still necessary to bribe the officer (*qarāwul*) at the checkpoint; otherwise, as is now common, he will confiscate the permit, charge the merchant with having contraband in his possession, and then torture him half to death, after which the latter will abandon any wish to ever again come to the city. This is why the people of Kabul are without food and clothing and why, for the residents of the surrounding region, there is nothing to be gained by providing them.

A new road was built from Kabul to Paghman by order of the late Amir Habib Allah. For its entire length shade trees were planted on both sides. When traveling along the road, drovers were required to muzzle their livestock to prevent damage to the trees. The decree that laid this down contained only the word "road," without specifying the road to Paghman. It was then applied, absurdly, to all roads and caused much torment to livestock owners. Donkeys, camels, and cows were supposed to be muzzled even in the center of the city. Anyone who violated this ordinance had to pay a fine to the police of from one qiran up to one or two rupees to redeem his animals. This decree remained in effect until the assassination of Amir Habib Allah [in 1919]. The present amir and his supporters don't seem to understand that, unlike livestock, spies and felons can travel along secret paths by day or by night to accomplish their ends. And no one can stop them.

Assassination Plots

While Habib Allah was urging the capture or assassination of his rival, Nadir Khan, he was having to face attempts on his own life in Kabul. He responded to these attempts, imagined and real, with characteristic harshness.

April 1: This evening thirty-two high-ranking figures from Aman Allah's government were arrested and accused of conspiring against Amir Habib Allah. It is said that their arrest most directly affected residents of the Eastern Province who support Hashim and the people of Qandahar who back Aman Allah.

April 7: Today, by order of the amir, two men who were planning an attempt on his life were arrested and beaten to death in the Arg prison. Mahmud Khan Yawar, who was also sentenced to be caned to death, managed to ransom his life for thirty-five thousand rupees.[180] With staves and rifle butts Habib Allah's soldiers beat and then imprisoned Brigadier-General Muhammad Hashim Khan, son of Muhammad Yusuf Khan, a Qizilbash. The reason was that he had been an officer in Aman Allah's army. (His grandfather was Habib Allah Khan, son of Khan Shirin Khan, son of Amir Aslan Khan Jawanshir.)

April 10: Two young Kabulis were arrested at two o'clock today. They had assembled a grenade with which they planned to assassinate Habib Allah in the mosque during the Friday service. The grenade was found when their house was searched. One of the men, whose name also happened to be Habib Allah, was the son of a carpenter, Hajji ᶜAbd al-Ghaffar. The other, ᶜAbd al-Rasul, was the son of an Indian servant (*khānasmān*), Khanji Khan, who had enjoyed a certain prominence during the reign of Amir ᶜAbd al-Rahman. They were betrayed by Qari Dust Muhammad Laghmani, who claimed to be a mulla but was in fact nothing but a swindler. He first incited them to commit the act and then, after the grenade was ready, turned them in. When Habib Allah and ᶜAbd al-Rasul were interrogated, they claimed that the *qārī*[181] had been the instigator and forced them to undertake the deed. So Habib Allah gave the order for his arrest. He was found at his shop in the building known as the Samar Company Building (*Shirkat-i Samar*) where he was working, unaware of the arrest order. The amir, who had been heading for Khwajah

Rawash to watch artillery practice, caught sight of him, beckoned him over, had him sit in the car beside him and took him to the gunnery range where all three were put before a firing squad. As they tied him to a tree, Qari Dust Muhammad cried out, "Amir-sahib, don't kill me. I've done a lot for you and I will do even more." But, he was unable to save himself and the death sentence for this vile devil was carried out. Oh, if only all the false mullas instigating sedition and destruction in the land could experience the kind of reward this one did!

April 29: Today at nine in the morning, they hanged a man on the Chawk, a Waziri nomad and supporter of Aman Allah. Two other men were put before a firing squad and fifteen had their faces blackened with filth and were paraded through the bazaar. As they were led around, a herald would cry out, "Whoever opposes the padishah of Islam and the servant of the religion of God will be arrested and punished, so let this be a lesson."

May 25: Some residents of Kabul, sick and tired of the violence and oppression of the northerners, concocted a plan to assassinate the amir. Twenty-five bombs were buried in the ground beneath a tent that had been set up for the amir on the Chaman-i Huzuri, the parade grounds. Habib Allah learned about the plot from an informant and invited the four or five thousand soldiers stationed in and around Kabul, in particular those stationed on the mountains near the city, in Chardihi, Arghandah, and Butkhak, to come so that he could demonstrate to them the hostility of the citizens of Kabul. To incite them, he first stirred them up with a speech in which he voiced his grievances against the residents of Kabul. He concluded by telling them about the buried bombs. When they saw them, the soldiers began to go after the onlookers who had gathered at the parade ground and who were themselves looking at the bombs with curiosity. Wielding their rifle butts, the soldiers drove them back to their homes. The soldiers then followed the amir's car back to the Arg, cursing any citizens they met en route. Afterward, they returned to their positions.

May 26: Word spread around the city that Aman Allah's partisans had planted two bombs in the ᶜİdgah Mosque on the eve of the Feast of the Sacrifice underneath the bricks at the very spot where Habib Allah would perform his prayers. But by the will of God, the bombs did not explode either when he knelt down or when he stood up. A day or two ago, while cleaning, a janitor stepped on the spot and the bomb went off, killing him and another man. This incident increased even more the indignation and hatred that Habib Allah felt toward the people of Kabul. God's will is unknowable.

Sexual Improprieties

The two subjects on which the new regime was most culpable in Fayz Muhammad's eyes were sexual misconduct and religious fanaticism. Given the considerable space that he allots to both, it is difficult to say which he considered more reprehensible. The various kinds of sexual misconduct reported range from the relatively mild—such as placing the wives of prominent people in situations guaranteed to call into question the husband's honor—to the heinous, including assault and rape. The most notable case of the former was the detention of the wives of Nadir and his brothers. But it is the latter type of incident that most concerned our author.

One day in February, a handsome young boy living in the Andarabi Quarter of Kabul went to the bath with his aged father. At the bath, three or four of Habib Allah's brigands grabbed the boy, tore away the cloth he had tied around his waist, and began to fondle him. Fifty men of honor who had finished their bath and were getting ready to leave escorted the boy and his father to Sayyid Husayn to lodge a complaint. But one of the perpetrators managed to get there first and tell a completely contrary story so that as soon as the group with the boy and his father came to the house of Sayyid Husayn, his minions pounced on them and beat them up. After driving them away, they let the boy and his father in to see Sayyid Husayn. He merely scolded the culprits and said to the father and his son, "The fact is, they gave you money and you yourselves consented to the act." He then forbade the men from any further assaults on women, young girls, or boys. In this fashion did he try to placate both sides. This case is only one of hundreds of similar incidents that occurred throughout the country.

April 1: This evening, the brother of Sayyid Husayn's wife sent a letter to ᶜAbd al-Wasiᶜ, a good-looking boy and the son of Zaman al-Din

Khan. Zaman al-Din, the son of Prince Hasan Badakhshani, served for a time as advisor to the Ministry of Foreign Affairs under Aman Allah and then was appointed governor of the Central Province. While serving as governor, he had gone to the Hazarahjat to investigate some matter. There, at the instigation of Amin Allah b. Arslah Khan Ghilzai, who had a fanatical hatred for Hazarahs, Zaman al-Din transported nine Hazarah elders from Bihsud and Day Zangi to Kabul and tried to have them exiled permanently to Qunduz in Qataghan, Tukharistan. When the Mangal tribe rebelled in 1924, these Hazarahs were pardoned and allowed to return home. Zaman al-Din, meanwhile, was named governor of Herat but unexpectedly passed away there.

In the letter, Sayyid Husayn's brother-in-law proposed to ᶜAbd al-Wasiᶜ that they become lovers. If ᶜAbd al-Wasiᶜ refused, he would use force. But ᶜAbd al-Wasiᶜ's mother hid him and gave the letter to Zaman al-Din's uncle, Muhammad Wali, who had been wakil and close to Aman Allah. But Muhammad Wali was afraid that he would be arrested and his property confiscated and so begged her not to mention his name. Instead he advised her to bring the letter to Sayyid Husayn's attention. Perhaps he would then exert his influence to prevent this abomination from happening. I have no idea how this shameful business was concluded. One should perhaps regard the effects in this case as heavenly punishment for the sins of the father and Muhammad Wali Khan's treachery to Aman Allah. You reap what you sow.

May 22: Today, as divine retribution for the misdeeds of the northerners, a giant swarm of locusts swooped down along the Logar road between Charasya and Kabul. News also came that five thousand nomad Pushtun households had gathered in the region of Shiniz in Wardak, having decided to make their migration into the Hazarahjat. But soldiers from the amir's army stationed at Ghazni violated the honor of a girl from one of the nomad families. The nomads then attacked the soldiers, killing them all. News of this reached the ears of other "servants of the religion" including the governor-general, Malik Muhsin, who visited the nomads to placate them. Using cunning, he patched up the business, the story of which had spread all over the country.

More obscure to the reader today are the portents that Fayz Muhammad embeds in a brief passage about the marriage of the amir's brother, Hamid Allah, on May 31.

This evening, Hamid Allah, who had decided to marry the daughter of a butcher named Jan Muhammad, made arrangements for the wedding to take place at the palace of the late Na°ib al-Saltanah, Sardar Nasr Allah. At the time of the wedding feast, his eyes lit on a verse inscribed on the wall: "The amir's palaces are in ruins. The people have all become a mob of ravens and owls."

Fayz Muhammad reports a number of occasions on which the northerners compelled or tried to compel Kabul women to marry them, an act tantamount to assault in his eyes. The report of the involuntary marriages arranged on the basis of the registration list of the Masturat School[182] *was one such occasion. Fayz Muhammad documents other attempts, involving the amir, to compel certain women into marriage, but these had a clearly political motive, to ally Habib Allah with the Muhammadzai clan. Fayz Muhammad presents his actions simply as an outrage against propriety, but another interpretation would be that by these liaisons the Tajik ruler was making a deliberate effort to give his regime a somewhat more legitimate veneer.*

April 1: Habib Allah, who already possessed a large harem, decided to take as wives the daughters of the late Sardar Nasr Allah and Amin Allah [who was in prison], sons of Amir ᶜAbd al-Rahman. But the women rejected him and when he found out that they were already married, he did not try to force the issue. He then made overtures to the lovely daughter of Sardar Muhammad ᶜAli, the son of Pir Muhammad, grandson of Sardar Sultan Muhammad, and grandnephew of Amir Dust Muhammad. When she too refused him, he decided to take her by force. But the girl made up her mind to kill herself rather than submit and took poison to save herself from his clutches. But thanks to God's mercy, she survived.

About two weeks later the amir made another attempt to persuade the girl to marry him.

April 16: Habib Allah resolved to take by force if necessary the daughter of Muhammad ᶜAli and again ordered her brought to him. But she again refused. He then sent to her mother's house some soldiers notorious for brutality. The mother and daughter had decided it was better to die than go to Habib Allah but in the end they were forcibly taken to him. However, in response to the young girl's entreaties he did not molest them.

These women, the wife and daughter of Muhammad ᶜAli Muhammadzai, turn up once again in Fayz Muhammad's account when he reports, under the events of May 7th, that the amir had transferred his harem, with the exception of these two women, from the Arg to the residence of the late prime minister ᶜAbd al-Quddus Khan, which adjoined the Burj-i Yadgar and the Shahr Ara Palace. Fayz Muhammad gives no clue as to what the significance of such a move was and why these two women should have been left in the Arg. Then once again, later in the month, the amir made another attempt at a Muhammadzai woman. Here one senses mixed feelings on the part of the author, contempt for the Tajik amir and his close friend and colleague Sayyid Husayn on the one hand, and at the same time a certain sense of satisfaction at the comeuppance of the Muhammadzai, which comes through in the speech he puts in Sayyid Husayn's mouth.

April 26: Tonight Habib Allah Khan ordered the daughter of the late Sardar Nasr Allah forcibly brought to the Arg. Her mother—also the mother of ᶜAziz Allah Khan—was the daughter of Sardar Faqir Muhammad Khan. He wanted to amuse himself with her and make her his concubine. But she said that a marriage between her and Aman Allah had already been contracted. Aman Allah's chaplain (*imām-i namāz*), Hafiẓ Muhammad Hasan Khan, and other witnesses who had attended the matrimonial contract ceremony confirmed the emotional declarations of the princess. Habib Allah warned them that if, after investigating, he discovered that they were lying, he would punish them severely. He kept the woman with him for a night and in the morning let her go home.

The next evening Sayyid Husayn summoned the princess to his house to check whether she had in fact consummated her marriage with Aman Allah. "Prepare a bed for her in a far room," he commanded, "where I can examine her." He spent the whole night with her and at dawn left the house saying that he had ordered that she, her sister, and the women and girls of the late Amir Habib Allah's harem now be rewarded in the same way that the girls and women of the Hazarahs had been rewarded by Amir ᶜAbd al-Rahman and his son Habib Allah.[183] Their family had now received a well-deserved punishment and other people would learn a lesson from this.

Religious Deviation

*Along with charges of sexual outrages, accusations of religious zealotry that violated Islamic norms recur throughout Fayz Muhammad's memoir. As a minority Hazarah Shi*ᶜ*ite he was particularly sensitive to both ethnic discrimination and religious bigotry. He also was especially disdainful of the use of religion and religious slogans by people who were ignorant of Islamic history and scholarship. To him, Habib Allah was just such an ignoramus.*

In Afghanistan partisanship was and still is expressed in an Islamic vocabulary. As we have seen above,[184] *when Habib Allah publicly declared the illegitimacy of any claims by Nadir Khan to the throne he did so in religious terms. Asserting the purity and unexceptionality of his own beliefs and conduct was an indispensable part of Habib Allah's search for legitimacy and his struggle for wider popular support. He emphasized the religious shortcomings of his enemies and his own contrasting piety. Fayz Muhammad finds his efforts misguided, uninformed, and in some cases ridiculously transparent.*

The incidents related by the Hazarah diarist show three recurring themes: assertions of the irreligion of both the deposed Amir Aman Allah and Nadir Khan; the contrasting self-asserted piety of the Tajik leader which he expressed through formal devotional acts as well as public words, and Fayz Muhammad's tacit confirmation (by reproducing the words of the amir) of his charges against Aman Allah and Nadir Khan and simultaneous rejection of Habib Allah's claims to any special status as devotee of Islam. The amir tried to demonstrate religiosity in a number of ways, including shrine veneration.

April 12: Killing is prohibited during this month [Zu'l-Qaᶜadah, corresponding to April 11–May 10, 1929]. However, Muslims today, not being true Muslims or champions of the religion, violate the regulations of God and the Prophet and shed blood, plunder property, and take other Muslims captive. But the Almighty knows just what they are doing. Habib Allah, accompanied by his brother and leading figures from Kuhistan and Kuhdaman, today went to the shrine (*mazār*) of Khwajah Safa, which overlooks the city. In antiquity it was the site of a village of idol worshippers and idols were discovered here during the reign of the late Amir

Habib Allah.[185] Afterward, they attended the Redbud Blossom Festival. They did not go to the Friday service but spent the day looking at the buildings of the city through binoculars and firing their weapons.

May 31: Habib Allah is basically an ignoramus, but in order to underscore his amirid dignity today he ordered a carriage for a trip to Mazar-i Khwajah Musafir so that he could go and read the Kufic inscription on the brick walls of the tomb. The shrine is near the village of Chihil Tan above the village of Shaykh Muhammad Riza-yi Khurasani.[186]

Habib Allah also inserted himself into the complicated issue of time-keeping for religious purposes, or at least lent his name to production of an almanac. Fayz Muhammad takes exception to the times fixed by the almanac, in this particular case for the onset of the Feast of the Sacrifice (ᶜĪd-i Qurbān *or* ᶜĪd al-Aẓḥāʾ).

May 19: Although the new moon for this month has yet to appear,[187] on Friday evening Habib Allah declared today [Sunday] to be the holiday [10th of Zu'l-Hijjah—Feast of the Sacrifice] on the basis of a calendar which he devised, the *Taqwīm-i Ḥabībīyah.* Although he has no special knowledge of astronomy, he thinks himself a veritable Avicenna among ignoramuses. Since the new moon was not visible in the sky on Friday and, had it appeared on Saturday eve, today would still be only the ninth [of Zu'l-Hijjah]. According to jurisprudence (*fiqh*), the holiday prayers are forbidden on the ninth, the day of ᶜArafat.[188] Possibly, someone sighted the new moon on the Friday [a week ago] and therefore the qazi declared the holiday. But if there is any doubt, then, according to Islamic law, the 10th of Zu al-Hijjah should correspond with the same day of the week as the first of Ramazan and this year that day was a Monday. Therefore the 10th of Zu'l-Hijjah should be celebrated on Monday and festivities and holiday prayers are not permissible today, the 9th.

The accusation of unbelief (kufr) *was an integral part of political rhetoric. Since idol worship was de facto proof of unbelief in the Islamic code, evidence of idol worship could thus be used to support charges that someone was an infidel.*

March 31: Thirteen Mangal tribesmen, informants for Nadir Khan, arrived in Kabul. They said that they had come on behalf of their tribe to express their obedience and deliver an oath of loyalty. Habib Allah accorded them the honor of an audience, presented each of them with a turban or thirteen rupees, which was equal to the cost of a turban. The amir also showed them Buddhist idols which were found at excavations in Jalalabad and Kuhistan and kept at the museum. He accused Aman Allah of idol worship but then himself took the statues home to add to his own collection. By charging the former amir with being an unbeliever, he hoped that the Mangals, barely knowledgeable in religious matters though they consider themselves devout Muslims, would spread the rumor of Aman Allah's irreligion among the wild tribes of the border zone. There is no other evidence than this of any lack of belief on his part.

April 8: Today the amir invited elders, tribal leaders including representatives of the Shinwari, and notables from Kabul and the Logar Valley to the Dilkusha Palace. He addressed them as follows:

> No one should reproach me for having taken the throne. Aman Allah turned his back on Islam and took up idol-worship. He wanted to force all the people of Afghanistan to prostrate themselves before him. Some people, who joined with him in idol worship, insulted, ridiculed, and humiliated those who remained true to Islam and even cursed their own fathers and grandfathers as stupid and cowardly. Things remained this way until I, risking my life, decided, in accordance with the command of the ulama and the religious leaders, to get rid of him. I achieved my goal and now that the majority of Muslims and their leaders and the ulama recognize me as amir, I will apply all my strength to defend and promote Islam and the Light of the Shari^{c}ah, the Lord of the Prophets, and to provide peace and prosperity to my brother Muslims.

He then removed the coverings on the idols which had been found near Jalalabad, Kuhdaman, Kuhistan, and elsewhere during excavations of Buddhist temples carried out by the French archaeologists Monsieur Foucher François [*sic*] and Monsieur Barthoux.[189] These men took some of the objects they found to Paris, and handed over to the government here the part which, by agreement, belonged to Afghanistan. These idols, and others found at Mazar-i Khwajah Safa in Kabul, Qal^{c}ah-i Murad Beg in Kuhdaman, and in Kuhistan, Bagram, and other regions of the north during the reigns of the late amirs ^{c}Abd al-Rahman and Habib Allah, had been deposited by Aman Allah in the museum in order to show the places where the idol-worshipers' ancestors had first settled.

After displaying these once sacred statues to his audience, Habib Allah declared, "Look at what he worships! You can see them with your own eyes." Two or three days ago, he had given the Shinwaris the chance to see them. They had kissed his hand and said in Pashto, "We bow down before you. You are the true padishah and the enemy of idol worship."

Habib Allah imagined that the idols would produce a great impression on people who had no grasp at all of either history or religion. In conclusion, he told those present that Aman Allah had reached Ghazni with his army, Muhammad Nadir Khan was in Logar, and Hazarah formations were in Ghurband and at the Unay and Khirs-Khanah Passes. Then he said, "If, O great people, you wish to hand over the reins of the government, country, and nation to someone else, then appoint a havildar (*ḥawālahdār*)[190] for me, for I would rather put my head on the block than worship these idols. I have no ambition for high rank and would be happy with just the clothes and food to which I am accustomed."

Habib Allah felt compelled to make this speech because he had received information from his informants that people—men, women, and children alike—were outraged by the abuse, oppression, and humiliation that they were forced to endure from high-ranking persons as well as the soldiers of his army. Indignant at the thievery and coercion being perpetrated, people have turned against him and pray to God for the return of Aman Allah, whom they once despised.

But outwardly the Kabulis declared, "We recognize you as padishah." One old man stood up and said, 'We have just one request and that is that you don't leave any of Aman Allah's ministers alive. They corrupted the nation and corrupted him. This especially applies to the minister of finance [Mir Hashim]. If he is drawn and quartered and you bring me his flesh, I will eat it with pleasure." Habib Allah responded, "I will kill them all except Mahmud Khan Yawar, who made an attempt on my life. Him I will imprison but not kill. You should tell me every detail of the oppression that has been visited on you, and in due course, I will give you total security."

May 19: Today, the amir ascended the pulpit of the ᶜIdgah Congregational Mosque and delivered this speech,

> I was a poor man, hiding from the government up in the mountains, in fear of being punished for my banditry. When Aman Allah decided to

> undermine the foundations of religion and turn the nation of believers into atheists, I opposed him and was victorious. He fled. As for me, I am unworthy of ruling the country and so I sent a large sum of money to Muhammad Nadir in France and invited him to take charge of the most important matters of government and put things in order. But he refused. Instead he came to the Southern Province and has busied himself there inciting the people to provocative acts. Today he is causing bloodshed and wants to destroy the government and the nation and to annihilate the people. But if he returns to Kabul now, it is still not too late to end the rebellion and the killing of Muslims.

Those who were present cursed him through clenched teeth for having destroyed the government, plundered its reserves, and demolished the tranquillity of the nation through murder and violence.

For Fayz Muhammad, the most dangerous weapon that the amir could wield was the fatwa (religious opinion). On April 15, a fatwa of takfir *(declaring an enemy to be an unbeliever) anathematized the Shi*^{c}*ite Qizilbash and Hazarahs as kafirs. In our author's eyes there were several levels of danger faced by the Hazarahs. First, there was the underlying racism in Afghan society that relegated Hazarahs to the bottom ranks of society. That racism had powerful economic as well as social motives and could always be activated on religious grounds since the vast majority of the Hazarahs were Twelver Shi*^{c}*ites. Second, there was a long-standing struggle for resources between Pushtun nomads and Hazarah farmers. The Pushtun nomads, most notably at this time the Sulayman Khayl, summered with their flocks and herds in the mountains of the Hazarahjat, and the tension between them and the Hazarah villagers was an ancient and unresolved one. It was not uncommon for the government in Kabul to lend its support to one side or the other in order to achieve a goal of its own. Habib Allah was well aware of the opportunities that this longstanding conflict presented. Third, there was the issue of religious difference, which the government could exploit when it served its interests.*

April 21: Tonight a group of Sulayman Khayl tribal elders arrived in Kabul hoping to obtain money, rifles, and ammunition. Alhough they gave an oath of allegiance, they did not get what they wanted. Habib Allah summoned them and encouraged them to attack the Hazarahs, on the grounds that the latter support Aman Allah and are Shi^{c}ites and unbelievers. In urging them to attack the Hazarahs and plunder and destroy their homes, crops, and property, he said, "As ruler, I can authorize you to act in this fashion. There is no need to fear any consequences because I do not consider such acts sinful and will never hold you responsible for them."

I do not know how much longer this uprising and the bloodshed and plundering of the people will last if such barbaric provocations continue.

Although Fayz Muhammad's sources told him that an anti-Shi^{c}ite proclamation was printed up on April 15, on the 23rd it appeared that the Islamic Regulatory Commission, to which the amir had appointed supposedly docile members when he took the throne, was not so ready to accede to the amir's plan. Sayyid Husayn also appears to have been opposed to any fatwa of takfir against the Shi^{c}ites. But pressure was building as Pushtun nomads began to respond to the opportunity opened to them.

April 23: Because the Hazarahs,who are Shi^{c}ites and followers of the Twelve Imams, have not yet given oaths of allegiance to the amir, a declaration was drawn up at a session of the Islamic Regulatory Commission accusing them of unbelief. It was supposed to be published once the Hanafi ulama confirm it.

The Sulayman Khayl nomads, in conformity with the decree of Amir Habib Allah Khan, declared a jihad against the Hazarahs. They resolved to march to the Hazarahjat and launch a religious war as far as the borders with Iran, which is a Shi^{c}ite state, with the help of Malik Muhammad ^{c}Alam Shinwari and a group of his fellow tribesmen who are in Kabul and cannot return to their own lands because of fear of Hashim Khan and the wrath of the Mohmand and Afridi tribes for violating the intertribal agreement and wreaking havoc on Jalalabad. But the Islamic Regulatory Commission, fearing a sectarian outbreak and the prolongation of war and bloodshed, would not affirm the declaration. In support of their decision, they said that in every country under the protection of any government, Christians, Jews, Zoroastrians, idolators, Buddhists, Shi^{c}ites, Sunnis, pagans, Isma^{c}ilis, and even all seventy-three sects of Islam live peacefully together. They obey their governments and do not interfere in the religions of others. Each upholds those norms of human conduct that do not contradict the holy code of his own religion.

Citing these reasons, the members of the Commission unanimously concluded that a list should be compiled of all the inhumane deeds that had been inflicted on the Hazarahs during the reigns of ᶜAbd al-Rahman, Habib Allah, and Aman Allah. These included burning Hazarahs alive, enslaving them, and giving their lands to the Pushtuns. These amirs persecuted the Hazarahs and drove them from the country. It was proposed to send this declaration to the Hazarahs themselves so that they would stop supporting Aman Allah, because all they had ever witnessed from him was annihilation, injustice, and inhumanity.

April 24: The amir today ordered distribution of a declaration signed by the mullas which authorized robbing the Qizilbash and murdering the Hazarahs of the city on the grounds that they had not given an oath of allegiance and were still supporters of Aman Allah Khan. However, Sayyid Husayn blocked implementation of this evil plan.

April 30: During the night, Habib Allah summoned Malik Muhammad ᶜAlam Shinwari, Malik Qays Khugyani—both of whom had arrived in Kabul almost simultaneously—and also members of the Sulayman Khayl tribe who were staying on in Kabul hoping to obtain money, rifles and ammunition. At the time of his discussions with them, the amir said that the population of the Hazarahjat had refused to submit and had decided to support Aman Allah. Therefore they were to wage war on them and consider Hazarah lands, wealth, families, and children as their own. In reply, those savage people, all of them ignorant and fanatical, vowed to fulfill his request.

Moreover, he declared that the Qizilbash are Shiᶜites just like the Hazarahs who have evaded giving their allegiance. Therefore the tribesmen could plunder the districts of Chandawul, Murad Khani, Mahallah-i ᶜAli Riza Khan, Chubfurushi, and Qalᶜah-i Haydar Khan in Kabul itself. This declaration thoroughly alarmed all Hazarahs, as well as the Qizilbash of Kabul and of several nearby villages, and they spent night and day in unrelieved terror. But we will see what it is that pleases God.

Today the heads of three dead Hazarahs and nineteen Hazarah prisoners from Shaykh ᶜAli, two of whom were Shi'ites and the rest Sunnis, were brought to Kabul. The severed heads, which had been scorched by fire, were nailed to wooden stakes and the prisoners were paraded around the bazaars so that the people would realize what the policies of "the servant of the Prophet of the holy religion of Islam" consist of.

May 27: Up to now, the Hazarahs, who support Aman Allah Khan and the government of the Pushtuns, have given neither an affirmative nor a negative answer to the amir's overtures. It is possible that now that they know about Aman Allah Khan's departure from the country, they will offer their allegiance and end the bloodshed.

In this regard, Habib Allah ordered that twelve thousand families of Pushtun nomads be detained in Butkhak and on the slopes of the "Kark" Mountains.[191] They were en route to the Hazarahjat from Peshawar and Jalalabad. Even before this, he had taken pack animals and other livestock from them, including the camels that transported their household goods as well as their trade goods, and ordered the animals sent to Qataghan, Badakhshan, Mazar-i Sharif, the Hazarahjat, Qandahar, and the Southern Province to transport war materiel. These actions aroused the nomads' anger. At the same time, the amir secretly invited their elders to come see him. With a fatwa from his pseudo-mullas in hand, he began to incite the nomads to holy war against the Hazarahs, promising them their lands.

But he seems not to realize that having deprived the Pushtuns of the source of their power, he has made an enemy of them. And now, through intrigue, he wants to push them into war with the Hazarahs who rose to the support of the Pushtuns. He hopes thereby to keep power in his hands, although he is an ignoramus and understands nothing about how to administer the country.

June 5: During this time, elders of the Sulayman Khayl, who coveted the lands and property of the Hazarahs, arrived in Kabul and volunteered to attack them. The amir was pleased with their offer but refrained from giving them definitive permission until the issue of whether the Hazarahs would offer allegiance or not was clarified. He also does not seem to realize that the influence of England and Russia in Afghanistan is very great today. He seems unaware that the Russian government is pushing Ghulam Nabi in Afghan Turkistan to attack British India and is giving him support in order to get control of the territory up to the Hindu Kush, while England, with the help of Nadir, is trying to transform the lands stretching up to the Hindu Kush into a colony of its own and is inciting an unholy alliance of the Pushtuns to impede Russian plans. Despite the intrigues of the two governments, Habib Allah imagines himself secure on the throne, and sets the beleaguered people of the country against each other. But, God willing, he will not remain so much longer.

June 6: The Sulayman Khayl, Andar, and Kharuti tribes violated the agreements they had with each other and are now at each other's throats. Before long, all those who have been following the guidance of Hazrat Shayr Aqa [Mujaddidi] will be annihilated for their misdeeds.

As instructed by the hazrat, a group of Sulayman Khayl elders had arrived in Kabul and expressed their willingness to attack the Hazarahs and take their lands. Habib Allah today agreed, distributed one hundred twenty thousand rupees to them as a reward, and issued a decree transferring Hazarah property to their ownership.

As has already been noted, Fayz Muhammad held the Naqshbandi establishment as represented by the Mujaddidi family particularly culpable for the push to anathematize and isolate the Twelver Shi^cites of Kabul. Here it was not just the Hazarahs who were vulnerable but the Qizilbash, a generic name given to groups of Iranian origin whose presence in Kabul dated back to the mid-18th century, when the region was conquered by Nadir Shah Afshar. The Qizilbash filled a very different social niche from the Hazarahs. For a long time they had formed a class of bureaucrats, secretaries and clerks in service to the Saduzai and Muhammadzai dynasties. They were well-to-do, occupied the upper echelons of Kabul society, and found their sudden association with the Hazarahs, their coreligionists but social inferiors, disconcerting and threatening.

April 25: The Hazrat of Shor Bazar [Gul Aqa Mujaddidi] issued a fatwa today authorizing the killing of the Hazarahs who are residents of Kabul. The great majority of them have been born in the city, built their homes here, and some have lived as long as fifty or sixty years here. Sayyid Husayn did not recognize this fatwa as binding, however, and admonished him, "When we were fighting with Aman Allah while he was still on the throne, he did not take it out on a single Kuhistani who lived in Kabul, let alone hundreds or thousands."

This hazrat, who thinks himself a great Muslim and an influential leader of Muslims, continually engages in such provocative acts. I do not know whether he has ever read the verse in the Qur'an, "Every soul earns only to its own account; no soul laden bears the load of another."[192] To hell with such a person, who claims to be a Muslim and doesn't know the blood of a thousand Hanafi Muslims has been spilled and is being spilled and that they are all of his faith. Thousands of homes plundered, hundreds of women and children assaulted—all this is a result of his fanaticism and ignorance. The All-High will punish him for this and send him to hell along with other enemies of the faith.

May 1: The forces of Habib Allah today carried out a raid on the village of Khushi in Logar and plundered its inhabitants. The fact that they were Shi^{c}ites and have not provided any recruits for the army served as the pretext. The soldiers slaughtered infants even while they were feeding at their mother's breasts and decapitated five- to seven-year old children.

May 11: The home of the chief financial officer of the treasury, Mirza Muhammad Isma^{c}il [a Qizilbash], was thoroughly searched today. The excuse given was that the residents of Chandawul have been concealing weapons in their compounds. Doors, floors, ceilings, and any other place that seemed suspicious were ripped out but no weapons were found. It will cost Mirza Muhammad Isma^{c}il an enormous amount to repair the damage. Other homes were similarly vandalized. Does the religion really consider such vandalism legal?

May 25: On the night of the looting of the house of the late Mir Zaman al-Din,[193] Muhammad Mahfuz, the deputy of the Mu^{c}in al-Saltanah Hamid Allah, trapped the Qizilbash in a situation from which they will find it very difficult to extricate themselves. He received an order by telephone from Hamid Allah to assemble several Qizilbash at the Ministry of Defense and send them to the Hazarahs to obtain oaths of allegiance. At 11 p.m. he summoned Nur al-Din Khan Jawanshir; Hajji Muhammad Ya^{c}qub Khan, the son of Mirza Muhammad Yusuf Khan [a military scribe—*amīn-i niẓām*—during the reign of ^{c}Abd al-Rahman Khan]; Mulla Mir Aqa, the son of Sayyid Husayn Sha^{c}rbaf, whose nickname is "Aqa-yi Bulbul Rawzah-khwan;"[194] the Iranian citizen Shaykh Muhammad Riza-yi Khurasani; Khalifa Ghulam Hasan; ^{c}Abd al-Wahid, the son of Mulla Malik; and a few others. He threatened them and told them they would have to go to the Hazarahjat and obtain an oath of loyalty from the Hazarahs. He gave them three instructions: first, to select a governor and a governor-general from among the Qizilbash;[195] second, to prepare to send a delegation to the Hazarahs and to specify the amount of money needed for its expenses; and third, to compose the text of a message, making use of their co-sectarianism with the Hazarahs, which would persuade the latter of the necessity of submitting to the amir.

The Qizilbash met that same night, prepared a response, and returned to Muhammad Mahfuz. They declared that even at the time of the Hazarah uprising, which dragged on for almost three years, Amir ᶜAbd al-Rahman did not send Qizilbash to the Hazarahs, although many of them held important positions in the government and enjoyed the respect of the amir. If one were to rely on co-sectarianism as a persuasive force, then it would follow logically and be just as effective to send from Kabul coreligionists [i.e. Sunnis] of the tribes of the Eastern and Southern Provinces to obtain their allegiance. More to the point, there is little love lost between Qizilbash and Hazarah. When Habib Allah took Kabul, the Qizilbash not only failed to protect the eighteen hundred Hazarahs who were in the city, but even disarmed eight hundred of them in Murad Khani in the presence of the "Sardar-i ᶜAli," the Muᶜin al-Saltanah [Hamid Allah] and gave their weapons to his men. Not one Qizilbash gave a single Hazarah asylum in his home. Habib Allah's soldiers then divided the Hazarahs up and robbed them of all the goods they had stored in caravanserais.

In prior attempts to persuade the Hazarahs to swear an oath of allegiance, a Qizilbash governor, Mirza Muhammad Muhsin, along with a delegation, and a sayyid and a mulla from both the Sunnis and the Shiᶜites had been sent to them but had returned empty-handed. Now, when the lands of the Hazarahs are occupied by forces loyal to Aman Allah Khan, to whom they have offered their allegiance and given support, no Qizilbash can possibly carry out such an order. Moreover, for forty years the Qizilbash have been treated as outcasts by the government and the nation. As for the Hazarahs, neither respect nor goodwill has ever been shown them. Therefore, not only do they not follow the principle "Shall the recompense of goodness be other than goodness?"[196] but, to the contrary, they live for revenge and retribution.

No one can say whether oaths of loyalty will ever be obtained from the Hazarahs. For now, this was the response the Qizilbash gave, and they were dismissed.

This was the beginning of a concerted government-sponsored attempt to extract oaths of loyalty from the Hazarahs of the Hazarahjat. With

Aman Allah's retreat from the fight, it was an opportune moment to press for their submission. As Habib Allah was aware, the Hazarahs were no more united as a group than any other ethnic element in Afghanistan, although the pronounced anti-Shi[c]ism of the government did tend to provide a motive for a common front. The plan to use the Qizilbash, who depended on the government for their livelihoods, to win the Hazarahs over may have seemed logical because of their shared religion. But as Fayz Muhammad repeatedly notes, there was a social gulf and little common ground between Hazarah farmers, herders, and day laborers and well-educated Qizilbash bureaucrats.

It should be added that there were groups of both Hazarahs and Qizilbash who were Sunni, most notably the Shaykh [c]Ali Hazarahs of the Ghurband region and the Kacharlu (Qājārlū?) Qizilbash of Kabul. There were also non-Twelver Shi[c]ites among the Hazarahs, notably the Isma[c]ili Shaykh [c]Ali Hazarahs led by the Kayani family. But for Fayż Muḥammad these groups do not significantly affect his construction of the Sunni-Shi[c]i bipolarity of Afghanistan in which the Hazarahs and Qizilbash, as Shi[c]ites, were very vulnerable to the oppression of the majority Sunnis, whether Tajiks or Pushtuns.

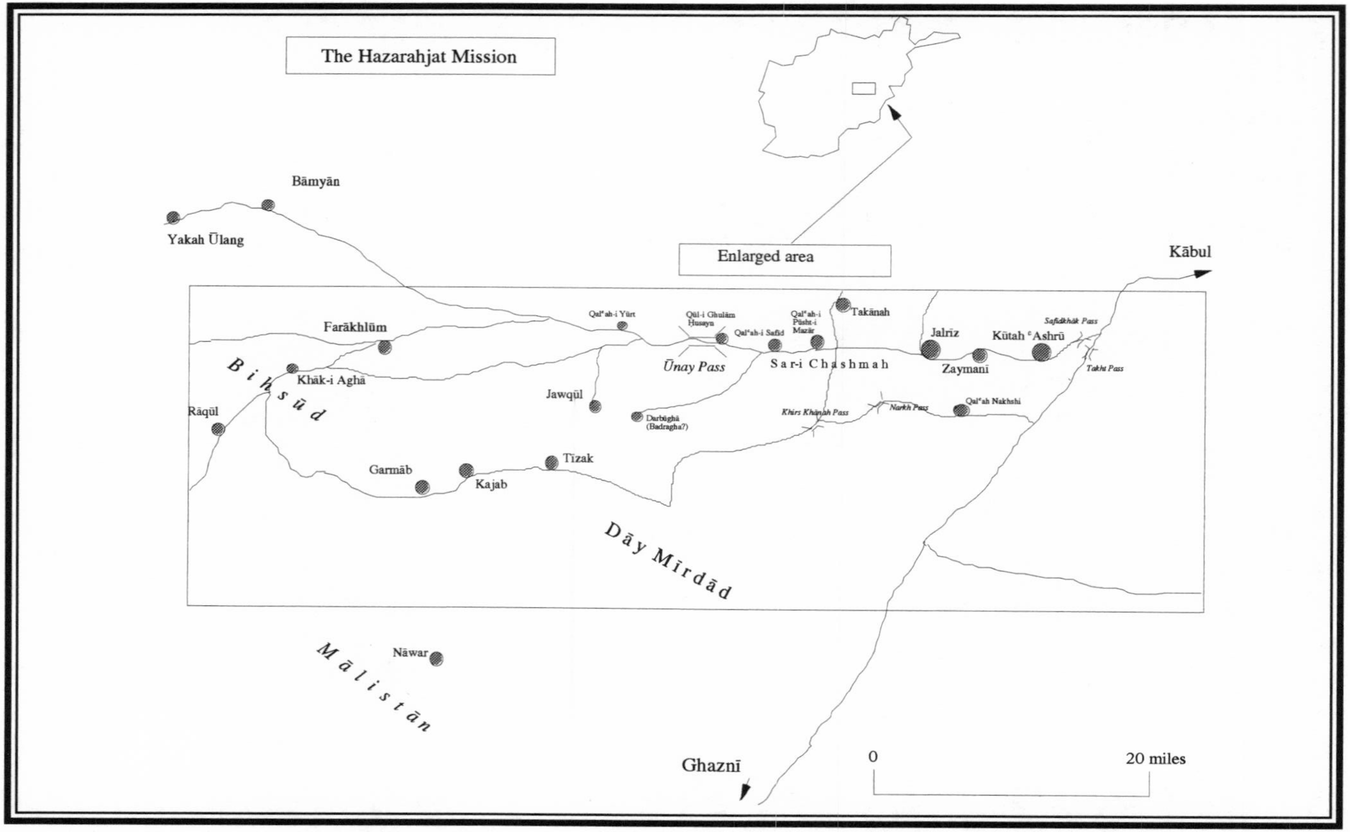

The Hazarahjat Mission
Enlarged area
Bāmyān
Yakah Ūlang
Kābul
Farākhlūm
Qalʻah-i Yūrt
Qūl-i Ghulām Ḥusayn
Qalʻah-i Safīd
Qalʻah-i Pusht-i Mazār
Takānah
Jalrīz
Kūtah ʻAshrū
Safīdkhāk Pass
Takht Pass
Zaymanī
Sar-i Chashmah
Ūnay Pass
Bihsūd
Khāk-i Aghā
Rāqūl
Jawqūl
Darbūghā (Badragha?)
Khirs Khānah Pass
Narkh Pass
Qalʻah Nakhshi
Garmāb
Kajab
Tīzak
Dāy Mīrdād
Nāwar
Mālistān
Ghaznī
0
20 miles

PART THREE

Habib Allah and the Hazarahs

If there is a central theme guiding Fayz Muhammad's story of Habib Allah Kalakani's seizure and occupation of Kabul, it is the relationship of the Hazarahs, especially those of the Hazarahjat, with the Tajik regime. Fayz Muhammad's sympathies for his fellow Hazarahs are never far below the surface of his work. His ethnic loyalty is strong and the story of the Hazarahs during this period is given more space in the narrative than any other group. Whether they played the pivotal role that he implies they did remains an open question. Except for his account, there is little information anywhere about them. Just as today the role of the Hazarahs in fighting the Taliban is little known, they are equally invisible in the extant accounts of the 1929 uprising, except in Fayz Muhammad's memoir.[197]

But this is possible to explain, as he probably would have done, in part as a consequence of their marginality and low status in Afghan society. Regardless of Hazarah achievements, their stories would always be of less consequence than those of the Pushtun majority in the construction of Afghan history. In addition, the Hazarah regions have been difficult of access to outsiders. Afghanistan itself has always been off the beaten track and within the country there are regions, one of them being the Hazarahjat, to which access has been difficult even for non-Hazarah Afghans. Of people outside Afghanistan, only their coreligionists, the Iranians, emerge as supporters and spokespersons for the Hazarahs both in 1929 and in the Soviet and post-Soviet periods.

It is possible, although Fayz Muhammad never directly says this was the case, that some groups of Hazarahs quickly found accommodation with the new regime, or at least did not immediately declare their opposition. In January 1929, the prospect of Tajik rule might well have seemed the least of many evils for Hazarahs as a group. In recent memory, Hazarahs had been treated abominably by the Pushtun Muhammadzai

Fayz Muhammad

ruling caste. Beyond institutionalized and routinized ethnic and religious discrimination, they were constantly prey to random violent persecution, persecution which might be officially encouraged, as we see here. Previously, government-sponsored persecution had reached a peak in the war that the amir, ᶜAbd al-Rahman, waged against the Hazarahs from 1891 to 1893. According to Fayz Muhammad, Aman Allah had been more tolerant and evenhanded in his dealings with them, but the extensive corruption that he condemns in Aman Allah's ministers indicates a general unhappiness with the regime and perhaps reflects a rise in ethnic anxiety among the Hazarahs. On Habib Allah's part there seemed reason, if Fayz Muhammad's reports are at all accurate, to worry about continued support from the Hazarahs for Aman Allah. To prevent a general pro–Aman Allah rising of the Hazarahs, Habib Allah had taken up, with a somewhat misplaced enthusiasm, the idea of sending delegations, at first Hazarahs, later mixed delegations of Hazarahs and Qizilbash, to the Hazarahjat to obtain pledges of loyalty and obedience to his government.

The first unambiguous sign that Habib Allah's administration might be as hostile to Hazarah interests as the Muhammadzai emerged in early April with the arrest of a prominent Hazarah and former government official, Ahmad ᶜAli, and the harassment of Hazarahs who had come to Kabul from the Hazarahjat.

April 2: Tonight the chief equerry (*mirakhur*), Ahmad ᶜAli, a Hazarah from Day Mirdad, was arrested. He had been his tribe's deputy to the National Council, during the time Shayr Ahmad,[198] son of Fath Muhammad Khan and grandson of Sardar Zikriya Khan, presided over it. [At some point] Aman Allah had dismissed him as chief equerry. On

January 13 he came to Kabul with a force of some fifteen hundred Hazarahs from Bihsud [perhaps in answer to the call for volunteers to fight the Shinwari]. But because the road was thereafter closed, he has had to remain in the city until now and has endured much hardship. When he was arrested, Muhammad Na^{c}im Khan was also taken into custody. The latter's father was Mir Iqbal Beg, a Hazarah sepoy from Day Zangi. Four prominent men from Bihsud—Ghulam Nabi Khan, Muhammad Ishaq Khan, Muhammad Hasan Khan son of Riza Bakhsh Sultan, and Qazi ^{c}Ali Khan the son of Sardar ^{c}Ali Khan—were also arrested. They are accused of being allies of Hayat Allah, the brother of Aman Allah, who was originally a backer of Habib Allah [but now in custody]. Also arrested were Mahmud Khan, deputy minister of defense under Aman Allah; Mirza Hashim Kur Kashmiri; Sultan Muhammad, Aman Allah's tailor; and several members of the Kabul aristocracy. It is said that these people had agreed to link up with the Hazarahs of Surkh-i Parsa who were coming via Paghman. Then, with the help of the Hazarah force in Kabul under Ahmad ^{c}Ali and the army advancing from Qandahar through the Hazarahjat, they planned to incite a general uprising and drive Habib Allah out of the capital. Some of the detainees were beaten. The soldiers who arrested them first extorted sums ranging from forty to five hundred and a thousand rupees and then confiscated their houses and property.

Another story regarding the arrest of the Hazarahs relates to Habib Allah's governor of Bihsud, Day Zangi, and Day Kundi, Mirza Muhammad Muhsin, better known as Kaka Muhsin. His father, Mirza Muhammad Afzal, is a Kabuli and belongs to the Sunni Kacharlu Qizilbash clan. Kaka Muhsin earned the patronage of Habib Allah thanks to his brother, Ghulam Husayn. When Habib Allah and Sayyid Husayn made their first assault on Kabul, Ghulam Husayn helped them by providing fodder for their animals and putting his fortress and houses and also the houses of other people of Chardihi at their disposal. For this he was rewarded with the rank of colonel. But later he was captured by Aman Allah's supporters and hanged. His older brother, Kaka Muhsin, was appointed governor of the Hazarah districts on January 27th. But because Mir Muhammad Husayn Khan, brother of the late Mir Ahmad Shah Khan, had been named governor there in November or December, refused to recognize the new regime, and was still in control there, Kaka

Muhsin was unable to establish his authority and found himself under siege in his home village of Kharbid. So instead, Kaka Muhsin wrote to Sayyid Husayn, "The Hazarahs who are under Mir Muhammad Husayn's authority refuse to submit and swear an oath of loyalty. You should arrest the Hazarah elders who are in Kabul and send an army to the Hazarahjat so that they will end their support for Aman Allah and express their obedience instead." Sayyid Husayn thereupon ordered their arrest. Eventually, realizing that the Hazarahs were irreconcilably hostile to Habib Allah, Kaka Muhsin made his way back to Kabul via the Khirs Khanah Pass with the help of the son of Shah Nur, a well-known Hazarah thief.

Word is that Aman Allah has sent six thousand rifles and a vast quantity of ammunition to Day Zangi and another six thousand rifles to Bihsud. Despite the fact that the population of these regions had endured a great deal of misery at the hands of Aman Allah and bear grievances against him, still they continue to support him to spite the Tajiks of the north. A force from Bihsud has occupied the Unay Pass and reached agreement with the militias of the Surkh-i Parsa, Turkman, Bamyan, Balkhab, and Shaykh ^{c}Ali Hazarahs for them to attack Kuhistan and Kuhdaman via the Ghurband Valley road while it simultaneously attacks Kabul via the road through Maydan.

April 4: Today [Thursday] Sayyid Husayn left for Khwajah Sayyaran near Charikar to make preparations for receiving the amir who has promised to go there on Friday. Baba Khan Kuhistani advised Sayyid Husayn to arrest those Hazarahs who a few days earlier had promised to get oaths of loyalty from the Hazarah tribes and then had left for the Hazarahjat. They were arrested but eventually released. Today there were more arrests. Soldiers who were assigned to conscription duty extorted money from those called up as well as from their neighbors who had no connection with the call-up at all. For instance, they seized two thousand rupees from the son of the late lieutenant general, Sayyid Shah Khan, in whose fort they found a horse belonging to the Hazarah chief equerry, Ahmad ^{c}Ali. In Sar-i Chashmah [a town on the east side of the Unay Pass] they arrested oil merchants and fined them three hundred rupees because a Tajik from Jalriz [a town to the east of Sar-i Chashmah] complained that several years earlier, the Hazarahs had been responsible for the death of his son. From the house of a Hazarah named Bula who was not at home at the time, they stole three hundred rupees. They also arrested several other people and confiscated their real estate and possessions for the treasury (*dīwān-i imārat*).

April 6: This evening, Kaka Muhsin returned to his home in Kabul following his futile attempt to take his position as governor of Day Zangi, Day Kundi, and Bihsud. During the day, he was received by Habib Allah and criticized for his failure to establish his authority. After his return to the capital, rumors spread that the governor-general of Qandahar, [c]Abd al-Karim, had, at Aman Allah's order, delivered seven thousand rifles to Bihsud by way of Gizab, Tamazan, and Sipahi. Four thousand men were said to be manning positions in the Unay Pass and two thousand at the Khirs-Khanah Pass. But this turned out to be mere rumor.

April 7: Today Habib Allah's army, advancing along the road not far from Ghazni near Shiniz in Wardak, was defeated in a fight and suffered many casualties. The army telephoned for reinforcements from Kabul and the thousand-man force preparing to march to the Hazarahjat via Sar-i Chashmah set off to assist those under fire.

An order also went out from Kabul to the people of Wazirabad that, although they had no firearms, they were to advance to Sar-i Chashmah armed with knives, axes, and swords and block the path of the Hazarahs, their coreligionists. Because they were coreligionists, it was thought the attacking Hazarahs would not harm them.

April 13: There are also rumors that not far from Ghazni, Hazarah detachments have attacked and pillaged the homes of those Tajiks who supported Habib Allah, and have also routed the Sulayman Khayl tribe, which had declared its opposition to Aman Allah.

April 14: Today we hear that the Hazarahs of Bihsud have sworn an oath of obedience to Habib Allah Khan to keep him from sending an army into the Hazarahjat. But as soon as Aman Allah gets things sorted out and the Hazarahs are assured of the support of the mullas and the Pushtun who oppose Habib Allah, they will attack his army in a joint operation with the Pushtuns and other tribes supporting Aman Allah. Habib Allah has only twenty thousand men and they have all been conscripted against their will. Moreover, the roads are cut and exact information is not reaching Kabul from a single place in the country. The mail and the telegraph are shut down and getting reliable information from eyewitnesses has become well-nigh impossible. The delivery of food and fodder has also stopped.

Today, Malik Muhsin, acting on the suggestion of Kaka Muhsin, ordered some of the Hazarah leaders, who were in Kabul because the roads were shut, to go to the Hazarahjat, extract an oath of allegiance from the Hazarahs, and persuade them to open the roads and the Unay Pass. Prior to this, it had been decided to send Kaka Muhsin there again, accompanied by Mulla Mir Aqa and Mirza Muhammad Isma^{c}il Khan Shahi.[199]

April 15: Today the amir ordered the printing of a proclamation in which the Hazarahs are accused of unbelief. However, in the evening, several Hazarahs from Bihsud arrived in Kabul and swore an oath of allegiance in order to collect a reward. Meantime the Hazarah delegation that had been assigned to obtain oaths of allegiance was still in Kabul, its departure delayed.[200]

April 17: At the request of Kaka Muhsin, an ambitious and vain man who aspires to rule over the entire Hazarahjat, a farman was drafted today, addressed to all Hazarahs. However, it remained unsigned because Sayyid Husayn had left for Charikar.

The Bihsud Hazarahs, armed with the six thousand rifles sent by Aman Allah along with instructions to delay their attack on Kabul for four days, today sent a message to Habib Allah seeking forgiveness for their failure to send oaths of allegiance. They hoped to deceive him with this letter. Their message was conveyed to Habib Allah by the Bihsud Hazarahs in a delegation from Sar-i Chashmah.[201] For this each of the delegation's seven members (Sayyid Zayn al-^{c}Abidin, the son of Sayyid Shahanshah from Takana; Ghulam Habib, son of the Qizilbash, Ghulam Hasan Khan, who had control of the land and fortress in Unay; the father of the governor of Maydan; and four Hazarahs from Sar-i Chashmah) was rewarded with a Kabuli turban made of rayon. As for when they would send their oaths of allegiance, the Bihsudis swore to His Highness that they would do it in ten to fifteen days. Habib Allah agreed to this and even said some words commending the Hazarahs for their virtue and piety, although only a day or so before he had ordered a proclamation printed up accusing them of unbelief and had obtained a fatwa from the mullas that labelled Shi^{c}ites as apostates.

April 20: Today, the Hazarah chief equerry, Ahmad ᶜAli, along with the son of Sardar ᶜAbd Allah Khan Tukhi (whose brother—ᶜAta Muhammad—had raised a rebellion in Mazar-i Sharif against Habib Allah), was hanged in Shayrpur [a quarter of Kabul and site of a prison], along with a member of the Taraki tribe and a Qandahari, for conspiring against the amir. Twenty-four other conspirators were imprisoned in iron cages.[202]

May 7: After promising [on April 17] that in ten or fifteen days the Bihsud Hazarahs would swear an oath of allegiance, the seven-man delegation from Bihsud had set off for home. Now the agreed-upon time had expired and no oath of allegiance was forthcoming. The Bihsud Hazarahs sent this explanation:

> We are Muslims and adherents of truth and religion. Since we gave an oath of obedience to Aman Allah, we are bound, by the regulations of the Shariᶜah, to support him, lest we have to answer for our actions to God and the Prophet. To fulfill our oath we are ready, from the least of us to the greatest, for any struggle. As long as we live, we will fight, and in the fight will devote ourselves to the service of religion and our homeland and to the defense of the nation and the government from the raids and pillaging of savage thieves. We cannot allow two riders [i.e. Habib Allah and Aman Allah] to share one saddle lest we bear the responsibility in this world and the next.

Twelve thousand Hazarahs then occupied the Unay Pass, prepared for battle, and issued this declaration:

> Aman Allah greatly oppressed us early in his reign and failed to punish the Pushtun nomads who destroyed our homes, killed us, threw us alive into the fire, took away our lands, and carried off our wives and daughters nor did he demand an explanation from the officials and governors who robbed us of several hundred thousand rupees, and for that he will be charged before God. But we have given our oath of allegiance and do not engage in treachery the way the Pushtuns do.

They then adopted the following plan of action.

> If we attacked Kabul by day, we would sustain heavy losses from the artillery on the heights of Chihil Tan, Dukhtar-i Kafir, Shah Mardan,

> Asmaʾi, Shayr Darwaza, and Takht-i Shah that overlook Chardihi and our attack would fail. Therefore, we must make our way to the summits of the mountains of Begtut and Quruq [near Paghman] and hide there for a day so as to attack the heights where the guns are at night. As soon as we get to the lower slopes of the mountains, the cannon fire will not cause us any harm. Then after climbing the heights, with the help of God, we must capture the guns and occupy the positions that command Kabul and Chardihi. In this way, success may be possible.

But Aman Allah asked them to postpone their attack on Kabul until his own forces approached Maydan. He planned to combine both forces and then launch his assault. So up until today [May 7], the Hazarahs are positioned on the lower slopes of the Paghman, Shakar Darrah, and Unay mountains, and are impatiently awaiting the beginning of the assault on Kabul.

Throughout the day, there has been talk everywhere about the arrival of Hazarah units at the Safidkhak Pass, which overlooks Arghandah and Maydan, as well as about the approach of Nadir from Logar, Hashim from the Eastern Province, and the military activities of the Hazarahs in Kuhistan. Habib Allah was quite concerned and ordered two thousand men to Butkhak (to defend against an attack from Logar) and a large unit to Kuhistan.

But as was often the case with coordination of forces from different ethnic groups linked by poor communications, nothing came of this plan. Fayz Muhammad remains ever hopeful, however. For the Tajiks in Kabul, the threat of such a joint action was ever present and steps were continually taken to counter it. On the one hand, Hazarahs under the direct control of the Tajik government were treated, according to Fayz Muhammad, with unremitting harshness to keep them docile. On the other, conciliatory overtures were made to those beyond government control in the hopes that they would renounce their support for Aman Allah and, after him, for Nadir, and recognize Habib Allah's amirate. (Similar tactics have reportedly marked the policy of the Taliban toward the Hazarahs in the late 1990s.)

May 23: Today, while freeing two hundred captured Wardaks, Habib Allah ordered his people not to release any Hazarahs but instead to send them to the prison in Shayrpur. He said he would have a talk with them later about their support for Aman Allah.

May 27: The governor-general, Malik Muhsin, left for Jalriz and Takana today intending to get an oath of allegiance from the Hazarahs. In the meantime, they have set up strong barricades at the Unay Pass and are preparing to attack Kabul. Malik Muhsin had first sent a number of people to the Hazarahs so they would give their oaths of allegiance and express their submission but they refused and instead proposed that he come to Sar-i Chashmah and negotiate there. But he was afraid to go to Sar-i Chashmah and instead returned to Kabul. He then left again for Jalriz and sent a group of elders from Maydan, Jalriz, Takana, Sanglakh, and Sar-i Chashmah to the Hazarahs with a message that said that if they refused to express their obedience and give an oath of allegiance, then the Pushtun tribes that migrate into the Hazarahjat, and are now in Kabul awaiting permission to set off, will occupy the Hazarahjat, and with the help of army units make short work of the Hazarahs.

May 29: Earlier, Muhammad Mahfuz had proposed an undertaking calculated to provoke the Qizilbash.[203] He and his father, Ahmad Jan,[204] a physician at court from the beginning of ᶜAbd al-Rahman's reign up to the present, were both in government service in high positions. But being of lowly origins, they did not show much gratitude for the favoritism shown them by the amirs ᶜAbd al-Rahman, Habib Allah, or Aman Allah, and both Muhammad Mahfuz and his father came out in opposition to the latter. Once he took power, Amir Habib Allah, at his very first reception, greeted Ahmad Jan like a close friend and appointed Muhammad Mahfuz as aide-de-camp to his brother, Hamid Allah.

The groundwork for exterminating the Qizilbash who live in Kabul was laid in the following way. Muhammad Mahfuz proposed getting an oath of allegiance from the Hazarahs because representatives of Aman Allah such as the governor-general of Qandahar, ᶜAbd al-Karim, and two sons of the late Amir Habib Allah[205] are now on Hazarah territory helping them prepare to overthrow the Tajik regime. Mahfuz had summoned seven Qizilbash to the ministry at night and ordered them to obtain an oath of allegiance from the Hazarahs. He thought that they would be unable to cope with this task, it would be possible then to accuse them of encouraging the Hazarahs to refuse to tender their allegiance, and he would get what he wanted, an excuse to destroy them. But the Qizilbash had a plausible reason why they could not do it and so had been excused.

Still in pursuit of his ignoble goal, Muhammad Mahfuz now presented their arguments to Habib Allah in such a way that the amir assigned Muhammad Mahfuz himself to make them fulfill the charge. Mahfuz then named Muhammad A^{c}zam, the son of Jalandar Khan, to work with him. The Qizilbash were again summoned and ordered to go to the Hazarahjat and get the oath of allegiance that the amir wanted. Realizing they were in mortal danger, the Qizilbash agreed to fulfill the command, but only on condition that Muhammad A^{c}zam himself lead the delegation to witness that the dealings of the Qizilbash were aboveboard and so ensure that they would not be unjustly blamed if the mission failed. Muhammad Mahfuz agreed, and with Habib Allah's sanction, ordered several Qizilbash to come to a meeting.

Today at 2 p.m. some fifty Qizilbash elders received invitations to the meeting. At four p.m. they appeared before him.

This was the second effort by the amir to assemble a delegation that he could send to the Hazarahjat to obtain oaths of allegiance from Hazarah leaders there. The story of this delegation makes up a major part of Fayz Muhammad's memoir not only because he was a member but because it is the most self-consciously autobiographical portion of the memoir. Here he portrays himself as the behind-the-scenes mastermind, whose objective was to undermine the mission and persuade the Hazarah leaders with whom the delegation negotiated to withhold support from the Tajik amir. At the same time he wanted to appear to the Qizilbash leader of the delegation and to the powers back in Kabul to be acting in accord with the amir's wishes.

The key members, as portrayed in Fayz Muhammad's account, were its leader, Nur al-Din Jawanshir; Mir Aqa, whose learning and wide reputation in the Shi^{c}i regions of Afghanistan at one point would rescue the members of the delegation when they were taken hostage; Muhammad Zaman, a Sunni Tajik from Parwan who was there to guarantee the otherwise Shi^{c}ite delegation did not behave in an untoward manner (Muhammad A^{c}zam, despite what is said above, did not accompany the group); and, of course, Fayz Muhammad himself.[206] *Important dramatis personae in the account who were not part of the delegation include the commander of the Hazarah forces at the Unay Pass, Fath Muhammad,* *and Sardar (Prince) Muhammad Amin, the Muhammadzai governor on behalf of the now-absconded Aman Allah. The delegation never got to meet with him at his residence at Raqul but his negotiations with them and his reaction to their arrival play a large part in the narrative.*

Besides its portrayal of the political situation in the eastern Hazarahjat, Fayz Muhammad's account offers glimpses of daily life in this inaccessible region, the depth of Hazarah attachment to the religious practices of Twelver Shi^cism, the high degree of local autonomy, and the general absence of any central government institutional presence in the region.

He begins with a description of the recruitment and organization of the delegation and sets forth some of the problems he thought it would face.

The Second Mission to the Hazarahjat

May 30: Yesterday at 4:00 p.m. the president of the Islamic Regulatory Commission, Muhammad A^czam, gathered together the fifty-three Qizilbash who were supposed to go to the Hazarahjat to obtain an oath of allegiance from the Hazarahs. When Nur al-Din, the son of Qazi Qutb al-Din Jawanshir, and two other Qizilbash saw Muhammad A^czam in their quarter of town, they realized that something was afoot and so they too headed for the Arg.

Sometime before 6 p.m. they were waiting outside the amir's office. Earlier, Nur al-Din had turned Muhammad Mahfuz against the Qizilbash clans, but when they had given a reasonable answer [as to why they should not be sent to the Hazarahjat], he had been thwarted. But now he had a plan for Muhammad A^czam. By the time Habib Allah emerged from his office, Nur al-Din had somehow persuaded Muhammad A^czam to get verbal instructions from the amir to the effect that the Qizilbash must leave for the Hazarahjat to obtain the oath of allegiance and that Nur al-Din himself should head the delegation. It was he who decided that seven people would make up the delegation.

At the request of the Qizilbash present at this meeting, Muhammad Zaman Khan, the son of Sarwar Khan of Parwan, was also included in the delegation. His role was to bear witness to any double-dealing by members of the delegation or its leader.

At 7 p.m. the Qizilbash were dismissed. Anxious about the scheming of Nur al-Din and Hajji Muhammad Ya^c^qub Khan, they parted company and headed home in a gloomy frame of mind. Because of the outrageous behavior of these two ignorant fellow clansmen, who out of self-interest and avarice are prepared to destroy everything of this world, they could only invoke the help of God who, perhaps, would defend them from evil, ignorance, and greed and save them from being murdered and robbed.

How dangerous the times have become and how incapable the government is of following a proper policy! How is it possible for the Hazarahs to give an oath of allegiance when the chief governor of Day Zangi, Day Kundi, and Bihsud, Mirza Muhammad Husayn, who is a fervent supporter of Aman Allah; the brother [Prince Muhammad Amin[207]] of the former amir; and ^c^Abd al-Karim, the governor-general of Qandahar, remain in the Hazarahjat, working hard for the defeat of Habib Allah?

If Nur al-Din possessed any sense at all he would not act in such an underhanded way. As long as the Hazarahjat is in the hands of partisans of Aman Allah and there is war between the northern Tajiks and the Pushtuns, sooner or later the Afghans will drive Habib Allah from the throne. Nur al-Din will then be in for an unpleasant surprise.

Even if the Hazarahs give an oath of allegiance in order to save themselves and their honor, without their governor, the brother of Aman Allah [Prince Muhammad Amin], and his partisans in the Hazarahjat finding out, then Habib Allah will want them to fight against the Afghans. But they will never agree to this and then the Qizilbash will be forced to bear the brunt of Habib Allah's anger. Unfortunately, Nur al-Din is a complete ignoramus and lacks any semblance of a conscience or sense of honor. Today he ordered the members of his delegation to prepare to depart. Against my will, I was enrolled in the delegation despite having no financial resources and being seriously afflicted with a swelling that has appeared on my neck.

June 1: Nur al-Din, head of the delegation, has enlisted men of sound judgment from Chandawul, Murad Khani, Qal^c^ah-i Haydar Khan, Afshar, and Wazirabad.[208] He asked the government to provide ten riding and ten pack horses for the delegation, ten rifles with ammunition, and fifteen thousand rupees for travel expenses.

June 2: Today Nur al-Din invited to his house the seven Qizilbash men who are to serve as members of the delegation as well as other leading Qizilbash figures. At first the men chosen for the delegation refused to go, citing the miserable state of their finances and the fact that physically they were not up to such a journey. But he warned them that the government would punish them if they refused to go and so they were forced to submit.

When a rumor circulated that the Hazarahs were ready to swear an oath of allegiance after learning of the flight of Aman Allah, part of the amir's army was sent to Sar-i Chashmah. It was ordered not to fire on anyone who swears allegiance as long as they are unarmed.

June 5: Out of fifteen thousand rupees envisaged as necessary for the travel expenses of the members of the Hazarahjat delegation, Habib Allah has approved only ten thousand. He said that since the government had no money and the army had to be paid first, the fellow clansmen of the members of the delegation should help with the provisioning. But the Qizilbash are all living hand-to-mouth and are continually exposed to mortal danger. Consequently, the members of the delegation were pleased to receive two hundred rupees each, which had been approved by Habib Allah as their modest compensation. With this money each man could buy ten to twenty seer of flour. One seer of flour today costs four to four and a half rupees; one seer of oil, thirty-five to forty rupees; one seer of meat, twelve rupees and six *fils*. Firewood by weight is one rupee for one and a quarter seer; one paw of buttermilk is ten *paisā*; one khurd of cheese, six paisa; twelve eggs, one rupee. Each of them could also buy fabric for clothing and have enough left over to supply his family with money for five to ten days. The total of two hundred rupees was also enough to acquire a saddle and harness and the clothes necessary for the trip.

June 7: Aman Allah, who fervently longed for the progress and civilization of the country and the nation and dreamed about the well-being of its people and the prosperity of its cities, finally despaired and left Afghanistan and its benighted people for Europe. Meanwhile, the governor-general of Qandahar, ᶜAbd al-Karim,[209] a son of the Chief Justice Saᶜd al-Din, had already been in the Hazarahjat for some time working on Aman Allah's behalf and had persuaded the Hazarahs to fight for him. But ᶜAbd al-Karim has now decided to switch sides. After Habib Allah confiscated his property in Kabul, he sent a message to the amir in which he expressed his allegiance and asked for a guarantee of safe conduct. "If my safety is guaranteed," he wrote, "I will deliver Muhammad Amin, Aman Allah's brother, to you. He is now in the Hazarahjat with me. I will also bring an oath of allegiance from the Hazarahs." When they got wind of his duplicity, the Hazarahs thought about arresting him. But since they had only their suspicions and no hard evidence, they continued to treat him as a refugee and guest of their tribes in accordance with the maxim "Honor the guest even if he is untrustworthy."

Today rumors spread that three airplanes, which had taken off from Mazar-i Sharif, landed on a specially prepared airstrip at Bad Asya, in Bihsud. The pilots told the Hazarahs that the planes were going to bomb Kuhdaman, Kuhistan, and the Arg in Kabul. They then flew back to Mazar-i Sharif.

Despite the fact that Habib Allah Khan had already dispatched a delegation to the Hazarahjat, today he ordered five units numbering sixty-five hundred men to that region. He also sent a large shipment of hand grenades to Gardiz and Khust for his lieutenant-general Muhammad Siddiq.

The delegation left Kabul on June 8. The members spent the first night at Afshar, just on the edge of Kabul, and then made their way to Kut-i Ashru in Maydan on the road west to the Unay Pass on the 9th. The next morning, Nur al-Din and six others went to Jalriz and Takana to meet with the leaders of those areas while Fayz Muhammad and the baggage continued on to the Qal^{c}ah of Pusht-i Mazar just west of the village of Sar-i Chashmah. There he was rejoined by the others. The delegation stayed there for a week (from the 11th to the 18th), during which time there was a good deal of to-ing and fro-ing by messengers. The ability of the party to conduct business was somewhat hampered by its timing. It was the first week in Muharram and people were busy preparing for the holiday on the 10th (June 18) and not particularly interested in the delegation's concerns. The week's activities did produce an agreement to meet with the Hazarah commander at the Unay Pass, Fath Muhammad. On the 18th at least part of the delegation left for the Unay Pass and at that point became little more than a political football passed from one faction to another.

June 8: Nur al-Din left Kabul today with the delegation for the Hazarahjat. Various rumors are circulating: one is of the imminent approach of Ghulam Nabi from Afghan Turkistan, although there is no hard news yet that he has left Mazar-i Sharif. Another is that large tribal forces in the Eastern Province have come together under the leadership of Hashim and another is that the Pushtun tribes under Nadir have begun to fight. Because of these rumors, Nur al-Din spent the night in Afshar at the home of Muhammad Mahdi Khan, a grandson of Sultan Khan. At daybreak on Sunday, June 9, Nur al-Din and the delegation, of which I was a member, left Afshar for the Hazarahjat.

June 9: Nur al-Din arrived in Kut-i Ashru today and took lodgings in the caravanserai there. There is talk here that the Tajik residents of Takana, Jalriz, and Kuhnah Khumar, who are under the jurisdiction of the governor of Maydan, enthusiastically support Habib Allah's government and send false and compromising information about the residents of Sar-i Chashmah, Unay, and the Hazarahjat to the the intelligence service (*idārah-i żabṭ-i aḥwālāt*) in Kabul. On the basis of these false charges, many people are arrested, robbed, and murdered. Having witnessed with their own eyes this unhappy state of affairs, the members of the delegation were fearful that if, God forbid, the Hazarahs did not tender their submission and recognize the infidel and thief as amir, then they themselves might be accused and punished, and since the Qizilbash did not have a homeland of their own, they too would be vulnerable to being robbed and killed.

I was at a teashop where a group of people had gathered. I turned the conversation to politics, trying to defend the delegation against accusations by people who might equate its members with the devils resident in Kuhnah Khumar, Jalriz, and Takana. Those people are noted for their savage fanaticism and inborn hatred for Shiᶜites, especially Hazarahs. I said, "I don't understand why the Hazarahs do not tender an oath of allegiance and express obedience to the government of the Tajiks, who have always treated them well and with whom they share the same language. You know, ever since the days of ᶜAbd al-Rahman down through the reigns of Habib Allah and Aman Allah, Hazarahs have been oppressed, robbed, and killed; thousands have perished, been taken captive, fled their ancestral homes, and seen their lands transferred to the Pushtuns. Moreover, before the reign of ᶜAbd al-Rahman, permission was never given to the Pushtun nomads to pasture their herds on the grazing grounds of the Hazarahjat. In his time and after, nomads frequently invaded the Hazarahjat, aided and abetted by government officials, and robbed and killed Hazarah families and destroyed their crops. The government never tried to resolve this issue. As a consequence, this beleaguered people has left and continues to leave its lands, seeking refuge in other countries. But, God willing, when we in the delegation reach the Hazarahjat, they will learn of the tragic fate that has been prepared for them by the Pushtun tribes and so will express their allegiance and put an end to the fighting."

I was sitting behind a wall and my remarks were overheard by Muhammad Zaman Parwani whom we had asked to go with us to witness what we did. When I went off to my room in the caravanserai, he thanked me for what I had said and the sincere feelings I showed for the government of Habib Allah. I rested easier because now no one can make accusations. This man is my witness, and if it becomes necessary will confirm what I said.

June 10: Today, when talk everywhere is about an imminent attack on Kabul by the tribes of the Southern Province under Nadir and the Pushtun tribes of the Eastern Province under Hashim, we left Kut-i Ashru and set off for Sar-i Chashmah. Nur al-Din made a detour to Takana and Jalriz with six other members of the delegation, his son and son-in-law, and seven armed riders—sixteen men including himself. He visited the homes of the elders there and made a display of his innate arrogance. At each home he boasted of his authority, smoked a water pipe (*qalyān*), and drank some water. He paid a visit to the home of the head of the Ahmadzai tribe, Hazrat Muhammad Khan, a man with a sensible head on his shoulders. There, though it was well before evening, he dined and continued his bragging. Meantime I, who had been forced to join the delegation despite my illness, arrived in Sar-i Chashmah with the train of eleven pack animals. I took lodgings near a pond next to the Qalᶜah-i Pusht-i Mazar fortress—at that time the only fortress on the road from Sar-i Chashmah to the Unay Pass. Exhausted and somewhat depressed, I sat down beside the pond. Hasan Riza, the son of the late Zaddar [Sardar?] ᶜAbd al-Ghiyas, and the proprietor of the fort, Hajji Sultan Muhammad, a man who owned a hundred houses, prepared food and tea.

As the latter had known me for a long time as a fellow clansman [the Muhammad Khwajah Hazarah clan] and had great regard for me, he asked, "What would you like for dinner—lamb or some chicken?" I was angry with Nur al-Din for having forced me to come to the Hazarahjat and so I answered, "Nur al-Din received ten thousand rupees from the government for travel expenses. Don't trouble yourself over me. When he comes, he will tell you what to prepare."

At sundown, Nur al-Din arrived and in an arrogant tone of voice ordered the residents of the fort to prepare dinner for a certain sum of money. When I tried to express my disapproval of his bad manners, he came up to me and chastised me saying that since I was only an employee of his, my position did not allow me to criticize. I replied, "You have not yet reached the kind of rank and position that allows you to insult me. If the Hazarahs hear about this, they will never show you any respect. They will refuse to recognize you as leader of the delegation and will never give you an oath of allegiance for the one to whom you willingly made a promise to go to the Hazarahjat and so put all Qizilbash under the threat of death. You will not succeed in getting anything done if you insult me."

A few moments later he regretted what he had said and came to see me in my tent to apologize, bringing other members of the delegation to intercede on his behalf. But in accordance with the Qur'anic verse, " . . . and when they pass by idle talk, they should pass by with dignity,"[210] I kissed him before he could open his mouth to apologize, and said, "For the sake of Islam and so that no harm befalls our mission, I harbor no feelings of enmity nor of hatred, so please don't worry." He was reassured and left.

June 11: Today, without consulting the other members of the delegation, Nur al-Din asked Col. Ghulam Nabi to go to the fort of his fellow clansmen and press them for an oath of allegiance. Ghulam Nabi was the son of Ghulam Riza and the grandson of Arbab Yusuf. He held the rank of colonel because his mother had been wet nurse to Sultan Jan Nur al-Siraj, the full sister of His Highness Aman Allah.[211] After the watercarrier's boy, Habib Allah, conquered Kabul, the colonel himself was out of work and so I invited him to join the delegation. I now took him aside and advised him that this was an opportunity to go and raise the Hazarahs against Habib Allah. By no means should he encourage them to tender an oath of allegiance and under no circumstances should he rejoin the delegation. But he should tell Nur al-Din just the opposite to reassure him.

Nur al-Din entrusted to Wali Muhammad, the son of Muhammad ᶜAzim Beg, several royal farmans. These contained promises of military appointments to Hazarahs up to the rank of lieutenant general and civil appointments as high as governor. The farmans also spoke of giving them certain land privileges and contained a vow that nomadic Pushtun tribes would not appear again in the Hazarahjat or in other places where even one Hazarah was found to be living. Wali Muhammad lives in the village of Seh Pay in Day Zangi. His father was killed by Amir ᶜAbd al-Rahman. He was supposed to distribute these farmans to the arbabs of the Day Zangi, Day Kundi, and Bihsud Hazarahs and was given two hundred rupees for doing so.

Nur al-Din handed several other decrees addressed to the elders of the Jaghuri and Malistan Hazarahs to nine schoolboys to take with them. These boys had been in hiding in Kabul, fearful that the northerners would force them to come to their lodgings and there molest them. They were now heading home with the delegation. Each had been given ten rupees for travel expenses. Nur al-Din also sent a personal message to Day Zangi and Day Kundi full of sayings of the Prophet and verses from the Qurᵓan.

At the time of the delegation's departure for the Hazarahjat from Sar-i Chashmah, I secretly instructed the boys to take all these documents to Fath Muhammad, the military high commissioner of the Hazarahs at the Unay Pass. These farmans ought to be put in the hands of Prince Muhammad Amin so that he can keep the amir's instructions from circulating in the Hazarahjat lest they mislead the Hazarahs and raise doubts about Nadir Khan. The boys followed my instructions.

June 12: Tonight Ghulam Habib Khan, the son of the Qizilbash Ghulam Hasan and a resident of Qalᶜah-yi Safid, returned to Qalᶜah-yi Pusht-i Mazar in Sar-i Chashmah [where the delegation was staying] with a letter from Col. Ghulam Nabi. Ghulam Habib, incidentally, was not on good terms with the Hazarahs of the Unay Pass whose lands bordered his fields and pastures. Ghulam Nabi had written, "I met some arbabs who are inclined to offer an oath of allegiance in order to end the hostilities. All this makes me confident of achieving our goals. From the Unay Pass,

I am setting off for the land of my clan to meet with my friends. I will persuade them all to submit to Amir Habib Allah." Nur al-Din was very pleased with the letter.

After convincing myself of the trustworthiness of two men—Ahmad ^{c}Ali of Sar-i Chashmah and Ghulam Husayn from Yakah Ulang (who along with Mir Faqir Bihsudi and Shah Mirza Husayn had led the fight in Bamyan against the army of Habib Allah)—I sent a message through them to Fath Muhammad, Mihrab ^{c}Ali, and other Hazarah leaders in Unay about Col. Ghulam Nabi's letter. I called on them to resist Habib Allah and refuse to give an oath of allegiance. I also promised to find out what I could of the situation in Kabul, about Nadir and Hashim and the tribes of the Southern and Eastern Provinces, and to pass on any information I might collect to Fath Muhammad via these two men who are able, with permission from one of the amir's colonels, Nizam al-Din, to travel back and forth to the Unay Pass under the cover of purchasing wheat, oil, and mutton. In the letter I wrote, "Once you get the information, begin preparing your forces and if possible move against Kabul. According to the leaders with whom I've met, if they're telling the truth, the residents of Kabul, Paghman, Begtut, and Maydan are all on the side of the Hazarahs."

June 13: Today Ghulam Habib returned and gave Nur al-Din the welcome news that last night he had gone to the Unay Pass and met there with the leader of the Hazarah tribal forces, Fath Muhammad. He said, "I negotiated an agreement with him that on Friday [the 14th] he would invite you and the other members of the delegation to come to my fort, Qal^{c}ah-i Safid, as his guests. He will be there with three or four elders of the tribe. Together you will discuss the questions of peace, a cessation of hostilities, submission, and an oath of allegiance. Based on what the two sides agree to, a resolution will be adopted to end the carnage."

It was not entirely clear from this whether Ghulam Habib was telling the truth. It seemed that it was his intent to arrange a meeting of the two sides, use cunning to achieve an outcome advantageous to himself, and persuade them to submit to Habib Allah. Afterwards, he and his brother ^{c}Ali Ahmad would receive high rank and status and a monetary reward from the amir. Having delivered the invitation for Friday to Nur al-Din and the members of the delegation, Ghulam Habib today returned home.

June 14: In response to the invitation from Ghulam Habib, Nur al-Din and the rest of the delegation set off today to join him at Qalᶜah-i Safid. There they dined while awaiting the arrival of the three or four Hazarah elders whom Ghulam Habib had mentioned. When they did not appear, Ghulam Habib sent one of his own horsemen to the Hazarahs who sent back the following message: "The elders left for home to celebrate the feast of the son of the 'Impetuous Lion' (*Ḥaydar-i Karrār*), and the nephew [sic] of the Prophet of God.[212] Without their consent we cannot negotiate, otherwise disputes might arise."

Before the arbabs left Unay Pass heading home, they vowed that each would choose one man of every four from among the braves under their authority and, on June 22, when the mourning for Imam Husayn was over, they would send them to the Unay Pass. Two thousand men would take up positions in the Unay Pass, another two thousand in Sar-i Chashmah, and a further two thousand would occupy the heights commanding Jalriz and Kut-i Ashru. After preparing their positions, they would wait for an order to attack Kabul. Then if the forces that are to carry out the initial assault on Kabul are weakened, the first rearguard unit of two thousand will attack Kabul while the second two-thousand-man unit will move into its position and the third force of two thousand will immediately move into the position of the second. Four thousand men will proceed to Paghman, Shakar Darrah, and the Quruq Mountains along the road between Sanglakh, Qalᶜah-i Kuh, and Paghman, while another four thousand would march there along the road linking the Safidkhak Pass, Maydan, and the Takht Pass. After the night prayer, under cover of darkness, they would begin the assault on the capital via Khayr Khanah Pass, Qarghah, Chihil Tan, Qalᶜah-i Ghazi, and Dar al-Aman and carry the attack up the Asmaᵓi, Shayr Darwazah, and Dukhtar-i Kafir heights. Were they to attack by day, they would suffer heavy losses from the concentrated fire coming from the Chardihi and Biyaban forts standing between the Khayr Khanah Pass and Chimtal and on the plain between Qarghah and Afshar, and so be unable to capture the heights. At night, however, gunfire presents no danger and they will be able to take the heights easily. After this, they can take the Arg, shoot down the supporters of Baçça-i Saqqaw, and cleanse the city of the northern contamination.

Primarily because of this agreement, the arbabs had decided not to attend the meeting at Qal^{c}ah-i Safid arranged by Ghulam Habib. In addition, they resolved that whatever happened, they would seize and execute Nur al-Din and Muhammad Zaman of Parwan and put the other members of the delegation under arrest.

June 15: Ghulam Habib left by himself today for the Unay Pass to meet the Hazarah leaders and to relay to them in a friendly way the concern of Nur al-Din and the members of the delegation that they had not shown up for the promised meeting. The Hazarahs replied, "We Hazarahs always conduct our mourning ceremonies through the 12th of Muharram, i.e. for three days after the murder of the 'Lord of Martyrs,' and although we are today under the gun ourselves, nonetheless we cannot ignore the sufferings of that son of the holy sayyid [^{c}Ali b. Abi Talib] and go about business as usual. We regret that Nur al-Din, who claims to hold high rank among Muslims and who puts his house in Kabul at the disposal of the padishah, ministers, and high-ranking officials as a husayniyah,[213] now pressures us and demands that we either express our obedience to the watercarrier's boy or he will summon an army from Kabul to force us to do so. His claim that he is a pious Muslim is an out-and-out lie and utter hypocrisy. He does not seem to know that the Muslims of the world, including those of India, put aside all other business on the 10th of Muharram and mourn in honor of the tormented imam, and spare nothing to do so. But Nur al-Din is quick to line his pockets and oppress us. Until the 12th of Muharram (June 20) we will not engage in any other business, nor are we worried about an attack by the army of Habib Allah."

Ghulam Habib found Nur al-Din in Sar-i Chashmah and delivered the Hazarahs' response. Beside himself with anger, Nur al-Din cursed them in the foulest language and ordered Ghulam Habib to take them a message in which he accused them of breaking their promise to attend the meeting. The Hazarahs, in accordance with my instructions which I had sent via Ghulam Husayn, responded to Nur al-Din through Ghulam Habib that they would never swear an oath of loyalty to Habib Allah until the situation in the Southern and Eastern Provinces and the circumstances of Ghulam Nabi in the region of Mazar-i Sharif had been resolved. Nur al-Din described the situation in a letter to the amir and sent it to Kabul on Sunday the 16th by courier.

June 17: Today Shaykh ^{c}Abd al-^{c}Ali, the son of Mulla Malik, who has settled with his family in Unay Pass and is living off the food handed out after the fasting of early Muharram and on alms from the Hazarahs, came to Sar-i Chashmah to meet with one of the members of the delegation, Mir Aqa, a specialist in Twelver Shi^{c}i law, and a man well-respected among both Hazarahs and Qizilbash. At Sar-i Chashmah, Shaykh ^{c}Abd al-^{c}Ali began to boast that he had a great deal of influence and authority among the Hazarahs. Mir Aqa confirmed this to Nur al-Din. Shaykh ^{c}Abd al-^{c}Ali suggested that they send him secretly to the commander of the Hazarah forces, Fath Muhammad. Nur al-Din, after hearing Mir Aqa's corroboration of his claim of influence, believed him and sent him to Fath Muhammad with a message that suggested that he name a time and place for a meeting and provide guarantees of safety for the leaders and members of the delegation. ^{c}Abd al-^{c}Ali departed with the letter as well as greetings for Fath Muhammad from Mir Aqa, whom Nur al-Din also believed was very influential among the Hazarahs. He promised to return the next day and report the outcome.

On the advice of the military high commissioner of the Hazarahjat, Prince Muhammad Amin, his deputy Khwajah Hidayat Allah, and Ghulam Husayn, Fath Muhammad designated a small village near the pass as the meeting place. There he planned to capture and murder Nur al-Din and Muhammad Zaman Parwani.

Nur al-Din was in an optimistic frame of mind at this point. When he fell asleep, he was at peace, confident that tomorrow would bring success. Nur al-Din was also pleased that those gifts which the Hazarahs had presented to Mir Aqa, he had been able to add to his own, and that ever since the first of Muharram, the funds allocated for travel expenses continued to fatten his own purse because the delegation was living off the hospitality of the people of Sar-i Chashmah. Still he carefully noted the daily expenses, of which in fact there were none, in his account book.

June 18 (the 10th of Muharram): Today is the day Muslims celebrate as the Day of Atonement. Nur al-Din has been waiting impatiently since sunrise for the return of Shaykh ^{c}Abd al-^{c}Ali, who should have been bringing back information about the time and place of the meeting with Fath Muhammad. But the shaykh did not appear. Finally, along with some of the members of the delegation—Mir Aqa, Mulla Ghulam Hasan, Mirza Qasim, and Muhammad Mahdi Afshar—Nur al-Din left for the husayniyah to participate in the ceremonies mourning the "Lord of Martyrs."

When Shaykh ᶜAbd al-ᶜAli, dressed in a long *chūkhā* with wide sleeves, finally came galloping up on his horse, I was sitting alone in my tent. Although he did not want to talk to me, I called out to him and invited him to join me. "Sit for a bit," I said, "Nur al-Din and Mir Aqa will return after finishing the *rawzah-khwānī*."[214]

I asked him about Fath Muhammad. But he wouldn't tell me anything. He sat for a while, waiting for Nur al-Din and Mir Aqa. As soon as they appeared, he jumped up and headed for their tent which stood on the same ridge of the mountain. He joined them and they entered the tent together. Muhammad Zaman [Parwani] was also one of the group. Out of my earshot and sight, Shaykh ᶜAbd al-ᶜAli relayed Fath Muhammad's message that the members of the delegation and Muhammad Zaman should come to the husayniyah in the village of Qul-i Ghulam Husayn to attend prayers in memory of the Lord of Martyrs and meet and negotiate a truce on the Day of Atonement (*ᶜĀshūrā*), i.e. today.

Nur al-Din selected Mir Aqa and me to go with him. Since I was in the dark about what was going on, I refused to go, using as an excuse the fact that it was the Day of Atonement. In reply I was told that the members of the delegation and Fath Muhammad were invited to celebrate together. So I had to go. I turned to Shaykh ᶜAbd al-ᶜAli and said, "In this chukha with its wide sleeves will you be able to provide the delegation with security and guarantees that Fath Muhammad and the others will not arrest its members?" He did not answer. Mir Aqa, who was his comrade-in-arms, was considered a *mujtahid*,[215] and was always collecting the *khums*,[216] answered for him, "Yes, I guarantee it." As a result of these casual words, I had no choice but to go.

Muhammad Zaman, however, had no intention of going. After ordering his horse saddled, Nur al-Din happily mounted and led the party off—Mir Aqa, two armed Wazirabadi horsemen, and me. An order was also given to Khalifah Ghulam Hasan to come along. He was officially a member of the delegation, but had not been selected for this excursion at first and was standing off to one side about to perform his ritual ablutions before praying. We then all left, accompanied by Shaykh ᶜAbd al-ᶜAli, who had conspired with Fath Muhammad and exposed to mortal danger the head of the delegation and three of its members.

Fayz Muhammad makes it clear that Fath Muhammad, local commander at the Unay Pass, and his men were unbending in their hostility to the mission and despite guarantees of safety, the Hazarahs at the pass took the party hostage. Fath Muhammad was particularly eager to lay hands on the Tajik from Parwan, Muhammad Zaman, who, however, had refused to leave Sar-i Chashmah, rightly believing his life to be in danger. When he did not show up at Qul-i Ghulam Husayn, the appointed meeting place in the Unay Pass, Fath Muhammad took his anger out on Nur al-Din.

So our group rode to Qul-i Ghulam Husayn, a Hazarah fort. After greeting Colonel Hashim, the customs officer of Bihsud, Mirza Zaman Shah, and other people there, we sat in the imambarah[217] which they had started to build in part of the mosque but hadn't yet finished. After a few minutes, Fath Muhammad showed up with an armed force of three hundred men, his tardiness explained by the fact that he was performing his prayers. Nur al-Din greeted him and then showed Fath Muhammad a farman from Habib Allah authorizing him to act on the amir's behalf.

We sat down for a meal of lamb stew in memory of the suffering of the imam and an entire recitation of his passion was performed. Then Khalifah Ghulam Hasan and I began the prayer in his memory. But Fath Muhammad, claiming he needed to consult Nur al-Din, led him outside and told him to send a message to Muhammad Zaman Parwani and the other members of the delegation to come as his guests. Nur al-Din, failing to grasp the situation he was really in and believing himself respected and influential among both Qizilbash and Hazarahs, was afraid that Fath Muhammad would arrest and murder Muhammad Zaman and so refused to comply.

Knowing full well that Nur al-Din had freely volunteered to obtain an oath of allegiance from the Hazarahs, Fath Muhammad was angered at his refusal and signaled for a bugle to be sounded. Pulling Nur al-Din from his horse, he disarmed him and while still mounted on his own horse drove him before him to the Unay Pass. To three other members of the delegation he said, "Get on your horses and follow me."

I had established a good rapport with Fath Muhammad. I had given him a full and accurate account of the situation, advised him regarding the strengthening of his positions and the readiness of his units, and convinced him not to tender an oath of allegiance. Now I approached him and quietly said, "If we go back, the amir will kill us. All the Qizilbash whom that opportunist Nur al-Din recruited for the delegation expect to die. Please take this into consideration and consult with the arbabs. But you must send me off as if I too am under arrest." Fath Muhammad complied and announced that the rest were all under arrest too and ordered them mounted on their horses and sent off.

A centurion (*ṣadbāshī*) from the Herat Troop, Colonel Gul Muhammad, had joined forces with the Hazarahs and was at Unay Pass, having been sent by Prince Muhammad Amin. When he learned from Colonel Ghulam Nabi that Nur al-Din had volunteered to obtain an oath of allegiance from the Hazarahs and had threatened the members of the delegation with arrest if they refused to go to the Hazarahjat, he was extremely angry and struck Nur al-Din so hard that he bloodied his cheek. One of the Hazarahs then took Nur al-Din's pistol and watch. Colonel Gul Muhammad unleashed a barrage of curses at Nur al-Din, "You wretched creature! Did the murdered Amir (Habib Allah the son of ᶜAbd al-Rahman) and His Highness Aman Allah show you so little kindness that you felt you had to toady to the watercarrier's boy for whose sake you are now prepared to sacrifice yourself? This, in order to undermine the strength of the community of Hazarahs who, being valiant and faithful to God, rose to support the Afghan [Pushtun] government and to drive out the 'boy' from Kalakan? You volunteered to obtain an oath of allegiance from this brave and courageous tribe in order to disgrace the feeble tribe of the Qizilbash and to drive it to the brink of death and destruction." Ashamed at his own behavior, Nur al-Din could only mutter repeatedly, "But the amir made me do it."

Then they took him and the three other members of the delegation to Fath Muhammad's tent. After tea, at sunset, the tax collector (*maʾmūr-i māliyah*) and today governor of Bihsud, Muhammad Ishaq, the son of Khalifah Ghulam Rasul Kabuli, arrived.[218] He brought Fath Muhammad an order from Prince Muhammad Amin to send Nur al-Din and his companions to the prince in Raqul. He also brought a supposed farman of Aman Allah's which proclaimed the latter's arrival in Qarabagh in Ghazni. This farman had been forged by Khwajah Hidayat Allah, the deputy of Prince Muhammad Amin, in order to bolster the spirits of the

Hazarahs in their struggle against Habib Allah. After the reading of this farman those present began to congratulate each other on the return of His Highness. At that moment, Col. Gul Muhammad turned to Nur al-Din and said, "If you are telling the truth that the watercarrier's boy forced you to try to get an oath of allegiance from the Hazarahs and you are really a sincere supporter of the Afghan government, then what kind of present did you bring the prince?"

Nur al-Din replied, "A pistol and a watch. But you took them away. Anyway, we were invited here and so did not have to bring gifts."

The colonel responded, "Muhammad Zaman Kuhistani Parwani whom you should have brought with you was your gift. Since you didn't bring him the first time, write him now so that he will come from Sar-i Chashmah to Unay Pass with the rest of the delegation." But Nur al-Din refused. I warned Fath Muhammad that if this order were carried out and they killed Muhammad Zaman as they had killed ᶜAbd al-Rahman, the son of Dad Muhammad Kuhistani, then all the Qizilbash in the delegation would be put to death and their property seized.

However, he paid no attention to what I said. To force Nur al-Din to write the letter in his own hand, they grabbed him so hard around the throat that his breathing was cut off and you could hear his vertebrae cracking. Licking his lips, he begged and pleaded for mercy. But the colonel was implacable. Mir Aqa removed his turban and also began to plead for mercy for him. The Hazarahs then interceded and so kept Colonel Gul Muhammad from doing Nur al-Din any real harm.

At this point, still the 18th, three members of the delegation, Fayz Muhammad, Nur al-Din, and Mir Aqa were sent off under guard to Prince Muhammad Amin, but they never reached his residence at Raqul. They spent the night of the 18th in very uncomfortable circumstances in a mosque at Qalᶜah-i Yurt and on the 19th continued on toward Raqul. En route, the party was intercepted by another group of Hazarahs under a local official, a dafᶜahdār *named Sayyid Jaᶜfar, who rescued them and took them to his own fort at Khak-i Agha. Here the fame of Mir Aqa was a major factor in their rescue.*

The complexities of politics in the Hazarahjat can be only dimly made out here. Fayz Muhammad is not particularly helpful about explaining the various factions that were encountered—perhaps he was uncertain about them himself—but it can be inferred from his account that Sardar Muhammad Amin, Aman Allah's representative, was still a significant factor. His position had probably been stronger before Aman Allah unceremoniously fled the country. Certainly by this time there was no longer widespread backing for Muhammad Amin, or at least many of the Hazarahs were now uncommitted and may have been interested in hearing what the delegation had to offer. Fayz Muhammad, whose position is clear and consistently anti-government, cannot be relied on to help us sort out all the factors that impelled any particular Hazarah village or region toward or away from giving the oath of allegiance to the government of the Tajiks.

Sayyid Ja^cfar, who extended protection to the delegation at Khak-i Agha, though locally powerful, was clearly subject to larger forces, for on the 20th he surrendered the three members of the delegation under his protection to a man whom Fayz Muhammad believed had already offered his support to Habib Allah, a certain revenue official (taḥṣīldār[219]*) named Riza Bakhsh. In the meantime it appears that the other members of the delegation had either stayed in Sar-i Chashmah or were released to return there by Fath Muhammad, for later Fayz Muhammad, Nur al-Din, and Mir Aqa would rejoin them there.*

Tonight, Nur al-Din, Mir Aqa, Ghulam Hasan, and I were sent off on horseback to Prince Muhammad Amin in Raqul. The two armed Wazirabadi horsemen, their heads bared, were also sent. All of us were being guarded by Col. Hashim, Mirza Zaman Shah, and seven armed Hazarahs. When we stopped for the night near Qal^cah-i Yurt, a Qizilbash official (*^carż-begī*—court usher) named Ahmad ^cAli arrived. At the request of Mir Aqa and me, they put us up in a mosque that was swarming with fleas and reminded us all of a jail.

The grandson of the ^carz-begi, a considerate lad, brought us bread and soft-boiled eggs after the *namāz*-prayer. It was impossible to sleep because of the plague of fleas, whose bites were very painful. I sat on the bed and scratched myself with both hands. Besides the bites, I had a fever and my body ached all over. Colonel Hashim, who was also spending the night in the mosque, called out to the Hazarah guards assigned to the prisoners and posted at the door and on the roof of the mosque. One of the guards replied, "I'm not asleep." I then asked Hashim, "Now that you've decided to take the leader of the delegation prisoner, do you know the situation of Nadir in the Southern Province and that of the Hazarah settlers in Turkistan? Do you have contact with them and are your reserves of war matériel sufficient to defend yourself against attack from the amir? If you don't have reserves, then arresting the members of the delegation is foolhardy. When Habib Allah finds out, he will kill you and the Hazarahs won't be any better off." But he didn't reply and his silence worried me. So I said, "I was wrong to say that. But be that as it may, another month or two enduring the humiliation and insults of Habib Allah will be required to clarify the real situation of Nadir and Hashim in the Southern and Eastern Provinces and then to act in conformity with the regulations of the holy lawgiver." Again Hashim gave no reply.

June 19: After morning prayers and tea brought today by Ahmad ᶜAli, the ᶜarz-begi, those arrested were sent off. [Ahmad ᶜAli was subsequently killed by the Hazarahs who claimed his land.] At about 11 a.m. we stopped for lunch at the fort of the Qizilbash Mirza Ghulam Nabi, who had been appointed tax collector of Bihsud.[220] Nur al-Din, although he knew that he had been condemned to death, still hoped for mercy or rescue. Mirza Ghulam Nabi prepared a meal for us. When we sat down to eat with him and with a sad-bashi and three or four soldiers, Mirza Zaman Shah arrived. He had overtaken us along the way and said he needed soldiers from the Herat Troop, which was stationed at the caravanserai in Jawqul. When he entered the house he began to insult us. Ghulam Nabi brought bread, buttermilk (*dūgh*), butter, and fried eggs. We ate without much appetite, distressed by the fact that we had not been able to send anyone to Shah Muhammad Husayn, our intermediary with the Hazarahs of Bihsud, to intercede for Nur al-Din. In despair, we set off again and at 3 p.m. approached a fort situated near the caravanserai at Bad Asya. We knocked at the gate, intending to make a stop to smoke a pipe and drink some water. An elderly grey-haired woman brought water and asked Mir Aqa, who was squatting by the road, "Which one of you is Mir Aqa?" "I am," he replied. The woman then burst into tears and began to kiss his hands and feet. "When we learned of your arrest on ᶜAshura, the people blocked all the roads to Raqul so that they would not be able to deliver you to the Sardar (Muhammad Amin) and Nur al-Din would not be killed."

Other women and children then ran up. They kissed Mir Aqa's hands and the hem of his garment, swore oaths on the heads of their children, and wished him long life. The first woman then informed him that an officer (*daf^{c}ahdār*), Sayyid Ja^{c}far, had sent someone to warn the prisoners not to go right away to Raqul but to stop at his fort in Khak-i Agha for awhile. With Sayyid Ja^{c}far's warning in mind, we set off again. Near the caravanserai we saw several soldiers with two field pieces. They had come here after their defeat in Bamyan at the hands of Habib Allah. At Bamyan the Hazarahs under Mir Faqir (a thousand men from the village of Dawlat Pay in Bihsud), Sayyid Shah Mirza Husayn with his people from Yakah Ulang, and the Hazarahs of Bamyan itself had surrounded Habib Allah's troops. But Mir Faqir then went home to celebrate ^{c}Ashura and Shah Mirza Husayn, having received twelve thousand rupees from an officer of the surrounded force, gave an oath of allegiance to the government of Habib Allah and returned to Yakah Ulang. This was the cause of the defeat.

Not far from Khak-i Agha, a horseman appeared on the road ahead. As he approached we could see it was the daf^{c}ahdar, Sayyid Ja^{c}far, and he was looking for us. He jumped down from his horse and greeted us warmly. After examining Mir Aqa and me, he began berating our guard, Colonel Hashim, in the harshest language, rudely ordering him to dismount and then said, "You're a treacherous enemy of the faith, just like that damned Ibn Sa^{c}d.[221] You are guarding a sayyid and a mulla whom Habib Allah forcibly sent to get an oath of allegiance from the Hazarahs. These men are like the prisoners of Karbala[222] taken into custody by that 'Shimr,'[223] Fath Muhammad, on the Day of Atonement and sent to Sardar Muhammad Amin. But he is already well informed about them and knows that they are opponents of Habib Allah and will not serve that scoundrel. So why are you driving them under guard like prisoners, along with Nur al-Din?" Hashim and Zaman Shah, seeing a large number of armed men standing in front of Sayyid Ja^{c}far's fort, were afraid that they would be killed. They began to cringe and in voices shaking with fear babbled, "We have treated them with respect and brought them here with honor."

Meanwhile, although we had endured all manner of hardship, we thought it right to end the confrontation and save Colonel Hashim and

Mirza Zaman Shah from death and so turned to Sayyid Ja^{c}far and said, "They really treated us well and showed us all due respect."

When he heard this, Sayyid Ja^{c}far stopped abusing the two men. Then everyone mounted up and rode to Sayyid Ja^{c}far's house. Near his fort, we were met by five hundred Hazarahs who had gathered to prevent our being taken to Raqul to Prince Muhammad Amin. At the sight of Colonel Hashim and Zaman Shah (whom they recognized as our guards), they surged forward and shouts went up. Some, weapons cocked, wanted to shoot the two. But Mir Aqa, Khalifah Ghulam Hasan, and I, taking our turbans off, rose to their defense and saved them from being killed.

After everyone had had his say, we were accommodated in Sayyid Ja^{c}far's guest house, which was furnished with carpets. Altogether some two hundred people crowded into it. We were still worried that Sayyid Ja^{c}far's people might kill Colonel Hashim, Zaman Shah, and the seven sepoys under their command, so we took them to one of the rooms in the inner sanctum of Sayyid Ja^{c}far's home and locked them in. The Hazarahs did not disperse until sunset when they rode off to spend the night in the nearby villages.

Although I was ill and had eaten nothing, nonetheless, after performing my prayers I passed this night in peace and in gratitude for the integrity and loyalty of the Hazarahs.

June 20: After tea today, those who had spent the night at different Hazarah forts returned in groups. All told, about one thousand men had now gathered. Sayyid Ja^{c}far, Shah Haydar, Shah Muhammad Husayn, and other ulama sent a messenger to Prince Muhammad Amin. In their letter, they said that they would not allow the prisoners to be sent to Raqul until all arbabs had been assembled and those arrested were given guarantees of personal safety. After the messenger went off, the Hazarahs began to prepare dinner. They were worried, however, that the prince would send the Herat Troop with cannons and take Nur al-Din off to Raqul by force to the fate that awaited him there. Moreover, they had received a message from the tahsildar Riza Bakhsh[224] in which he demanded that they not leave the prisoners with Sayyid Ja^{c}far but send them to him under guard to prevent, God forbid, any misunderstanding from arising. So it was that without having had time to eat, we were delivered to the tahsildar in Jilgah-i Kajab at 3 p.m. escorted by a guard of five hundred armed infantry and horse. We dismounted onto a large raised platform, twenty by ten *gaz* [about sixty by thirty feet], surrounded on four sides by tall plane trees and covered with large colorful carpets. Braziers stood at the four corners. Bread, tea, halvah, meat, fried eggs, and bowls of buttermilk were served. We and our five hundred guards ate and drank until we were full. Then the horsemen were dismissed, having been given notice that tomorrow they were to accompany us to the assembly in order that there would be some protection for us should the prince try to kill Nur al-Din.

The infantrymen who had been appointed to guard Nur al-Din stayed behind, a small number of them scattering to nearby forts.

From Riza Bakhsh's behavior I sense that he is a partisan of Habib Allah. Sayyid Ja^{c}far warned me about this. "I hope he doesn't deceive you or force you into getting an oath of allegiance from the people." I replied, "It won't do him any good if he tries."

In order that no one should harm Nur al-Din, Riza Bakhsh took him to spend the night in a special tower in the inner part of the fort, the same place where he had given sanctuary to Nazar Muhammad, the son of Mahmud Taymani. Some time before, Nazar Muhammad, en route to Dakka,[225] had lost sixteen thousand rupees, for which he spent a long time in prison. When Habib Allah seized the throne, he released him and appointed him a governor in Bihsud. But Riza Bakhsh, worried that Prince Muhammad Amin would kill Nazar Muhammad, gave him sanctuary. [Later] Riza Bakhsh sent Habib Allah an oath of loyalty through him and prevented a popular rising against the amir.

The three of them [Riza Bakhsh, Nazar Muhammad, and Nur al-Din] now had a talk and it's my understanding that they want me to persuade people, using proof-texts from the Koran, to submit to Habib Allah. But they haven't taken into account the fact that I have a conscience and cannot act in this way.

Fayz Muhammad provides a very vague rationale for Sayyid Ja^{c}far's turning them over on June 20. He says that Riza Bakhsh demanded they be turned over to him "lest misunderstandings arise" and Sayyid Ja^{c}far immediately complied. What those misunderstandings might have been he does not even hint at. Fayz Muhammad still paints Sayyid Ja^{c}far in favorable colors, that is, as a staunch enemy of the Kabul regime. But his first *rescuing the delegation from the escort taking them to Muhammad Amin but then turning them over to Riza Bakhsh, someone our author strongly felt was a supporter, if a clandestine one, of the Kabul regime, suggests the opacity and fluidity of the political situation.*

By now the delegation was too caught up in internal Hazarah politics and any hope of a general pledge of support for the Habib Allah regime must have seemed very faint. Indeed, for some of the members, notably its leader, Nur al-Din Jawanshir, the hope of a successful outcome that would satisfy the Tajik amir was overtaken by the thought that they would be lucky to escape the Hazarahjat with their lives. They spent the night of the 20th at Jilgah-i Kajab, the residence of Riza Bakhsh. On the 21st, Khwajah Hidayat Allah, Sardar Muhammad Amin's personal representative, arrived and after a secret discussion with Fayz Muhammad, or so he presents it, the latter drafted a set of terms on behalf of the Hazarahs that he believed would satisfy the amir's demand for an oath of allegiance without actually giving him one.

June 21: Today a number of infantry and horsemen arrived after breakfast. They reported that some arbabs had come to Muhammad Amin in Raqul and he had spoken to each of them individually about those of us who were detained. No one knows what they agreed to. Hearing this, Nur al-Din feared that the arbabs had decided to hand him over to the prince who would hang him. Frightened out of his wits, he began babbling senselessly. Riza Bakhsh turned toward him and said, "Khan-sahib! Everything is fine, there's nothing to worry about." He then placed a cushion on his seat and said, "When sitting down, you should be higher than others, but don't say anything that might spoil things. Let Fayz Muhammad speak." After these words of Riza Bakhsh, I realized that either Nur al-Din had disobeyed the instructions given to him at night in the tower, or he wanted to provoke me to speak out. But I said nothing.

At this point Muhammad Amin's deputy, Khwajah Hidayat Allah, came in accompanied by two or three sayyids and arbabs. According to his instructions from the prince, Hidayat Allah expressed pleasure and satisfaction with Mir Aqa, Khalifah Ghulam Hasan, and me. He particularly complimented me on the fact that, according to Colonel Ghulam Nabi and others, I had not yielded to the blandishments of Habib Allah but, in the presence of witnesses and the amir himself, I had recited several verses from the Koran and accused the amir and his supporters of being unbelievers and so was forcibly sent to the Hazarahjat. Hidayat Allah said, "The sardar is very pleased with you; you never forgot the regard shown you by his father, the late Amir, and by his brother, His Highness Aman Allah. You refused to serve Habib Allah Kalakani and you gave encouragement to the Pushtuns in Kabul when you addressed them saying, 'What happened to your devotion to the religion, your valor, your Afghan honor about which so much used to be said in bygone times? You have submitted to a thief, a drinker of blood, and a lecher. You are cutting off the very limb on which you sit and betraying your own government and people, undermining the faith and unity, and are setting foot on the path of murder and looting.'"

This was all in a letter from Muhammad Amin that was addressed to me. Hidayat Allah wanted to present me with this letter, which in the future might serve to confirm the efforts we had made. But Mir Aqa and I demurred saying, "It will make no difference. If Habib Allah learns about this letter he will kill us."

So Hidayat Allah then read to us another letter signed by the prince and addressed to the sayyids, arbabs, and Hazarah units that showed their support for Nur al-Din by not allowing him to be taken to Raqul and certain death. From it he read, "You showed sincerity, steadfastness, and honor in support of the Afghan government and you not only refused to express obedience to Habib Allah but you encouraged confidence among the Pushtuns and helped unify their tribes. You may excuse Habib Allah and the tribes may forgive him. But what about his partisans like Nur al-Din? This man ought to leave here. You should not let him stay one more day with you or it will be taken as a provocation."

Hidayat Allah handed the sardar's letter to the Hazarahs. Then he took me and Sayyid Muhammad Akbar aside and said, "I want a word with the two of you in private." Sayyid Muhammad Akbar, a Hazarah and descendant of the Prophet, is distinguished by a noble character and penetrating mind. We moved away from the gathering and sat down under a tree on the bank of a canal. Hidayat Allah tried to guess the intentions of Riza Bakhsh, who, unbeknownst to Prince Muhammad Amin, had sent an oath of allegiance to Habib Allah and, in spite of the wishes of all the tribes including his own, expressed his loyalty. Hidayat Allah said to me,

"When you return to Sar-i Chashmah, you will have to endure a great deal at the hands of Habib Allah for failing to obtain an oath of allegiance." He said this so that if Riza Bakhsh should lead the discussion around to the subject of an oath of allegiance, then we should give him to understand that it was fully our intention to get it. I raised no objections. Hidayat Allah reflected, "We must think this through so that your actions do not bring you any harm." So Hidayat Allah, Sayyid Muhammad Akbar, and I fell to thinking about the problem but could not come up with a way that would guarantee security for the members of the delegation and Nur al-Din.

Then I asked for some paper and wrote a message that the Hazarah elders could send to the leader and members of the delegation. It said, "The leader and members of the delegation have familiarized us with the decrees and plenary powers entrusted to them. Since the leaders and elders of the Hazarahs have scattered to their homes because of the Feast of Atonement, and since the territory of Bihsud is vast, it will be a few days before they return. On their return, they will set forth their conditions and send them with the delegation, which should then deliver them to Kabul for the amir's approval. This same delegation should then convey back to us those conditions that have been accepted. If our interests are sufficiently taken into account, naturally, we will give an oath of allegiance."

I then made a clean copy of this message, disguising my handwriting, and tore up the draft. I told Hidayat Allah, "If the arbabs, sayyids, and ulema sign this statement and send it to the amir, that will be good on two counts. First, the correspondence will drag on for at least a couple of months, there will be a ceasefire while it does, and the situations of Nadir in the Southern Province, Hashim in the Eastern, and the Hazarah settlers in Mazar-i Sharif will become clearer. Then the appropriate steps can be taken and Habib Allah will be crushed. Secondly, once he receives this message, Habib Allah will have some hope that the Hazarahs will eventually give an oath of allegiance and therefore will not punish the members of the delegation."

Khwajah Hidayat Allah and Sayyid Muhammad Akbar approved my solution and agreed that after the elders sign it, they will give it back to me to take to Kabul. I then called Mir Aqa out of the majlis so that no one would accuse me of talking with these other two alone and inform Habib Allah that I had. Under my breath, I told Sayyid Muhammad Akbar that I would be happy to draft the conditions on which the Hazarahs would give an oath of allegiance. Then the four of us returned to the majlis and Khwajah Hidayat Allah left to rejoin Muhammad Amin.

When we were still at Sar-i Chashmah, Nur al-Din had written Mulla Muhammad Zaman, who he thought was very influential, to help persuade the Hazarahs to give an oath of allegiance. Muhammad Zaman now arrived from Qal^cah-i Nakhshi, about a day's ride away. Under instructions from Riza Bakhsh and Mir Aqa, Muhammad Zaman threatened the Hazarahs that if they did not give the oath of allegiance they would be killed and their belongings plundered. The Hazarahs, hearing what these mullas had to say, were confused and frightened. On the pretext of answering a call of nature, I walked out of the majlis and advised those Hazarahs who had also gone out of the majlis not to give an oath of allegiance nor to stop fighting Habib Allah. I encouraged them to continue the struggle in the name of the Shari^cah.

Vis-à-vis my promise to Hidayat Allah and Sayyid Muhammad Akbar to set out the conditions under which the Hazarahs would express allegiance to Habib Allah, I crafted the following terms. First, since an oath of allegiance is, according to the Shari^cah, an expression of free will, therefore one cannot obtain such an oath by force. Second, because the throne was taken away from the Pushtuns and they are fighting to get it back, the Hazarahs will not give the oath of allegiance until all the Pushtuns have submitted. Third, the taxes for this year are not to be reimposed since they were already collected by Muhammad Amin, Amir Aman Allah's appointee. Fourth, since the Pushtun nomads are wont to kill and rob Hazarahs, the government cannot confiscate the weapons of the latter which they have purchased to defend their property, crops, and families. Fifth, after these terms are acknowledged and an oath of allegiance given, the Hazarahs would not take part in any fighting against the Pushtuns. Not only have God and His Prophet forbidden the shedding of the blood of Muslims, they have damned those who do and promised to send them to Hell for eternity. Sixth, to avoid offending Hazarah honor, the government should withdraw its garrison from the Hazarahjat and not send troops into this territory in future. Seventh, a guarantee of safe passage should be given to Muhammad Amin, his deputy, and his retainers. If he agrees and comes to Kabul, then the government is obligated to pay him a salary equivalent to what is suitable for a prince. Eighth, if he does not accept the terms and return to Kabul, then we will escort him across the borders of Afghanistan to either Russia or Iran. The government should accept the responsibility of providing a guarantee that governors and police officers will not interfere when he crosses through their territory lest future generations of Hazarahs bear the shame that their forebears denied him assistance. Ninth, there is to be no punishment and no censure for the Hazarah tribes that previously refused to express allegiance and give an oath of loyalty but rose up only to defend themselves.

I handed these terms to Sayyid Muhammad Akbar, tore my draft up into little pieces and disposed of them in the canal.

On the 22nd, the group headed back to Sar-i Chashmah, stopping for the night at Tizak, escorted partway by Riza Bakhsh. At Sar-i Chashmah, which they reached on the 23rd, they found that Muhammad Zaman Parwani had gone to Takana, a Tajik village, where he obviously felt safer. It was clear by now that there was virtually no chance that the delegation would obtain a meaningful pledge from any of the various Hazarah factions. On the 25th some of the members headed back for Kabul, spending that night in Jalriz. The rest, including Nur al-Din and Fayz Muhammad, remained at Qal^{c}ah-i Pusht-i Mazar near Sar-i Chashmah on the slender hope that some kind of pledge would be forthcoming from the Hazarahs.

June 22: Tonight [that is, the night of June 21], the tahsildar, Riza Bakhsh, again escorted Nur al-Din to his accommodations in the tower. There the two of them plotted with Nazar Muhammad. After the sun rose, the three of them had their breakfast outside the walls of the fort. During breakfast, Riza Bakhsh, who was sitting with me, whispered in my ear, "Let me know as soon as Habib Allah's army comes to Sar-i Chashmah, so that we can immediately send a general oath of allegiance." When I heard this, I thought that Nur al-Din, Nazar Muhammad, and he had agreed that if, after the arrival of the delegation back in Sar-i Chashmah, the Hazarahs do not send terms like the ones set forth in my letter, then the delegation would summon military units from Kabul to Sar-i Chashmah which would force the Hazarahs into sending an oath of allegiance to Kabul. After breakfast I discussed my supposition with Sayyid

Muhammad Akbar and advised him that the Hazarahs should not give an oath of loyalty nor submit to any tricks of Riza Bakhsh that would disgrace them.

Soon some three hundred infantry and cavalry, which yesterday Riza Bakhsh had assigned to escort the delegation, arrived. We left Riza Bakhsh's house and headed back to Sar-i Chashmah, stopping for lunch at the mosque of the Garmabi Sayyids. Its imam and caretaker was a Hazarah, Ghulam Rasul. Lunch began after Mir Aqa and Khalifah Ghulam Hasan led the noon prayer. During the meal, I reminded Sayyid Muhammad Akbar, who was sitting next to me, of my earlier admonitions. After lunch, we continued on our way and reached the village of Tizak in Day Mirdad in the afternoon and stopped at a public imambarah.

June 23: We spent the night as guests of the people of Tizak. An encounter on the road today with two horsemen from the Wardak tribe brought much joy to me and other members of the delegation. The riders were on their way to Prince Muhammad Amin to tell him of Nadir's successes in the Southern Province. But Nur al-Din, Riza Bakhsh, and Nazar Muhammad, who were traveling with us, immediately downplayed this information, declaring that the Wardaks were spreading false rumors and propaganda in order to provoke the Hazarahs into a war with Habib Allah.

Yesterday a courier had arrived from Malik Hazrat Muhammad Ahmadzai, a nomad and a landowner in Takana. I had heard enough evidence from the messenger about Nadir's doings to be able to refute what those three men were saying. The messenger also brought news to Nur al-Din of the move of the rest of the members of the delegation from Sar-i Chashmah to Takana. Nur al-Din gave him twenty rupees and a turban and sent him back to the other members of the delegation with the message that he was on his way from (Jilgah-i) Kajab to Sar-i Chashmah.

After breakfast we set off for Sar-i Chashmah. People on the road warned us that Hazarahs who occupied the Unay Pass were bent on killing Nur al-Din, Nazar Muhammad, and Riza Bakhsh because they were allies of Habib Allah. Nur al-Din and Nazar Muhammad were deeply worried and wanted the party to change direction at the Khirs Khanah Pass, take the road to Qal^{c}ah-i Nakhshi, cross the pass at Narkh in two days time, arrive in Maydan, and from there continue on to Sar-i Chashmah. I was not happy with their decision and galloped off with the

Hazarahs who were escorting us. Other members of the delegation who had been trying to give Riza Bakhsh some encouragement came with me. At the summit of the Khirs Khanah pass, we dismounted and said our farewells to Riza Bakhsh and the three-hundred-man escort. Nur al-Din, who was afraid of being captured, pleaded with the Hazarahs to take him as far as the positions occupied by Habib Allah's units, which included people from Maydan, Kuhnah Khumar, Jalriz, Takana, and Sar-i Chashmah. But I objected, saying, "God forbid. This would surely lead to fighting. The Hazarahs should not ride down from the pass with us." Then I turned to Riza Bakhsh and said, "You should act as Sayyid Muhammad Akbar was ordered to do. God forbid that you should act in any other way."

Parting ways, we set off and reached Sar-i Chashmah without incident. Nur al-Din wanted to head straight for Takana to rejoin the members of the delegation who had stayed behind and then gone there, fearing a Hazarah attack. I did not agree. "I'll never go there, otherwise we would be disgracing the honor of the people of Sar-i Chashmah. Word will get out that the people of Sar-i Chashmah are partisans of the Hazarahs and that is why the leader and members of the delegation went to Takana."

At this time, a rider joined us from Takana. He was the one who had carried the message to the members of the delegation that they should return to Sar-i Chashmah. He also brought a letter from Muhammad Zaman Parwani, whom the people of Takana and Jalriz had bullied into leaving Sar-i Chashmah for Takana so that they could accuse the people of Sar-i Chashmah of supporting the Hazarahs, thereby dooming them to attack by Habib Allah's forces. What they had told him was, "Tonight, the people of Sar-i Chashmah will bind you hand and foot, hand you over to the Hazarahs and then, in the confusion, will shoot you and say that the Hazarahs attacked and kidnapped you. They will carry you away and kill you as they did [c]Abd al-Rahman Kuhdamani."

Muhammad Zaman's message said, "I won't come back to Sar-i Chashmah. The rest may decide for themselves whether to go or not."

I said I wouldn't go to Takana because the people of that region and also Jalriz are religious fanatics and are a danger to Sar-i Chashmah. Muhammad Zaman did not come today from Takana but the remaining members of the delegation came at night and explained why they had gone to Takana. "When we received the letter from the Hazarahs saying that Nur al-Din and other the members of the delegation had gone as guests to Farakh-i ᶜUlum [Farakhlum] and had asked the writers of the letter to tell us to leave Sar-i Chashmah, we understood this to mean that they had arrested you. So if we were to remain here, we thought they might attack us at night and arrest us. Hence we decided to go to Takana. But the people of Sar-i Chashmah pleaded with us not to leave, assuring us that each of us was perfectly safe amd no one would cause us the slightest harm. We believed them and refused to go to Takana. However, the people of Takana, having intimidated Muhammad Zaman, began to abuse the people of Sar-i Chashmah and we were unable to stay here. Muhammad Zaman will come tomorrow."

June 24: At the time of the evening prayer, I handed Nur al-Din the Hazarahs' letter in which their terms for an oath of allegiance were set out. In a separate letter to Habib Allah, Nur al-Din described his detention and accused Fath Muhammad of being responsible. But I kept him from signing the letter, saying, "Look, the Hazarahs only wrote in their letter that a colonel and his sepoys had arrested the leader and members of this delegation. If you implicate Fath Muhammad in this, then Habib Allah will try to take revenge on him and the Hazarahs, feeling threatened, will begin to revolt." So together we altered the text of his letter and sent it to Kabul to the godless one, the king of the thieves.

Muhammad Zaman Parwani also now returned from Takana. He was relieved when he heard what the people of Sar-i Chashmah and I had to say and asked me to tell Nur al-Din that his legs were bothering him and that he wanted permission to go back to Kabul. I promised to help him, passed his request on to Nur al-Din, and got permission for him to return to the city.

At this time Malik Hazrat Muhammad Ahmadzai, Sayyid ᶜAbd al-Qasim, and Sayyid Zayn al-ᶜAbidin arrived. Zayn al-ᶜAbidin had received the title "brigadier of the army and the country" (*birgid-i lashkari wa kishwari*) from Governor-general Malik Muhsin for having promised, as mentioned earlier, to get the Hazarahs to give an oath of allegiance. They had come to find out about the situation of Nur al-Din and how things had turned out with the Hazarahs, specifically whether the Hazarahs were going to give an oath of allegiance or not.

When they learned that the Hazarahs had promised to give an oath of allegiance but only after their terms are accepted, these men were pleased. Taking me aside, Malik Hazrat Muhammad said, "May God grant that the negotiations drag on for a long time, or at least until the situation of Nadir and Hashim, the question of the alliance of the Pushtun tribes of the Eastern and Southern Provinces, the activities of the Hazarah settlers of Turkistan and Darrah-i Suf[226] and also the outcome of the struggle in Bamyan between Mir Faqir and the forces of Habib Allah under Brigadier-General ᶜAbd al-Rashid are all clarified. By that time, with the help of the Almighty, Habib Allah will have been defeated, Nadir with his brothers and the valiant Pushtun will have taken Kabul, and it will not be necessary for the Hazarahs to give an oath of allegiance." Malik Hazrat Muhammad questioned me at length about military activities in Bamyan and about the encirclement there of the forces of Habib Allah. I told him that at the request of Nur al-Din the Hazarahs had sent a letter to Mir Faqir (who, though defeated once, had again gone to Bamyan and renewed military operations there) to end the fighting and hold his positions until it became clear whether they were going to recognize Habib Allah or not. After this, Malik Hazrat Muhammad gave a Pushtun twenty-five rupees and sent him to the Southern Province to find out what the situation there was. He promised to pass any information that he received on to me so that I, in turn, could bring it to the attention of the Hazarahs.

June 25: Muhammad Zaman, Nur al-Din, and Nazar Muhammad spent the night [of the 24th] inside the fort of Qalᶜah-i Pusht-i Mazar in Sar-i Chashmah worried about a possible Hazarah attack. They had decided that only an overwhelming military presence would compel the Hazarahs to obedience. Otherwise, hoping that Nadir would arrive in Kabul, the Hazarahs would just put off any oathtaking on various pretexts. So, the three men concluded it was essential to send a powerful force from Kabul to Sar-i Chashmah that would terrify the Hazarahs and force them to give an oath of allegiance immediately. Apparently Riza Bakhsh, who had earlier secretly given an oath of allegiance, urged Muhammad Zaman and Nazar Muhammad to press for such a policy. Probably Riza Bakhsh had this in mind when he had said to me, "As soon as the army comes from Kabul to Sar-i Chashmah, tell me so that I can send an oath of allegiance right away, without waiting for the acceptance of the terms set by the Hazarahs."

Muhammad Zaman and Nazar Muhammad left Sar-i Chashmah for Kabul and spent the first night [the 25th] in Jalriz. There they listened to inflammatory statements from a resident of Kuhnah Khumar, a Tajik named Muhammad Aman, who was district chief, and also from local Tajiks who were inciting riot, bloodshed, and plundering in Maydan and Sar-i Chashmah against the Hazarahs.

Also today Malik Hazrat Muhammad received information through his courier about the situation in the Southern Province and told me of the treasonous activities of Mulla Shah Nazar and other pseudo-mullas who, using malicious propaganda, are causing the Sulayman Khayl, Ahmadzai, Matun, Sabri, Muqbil, Jaji, Jadran, and Mangal tribes to forget their Afghan honor and are keeping these tribes from joining forces and fighting alongside Nadir. He is now isolated while Habib Allah, through proclamations and informants, is promising large monetary rewards to the pseudo-mullas and tribal elders. By bribing and suborning the Pushtun tribes he has shattered their alliance with Nadir and is winning them to his side. The son of Khwajah Jan, Major-General Ghulam Siddiq, is trying with all his might to hinder Nadir. God knows how all this will end up.

I was quite upset when I received this information from Malik Hazrat Muhammad. I can only put my trust in the help and will of the Creator.

June 26: Muhammad Zaman and Nazar Muhammad traveled from Jalriz to Kabul today. I had asked Muhammad Zaman to deliver to my family some money which I had collected from someone to whom I had made a loan and he did so. He still believed that I was sincere in my service to Habib Allah because I had managed to obtain a letter from the Hazarahs in which they promised to provide an oath of allegiance and express their obedience. He was not aware that I had in fact prevented Habib Allah from realizing his plans in the Hazarahjat and had actually kept the Hazarahs from giving an oath of allegiance.

Today, with flags flying, drums beating, and shouts of "O Four Friends" (ya chahar yar), some two hundred Wardak men marched against Prince Muhammad Amin in aid of the Hazarahs. They took the road to Raqul through Tizak and Kajab. This was distressing to the supporters of Habib Allah and heartened the Hazarahs and all true Muslims.

This evening a Pushtun from the village of Zaymani in Maydan arrived, as did a rider sent by the sayyids of Takana who had been calling for an alliance of Pushtuns and Hazarahs against Habib Allah. These two men, who had been keeping the Hazarahs informed of the course of military activities, arrived at the Unay Pass under the cover of buying wheat. They each brought letters from Nadir Khan. Despite the fact that Nur al-Din, Mir Aqa, Khalifah Ghulam Hasan, Mirza Muhammad Qasim, and Muhammad Mahdi Afshar were all there, I nonetheless took both letters and said that I would hide them from them. I thanked the men and asked them to deliver a message to the Hazarahs encouraging them to stand firm.

On the 27th, Fath Muhammad sent another messenger to Nur al-Din, perhaps to open negotiations again. In any case, the arrival of Hamid Allah, the amir's brother, with some machine-gun toting cronies, brought a swift end to the faltering negotiations. The members of the delegation still at Sar-i Chashmah now went home to Kabul, with considerable trepidation about the consequences of their failure.

Although Fayz Muhammad, as well as Nur al-Din and Mir Aqa, would pay dearly for the unsuccessful outcome of the mission, our author presumably derived some satisfaction from the delegation's inability to win a single expression of support for the Kabul regime, an outcome that he himself had worked to achieve, or so he asserts throughout.

June 27: Fath Muhammad, the military commander of the Unay Pass, sent Zavu, a mutton-seller from the Hazarah clan of Chuli, to Nur al-Din today, ostensibly to negotiate a truce but in fact to ascertain what his and Habib Allah's plans were regarding the Hazarahs. Nur al-Din gave the messenger a silk turban and seventy rupees worth of vegetable oil as a present as well as a message to Fath Muhammad which said that without waiting for approval of the terms submitted by the Hazarahs, he should send a tribal and general oath of allegiance in order that he subject neither himself nor the Hazarahs to death and destruction. In addition, he should also return what he had confiscated from Nur al-Din—the farman that authorized his mission, the amirid decrees, and his watch, pistol, and knife. If he did, then everything would be fine. Zavu, having deduced the real plans of Nur al-Din, had decided to depart for the Hazarah positions at the Unay Pass when I called him aside and told him that the residents of Kabul, Chardihi, Maymanah, Arghandah, Maydan, Logar, and Wardak were united with the Hazarahs and were waiting for their attack on Kabul along with Nadir's attack on Logar. Having thus been given new hope, Zavu took the message to Fath Muhammad not to be hasty in providing an oath of allegiance, for with the help of various devices, things could be dragged out until Nadir's situation was clarified.

At this time the Qizilbash, Ghulam Habib, approached Nur al-Din carrying a jug of yoghurt and some meat pies. He owned a fort in Unay Pass and had a dispute going with the local Hazarahs, in particular the Hazarahs of the Qal^{c}ah-i Karim fort, over water and pasture. Nur al-Din, who was a relative of his, asked, "Why haven't the Hazarahs up to now presented terms?" He answered, "If the residents of the Unay Pass would allow it, then the Hazarahs would give an oath of allegiance and right away let you cross my land. But instead the people of Unay Pass say all sorts of things to them about Nadir and keep them from giving an oath of allegiance and expressing their obedience."

I was indignant when I heard this. "How is it possible for you, who think of yourself as an adherent of Islam and a sinless Shi^{c}ite, to heap dirt on the peasants who pay one-quarter of their earnings in taxes and who, day in and day out, supply the soldiers with provisions, delivering fifty kharwars of wheat, flour, barley, mutton, firewood, and cooking oil. You slander them because you have designs on their land and water and are just looking for an excuse to attack them." I then recited a verse from the Qur'an which forbids this sort of behavior. He repented and uttered a few words affirming his devotion to Islam and his willingness to help other Muslims.

Today Habib Allah received the letter from the Hazarahs, containing the terms under which they would give an oath of allegiance. Muhammad Zaman and Nazar Muhammad also gave him the message from Nur al-Din. Habib Allah was furious when he learned from Colonel Nizam al-Din and the district chief of Kuhnah Khumar, Muhammad Aman, that the Hazarahs had advanced about two miles from the Unay Pass towards Sar-i Chashmah, and taken up positions. He ordered his brother, the "Mu^{c}in al-Saltanah" Hamid Allah, to go to Sar-i Chashmah the next day with five hundred bloodthirsty cutthroats and find out what is going on. If the Hazarahs had advanced even half a mile, then he should bombard them with artillery and rifle fire and drive them back.

Hamid Allah

June 28: At 8 a.m. I was in my room, an antechamber to Nur al-Din's room, writhing from side to side with abdominal pains when I heard the sounds of an automobile horn and people shouting. A few moments later, Hamid Allah walked into the room. He was on his way from the capital to Sar-i Chashmah with a group of his associates, a bunch of hardened thugs, some of whom had submachine guns. They had left their car on the main road as there was no driveway up the mountain to the house where Nur al-Din was staying.

Frightened, Nur al-Din called me to join them. To Mirza Muhammad Qasim he said, "Send a message to the Hazarahs who are in their positions at the Unay Pass and ask them why we don't yet have their terms for an oath of allegiance?" When I heard this coming from the terrified Nur al-Din, I thought that if fighting did break out, they would accuse the members of the delegation of provoking the Hazarahs, persuading them not to send terms, and of warning them of the arrival of Hamid Allah. I quickly asked Mirza Muhammad Qasim for the delegation's file, opened it, and showed it to Hamid Allah who had come in but had not uttered a single word of greeting. I said, "There's no need to send the Hazarahs a message. Here, look at the file. It's clear from it that things are nearing completion. There's no need to be hasty or overanxious." But Hamid Allah is a stupid opinionated person of low background who once earned his living as a dancer at weddings, later participated in the robberies of his brother, became used to a debauched life and now, as a result of the shameful behavior of dishonorable pseudo-mullas, is honored with the title "the King's Helper" (mu^{c}in al-saltanah) and is puffed up with conceit and self-satisfaction like a big red balloon. He showed absolutely no interest in the file or the notes in it and headed for the summit of the mountain on foot. Nur al-Din and Muhammad ᶜAli, the son of Fath Muhammad, a descendant of the Qizilbash Khan Shirin Khan of the Jawanshir clan, accompanied Hamid Allah and the other brigands up the mountain that overlooks the forts of the Unay Pass.

From there, they descended to the Qalᶜah-i Safid, where Ghulam Habib lives. They asked him about the peasants of Qalᶜah-i Karim, well-to-do oilsellers: "And these people, are they with you or against you?" That infidel, lacking any conscience and at odds with them over land, pasture rights, and water, said that they were the enemy and partisans of the Hazarahs. Hamid Allah, an ignorant libertine who would do anything that he felt like doing, ordered his men to open fire on the Qalᶜah-i Karim fort with rifles and cannons. One man was killed and an eight- or nine-year-old girl was wounded. The men of the fort fled into the mountains. That heartless infidel then ordered his gangsters to set fire to the fort and to carry off the valuables of its inhabitants. The residents of Takana, Jalriz, Kuhnah Khumar, and Qalᶜah-i Majid, religious fanatics all, had long been awaiting that moment. Hundreds of men under the command of the unbeliever, Colonel Nizam al-Din, who had been guarding Sar-i Chashmah from Hazarah attack, poured down on Qalᶜah-i Karim, drums beating, banners flying, and shouting "ya chahar yar," and consigned it to fire and sword. They burned practically all the forts in the region up to Unay, drove off livestock, and looted anything movable. Hamid Allah himself set up a machine gun on a mountain and began to spray fire down on the Hazarahs who had descended the pass and pitched their tents there. The machine-gun fire forced them to quickly strike their tents and head for positions at the top of the pass.

Until late evening, the sound of rifle and machine-gun fire could be heard everywhere. That night, after the residents of Unay Pass had lost all their possessions and gone into hiding in the mountains, Hamid Allah took prisoner forty women and children and two young girls whom he took to Qalᶜah-i Safid and handed over to Ghulam Habib. After establishing positions at Unay, he returned to the city. During the evening, while fighting was still raging, Hamid Allah ordered Nur al-Din to provide one kharwar and forty Kabuli seers of provisions. Nur al-Din busied himself until midnight, delivering the one and a half kharwars of food to Habib Allah's troops, food that had been prepared for them by the people of Sar-i Chashmah while he himself spent the night in utter terror.

June 29: A member of the delegation, Muhammad Mahdi Afshari, now decided to return to Kabul. "Whether they allow me or not, I am going to leave anyway because when war breaks out, I will be in no position to cope with any questions relating to a peaceful settlement," he said. Mir Aqa also supported him and they both decided to leave. I warned the two of them that before they left they should consult with Nur al-Din as the leader of the delegation. They should be sure to act in such a way that Habib Allah would not suspect that they were returning of their own accord and would not avenge himself by persecuting the hapless Qizilbash tribe, to which they belong, even though they were selected for the mission against their will. As I had advised, an hour and a half later they approached Nur al-Din and it was decided that the entire delegation would return to Kabul together.

So, we rode out of Sar-i Chashmah. Following little-used paths, pretending we were on our way to Takana, we managed to get to the main road and make for Kabul. En route, I turned to Nur al-Din and Mir Aqa and said, "Words may or may not have an effect but if one remains silent they certainly won't. Whether you listen to me or not, I have to speak out. I think that we should go to the governor of Maydan and inform Habib Allah by telephone of our situation so that we are not persecuted for willfully leaving the scene without instructions."

Everyone seconded my suggestion and we headed for the governor's house in Maydan. At a shop near the caravanserai in Kut-i Ashru, we stopped for tea. I still had a high fever and consequently rode in last. There was an automobile parked near the shop in which armed men were sitting. I tried to pass unnoticed but a large, bearded fellow sitting in the car called out, "Whose convoy is this and whose riders are these?" I answered, "The Hazarahjat delegation. Since the Mu^{c}in al-saltanah has started fighting, we're returning to the city." Another sepoy sitting in the car whose beard was shaved off and whose appearance as a result seemed bloodthirsty, rudely said, "Hey you, get off the horse." I hesitated, answering, "Oh, I don't know if I can." Then I saluted them and apologized that I could not dismount, muttering, "I'm very sick. If I dismount

I won't be able to get on again." I then left and rejoined the other riders.

At that point they called over Nur al-Din. Since he had volunteered to obtain the oath of allegiance but had been unable to do so, the governor-general, Malik Muhsin, now dealt him more than a hundred lashes despite the fact that he was wearing only light summer clothing. Cursing him and his family, he asked, "What did you do with the ten thousand rupees?" After beating Nur al-Din black and blue, Malik Muhsin drove off toward Sar-i Chashmah to find out how the fighting was going. At the Unay Pass, meanwhile, Hamid Allah had dispersed the Hazarahs, of whom fewer than a hundred were still in position. Among those he killed was a Hazarah leader, Col. Khayr Muhammad Nizami, whose head he severed and sent to the city where it was hung on the Chawk. He then advanced to Qal^{c}ah-i Yurt, seized the pass, and occupied the Hazarah positions, after which he returned to the city with a satchel that had fallen into his hands and contained the correspondence of the slain colonel.

Nur al-Din and the rest of us had now changed our minds about going to Maydan and calling Habib Allah from there. Instead we headed directly for the city. Afraid of the governor-general, who might have arrested us on his return from the battlefield, we avoided the main road and rode to the capital by way of Qal^{c}ah-yi Ghulam Haydar Khan and Chihil Tan. On the way, Nur al-Din sent a large part of the delegation to their homes in the Afshar quarter of Kabul while he himself went directly to see the head of the Islamic Regulatory Commission, Muhammad A^{c}zam, his mentor and supporter, to tell him what had happened. This evening, together with his son, son-in-law, Muhammad ^{c}Ali, and me, he reached the capital and first headed for his own home. Then he met with Muhammad A^{c}zam, who was reassuring and told him not to be afraid of the governor-general.

June 30: Today Malik Muhsin ordered the arrest of Nur al-Din and the confiscation of what remained in his baggage train. Nur al-Din tried to placate him by sending the Qizilbash Hasan ^{c}Ali with some of the ten thousand rupees. Hasan ^{c}Ali was formerly clerk to Mahmud Yawar and was now working for Malik Muhsin. He used his position to extort money and confiscate property for the governor-general, who was consequently quite pleased with him. The governor-general, ten thousand rupees richer, rescinded the order for Nur al-Din's arrest.

The story of the delegation and the consequences of its failure is not quite over. But the severity of the reaction against its members was intensified by Hamid Allah's efforts to gain by force what the delegation had failed to achieve through diplomatic means. When his military operations proved equally unsuccessful, the delegation's members bore the brunt of his frustration.

June 30: Hamid Allah again rode into Qal^{c}ah-i Yurt. Since he had gotten as far as the caravanserai of Jawqul without encountering any resistance he thought that he would be able to capture all of the Hazarahjat. He had his forces occupy the mountaintop positions that the Hazarah troops had abandoned. Along the road from Qal^{c}ah-i Yurt to Jawqul he burned down every fort and his men made off with the livestock and other property. A small group of Hazarahs, whose homes had been burned, kept up resistance in the mountains. A delighted Hamid Allah came galloping into Sar-i Chashmah and from there returned by automobile to the city. He opened the satchel of the slain Col. Khayr Muhammad, whose head they had hung on the Chawk, and found a number of unsigned letters from residents of Chardihi, Paghman, Arghandah, Logar, and Maydan addressed to the Hazarahs. These expressed support for the Hazarahs' struggle against Habib Allah and promised to give them help whenever they decided to attack Kabul. Among the letters, he found one from the residents of Sar-i Chashmah signed on April 21 and addressed to the military commander of the Hazarahjat. It expressed the hope that the Hazarahs would release the son of Dad Muhammad Kuhistani, ^{c}Abd al-Rahman, a good and kind fellow, and resolve their problems in a peaceful manner. But the Hazarahs could not fulfill this request. They had put ^{c}Abd al-Rahman to death after Habib Allah hanged their own representative, the chief equerry, Ahmad ^{c}Ali.

Although this letter was addressed to the military commander of the Hazarahjat, Hamid Allah, a wicked man utterly lacking in common sense, had no idea when it was written and who the commander was to whom it was addressed (it was, in fact, Prince Muhammad Amin), and put all the blame on Nur al-Din and the members of the delegation who were Qizilbash. To get authorization to investigate, he took the letter to his older brother, king of the thieves, who had awarded himself the title of "servant of the religion of the Prophet of God," although in fact all he ever did was work to destroy the religion of the Prophet of God.

July 1: Hamid Allah went to Sar-i Chashmah today, having postponed his investigation of Nur al-Din, the members of his delegation, and the tribes of the Qizilbash. Because of the letter in which the people of Sar-i Chashmah asked the Hazarahs to think of them as sincere allies, Hamid Allah now ordered the looting and burning of their homes and forts, notwithstanding that the majority of the residents of Sar-i Chashmah were upstanding people who had earned the titles *ḥājjī* [pilgrim to Mecca], *karbalāʾī* [pilgrim to the Shiʿi holy sites in Iraq], and *zuwwār* [pilgrims to Mashhad or other shrines holy to Shiʿites], paid the *zakāt* [the 2.5% canonical tax on wealth] and the *khums* [the twenty percent due the ruler]. They were devout adherents of the religion, worked for the most part as oilsellers, and were fairly prosperous. He had many of them put before a firing squad at the cemetery of the shrine of Hajji Sultan Muhammad.[227] Also on his orders, his men looted the Tajiks of Takana, Jalriz, and Kuhnah Khumar who were actually enthusiastic supporters of Habib Allah. They plundered not only property that could be easily sold—oil, carpets, dishes, livestock—but even the mosques. The looting went as far as removing doors from houses.

Hamid Allah's men carted away their booty over the course of several days. It is said that they stole property worth 1.5 million rupees. Hamid Allah brought thirty-four male and forty female prisoners to Kabul. He decided to sell the women and so lodged them in a separate house. He ordered the men held in solitary confinement and gave them nothing to eat or drink. The Qizilbash, with the help of a kind and sympathetic municipal official (*maʾmūr-i baladiyah*), Muhammad Ibrahim, collected money and secretly passed it to some bakers who then baked and delivered bread to the prisoners for as long as they themselves were not punished for doing so.

July 2: Hamid Allah, formerly a dancer at weddings and now "the King's Helper," yesterday was defeated in a fight with Hazarah devotees of Islam in the region of Jawqul. He lost many soldiers, machine guns, six-pound guns, rifles, and ammunition. During the retreat, he was in a wild rage and mistook the inhabitants of Sar-i Chashmah for Hazarahs and although they are submissive subjects, he looted their property, took prisoners, and burned their forts, as noted above.

Taking these prisoners to Kabul, he decided to kill the men and, as already mentioned, sell their women into slavery. On the basis of a letter found in the satchel of the slain Col. Khayr Muhammad and the message of Nur al-Din sent through Nazar Muhammad and Muhammad Zaman, in which he asked that an army be sent from Kabul to Sar-i Chashmah to frighten the Hazarahs, Hamid Allah now accused Nur al-Din and the members of his delegation of a conspiracy, as a consequence of which the Hazarahs had started a war and he himself had been defeated. At night [on the 1st] he appeared before his older brother and received permission from that heartless thief to exterminate all the Qizilbash, sell their women and children into slavery, and expropriate their property.

At one o'clock in the afternoon, at the head of eight hundred bloodthirsty bandits, Hamid Allah headed for Chandawul through Bazar-i Sar-i Chawk and Baghban Kuchah. Stopping at Bazar-i Sih Dukkan, which is adjacent to the gates of Chandawul, he had his armed bandits stand guard at every door so that no man, woman, or child could leave their houses. Having issued this order, he tried to enter Chandawul and commence the killing and looting.

But other residents of Kabul realized that while today this misfortune might happen to the Qizilbash, tomorrow it could happen to them, and so they armed themselves as best they could, some with small lances, some with pistols, and some with axes. They concealed these weapons under their coats or chukhas and headed for Chandawul on the pretext of seeing what was going on. They were resolved, should the Qizilbash be slain, to slaughter the bandit-infidels and then let history judge. The mayor, Khwajah Taj al-Din, who in comparison with other Kuhdamanis and Kuhistanis was a good-hearted person and consistently defended the residents of Kabul and other areas from the assaults, killings, muggings and insults of the diabolical northerners, on seeing this scene unfold like the Day of Judgment, was deeply alarmed. Using every trick at his disposal, he tried to keep Hamid Allah from entering Chandawul. First he took him away to his own office, which is located next to the Qal^cah-i Baqir Khan and is adjacent to Chandawul, and asked him why he was so upset. Hamid Allah showed Khwajah Taj al-Din the unsigned letter found in the slain colonel's satchel and said, "Nur al-Din persuaded the Hazarahs not to give an oath of allegiance nor submit; he encouraged them to fight and then treacherously called for a force to be sent [that would be ambushed]. So, because of his plotting, we have failed and the Hazarahs have won. As a result, I got permission from the amir to punish the Qizilbash for their treason." Khwajah Taj al-Din read the letter and saw that it was dated April 21 while he knew that Nur al-Din left [the Hazarahjat] in late June. He then quietly explained to the ignorant Hamid Allah, "The residents of Sar-i Chashmah, expressing goodwill and sincere intentions towards you, wrote this letter in April to Prince Muhammad Amin, in order to save the life of ᶜAbd al-Rahman Kuhistani. Nur al-Din left the Hazarahjat in late June. There's a difference here of almost two months."

Meanwhile, Hamid Allah's nephew, Iskandar, and others under his command rounded up the members of the delegation and brought them to the home of Nur al-Din along with all the Qizilbash who had served in the administration of His Highness Aman Allah. It was his intention to make short work of them. But once there he had second thoughts. Iskandar, Sultan ᶜAli, the chief (*kalāntar*) of the quarter, and Nur al-Din's son, Nasr al-Din, dragged me and several middle-aged Qizilbash civil servants off to Nur al-Din's home. The Qizilbash, expecting to be robbed and killed, were hiding in their homes behind locked doors. I was sick and had been in bed. Standing above the crowd, Hamid Allah addressed the Qizilbash who were standing there under the scorching rays of the sun, expecting a sentence of death to be passed on them. Speaking in a disappointed voice, Hamid Allah said, "As long as I live I will serve the faith and nation of Islam. Yesterday, had the Hazarahs killed me in the fight that occurred because of the treachery of Nur al-Din, how would I, being dead, be able to serve the government and the nation? Since this delegation represents the Qizilbash, therefore I ask of you, greybeards and elders of the tribe, how should I deal with them?" The voice of Sayyid Tahmasp was heard, "Shoot them!" Mulla Husayn ᶜAli, who ought to have said, "Since they represent the Qizilbash, hand them over to their people and name a reliable person from your side. If it comes out that they have done wrong, then the tribe will shoot them," said only, "Pardon them!" Hamid Allah shouted at him, "Shut your mouth! How can I pardon them for such offenses when I was almost killed?"

Then he ordered us caned within an inch of our lives and after that if we were unable to get up and leave under our own power, we were to be shot and our corpses nailed to the doors of our houses. They chose Nur al-Din, Mir Aqa, and me. Twenty-four bloodthirsty Pushtuns from the Khud Khayl tribe along with Kuhdamani and Kuhistani bandits stood in a circle, holding bundles of cherry and almond sticks at the ready.

First, they knocked Nur al-Din and then Mir Aqa down to the ground and beat them almost to death. Nur al-Din could only utter, "For God's sake . . . for God's sake . . . "

While they were beating him, Mir Aqa managed to mumble a couple of times, "We were only doing our duty . . . " As for me, one stick caught me on the forehead and blood drenched my face and beard. I whispered the prayer of Abu Hamza from the *Shamāʾil-i Hażrat-i Sayyid al-Sājidīn*: "O God! Save me! Truly, You are the savior!" Nothing more passed my lips.

We three were supposed to die from the beating. But because there were so many of the bandits taking part, only three or four of the staves actually hit us; the rest of the time the executioners managed only to strike each other, and so we survived. After the beating, Mulla Muhammad Yunus, known as Mawlawi Jang, a truly evil person, demanded of Hamid Allah that he throw us in prison and confiscate our homes. But Hamid Alllah said he would allow us to go home. Mawlawi Jang said, "Several times you have vowed that if you caught any Shiᶜites, you would crush them into little bits, like breaking sugar with tongs. Now that God has delivered the opportunity to you, you should carry out your promise to the people of the faith and so merit the title ghazi." But Hamid Allah did not respond.

The Qizilbash and their relatives gathered up Nur al-Din and Mir Aqa, taking the former to his own home and the latter to his sister's home. Muhammad ᶜAli, a member of the delegation and nephew of Khan Shirin Khan Jawanshir, who had also been sentenced to a caning but then pardoned because he had accompanied Hamid Allah to the mountains at the Unay Pass, supported me under the arms and led me from the Qalᶜah-i Baqir Khan to a nearby canal.

Not only was I unable to walk, I could not even make my feet move. So Muhammad ᶜAli left me there next to the canal and went about his own business. When word got around, a tea seller named Sayyid Abu'l-Qasim and his uncle, Sultan ᶜAli, became alarmed and hurried to the canal. Abu'l-Qasim lifted me onto his shoulders, took me to his shop, and sat me down at the entrance. Then they brought a charpoy bed and laid me on it. In a soft voice I uttered, "Glory be to God. They arrested [me] on the 10th of Muharram and on the 24th of the month my beard, my face, and my whole body are covered with blood. Now, maybe, they will consider me a true follower of the Lord of Martyrs [Imam Husayn]." When they heard my words, people who were standing there and those who lifted the charpoy onto their shoulders began to weep. With tears in their eyes, they carried me home. There, my wife and children, along with other men and women who had gathered, burst out sobbing. Iodine was brought from the Iranian embassy and swabbed on my back and sides. The Iranian military attache, Colonel ᶜAli Khan, had received instructions by telephone from the Shah of Iran to do everything possible to aid and comfort the Shiᶜites of Afghanistan without interfering in the internal affairs of the country in a way that might invite an attack on Iran. At a meeting with ᶜAta al-Haqq, Habib Allah's foreign minister, Colonel ᶜAli Khan demanded that the persecution of Shiᶜites stop and he succeeded, to some extent, in reducing the number of attacks.

In the evening, Mirza Muhammad Ayyub and Mirza Muhammad Mahdi returned from interrogation. Mirza Muhammad Ayyub asked me, "Shouldn't the letter, which you wrote on behalf of the Hazarahs, have gotten to Habib Allah by now?" I answered, "I did my duty and sent the Hazarahs' letter in which they promised to give an oath of allegiance. I didn't do more than that nor write anything to anyone. So you may tell this ignorant government, with no qualms, that the delegation fulfilled its duty. Don't worry that anyone will harm your tribe or other members of the delegation." Mirza Muhammad Ayyub was reassured and left after about an hour. It was clear to him that this misfortune had befallen his people because of the foolish ambitions of Nur al-Din.

July 3: Today, Hamid Allah renewed combat operations against the brave Hazarahs. Nurturing hatred in his heart, he resolved today to deal as harshly with the Hazarahs as he had dealt with the residents of Wardak, Logar, Tagab, and Qandahar before this.

When he arrived back there with a large military force, he attacked the small contingent of Hazarahs living in the region. But he was unable to plunder their belongings, steal their livestock, or set fire to their homes and forts, for a force of Hazarahs unexpectedly surrounded him and opened fire. Their attack was such a surprise that Hamid Allah not only abandoned the fight but also lost the route by which he might have been able to retreat. Out of 84 bandits, including those who yesterday had caned Nur al-Din, Mir Aqa, and me, all but four were killed. Their machine guns, the six-pound field pieces they had dragged with them, and the stores of ammunition fell into Hazarah hands. As for that dog, Hamid Allah, he managed to scramble away from the battlefield in the evening like a cunning fox. But his arms and his legs were bleeding and covered with lacerations and contusions. A bandit from Maydan named A^{c}zam lifted him onto his shoulders, carried him through the village of Darbugha[228] to the car, and then drove him to Sar-i Chashmah. This same night he fled back to the city and told the leader of the blackguards and infidels what had happened. Already badly frightened by news about Nadir and Hashim, the amir's fear was compounded by this news and he said, "In general, I am not too worried about the Pushtuns because if I give them a few rupees, I can make them obey like donkeys. But the Hazarahs fought for three years against the army of ^{c}Abd al-Rahman which numbered 120,000 soldiers and had a hundred cannons and still they were not defeated. The amir managed to gain victory only after the Hazarahs were decimated by cholera. It is impossible to defeat them or force them to obey."

After thinking about this for a bit, he turned on his brother, "The Qizilbash delegation prevented the Hazarahs from unleashing war and attacking Kabul. Moreover, it obtained a letter from them in which they promised to give an oath of allegiance. They did therefore accomplish something. Perhaps, it's true, they would not have given an oath of allegiance right away but still it's equally true that they would also not have taken up arms against me. Now, having stirred up this hornet's nest, you've managed to create a combat zone in the west to add to the problem of Nadir and Hashim in the south and the east." Having said this, he pondered how to rectify the situation so that the Hazarahs would stop fighting and he might then enjoy the leisure to concentrate his forces on Nadir and Hashim.

July 4: After hearing of Hamid Allah's defeat and the Hazarah victory, the Qizilbash were gripped with fear. They live in terror because of the fatwa of the pseudo-mullas that has branded them unbelievers. As coreligionists of the Twelver Shi^{c}ite Hazarahs they are outcasts in the view of the government, the nation, and the Sunni community. Because of that fatwa they are now forbidden to work as civil servants and so are on the verge of annihilation, with no other protector or helper but God. Nor do they have the wherewithal to travel and so they are denied the possibility of leaving the country.

Instead of expressing their gratitude for the work the delegation accomplished in the Hazarahjat, the Qizilbash abused their relatives and wrote to Habib Allah offering to cane them. They even expressed gratitude to Hamid Allah for punishing their fellow tribesmen and interpreted his censure as instruction and guidance, hoping that in this way they would be able to save their families and possessions. They took this letter to the Arg and handed it to the minister of court, Shayr Jan.

With respect to the Hazarahs who had come down from the summit of the Unay Pass and pursued the remnants of Habib Allah's forces up to Sar-i Chashmah, the Qizilbash Mirza Sultan Husayn, referring to Hamid Allah's fight with them, asked the Minister of Court, "When the truce negotiations were going on, did the Hazarahs come down from the Unay Pass of their accord or did you force them to come down and start fighting?" By these words he wanted the minister to understand that Hamid Allah, though he had suffered a defeat, had himself instigated the fighting. The minister of court answered, "We forced the Hazarahs to come down and were ourselves responsible for starting the fighting."

Racking his brains over how to extricate himself from this situation, the amir now decided to print an appeal and send it to the Hazarahs through the Qizilbash. The minister of court prepared everything necessary and promised that he would present a new delegation to him the next day.

The Third Delegation to the Hazarahjat

July 5: Due to the criminal schemings of the partisans of Habib Allah against the entire downtrodden population of Afghanistan and because of the battles between the Hazarahs and the northern bandits, a group of fearful and anxious Qizilbash elders today began to do what was necessary to protect themselves, their property, and their honor. In line with the promise yesterday given to Habib Allah by the minister of court, they met at the home of Mirza Muhammad Mahdi to select members for another delegation to be sent to the Hazarahjat.

While members were being chosen, a rumor spread that I had died as a result of the beating I was given. This news was depressing to the Qizilbash and a local official, Muhammad Ibrahim, an honest fellow and a sincere Muslim [who had already helped collect money for food for the Hazarah prisoners from Sar-i Chashmah], sent some men to Afshar, Wazirabad, and other [Shi^cite] places on Meeker[229] bicycles, to invite the people he knew there to come to my funeral.

However, it quickly became clear that the story of my death was premature. So the funeral arrangements were called off and attention was again turned to choosing the members of a new delegation. Two groups were formed—one of four men and the other of eleven. The Qizilbash planned to tell the minister of court that their people had already served in a delegation and that although they had faithfully fulfilled their assignment, they had still been insulted and abused. If it was only necessary to deliver an appeal to the Hazarahs, the four-man delegation would suffice. But if it was thought necessary to send another negotiating team, then they would offer the eleven names to the government. They went to the Arg, presented their resolution to the minister of court, and suggested that he himself head the delegation. But he declined, saying that if he did, the governor-general and Hamid Allah would become his enemies. But he promised to present them to the amir the next day at Dar al-Aman.

July 6: Today, the amir and his courtiers set off for Dar al-Aman, renamed Dar al-Habib, to rest and relax. According to the promise made them by the minister of court, Shayr Jan, the Qizilbash also drove out to Dar al-Aman by car. There the minister of court presented them to His Highness and put their resolution before him. Habib Allah hated the Qizilbash because of his fight with the Hazarahs and because they were Shi^cites. Provoked by the pseudo-mullas, he continually sought ways to exterminate them. But now, hypocritically, he praised their outstanding service to the Afghan government over the past two hundred years, saying, "During this long period, you have not grown rich, for you did not come to plunder the wealth of the government and nation. Instead you lived only on your salaries as civil servants." Habib Allah then denounced the ministers of Aman Allah, who, despite being Sunnis, had, in a very short time, ransacked the nation and its glorious buildings, caravanserais, fields, and gardens and had betrayed Aman Allah in the process. He referred to each one by name, calling them swindlers and rogues. Then he agreed to send the four delegates who were supposed to distribute the appeal in the Hazarahjat and said he saw no need for the delegation of eleven to go at this time.

Just then, Mirza Hasan ᶜAli Qizilbash (who was Malik Muhsin's chief henchman in extortion) volunteered to go, saying "as a service to the government, I will deliver the appeal to the Hazarahjat myself." The governor-general, who believed in his loyalty, recommended him to Habib Allah and so he was included. Habib Allah also confirmed Hajji Rustam ᶜAli from Wazirabad, Mulla ᶜAbd al-ᶜAli from Murad Khani, and Mulla ᶜIwaz from Afshar, names put forward by the Qizilbash themselves. He said they should go to Sar-i Chashmah by car, thence to the Hazarahjat to distribute the appeal, and then return to the capital. The Qizilbash went home in an optimistic frame of mind, hopeful that their lives would improve after completion of this mission.

July 7: Today Mirza Hasan ᶜAli set off, after completing preparations for departure and receiving an automobile, four hundred copies of the appeal [prepared and printed on July 4], and a thousand rupees for the four men's travel expenses.

This is the text of the appeal, as prepared and printed by Muhammad Hasan Salimi:

> Let it be known to my ignorant subjects, the Hazarah tribes! As a result of the instigations of mercenary-minded and unfriendly people, you ceased being obedient. I put up with a great deal and came to you with good advice and even dispatched a delegation to you made up of your fellow-tribesmen and staunch supporters like Nur al-Din, Mulla Fayz Muhammad, and others. They were supposed to encourage you to take the path leading out of the wilderness of error. However, not only did you fail to heed their advice but, on the contrary, you advanced another step into the abyss of brutality and perfidy. I was therefore forced to send a small contingent from my triumphant army to overwhelm you. Now you flee from my soldiers in terror. In the capital I have prepared a mighty force that I am going

> to send to your region. Loyal tribes of Pushtuns also beg me every day to let them annihilate you. But the characteristic quality of padishahs is mercy and that of great people is leniency towards the creatures of God. The relationship of the padishah to his subjects is like that of a father to his children. Therefore I cannot allow you to put yourselves in a hopeless situation. I put it to you that if, starting today and for the next ten days, your deputies come to His Highness the padishah with oaths of allegiance and tender your obedience, I will forgive you and consider you subjects like all my other subjects. But if, at the expiration of this period, no pledges are forthcoming, then I will send a force against you and call up the Pushtun tribes to annihilate you and seize your land and belongings. When the troops and the tribal contingents are dispatched, your prayers for forgiveness will be of no avail and you will be undone by your own hand. Although I have put up with a good deal from you and more than once have tried to point you in the right direction, my actions have yet to produce the desired results. Now I consider it necessary to remind you one more time of this. Decide how you are going to behave. If you know your own best interests then you will not go so far as to put yourselves in front of the muzzles of cannons and rifles. 26 Muharram 1348 Hijri. [July 4, 1929]

The Qizilbash delegation reached Takana and satisfied itself that the road would be closed for the next several days. They opened negotiations with the Hazarahs, their coreligionists, declaring that they were on their side and had been forced to come to the Hazarahjat under pain of death. So, the Hazarahs escorted them, under guard, through the Unay Pass and brought them to Prince Muhammad Amin Khan in Raqul where they were treated as friends of the Hazarahs and enemies of Habib Allah. In any event, they were given a certificate signed by the prince and the Hazarah arbabs. In this way, the Qizilbash protected themselves.

Fayz Muhammad's account of this third delegation momentarily ends here but he returns to the story later.[230]

Fighting between Hazarahs and Tajiks Continues

July 8: The Hazarahs have now been fighting Habib Allah's troops for eleven days, inflicting a defeat on them each day. Today, following another victory, they returned to their trenches and positions in Unay Pass. Then they launched an attack on the place where a five-thousand-man regiment of Habib Allah, which included soldier-bandits, officer-extortioners, and infidels, was stationed. Armed with cannons and machine guns, these men were ready to fight, but the Hazarahs, shouting "ya ᶜAli," drove them back to Jalriz, killing, wounding, or capturing many of them and seizing their weapons and a large stock of ammunition. Many of the retreating soldiers, unable to withstand the onslaught of the Hazarah attack, dropped their rifles and bandoliers and ran. In revenge for Hamid Allah's burning the forts at Sar-i Chashmah, the Hazarahs set fire to the Qalᶜah-i Majid and several villages in Takana and Jalriz, and looted them.

The majority of Habib Allah's troops, who had been forcibly conscripted from Chardihi, Maydan, and the environs of Kabul and sent to the battlefield, ran home and hid, because of the amir's order that deserters were to be shot. Everyone is talking about the Hazarah victory. The residents of Kabul, Chardihi, Logar, Maydan, and Wardak, overjoyed by the way things were going, especially this most recent victory of the Hazarahs, prayed to the All-High to help them win out and liberate Kabul.

But the ulama now issued a fatwa that runs as follows:

> Because His Highness Aman Allah abdicated the amirid throne, the declaration of war issued by Sardar Muhammad Amin [whom Aman Allah had appointed to the post of military high commissioner] is null and void. In the event of an attack on Habib Allah, the Hazarahs themselves should look to their own defenses: they should defend their own lands, families, and belongings but not attack other Muslims, since both sides, the slayer and the slain, are answerable before God and the Prophet.

The Hazarahs now reversed their decision to march on Kabul. But they bravely continued the struggle to the end, sincere in their faith and having refused to give an oath of loyalty or to submit to Habib Allah.

Here is another disjunctive element in the narrative. Why, if the Hazarahs had the government forces on the run, as Fayz Muhammad suggests, they were dissuaded from continued fighting by this rather innocuous fatwa, is a mystery. It is more likely the case that the Hazarah leadership of the various factions did not have the same objectives that Fayz Muhammad attributes to them. Attacking Kabul would have taken them far from their home bases and put them, had they managed to take the capital, in the same kind of situation the northern Tajiks found themselves in, besieged from all sides. Politics tend to be extremely local in Afghanistan and once the Hazarah elders secured control of their own regions they had little further interest in fighting for more territory.

In the meantime, during the early part of July, Nadir Khan and his brother Hashim once again seem to have drummed up tribal support for a renewed offensive against the Tajik government. But Habib Allah was not unskilled at the arts of propaganda and persuasion. The imaginary words Fayz Muhammad put in Habib Allah's mouth earlier about the Pushtuns being donkeys susceptible to the carrot of a few rupees may have been only a reflection of Fayz Muhammad's prejudices. But there is little doubt that the services of the tribes in the Eastern and Southern Provinces were for sale to the highest bidder, and Habib Allah knew this as well as anyone. And unlike Nadir he had no ethnic ties to help him win support there but had to rely on the offer of money, offices, titles, and an invitation to the tribes to wage war on their neighbors in the name of religion.

July 9: Habib Allah, alarmed by the situation in the Southern and Eastern Provinces and the activities of Nadir and his brothers, which are all utterly reasonable and proper in light of the dictates of Islam, today ordered that a circular addressed to the elders of the Mulla Khayl, Sulayman Khayl, Kakar, Taraki, Andar, ᶜAli Khayl, Dawtani, Kharuti, and the nomadic and settled Ahmadzai be printed up. These are the same tribes that led the Afghan government and the nation to destruction by [originally] supporting Habib Allah of the ignorant Tajik people; these are also the tribes that volunteered to plunder and enslave Hazarahs and seize their lands and homes. By affixing his signature and the seal of his depraved amirate to this circular, Habib Allah called upon all of these tribes to attack the Hazarahs. Here is a copy of the farman addressed to Rahim Khan of the Kakar tribe that came into my hands and which I included in my journal of the rebellion:

> May it be known to Your Worship, Rahim Khan Kakar! Your piety and praiseworthy service to your Muslim government has been reported to His Highness by Brigadier Khattak Khan. I, the "Servant of the Religion of the Prophet," express satisfaction and gratitude for your service, and by this farman bring these things to your attention. In the future I want you to serve the pure religion of Islam and so earn the satisfaction of the All-High,

His Prophet, and me as the servant of religion. You and your tribe should declare war against the Hazarahs who have not expressed their obedience to the padishah of Islam. Any village that you capture will be yours and its belongings and lands will be given to you from His Highness, as compensation in both this world and the next. After the holy war comes to an end and the Hazarah issue is resolved once and for all, every tribal leader will receive a title and a gift, depending on his contribution to the victory. 1 Safar 1348 Hijri. [July 9, 1929]

The publication of this dissension-sowing decree pleased the foolish Pushtuns. It is not enough that they are infidels. They also utterly lack any sign of honor or conscience and have not the slightest inkling that they are cutting off the limb on which they sit. It never occurs to them that the result of this will be the humiliation of the nation, the enfeeblement of the government, the destruction of the country, and the plundering of its monetary and material resources and its arsenals, which have been accumulated over the course of one hundred years—at the cost of much blood—for the defense of the people, their honor, lands, and buildings, the independence of the country, and the repelling of attack by foreign enemies. But the Pushtun are interested only in acquiring lofty ranks in a world full of misery, futility, ignorance, and savagery.

As for this Rahim, he had already taken advantage of a similar government decree during the time of Aman Allah and had seized lands and forts in Pul-i Jangali, Gazak, and Arghandab that belonged to the Hazarahs of Jaghuri. Thus did he demonstrate his zeal for the Pushtun government. Habib Allah confirmed all this usurpation and destruction, and declared the Kakar tribe worthy of reward, calling what they had done a service to the government and the nation.

July 10: Today ᶜUmar Khan, an infamous libertine and the son of Malik Zayn al-ᶜAbidin Daᵓudzai,[231] promised the chief bandit, Habib Allah, that he would take upon himself the duty of either forcing the Hazarahs' submission or crushing them. Here are his very words: "Purdil Khan has taken Ghazni and captured Qandahar; Major General Muhammad Siddiq and ᶜAbd al-Qayyum Ibrahim Khayl Paghmani have advanced toward the Southern Province; and Muhammad ᶜUmar 'General Sur-i Satranj' has defeated the opposition in numerous battles. I don't want to lose ground to my peers here. I should be able to make short work of the Hazarahs and extract their submission."

His ambition was welcome and he set off for Jalriz with a contingent of veteran Kuhdamanis and Kuhistanis and some field guns. Linking up with the soldiers who had advanced against the Hazarahs and were skirmishing with them daily, he fought with a small force of Hazarahs that had arrived in Sar-i Chashmah and was conducting combat operations as far as Takana. The Hazarahs, showing courage, killed or wounded five hundred soldiers and fifteen of Habib Allah's officers. ᶜUmar himself was wounded in the leg. He thus never had the opportunity to achieve his goal and the artillery, rifles, and ammunition of his force were captured by the Hazarahs. His face red with shame, he was brought with the other wounded tonight by car to the city. The victorious Hazarahs returned to Unay Pass and re-occupied their positions. From the battlefield they carried off the heads of the slain, mounted them on poles, and planted those poles at the summit of the pass so they would overlook the bazaar in Kabul. The slain would never again eat mulberries but would stand at the summit of the pass as an imprecation against the evil oppressor, Habib Allah.

July 12: Habib Allah went out to Paghman today, ostensibly to relax but in fact because he was worried that the Hazarahs would come down out of the Paghman mountains along the road through Katan and attack Paghman and Kabul. Through the day, his men readied their positions and dug trenches.

Also today he telephoned the commandant of Kabul and told him to arrest Mir Hashim, the minister of finance in Aman Allah's administration, and his brother. Just prior to this, Mir Hashim received a letter from Nadir informing him of his imminent arrival in Kabul and encouraging him to rouse the people of Kabul and its environs against the bandit leader. An anxious Habib Allah also ordered the arrest of Prince ᶜAbd al-Majid,[232] the Qizilbash Mirza Sultan Husayn, and [ᶜAbd al-Wahid] the son of Mulla Malik, who were accused of secretly sending weapons and ammunition to the Hazarahs. After this, he directed that all the sons of the assassinated amir, Habib Allah, be assembled at the gates of the Arg. But there was nothing to be gotten from them; some of them were still quite young and their mothers had already paid out bribes of two, three, and four hundred rupees for their safety. So they were allowed to go home.

Executions in Kabul and Divisions in Hazarah Ranks

A rash of executions of suspected enemies of the Tajik regime occurred in the second week of July. Already mentioned was the grisly death of ᶜAli Ahmad Luynab, erstwhile claimant of the throne, who was blown from a cannon. Sunday, July 14 was a particularly tragic day for the Muhammadzai ruling clan as three of its princes were hanged. We also find Fayz Muhammad reporting serious defections at this time in the Hazarah ranks to the side of Habib Allah. Hitherto, his account had singled out individuals who had "secretly" given oaths of allegiance to Habib Allah. Now he mentions large groups—the Hazarahs of Day Zangi and Day Kundi of the western Hazarahjat, for example.

July 12: Qazi ᶜAbd al-Shukur and the mufti of Qalat, who had been arrested in Qandahar, were executed yesterday with ᶜAli Ahmad Luynab.[233] During Aman Allah's stay in Qandahar, they had issued fatwas charging Habib Allah and the people of the north with being infidels. Mulla ᶜAbd al-Wasiᶜ, arrested along with them, escaped death[234] only because his younger brother, ᶜAbd al-Karim, had betrayed Aman Allah in the region of Qul near Bihsud. He had done this by persuading the Day Zangi and Day Kundi Hazarah contingents (numbering nine hundred men), who had been conducting operations in Bamyan and at the Unay Pass, to stop fighting Habib Allah's army. Unbenownst to Prince Muhammad Amin, he and the governor of Day Zangi, Mir Muhammad Husayn, had sent a letter on behalf of the Hazarahs in which he pledged loyalty to the leader of the bandits and said he would see that an oath of allegiance from all Hazarahs was subsequently obtained. ᶜAbd al-Karim chose the path of treason to save his property from confiscation and also to receive high rank. Because of his treachery, the honor, dignity, and respect that his fathers and forefathers had enjoyed for 150 years, from the time of Shah Mahmud Saduzai[235] until now, were consigned to oblivion.

July 13: Today the former minister of finance, Mir Hashim, and his brother, Sayyid Habib, who, as already mentioned, had been in communication with Nadir Khan, and [also] the Qizilbash Mirza Sultan Husayn and ᶜAbd al-Wahid, the son of Mulla Malik, accused of delivering and selling rifles and ammunition to the Hazarahs, were arrested. Also arrested were the bakers whom the Qizilbash had paid to take food to the imprisoned men and women from Sar-i Chashmah. A day after being arrested, ^{c}Abd al-Wahid was released because his elder brother was a member of the delegation sent to the Hazarahjat to distribute copies of the appeal cited above. Mirza Sultan Husayn paid a bribe of three thousand rupees to the commandant [of the Arg? qal^{c}ah-begi]^{c}Abd al-Ghani and after a few days was also released. The bakers also bought their way out, escaping prison by paying bribes ranging from five hundred to a thousand rupees each.

Today the decree branding the Hazarahs unbelievers was broadcast on the radio. When they learned of it, the Hazarahs stepped up their struggle against Habib Allah and his gang, against this "servant of the religion of the Prophet of God" who is, in fact, its very nemesis. They declared that the oath of allegiance has the force of an agreement only when it is given voluntarily. This is according to the Shari^{c}ah and is the main basis of any oath. No matter, the pseudo-mullas still issued a fatwa accusing them of unbelief and declared that the theft of their property and the shedding of their blood was legal according to the Shari^{c}ah. From this there was no recourse for the Hazarahs but to defend themselves from destruction. Devoted to their religion, they could not offer their obedience to a libertine, thief, and murderer.

July 14: Today, at the order of the chief oppressor, Habib Allah, a number of high-ranking individuals were sentenced to death by hanging, although they had committed no offense. The order was immediately carried out. The victims included the deputy minister of defense under Aman Allah [Mahmud Khan[236]] and three members of the Muhammadzai royal family—two sons of the martyred Amir Habib Allah: Prince Hayat Allah,[237] known as "^{c}Azud al-Dawlah" ("The Right Arm of the State"), and Prince ^{c}Abd al-Majid—and Sardar Muhammad ^{c}Us̱man, son of the late Sardar Muhammad ^{c}Umar b. Sardar Sultan Khan. Sardar Sultan Khan had received the post of governor of Herat and the nickname "sarkar" from Nasir al-Din Shah Qajar.[238] The slain men were thrown into a pit. This was kept secret and for a time the guard at the gates of the prison ate the men's breakfasts and dinners so that their relatives would not discover what had happened to them and try to take revenge.

By mid-July, Fayz Muhammad has begun to reveal divisions in the

Hazarah ranks, notably the activity of ᶜAbd al-Karim to persuade the Day Zangi and Day Kundi Hazarahs to offer their allegiance. Still, it would be several more weeks before extended negotiations would seem to put them, if not in the amir's camp, at least safely out of the fray.

PART FOUR

Nadir Khan Fades Away and the Hazarahs Negotiate

From mid-July to the end of August when the memoir abruptly ends, the tide appears to move inexorably in favor of Habib Allah, despite Fayz Muhammad's interpretation of every sign of resistance as an indication of the amir's imminent overthrow. The unwary reader might well wonder how, given all the "defeats" which the amir supposedly suffered, he was able to cling to power. But Fayz Muhammad felt no compunction to seek corroboration of the rumors that reached him. He reported what he heard, and perhaps even embellished what he heard, according to his own predilection to see the defeat of the Tajik amir around every corner, as if a rumor that accorded with his hopes was as good as fact. On occasion he notes that a rumor proved to be false but much of the time the reader has to reach that conclusion for himself from contradictory information subsequently reported. Perhaps this is judging the work unfairly and does not take sufficient account of the unfinished state in which it has reached us. It is also true that Fayz Muhammad never claims to be an impartial observer.

The resistance to the Kabul government during the last six weeks covered by the memoir occurred on three fronts—the Eastern and Southern Provinces, where the Musahiban brothers continued to struggle to unite the Pushtun tribes; Tagab to the northeast; and the Hazarahjat to the west, where resistance appears to have come to an end when a Hazarah delegation made up of representatives from the Ghazni and Bihsud regions comes to Kabul. There was also some minor activity from Afghan Turkistan, where local Hazarahs and Tajiks combined against the regime and its Turkmen allies, and from a new source, the Ismaʿili Shaykh ʿAli Hazarahs led by the Kayani family.

Musahiban Activity in the Eastern and Southern Provinces

From mid-July to mid-August, Nadir Khan and his brothers continued to press their cause as best they could among the Pushtun tribes in the south and east. Although Fayz Muhammad's information about their activities was often contradictory from one day to the next, the reader does get a picture of the fitful nature of their efforts first to meld a coalition of tribesmen and second to organize its movements to coincide with the movements of anti-Saqqawist forces elsewhere.

The two-week period between July 14 and 27 seems to have been a critical time for the Musahiban leader, and the events of July 14 and 15, if Fayz Muhammad's sources were in any way accurate, especially telling of Nadir's inability to capitalize on apparent success.

July 14: This morning at 10 o'clock the courageous forces of Nadir entered Logar. At Padkhwab-i Rughani they clashed with Habib Allah's forces and defeated them. From there they advanced to Surkhab where they surrounded Muhammad Siddiq and his force at Kariz-i Darwish. He sent a courier to Kabul with a request for reinforcements.

Also today militia from the Karu Khayl tribe, intending to attack the force stationed in Butkhak, reached Chakari and Khurd Kabul. However, it was unable to win out over the unit of Habib Allah's army stationed there. The fighting lasted until night; then the Karu Khayl, carrying their casualties with them, withdrew in frustration.

July 15: The army that had taken Qandahar and only just arrived back in Kabul was dispatched to Logar today to help Muhammad Siddiq who yesterday asked for reinforcements. Two hundred of Habib Allah's soldiers have been killed in the fighting. They say that during the fighting, some of the soldiers fled into the mountains. Many were taken captive in Gardiz and Kariz-i Darwish. General Muhammad ᶜUmar, known as General Sur, was surrounded and Nadir's army won a victory that produced joy among the Kabulis and among all those who were trying to save themselves from the humiliation at the hands of the Saqqawists.

In a spirit of kindness, Nadir at first put his faith in his prisoners as Muslims. He distributed one British pound sterling in gold to each of them, took away their rifles and cartridges, and released them, warning them that they were not to fight any more against their fellow Muslims. But these are people about whom it may safely be said, "they bite the hand that feeds them." Then Nadir placed ten to twenty prisoners in the custody of each of the maliks of the Southern Province tribes, told them to feed them and in return make them work in the fields and gather firewood. In this way, he parceled out the prisoners among the maliks. But Nadir's money had now run out and some of his supposed tribal supporters began to look with envy on those who received money from Habib Allah. And so, despite the success that had been achieved, the brave tribes of the Southern Province disregarded their oaths and began to disperse and go home.

By the end of the day on the 15th, then, his "victory" had somehow been transformed into defeat and from this point until the memoir ends, nothing that threatens the Kabul government is heard from Nadir.

July 16: The force sent to help Major General Muhammad Siddiq[239] had not heard about the withdrawal of the braves from the Southern Province. Still worried they might attack, it stopped at the village of Muhammad Aghah near Logar and advanced no further.

Today a Paghmani, General of Artillery ᶜAbd al-Qayyum of the Ibrahim Khayl, was sent to Kariz-i Darwish to set up artillery positions. Habib Allah, who now had inadequate forces in Kabul, was worried. To conceal his fears from the people and prevent any uprising, today he ordered the printing of a proclamation. This is the text:

> Muhammad Nadir and his brother, Shah Wali, have fled and now are in some unknown quarter. Opposition to him has appeared among some of the Pushtun tribes. These villains, and we may call them just that, have abandoned all conscience, violated their alliance, the religion, and Afghan honor.

The purpose of this proclamation is to undermine the faith of those opposed to this ignorant and wicked government who expect the victory of the two brothers. Habib Allah was encouraged to publish this announcement because ignorant tribes like the Sulayman Khayl, and especially the Sultan Khayl clan of this wicked tribe, the Manzai clan of the ᶜAli Khayl, the Salih Khayl, Mamuzai, Khwazak, Lundizai, the Milen-olai clan of the Par Khayl tribe, the Ibrahim Khayl, the Zalui clan of the ᶜAli Khayl tribe, the Andar, the Sahak, the Ashuzai clan of the Durrah tribe, the Jadran, the Dari Khayl, the Fakhri, the Kharuti, and also the Tajiks living in Katawaz, Zurmat, Gardiz, and other regions, have come out against Nadir and in support of him.

Through the rest of the month Fayz Muhammad continues to report the skirmishes taking place with tribes from the eastern and southern provinces, though there is no evidence that they are now fighting for the Musahiban cause. One particularly tenacious group, the Karu Khayl, launched raids on the eastern part of Kabul, the area known as Khwajah Rawash and now the site of the airport. Fayz Muhammad suggests a reason other than support for Nadir and his brothers that might have prompted the raids. The Karu Khayl were, he says, "the tribe of the wife of Muhammad ᶜAli Khan, brother of Aman Allah, and the tribe of Aman Allah's mother."[240] *Perhaps some form of revenge was the motive here, but whatever it was, it is quite clear that the Karu Khayl were acting alone. There is little evidence at this point that Hashim had made any headway in the Eastern Province in forging the disparate Pushtun tribes into a coalition.*

When Fayz Muhammad made his entry for July 22, or when he revised the entry, he reflected on the the difficulty that Hashim was facing.

While on the one hand consoling themselves with these hopes [of a three-pronged Eastern Province, Southern Province, and Hazarah attack on the city], the residents of Kabul could not help but think, on the other, of the Hazrat-i Charbagh, the Khugyani and Shinwari tribes, ᶜAbd al-Rahman the son of ᶜIsmat Allah Khan,[241] Malik Qays, and ᶜAbd al-Rahman and Malik Muhammad ᶜAlam [Shinwari], who, with foreign backing, constantly strive to undermine the state and plunge the country into internecine struggle. They opposed the tribal and Islamic alliance and continually interfere with the work of Hashim. When residents of Kabul talk to each other they cannot conceal their worry that even if the Hazarahs join forces with the Pushtuns to crush Habib Allah, the savage and ignorant tribes of the Eastern Province will never stay on the paths of unity, the faith, and Afghan honor because of outside instigation and incitement from these persons, especially the Hazrat-i Charbagh.[242] They tell each other that ultimately they will have to rely on the Hazarahs and the people of the Southern Province and not on the Eastern Province tribes.

There was further fighting with Eastern Province tribes, notably the Khugyani, in a battle fought near Khurd Kabul on July 18. To get his men to the front Habib Allah had commandeered all the automobiles and horse-drawn buggies (gādīs) *in Kabul, ordering that anyone found concealing a vehicle would be shot in front of his garage. Fayz Muhammad asserts that this decree had the effect of rendering "four hundred government vehicles and private carriages" useless, presumably because their drivers were killed. But by July 19, the Kabul forces had matters under control and, Fayz Muhammad grudgingly admits, after many sleepless nights the amir now spent one in an easy frame of mind.*

As a sign of Nadir Khan's diminishing chances for victory in Fayz Muhammad's eyes, he reports in early August the arrival of a delegation sent by Nadir to try to win release of members of his family still held in Kabul. The delegation remained in Kabul for a week, then returned empty-handed.

August 7: Nadir, saddened by the disintegration of the alliance of the tribes of the Southern Province, today sent a group of ulama, tribal leaders of the Southern Province, and representatives of the Ahmadzai led by Adam Khan, the son of Malik Pir Dust, to Habib Allah in Kabul. Through them he asked the amir to release his and his brothers' families who were languishing in custody and send them to him. When that happened, he would abandon the ill-fated alliance of Pushtun tribes and leave the country. The delegation arrived in Kabul in three cars and was accorded a warm reception.

August 13: The group of ulama and leaders from the Ahmadzai and other tribes who came to Kabul to seek the release of the families of Nadir and his brothers presented a petition today to the ringleader of the oppressors to release these people. If they were released, Nadir would then extinguish the flames of rebellion, leave the country with his family and servants, and end the carnage. But Habib Allah, an ignoramus who did not know a good thing when he saw it, refused the request. After giving each member of the delegation a turban made of poor quality silk, he sent them back. The behavior of this imbecile, insulting to the family of Nadir, evoked the wrath of the delegation and during its return its members heartily cursed him.

Although Fayz Muhammad continues to report the rumors of distant fighting against the amir's forces, he devotes much of the rest of his memoir to matters closer to home, to things happening in Kabul itself and to the amir's changing relations with the Hazarahs.

July 20: Today an article was published in *Ḥabīb al-Islām* reporting on a banquet for the Hindus of Kabul that was held on July 7 at the Chihil Sutun palace, next to the village of Khandaqi.[243] Habib Allah, his ministers, Governor-general Malik Muhsin, the aide-de-camp, Muhammad Saᶜid, and other high-ranking figures were invited. The Hindus' message to the oppressor Habib Allah was read by Mangal Singh:

> May we be a sacrifice on behalf of the luminous and blessed *Amīr-ṣāḥib ghāz'*! We Hindus, residents of the province of Kabul, express our gratitude for the fact that the fortunate and valorous amir-sahib-ghazi has disseminated justice and surrounded us, like a loving parent for his children, with paternal concern and affection. For this cordiality of His Highness we will always pray to the Almighty not to shorten the shadow of the Phoenix, the amir-sahib ghazi, over the heads of the weak and unfortunate. Today our brothers in faith live in total tranquillity and boundless prosperity and we, a humble and weak tribe, to whom a strong wind has sent good news from Qandahar, cannot find the appropriate words to express our gratitude for the valuable concern of His Highness [Habib Allah], the Sublime Sardar [Hamid Allah], their excellencies, the occupiers of high positions, the respected governor-general and the aide to His Highness. For the paternal kindness and benevolence of our kingly father, we hardly know how to show our warm appreciation of the beloved padishah. Therefore, first of all, we raise our hands to the Almighty in prayer that he will assist you in realizing all your dreams and desires in this world. Amir-sahib-ghazi! Each time we bow in prayer, we pray to the Almighty to give you happiness and long life. For your love, we are ready to sacrifice ourselves. Long may the padishah be all-powerful. May the All-High aid and assist you. Our wish is that you make short work of your enemies. May they be like tent pegs—their heads beneath a stone, their bodies in the ground, and a rope around their necks! Rest assured that this humble tribe will always be praying for you. 30 Muharram 1348 Hijri [July 8, 1929]

This adulatory message, which hardly corresponded at all with the way things really were, was signed by Diwan Mangal Singh, Naranjan Das,[244] Kusanga Arjan Das, Diwan Mohan Lal, Diwan Hukm Chand, Mir Singh Lachman Das, Kash Singh, Sherbal Makan, Shuhi Bartarz, Bhagwan Das, Mir Singh, Amir Chand Dalal, Nanak Chand, Lachman Das, Tule Ram,

Lakhi Chand, Kaniya Lal, and some others.

Habib Allah replied in his Kuhdamani dialect of Persian in which he knows only such words and phrases as chicken, eggs, wood, selling grapes, and other nonsense. His minister of court, Shayr Jan, who was also the administrator of the press, published the reply in the paper under the headline "The Gracious Response of the Amir." It went as follows:

Naranjan Das and Mahmud Tarzi (1919)

> Mangal Singh and other Hindus! Truly, we have followed the guidance of our great leader who in 1348 Hijri [1929] again kindled the rays of the religion in the glittering palace [of the nation], spread justice to Muslim and non-Muslim alike, and took them under his shield and protection.[245] As concerns you, O Hindus, we have given you our support to the extent we have been able to. It is also necessary to recognize that we have allowed you civil and political freedoms equal to those of Muslims, Jews, and other subjects. We have not allowed anyone to have special advantages and privileges. From the perspective of religion, we protect you just as we protect others. What we say is confirmed by proofs we see in everyday life. In all my actions, I have maintained the principles of the sacred religion. Today, events are taking place before my eyes like those which took place at the beginning of this millenium between Iran and Rome. As it was then, so is it now and will be in the future. I assure you in all sincerity that no one will bring any harm to your religious freedom if civil calm prevails. You may live peacefully, maintaining the principles of the holy Shar^{c}ia, and your prosperity is our hope.

Thanks to such obsequious and servile declarations [as that of the Hindus], the unfortunate peoples of the East are always vulnerable to destruction and cannot find the right path.

Fayz Muhammad also speaks of the financial hardship the people of Kabul suffered because of the need to pay Habib Allah's erstwhile tribal supporters. He claims that, despite this heavy taxation, the amir's own troops, mostly Tajik, were not being paid while the bulk of the money collected from the civilian population was spent to win Pushtun support.

July 24: From January to the present, that is for about seven months, while fighting has been going on, each of the fifty thousand sepoys from the tribal forces has been paid 140 rupees a month. That means the residents of Kabul and the villages and forts surrounding it have shouldered the burden of paying out some 12 million rupees.

The ongoing, intolerable monetary extortions, the murders, looting, arson, the ransacking of the treasury and the arsenals, the disabling of automobiles, and the misappropriation of valuables, carpets, and household goods has brought the government, the nation, and the country to the brink of destruction. All of this can be blamed on the hazrats and mullas. 150,000 people have perished. If there were no further fighting in the country, it would still take a hundred years to return to the status quo.

July 27: Already Habib Allah's soldiers had not been paid for seven months and survived only by stealing from the peasants. Instead of paying the troops, the money in the treasury was used to bribe the avaricious and unscrupulous Pushtuns in order to neutralize them.

Besides the taxation to pay for the war, the confiscation of property owned by officials of earlier administrations went on. The home of the late prime minister, ᶜAbd al-Quddus, was confiscated and looted of carpets and valuables found secreted behind a false wall. In late August, Mīr Hāshim, the minister of finance under Aman Allah, and his brother, Sayyid Habib, were arrested because of a letter they reportedly received from Nadir, and their houses confiscated.

Other stories Fayz Muhammad tells relate to the appearance of counterfeit coins and problems of bribery in the Central Customs Office.

August 10: Rumors circulated in Kabul today that rupees and *qirāns*[246] minted with the name of ᶜInayat Allah, who had briefly taken the throne after Aman Allah's abdication, had appeared. ᶜInayat Allah had been forced into exile and settled in Tehran. But a few days ago, there was talk that he had returned to Jalalabad. Rupees and qirans minted in his name were circulated by Habib Allah's enemies. This news encouraged the people of Kabul. When they met, they told each other that there is at least a grain of truth in every lie. But ᶜInayat Allah is still in Tehran, and the Indo-British authorities, whose protégé is Habib Allah, will not allow ᶜInayat Allah to enter Afghanistan from Tehran through their territory. From this it follows that the coins with ᶜInayat Allah's name on them were probably minted by counterfeiters in Tirah. They may have acted on the instructions of Nadir in order to unite the Pushtuns by using ᶜInayat Allah's name.

This story was repeated for several days but gradually died down. It is not known who was behind it, but it brought no advantage to either Nadir or Hashim, for all Pushtuns by their very nature are untrue to their alliances and agreements and are more accustomed to thievery than honesty.

August 12: Hajji Muhammad Salih, the son of the Qizilbash Mirza Muhammad Tahir (who had given Habib Allah's minister of court, Shayr Jan, a bribe of four thousand rupees, hoping thereby to leave Kabul, go to Iran, and escape the tyranny of the Habib Allah regime), was appointed director of the customs office at Herat and left for that city. When he reached Ghazni, a resident of Kabul by the name of Ahmad ᶜAli complained to the minister of trade. Ahmad ᶜAli was an official in the Ministry of Trade to whom Hajji Muhammad Salih had promised, but not paid, a bribe before leaving Kabul. As a result of his accusations, the minister telephoned the governor of Ghazni and ordered him to send Hajji Muhammad Salih back to Kabul. He was brought from the caravanserai where he was staying to the Bala Hisar, looking like someone who had just committed murder or was guilty of a sin like fornication or drunkenness. They held him that night under guard and sent him the next day to Kabul. The five hundred rupees he had paid to get himself and a maidservant to Qandahar were for nought. When he arrived in Kabul, he was sent right away to Malik Muhsin. Hajji Muhammad Salih even offered him a bribe, fearful of the reason that he had been summoned back to Kabul. He told Malik Muhsin what had happened to him and showed him the farman of appointment from Habib Allah and the instructions of the minister of trade. The governor-general escorted him to Habib Allah along with his farman and reported that he was not guilty of anything. Hajji Muhammad Salih was considerably relieved and now asked Habib Allah not to appoint him to the customs post. After this, he swore before his relatives and friends that he would never again serve the government. He was convinced that all the Kuhistanis and Kuhdamanis were thieves.

Every seller of eggs, vinegar, grapes, firewood, grape syrup, and dates, having now taken up arms and strapped on a bandolier, wanted to be a minister, a qal^{c}ah-begi, an aide-de-camp to the amir, a military high commissioner, a governor-general, a field marshal, a lieutenant general, a brigadier, a colonel, or a governor. Every thief and ignorant unbeliever, every vagrant whose life had been spent in the hills and wastelands, every brigand, and every murderer of true believers, sees himself as padishah. It is clear that in such a government there is no place for a rational person. Hajji Muhammad Salih secured an appointment in Herat but wound up with nothing, after spending some thirty thousand rupees in vain. After this, he emigrated to Mashhad, travelling by way of Quetta and Durzab.

Fayz Muhammad also continues to raise the issue of the general immorality of the Tajik administration and in particular the sexual abuses committed against the people of Kabul, men and women alike, by Habib Allah's men, although with somewhat less intensity (whether he had become more inured to these incidents or there were fewer to report, it's difficult to say). One of his cases includes details well-chosen to stir moral outrage.

August 1: The governor-general, Malik Muhsin, today hanged the husband of a woman from Chardihi, whom one of the debauchers from Habib Allah's gang had raped and impregnated. The rapist himself was also caught. Malik Muhsin ordered the woman imprisoned until she gave birth and afterwards for her and her infant to be killed. The qazi-judge objected to killing the infant, declaring that this contravened the laws of the Shari^{c}ah. The governor-general replied, "Whether my order conforms with the Shari^{c}ah or not, it must be carried out. So don't argue!"

August 7: Last night Hamid Allah learned that a young man from the northern regions had been brought to the village of Bibi Mahru[247] to dance and sing at a wedding. Hamid Allah suddenly barged into the house with a gang of bandits and arrested more than a hundred people who were innocently enjoying themselves. Hamid Allah himself was a dancer and an incorrigible libertine but, in order to appear to be a devotee of Islam in the eyes of the people, he put those he arrested in shackles, took them to the city, and threw them in jail. Today they were paraded around the bazaars as a lesson to others and the young dancer was caned nearly to death. The rest were fined a total of twenty thousand rupees, each person having to pay a fine ranging from one to six hundred rupees. Hamid Allah also ordered the homes of the parents of the bride and the bridegroom confiscated. Despite the fact that during the time of his brother's brigandage Hamid Allah himself loved to dance and, at the time his brother came to power, would have his way with young girls and young boys at night and by day would molest people, he nonetheless took these steps to try to make himself appear to be a true Muslim and an upholder of the Shari^cah.

August 16: Rumors circulate that soldiers of Habib Allah in Qandahar abducted a young boy one night, forced him to dance for them, and then sodomized him. This shameless act of the Kuhdamani and Kuhistani brigands, miscreants, and infidels revolted the pious and chaste people of Qandahar and they denounced the perpetrators as unbelievers. They considered these acts a gross violation of the Shari^cah and decided that it was better to perish than subject themselves to humiliation at the hands of Habib Allah's band. They nourished the hope that someone might be found who would be able to rout the northerners and save the oppressed populace. They would give him any assistance to rid Qandahar of the gang of tyrants. They discussed this in secret but dared not start anything without the support of the tribes outside the city. The accursed northerners, having learned about the intentions of the residents of the city, began now to exert every effort to try to prevent news of their sexual escapades reaching the people outside the city and leading to an uprising. They therefore began to post misleading announcements to persuade the residents of the city of their piety and religious devotion.

How Fayz Muhammad was privy to such information he does not say. This story is somewhat uncharacteristic of him in its lack of specifics. But it does serve the purpose of further vilifying the "northerners" in language and image chosen for the greatest impact.

Probably affecting our author more directly and of more concern to him was a measure taken by the government to limit Iranian involvement in Afghanistan's politics. Iran interceded with the government not only on behalf of its coreligionists, the Twelver Shi^cites, but also on behalf of others subjected to what Fayz Muhammad depicts as government abuse. The Iranian Embassy had standing orders from the shah, according to Fayz Muhammad, to take whatever steps it could to assist Shi^cites. In Fayz

Muhammad's own case this had meant providing him with iodine to treat the wounds he suffered from the beating on July 2. But, as he reports here, members of the embassy also intervened on behalf of non-Shi^{c}ites as well, in this case a member of the royal family. But this time, the Tajik amir countered by isolating the embassy and forbidding Kabulis from entering it. In reporting this, Fayz Muhammad also indicates the importance the embassy had for him and, by implication, Fayz Muhammad's importance to the embassy.

August 2: The military attaché at the Iranian embassy, Colonel ^{c}Ali Khan, visited Prince Amin Allah Khan[248] because Hamid Allah and his elder brother had ordered him caned. However, at the petition of the minister of court, Shayr Jan, they commuted the caning but ordered the severing of all contacts with foreigners by Afghans. So the guard at the Iranian embassy was replaced and the people of Kabul were prevented from visiting the embassy. For eight years, I had visited the embassy twice a week. But after receiving word from the secretary at the embassy I stopped going there for a while. Prince Amin Allah now left Afghanistan.

In the midst of the seeming turmoil, Fayz Muhammad reports the somewhat incongruous news that people from some of the embassies in Kabul received permission for an outing to Jabal al-Siraj on July 27 to visit the power station there.[249] Since most foreigners had evacuated the city earlier, it is not entirely clear who made up the group of picnickers and why they would have been interested in the condition of the power station. Perhaps the amir's willingness to permit the outing was a sign that his hold over the countryside around Kabul at least to the north was fairly secure, despite the threats continually reported by Fayz Muhammad. It may also have been intended to aid in his quest to gain international recognition of his regime. Like the Taliban in 1997, Habib Allah found that control of the capital won him no international recognition.

Perhaps the hope of gaining diplomatic recognition, combined with a greater sense of security, also prompted the amir to begin preparations to celebrate Independence Day (August 19).

The Independence Day Celebrations

August 5: In order to win the people over to his side and to instill confidence in their hearts that the government is not afraid of fighting, Habib Allah ordered a Victory Arch built and flower beds planted from the Shah-i Du Shamshirah Mosque near the bridge up to the Monument to Knowledge and Ignorance which was erected by His Highness Aman Allah, and the road to Dar al-Aman decorated in celebration of Independence Day. He assigned the organization of the festivities, including recruiting singers, to the Minister of Education, Fayz Muhammad,[250] and to those sycophants who have continually curried the amir's favor. The amir warned them that if they did not make better preparations than had been made for the holiday in preceding years, he would have them all shot. And although Habib Allah had no conception of what constituted beauty, nevertheless, afraid of slanderers, these people zealously applied themselves to the holiday preparations.

August 14: At this time Habib Allah made vain attempts to get foreign regimes to recognize him as amir of Afghanistan and to resume diplomatic relations. By a decision of the National Assembly, the northerners sent telegrams to the Russian and English governments and requested they send a minister plenipotentiary to re-establish relations and conclude new agreements. But these two governments refused to respond to the overtures and instead hoped that Nadir or someone else towards whom the nation was not averse and who could consolidate power in the country and defend its borders and subjects would come to power. To conceal this rejection, the brigands circulated rumors that ministers plenipotentiary would be dispatched to Kabul after Independence Day.

August 18: Yesterday, the shopkeepers of Kabul were forcibly assembled in the southern part of Dih Mazang, which Habib Allah had designated as the site for the Independence Day celebrations. Originally, he had planned to hold it at Dar al-Aman but, worried about attacks from Nadir and the Hazarahs, he changed his mind and ordered the shopkeepers to decorate the shops in Dih Mazang. The director of the museum, Ghulam Muhyi al-Din, and his staff, busy with preparations for the celebration, had been assigned to decorate the streets and other spots planned as gathering places for the festival. They now began to hang colored banners and strings of electric lights. The minister of education, Fayz Muhammad, ordered to round up singers who were students in the schools, had done so but still he continued to fuss about as if he were still recruiting them, so that the chief tyrant, Habib Allah, would not punish him for being idle.

At this time, a frustrated and disappointed Nadir moved his headquarters to ᶜAli Khayl with the Jaji tribe, which has assured him of its unswerving loyalty. In the preceding seven months he and his brothers, Shah Wali and Shah Mahmud, have made every effort to forge an alliance with tribes utterly lacking in any sense of Pushtun loyalty, honor, conscience, and cooperation. Nadir spent his days and nights hungry and cold, sleeping on bare earth, stones, and camel thorn, in order to unite the treaty-violating Pushtuns who live in the mountains of the Southern Province. But some of them, completely devoid of any sense of honor or belief and possessed by an avarice that knows no bounds, offered themselves to Habib Allah and, in reward, he gave each of them from three to fifteen thousand rupees. Others pledged to murder Nadir and his brothers for a hundred thousand rupees.

Believing that Nadir's efforts have now failed, Habib Allah acts as if he were the legitimate amir of Afghanistan. But he is unaware that divine retribution awaits ignoramuses and tyrants like himself. God saves, and has mercy on, children and all good people who find themselves in hopeless situations. We hope that He will save the people of this country from the oppression and mischief caused by the supporters of Habib Allah and give us peace of a kind.

August 19: During the reign of His Highness Aman Allah, it was customary to celebrate Independence Day for eight days at Paghman, which would be specially decorated for the occasion. Money collected in the form of rental fees for cars and carriages and from the sale of tickets to the celebration—in all some sixty thousand rupees—and one lak of rupees from theater and cinema rentals—would be given in prizes to master craftsmen, wrestlers, and others. But today it was announced that the holiday would be only five days long and would be held in a field on the banks of the Kabul River near the southern section of Dih Mazang. Around eight in the morning, when they heard the town crier, all citizens were told to line both sides of the street from the Victory Arch which

August 1929—Independence Day celebrations, Hamid Allah shooting, Malik Muhsin far left

August 1929—Independence Day celebrations, ᶜAta al-Haqq, Foreign Minister, delivering speech

stands beside the Shah Du Shamshirah Mosque to the place where the celebration is to be held and await the arrival of Habib Allah's car. Although everyone was loath to even look at Habib Allah, still, fearing punishment if they did not, residents stood until 10 a.m. under the scorching heat of the sun. When the car with the leader of the brigands passed them, the people, overcoming their feelings, raised their hands to their foreheads in greeting.

Habib Allah drove up to the festival grounds, climbed up on a wooden stand before a large crowd and, imitating Aman Allah's statesmanlike appearance, opened the festival with a speech. However his homily, which had been written by the minister of court, who had also coached him on how to deliver it, most of all sounded like the peroration of a thief. He had not bothered to memorize the text and stood there telling lie after lie about the way things really were.

August 22: On holidays, and therefore today, the Pushtuns of the Southern Province, those who were supporters of Habib Allah, dance to drums for money as they did during the reign of Aman Allah. The Kuhistanis and Kuhdamanis are much amused and make fun of them: "Look how splendidly the Tajiks make you Pushtuns of the Southern Province dance." And the Pushtuns, having forgotten the meaning of shame, accept these insults in silence so that Habib Allah will not take back the two or three rupees he has paid them for dancing.

Three days after the Independence Day celebrations began, Nadir is heard from again with the issuing of a proclamation that was smuggled into Kabul.

August 22: Nadir addressed a general proclamation, which he sent out by secret courier, to the people of Kabul. This evening leaflets with the proclamation were posted in gathering places in the city. The text reads:

> Despite extremely difficult circumstances and bloodshed among Muslims, we have been calling for a ceasefire and a truce and have avoided raiding and attacking, so that perhaps the destroyer of religion, Habib Allah, who calls himself the "servant of religion," would come to his senses and put an end to subjecting the country to death and destruction and return to his former way of life where he was happy to herd two or three goats and sheep in the open air and enjoy the life which his father had led. However, the fact is that this ignorant unbeliever, having seized the throne,

> has not stopped boasting, "Even if hundreds of thousands of people perish and thousands of homes, the country, and the nation are destroyed, having taken the throne by sword and the help of God, I will never abandon it so long as I live." Having carried out his criminal plans, Habib Allah has plundered all the resources of the nation and brought the country to the brink of disaster by his sedition. The tribes of the Southern Province have joined forces and resolve to attack Kabul and cleanse it of Habib Allah and the larcenists who support him. This is the plan: a force of ten thousand militiamen will march on Kabul via Char Asya, ten thousand via Butkhak, and twelve thousand through Sar-i Chashmah and Maydan. In view of the resolution of the valorous Pushtuns of the Southern Province, the residents of the northern and other regions should either detain the villain or drive him out of the palace and the capital. Failure to do so will be the cause of serious loss to themselves.

A copy of this proclamation, which came into Habib Allah's hands, unnerved him.

At this point, the proclamation would seem to have been pure bluff. The tribes of the Eastern and Southern Provinces were in disarray, at least as far as Nadir's hopes were concerned. Fayz Muhammad, however, still continues to interpret all signs as pointing to the imminent collapse of the house of Habib Allah. But by the time his memoir ends on August 28, Nadir Khan was no closer to realizing his hope of taking Kabul than he had been when he arrived from France back in March.

The End of Resistance in Tagab

Tagab's importance in the narrative lies more in the boost it periodically seems to have given to Fayz Muhammad's morale than in any real threat it posed to the Tajiks in Kabul. Between early May and late July, Fayz Muhammad had found virtually nothing to report from the Tagab front. But then on July 24 he reports the hopeful, for him, news that a letter had been sent to the people of Tagab by Hashim, that a two-pronged offensive of Eastern Province forces planned to attack Kabul, with one force advancing on Kabul from the east along the road from Jalalabad and the second circling north through Tagab and into Kuhistan and then coming south down the Kuhdaman Valley, the heart of Tajik-land, and attacking the capital. The rumored letter sought Tagabi support.

Like all such grandiose schemes of coordinated attacks on Kabul, this one came to nothing. Still, the rumor had some effect. First, it led the amir to deal harshly with a problem Fayz Muhammad reported as being a major one for the Tajik leader—desertion.

August 2: The amir's forces, defeated in three regions (in Jalriz by the Hazarahs, in Logar by the Ahmadzai, and in Tagab by locals), saved themselves by flight. When he heard this news, a frightened Habib Allah ordered a decree posted in all the mosques of the city and villages. In it he warned the quarter chiefs (*kalāntar*s) of the city and the heads (*kadkhudās*) of the villages not to give shelter to deserters fleeing the battlefield but to hand them over to the authorities. The authorities, in turn, were to send them back to the places from which they had fled and there shoot them as a lesson to others. Should the kalantars or kadkhudas harbor anyone and be discovered, then the decree said that they would be subject to a fine of twelve rupees and the deserter shot. Every kalantar or kadkhuda who sheltered more than one deserter would be fined up to five thousand rupees. After the issuing of this decree, deserters sought refuge in the mountains.

Second, because of the letter and the rumored moves of Eastern Province tribes, four Tajik khans from Kuhistan who had come to Kabul—Muhammad A^c^zam from Tutumdara, a large village at the northeast corner of the Kuhdaman Valley;[251] *Muhammad Zaman from Jabal al-Siraj, and two men whose home villages or towns were unknown to Fayz Muhammad, Khwajah Babu and a man known as Mir Bachcha, the son of Mir Akbar, returned to Kuhistan on August 3, ostensibly to defend their families and property from the Tagabis. Then on August 5, Habib Allah sent a farman to the Tajiks of Kuhistan and Kuhdaman calling on them to form a 6,500-man force to resist any force attempting to enter Kuhistan from the direction of Tagab. There were some skirmishes between the 5th and the 9th prompted by Tagabi belief, or so Fayz Muhammad reports, that Eastern Province tribes were on the way there.*

The farman calling on the Kuhistanis and Kuhdamanis to prepare to defend themselves against the Tagabis either included instructions to them to take whatever weapons they had and go lay waste Tagabi farms and orchards or such instructions followed shortly. For Fayz Muhammad reports that on August 12, the Tagabis, having received none of the promised support from the Eastern Province tribes, now faced a concerted counter-offensive from Kuhistan and decided it was time to make their peace with Habib Allah.

August 12: A decree was sent to the people of the north with an order to arm themselves with saws, hatchets, and axes and cut down any fruit or other tree that they found in the region of Tagab. This kind of order from Habib Allah violates the precepts of the Prophet Muhammad, who, at the time of the conquests, had prohibited the army of Islam and his companions from cutting down trees, destroying crops, killing the elderly, women, or children of unbelievers.

Because of this decree, the frightened Tagabis now set out, Korans in hand,[252] to ask for forgiveness and to express their obedience. However, the northerners paid no heed to the Koran and went on cutting down their trees. The Tagabis had been incited to war by the lying provocations of the tribes of the Eastern Province, who had promised to come and help but did not, and now the Tagabis themselves had to bear the brunt.

August 13: Today, the Tagabis sent a message to the tribes of the Eastern Province in which they explained why they had submitted to Habib Allah. The reason was that the Eastern Province tribes had appealed to the Tagabis to stand up and fight and had themselves promised to come but had not. As a result, humiliation and even destruction threatened the Tagabis. In their message, they wrote, "You violated the agreement and from the very outset of the rebellion up to now you are to blame for all the destruction. Our misfortunes and sufferings are all due to you."

This marked the end of Tagabi resistance. Malik Muhsin, governor-general of Kabul Province which included Tagab, now went to the town to establish administrative control over it and took some of the more prominent Tagabis back to Kabul as prisoners. Fayz Muhammad has nothing more to say about Tagab after this.

The Hazarahs Make Their Peace with the Tajiks

Nothing was more important to Fayz Muhammad during the seven weeks after he returned from the Hazarahjat than that the Hazarahs continue to withhold their support from Habib Allah. But they too were becoming increasingly aware that there was no credible challenger to Habib Allah, and since Hazarahs had many kinsmen and business interests in the capital, it is not surprising that the voices of accommodation begin to make themselves heard during July and August as Nadir's threat diminished. For Fayz Muhammad, the Hazarah willingness to negotiate and cease hostilities was largely a matter of betrayal of the Hazarah cause by another Hazarah, Nadir ᶜAlī from Jaghuri, a district not far from his own home town of Qarabagh southwest of Ghazni.

After the delegation to the Hazarahjat in which Fayz Muhammad participated returned to Kabul, the fighting between Hazarahs in the Unay Pass region and forces loyal to Habib Allah intensified. No doubt the issuing of the fatwa branding them infidels, or at least the rumor of such a fatwa, was instrumental in hardening Hazarah resolve. In addition, Hamid Allah's defeat, after being lured through the pass, no doubt encouraged the Hazarah forces there to try to expand their control eastwards. But whereas the Unay Pass and west of it was predominantly Hazarah-land, just east of the Unay Pass, Takanah and Jalriz also had large Tajik populations and these sided with the Kabul regime.

July 17: At four o'clock this afternoon, shouting "ya ᶜAli madad" ("O ᶜAli, help us!"), Hazarah braves, who had heard about Habib Allah's proclamation in which he threatened to turn the Pushtun tribes loose on them, attacked his forces that were stationed in the Unay Pass and Qalᶜah-i Safid. They routed them and pursued them to Takana and Jalriz. After killing, wounding, and capturing many of them, the Hazarahs returned to the Unay Pass in triumph.

July 22: The brave Hazarahs, whose courageous struggle broke Habib Allah's morale, have resumed fighting. A force with siege weapons was sent from Kabul to Jalriz to assist the defenders there so that if the Hazarahs, in pursuit of the troops defeated at the Unay Pass, should get as far as Jalriz, then the artillery could be used to reduce the captured fortresses and make it impossible for the Hazarahs to stay in them and continue the fight.

July 23: Today Habib Allah seemed somber: the gallant Hazarah attack and defeat of his army has plunged him into despondency. After sending 450 soldiers with siege weapons yesterday to help his forces in Jalriz, not a single soldier remains in Kabul, since forces have been sent to Logar, Sar-i Chashmah, Butkhak, Khak-i Jabbar, and Tangi Gharu as well. Habib Allah had already dispatched even the 150 soldiers who guard the airport and the Arg to Sar-i Chashmah to defend it against the Hazarahs. Not only were there no tribal forces in the capital, there weren't even any policemen.

The chief thief himself, Habib Allah, departed today for Sar-i Chashmah and the governor-general Malik Muhsin for Logar. En route, the governor-general had four of the amir's soldiers shot for desertion. The soldiers who had fought at Logar and been defeated were outraged when they learned about the execution of these four and decided that as soon as Malik Muhsin approached they would dispatch him to the next world. But, in the nick of time, he realized what was afoot and returned to Kabul.

At Kut-i Ashru, Habib Allah disarmed and shot sixteen soldiers who had been in the fighting with the Hazarahs but had fled toward Kabul. Among those slain were four Shi^cites—residents of Wazirabad—who had been sent to the battlefield under duress. Their execution angered not only the residents of Wazirabad but also all Shi^cites.

Today, the Shi^cite sayyid Abu'l-Qasim, who had a house and plot of land in Takanah, prepared loaves of bread made from one and a half Kabuli seers of flour, a skin of fresh buttermilk, some oil, and a roasted sheep he had slaughtered at midday. He set off with the food to offer it to Habib Allah and his bandits who were hungry and thirsty. When the sayyid approached the leader of the thieves, he was asked who he was and where he came from. A Sunni Tajik from Jalriz, blinded by a savage, fanatical hatred for all Shi^cites, said he was a Shi^cite sayyid as well as a partisan who the night before had given shelter in his fort to a Hazarah, the son of Shah Nur.[253] When he heard this, Habib Allah was enraged. Without thinking, he fired seven shots from his pistol into the sayyid although what he should have done was thank him for the desperately needed bread, meat, oil, and buttermilk he had brought. Habib Allah then ordered his home burned to the ground and his belongings confiscated. He handed his two wives and his betrothed daughter over to the Kuhdamanis. Hamid Allah, the tyrant's younger brother, came running from the battlefield to participate in torching the fort, ransacking the sayyid's belongings, and seizing his wives and children. Tearing an eight-month-old son from its mother, he grabbed the baby by the feet and threw him to the ground with all his might, killing the infant. The Tajiks of Jalriz and Takanah dragged off everything in the sayyid's house. Since he had been quite well off, each Tajik made off with a substantial amount. In the evening, the Hazarahs learned that Habib Allah was in the region and attacked him from four sides, hoping to capture and send him to Nadir. But he escaped in his car back to Kabul. In the fighting with the Hazarahs, twelve of his men were wounded and several killed. The Hazarahs now command the countryside right up to Jalriz.

July 25: Today the Hazarahs, having learned of the murder of Sayyid Abu'l-Qasim, the torching and looting of his home, the holding of his wife and daughter, and the murder of the eight-month old infant, took revenge on Habib Allah's forces in Jalriz. Fifty wounded bandits, the backbone of Habib Allah's force, were loaded in vehicles and driven to the hospital in Kabul. The rest, bleeding and smeared with filth, became the prey of dogs and jackals. The Hazarahs also burned several houses in Takanah and shot three or four men who had participated in the murder of the sayyid.

Rumors circulated that the Hazarahs, having taken Jalriz, intend to come over the mountains through Sanglakh and attack Paghman and Kabul. Sayyid Haydar Shah Sanglakhi promised Habib Allah that he would not allow the Hazarahs to pass through Sanglakh. In return he received 150 English muzzle-loading rifles from the amir and set off for Sanglakh. But Sayyid Haydar Shah is really an ally of the Hazarahs and has advised them not to be too hasty in attacking Kabul through Sanglakh and Paghman, at least until it is known when the people of the Southern and Eastern Provinces will attack. It is doubtful whether the people of Maydan, Arghandah, Begtut, Paghman, and Chardihi, although they hate Habib Allah and await the attack of the Hazarahs on Kabul with impatience, can be relied on. The Hazarahs followed the sayyid's advice and suspended the offensive against Kabul and returned to their positions in the Unay Pass.

Throughout his narrative, Fayz Muhammad emphasizes the importance of the "religion card"—the usefulness to either side of condemning the other as kafirs, worthy therefore only of death. The problem with playing the religion card, especially in Kabul with its large and influential population of Qizilbash Shiᶜites, was that the regime could not function without some degree of cooperation from the Qizilbash. The incident that Fayz Muhammad describes here obviously overstepped the bounds of what was acceptable in the sectarian war of words.

July 26: Tonight Habib Allah summoned one of the pseudo-mullas from the Andar tribe, and assigned him to deliver a sermon at the Friday service in the Pul-i Khishti congregational mosque, in which he was to accuse the Hazarahs of unbelief and call for a pogrom against the Shiᶜites. This pseudo-mulla ascended the pulpit, recited some verses from the Qurᵓan and some words of the Prophet, texts that are completely inappropriate to the present situation, and then began to call for the killing, robbing, and enslaving of Shiᶜites. But the discourse of this ignorant mulla, on whom Habib Allah had pinned his hopes, angered those present who had had enough of the oppression and evildoings of Habib Allah and the northern infidels and fervently prayed for Hazarah success. The mayor, Khwajah Taj al-Din, took note of the people's unhappiness with the sermon and straightaway went to Habib Allah and received permission from him to arrest the mulla.

Then a group of Qizilbash who took this pseudo-mulla off to the prison in the Arg came to the mayor's office and complained, "Accusing the Shiᶜites of unbelief and heresy solely on the grounds that up to now the Hazarahs have not sent the government an oath of allegiance violates the ordinances of the Shariᶜah. This can only result in great carnage which no one will be able to stop. The defenseless Qizilbash will suffer, their property and homes will be ransacked and confiscated, and they themselves will perish. And this will only bring loss in this world and the next. If the Qizilbash of Kabul perish, this does not in any case mean that all Shiᶜites will be annihilated. Furthermore, if there is bloodshed, the other side will also suffer great losses."

After hearing the Qizilbash out, the mayor reassured them and said that the amir, carrying out the will of the people, had ordered the arrest of the libertine mulla and would put him on public display as a lesson to others. Tomorow several Qizilbash should come and verify this with their own eyes.

At this point, officials from the Iranian Embassy formally accused Habib Allah of ignorance and spreading lies [about Shi^cism].

July 27: Today the Hazarahs resumed combat operations in the Sar-i Chashmah area and entered Jalriz in triumph. The 1300-man brigade (*ghund*) of Habib Allah that was stationed there was unable to withstand the onslaught and scattered to their homes in Kuhdaman via Begtut and Paghman. They would not return to Kabul for fear of being shot as deserters.

July 28: Today, the mayor of Kabul, Taj al-Din, who had promised to make an example of the mulla from the Andar tribe who had denounced the Shi^{c}ites from the pulpit, sent a written invitation to the elders of the Qizilbash by the hand of Agha Jan, the son of Nawruz ^{c}Ali Khan, asking them to come to the municipal offices. In the message, he indicated that it would be judicious on their part to forgive the mulla. Some of the Qizilbash came to me for advice. They reported that a decree has been ready for publication for some days now accusing Shi^{c}ites of unbelief. Yesterday 120 mullas had signed it and thereby incited all Sunnis to a holy war against Hazarahs. They felt that if they were asked anything regarding issues of religion they would not be able to answer. The Qizilbash feared they might be humiliated at the municipal offices and asked me how they should behave.

Ever since the beating on July 2 my whole body has been in pain and I have been confined to bed. I recited Abu Hanifah's[254] precept: "It is wrong to consider a person an infidel if he is a 'person of the *qiblah*' (someone who prays toward Mecca). Regarding the unity of all Muslims, Abu Hanifah also says, 'Everyone who utters the words "There is no god but God, and Muhammad is the Prophet of God" is Muslim by consensus.' In the *Hidāyah*[255] Shi^{c}ites are considered Muslims on the basis of a fatwa from Nu^{c}man b. Sabit. Moreover, the law written down in the Shari^{c}ah reads as follows: 'Evidence given even by people who have erred is acceptable.' So how can they call people who profess the Muslim faith, infidels?"

However, the Qizilbash said that they would not be able to quote from the *Hidāyah* themselves and give a reply like mine at the municipality. Instead they proposed to carry me on a *dhooly* [litter] so that I could do it for them. But I could not move and reproached them, "O wicked, cowardly people! Can't you even cite a book written by the Sunnis themselves? You stay here and work for this government, and yet force me, a sick man, to respond on your behalf and quote their book to them?" I then asked them to send Shaykh Muhammad Riza, an exceptionally articulate man, so that he could quote from the book at the municipal offices. He would say that Shi^cites should be treated just like the followers of Abu Hanifah and that the Sunnis should stop accusing the Shi^cites of unbelief. So the Qizilbash departed and sent the shaykh to me accompanied by the kalantar of their quarter, Sultan ^cAli. But no matter how I tried to persuade Shaykh Muhammad Riza, he did not have the courage to quote the book at the municipality, fearing that he would be condemned for it.

A merchant from Tabriz, named Asad Allah, and an official from the Iranian embassy, Sardar, had come to visit me at this time. So, I sent the *Hidāyah* to the Iranian embassy by the hand of Sardar. The military attaché and his secretary went to see Habib Allah and conveyed their government's view of the need for him to exert more control over religious conflict. By the following day announcements were posted in mosques and in other frequented places, forbidding the denunciation of Shi^cites as infidels. Habib Allah was thus thwarted from publishing the proclamation which the pseudo-mullas had signed. Thanks to the actions of officials of the Iranian embassy, the denunciation of Shi^cites stopped and the Qizilbash were reassured. This evening, Qizilbash leaders went to the municipality to intercede for that infidel mulla [from Andar]. Habib Allah kissed him and released him.

July 29: The Hazarahs who had defeated the forces of Habib Allah at the Unay Pass pursued the fleeing soldiers to Jalriz. Fighting continues right up to this evening in Jalriz. However, the amir's forces, who have fortified their positions, are managing to hold out. At night, when both sides were tired from the fighting, two Hazarahs, one of whom was a sayyid from Sanglakh, stumbled into Habib Allah's troops. These Hazarahs had been returning home from the Hazarahjat where they had gone to buy meat and flour. Both were delivered to Kabul. The sayyid, who was loyal to Habib Allah and had not taken part in the fighting, was released. Habib Allah summoned the other Hazarah for questioning hoping to learn the situation of the Hazarahs, the state of their arms, and their intentions. The interrogation went as follows:

"If you don't tell me the truth, I'll kill you," Habib Allah threatened, "because I already have accurate information obtained from Pushtun nomads."

"I don't care whether you have the facts or not, I would not lie in any event because lying is the worst sin of all. I'm not afraid of dying. I joined the struggle, knowing in advance that I would perish. However, my life would be cursed if I were to submit to anyone except God and his Prophet, especially to some devil. Therefore if I die while defending my property, family, the honor of my tribe, the legal Islamic government, and my homeland, this will be a great honor for me."

"So why then do you fight against me? I am the padishah of Islam and I hold the reins of government in my hands."

"The padishah of Islam is His Highness Aman Allah, whom ignorant mullas accused of unbelief," declared the Hazarah. "But nothing that he has been accused of has been affirmed by the Shari^{c}ah. He was forced to abdicate but he remains devoted to the religion of Islam. The Hazarahs fight so that they can invite him back by telegram once they take Kabul and declare him amir despite the fact that he has never done anything good for them."

"And where are you going to get the rifles and ammunition to fight the government?" asked Habib Allah.

"In future we are going to get them just as we did in the past, by capturing them."

"You know, all the Hazarahs are going to perish and how is a dead man able to fight?"

"There are 2,100,000 Hazarahs and before they perish their numbers will double."

"Then according to you, the Hazarahs, who had promised to give an oath of allegiance, will not now give it?"

"Never! We promised to give an oath of allegiance in order to end the war and save ourselves from destruction. In fact, we are waiting for Nadir to approach Kabul to resume the struggle."

The Hazarah had told the truth so Habib Allah canceled the firing squad and imprisoned him instead.

For Fayz Muhammad, the outlook for the Hazarahs was closely tied to the success, or lack thereof, of Nadir. Although to this point, what he was reporting about the Hazarahs was encouraging (despite his tendency to overstate Hazarah successes), their willingness to fight outside the Hazarahjat was largely contingent on the oft-proposed multi-pronged coordinated offensive against Kabul actually materializing. The weak links in the offensive, at least as Fayz Muhammad presents the case, were the Pushtuns, not the Hazarahs. And nothing diminished Hazarah resolve like setbacks in the Eastern and Southern Provinces.

July 30: Today an article with the headline "Defeat for Muhammad Nadir Khan" was published in issue No. 20 of *Ḥabīb al-Islām* by its editor and chief bootlicker. It read,

> Muhammad Nadir Khan has tried to ignite rebellion and sedition in the Southern Province. To some degree he has succeeded in raising a few of the tribes against the central government. But he soon saw the regrettable outcome of his illegal activities. As you know from issue No. 19 of *Ḥabīb al-Islām* and as reliable facts at our disposal attest, Muhammad Nadir Khan is now nowhere to be found. His brother, Shah Wali Khan, has left Afghanistan for Parachinar.[256] The general situation of the tribes and the intentions of their leaders inspire confidence that soon all the tribes will express their submission to the lawful central government and will never again yield to the provocations of the enemies of Islam and the opponents of Pushtun honor and valor. Moreover, we are convinced that the English government, which is our neighbor, upholding the principles of good-neighborliness and of international agreements, will prevent the return to Afghan territory of persons who would bring harm to the security and general tranquillity of the country.

Lieutenant General Muhammad Siddiq, known by the nickname "No-Nose"[257] because his nose was cut off during a raid, sent this issue of the paper to the Hazarahs. They had pinned their hopes on Nadir and were now disappointed and returned to the Unay Pass from Jalriz. The report of the retreat of the Hazarahs, which I entered in my diary of the rebellion, greatly distressed me because I had persuaded them to step up their struggle against Habib Allah. I cursed the editor of the newspaper for being an ignoramus. I know that Kabul and its environs have been encircled from the very first day of Habib Allah's reign and there is not a single safe road. The whole country is engulfed in the flames of rebellion and Habib Allah's gang are busy killing and looting. Despite this, the editor calls the government with Habib Allah at its head the legitimate one—these brigands from the north, unbelievers, destroyers of the country, pseudo-mullas, people in whom not a single ounce of humanity remains—while the devout defenders of Muslim honor, who spend day and night in misery and deprivation, exerting every effort to drive out the gang of unbelievers and libertines, so as to bring tranquillity to the nation, end the rebellion, and restore the destroyed government and country, these the editor calls rebels, enemies of Islam, and foes of Afghan honor. He dares call the gang of bandits and despoilers of the country the legal government! May this report be accursed and that fiend be damned, who with the help of a secret agent conveyed it to the Hazarahs and detoured them from the path of what is right!

All these things—the abovementioned newspaper report; a Koran sent by Habib Allah to the Hazarahjat; the propaganda of Mirza Hasan ᶜAli, the scribe working for the governor-general, Malik Muhsin, who had arrived in the Hazarahjat and introduced himself to the backers of Muhammad Amin Khan; and the activities of Nadir ᶜAli, the son of Sultan ᶜAli, a Hazarah from Jaghuri who had obtained an oath of allegiance from the residents of Fuladi, Mir Adinah, Pushtah, Shayr Dagh, and Jaghuri—resulted in my admonitions going for nought.

July 31: A certain bandit from the Farrash Shiᶜites of Paghman has gathered some three to four hundred men and conducted raids against Habib Allah. Tonight he led a foray against Qarghah and skirmished with the local population. But later, after several such raids, he went into hiding on the heights of the Kuh-i Paghman and then escaped into the mountains. Malik Muhsin killed his brother, a man named Hasan, and confiscated two or three houses belonging to the poor people of Afshar, accusing its residents of having sheltered and fed this brigand.[258]

Today Habib Allah, fearing that Hazarah contingents having reinforced their positions on the Kuh-i Surkh might begin an offensive against Kabul, ordered a unit with artillery to go to Paghman and take up a position there.

The story of the Hazarah of Jaghuri,[259] Nadir ᶜAli, occupies a good deal of this part of Fayz Muhammad's narrative. He seems more than a little obsessed with Nadir ᶜAli, blaming him for betraying the Hazarahs and singling him out as the main culprit behind the Hazarahs' finding accommodation with Habib Allah. Particularly galling to Fayz Muhammad was Nadir ᶜAli's success in persuading other Hazarahs to support the Tajik administration, in other words convincing them to do exactly the opposite of what Fayz Muhammad had been urging.

Nadir ᶜAli, son of Sultan ᶜAli and grandson of Sardar Shayr ᶜAli, was a Jaghuri Hazarah. During the reign of Aman Allah, he had come out in opposition to the governor, for which reason he, the governor, and also the elders of Jumᶜa had been summoned to Kabul. There he was investigated and ultimately acquitted. Mirza Muhammad Yaᶜqub, the son of Muhammad Ayyub and nephew of Mirak Shah Kabuli, vice-president of the National Council, became his benefactor. Nadir ᶜAli was appointed to the National Council, a post he held for a year. In the first days of the rebellion, when Habib Allah captured Kabul, he was appointed governor of Jaghuri and Malistan but was unable to take up his post, getting only as far as Logar before he had to return to Kabul. Fearing that the governor-general, Malik Muhsin, would punish him because he had not reached Jaghuri, he went into hiding at the home of the mother of ᶜAbd al-Karim, a concubine of the late Amir Habib Allah.[260] While he was still a member of the Council, he had beguiled her into marriage.

At the first opportunity, Nadir ᶜAli fled on foot at night to Bihsud and from there made his way to Jaghuri. When rumors spread that Aman Allah Khan was intending to attack Kabul, Nadir ᶜAli concealed the farman of appointment issued by Habib Allah, went to see Aman Allah and received money and arms from him. After the latter's defeat, he allied himself with Muhammad Khan, whom Habib Allah named a lieutenant general (*nāʾib sālār*). He accompanied Muhammad's units to Muqur and Kalat, leading raids and forays along the way and trying with all his power to prove his devotion to Habib Allah.

Nadir ᶜAli now [July 31] extracted an oath of allegiance from his own people. Like a dog ready to serve whoever throws it a scrap of bread, he called Malik Muhsin on the telephone after arriving in Ghazni and reported that he had received the oath of allegiance from forty thousand men of his tribe—the Hazarahs of Malistan, Jaghuri, Mir Adinah, Pushtah, and Shayr Dagh. Nadir ᶜAli hoped that his tricks would be effective and he would be well received in Kabul. So he left for the capital by car. As soon as he arrived, Habib Allah told him to set off for Bihsud and get an oath of allegiance from the Hazarahs of Bihsud, Day Zangi, and Day Kundi in the same way that he had gotten one from the Hazarahs near Ghazni. But Nadir ^{c}Ali was loath to accept the commission and instead suggested that the amir summon the elders of the Muhammad Khwajah, Jaghatu, and other Hazarah tribes living in the vicinity of Ghazni and through them obtain an oath of allegiance from the Hazarahs of Bihsud.

But Habib Allah himself understood nothing of this and each of his supporters, yipping and yapping like dogs, constantly tugged him in this direction and that. Nadir ^{c}Ali, in fear of his life and afraid that the tribes which, according to him, had given an oath of allegiance, although in fact they had not, would unite with the Muhammad Khwajah, Jaghatu, and other tribes living in the vicinity of Ghazni, begin to fight the troops of Habib Allah and take him captive if he went there, persuaded Habib Allah to summon the elders of these three tribes to Kabul. He argued that it might then be possible to get an oath of allegiance from the obstinate Hazarahs. Once the representatives of these three groups arrived in Kabul, the Hazarahs of Bihsud might sever their alliance with other Hazarahs and swear allegiance.

Habib Allah called the governor of Ghazni and told him to send the leaders of these three tribes to Kabul. When they went to Ghazni to pay their taxes, the governor took them into custody and sent them by car to Kabul under escort.

Meantime the fighting with the Hazarahs in the Unay Pass continued. From the following it would appear that the Hazarahs had not been quite as successful as Fayz Muhammad earlier suggested when he reported the capture of Jalriz. Units of the amir's were well west of Jalriz by this time and in the Unay Pass. The amir's strategy in seeking agreement with the Hazarahs of Bihsud, Day Zangi, and Day Kundi here seems clear. If he could persuade them to give oaths of allegiance, then the Hazarahs fighting in the Unay Pass (whom we probably should understand as included in the Bihsud Hazarahs, anyway) would be outflanked since Day Zangi, Day Kundi, and Bihsud lie to the west of the Unay Pass.

August 1: The fact that Habib Allah had sent a Koran to the residents of Sar-i Chashmah was interpreted by the Hazarahs as a sign of weakness, and so they attacked Muhammad Siddiq "No-Nose," whose units were garrisoned at Qal^{c}ah-i Majid near Siyah Baghal and Qal^{c}ah-i Safid, a fort belonging to the Qizilbash Ghulam Hasan in the Unay Pass. They chased the forces of "No-Nose" as far as Jalriz. In response, Hamid Allah hitched up horses to several field pieces and sent them to Jalriz at 2:00 p.m. Accompanied by a band of brigands, he himself also set off for that region.

Today the hands of a Hazarah were cut off and his belongings confiscated after Habib Allah's soldiers found two rifles in his house. Friends of his had informed on him.

August 2: Habib Allah ordered the Hazarah leaders of Jaghuri, Malistan, Mir Adinah, Pushtah, Shayr Dagh, Muhammad Khwajah, and the environs of Ghazni who had been brought under escort to Kabul to go to Bihsud and extract an oath of allegiance from the militant Hazarahs.

All the Hazarah leaders, meantime, except for Nadir ^{c}Ali, had met with me even though I was ill. They wanted my advice on how they should act and I made some suggestions. They were upset by the scheming of Nadir ^{c}Ali, who hoped to force the Hazarahs into obedience. If he succeeded, all Hazarahs would be disgraced. So with apologies, they told Habib Allah that they had no tribal ties with the Hazarahs of Bihsud, Day Zangi, Day Kundi, Surkh-i Parsa, Turkman, Bamyan, Shaykh ^{c}Ali, and Balkhab, and knew them only by name. These tribes would not follow their advice or admonitions. Habib Allah did not castigate the Hazarahs of Ghazni for their refusal to go to Bihsud because just prior to this, he had sent them a Koran, and, separately, Muhammad Siddiq, had also sent a Koran, two sheep, and a message appealing to the Hazarahs to submit and promising to fulfill any of their demands. So now the amir said, "If you don't want to go yourselves, then just send them a letter containing some stern warnings over your signatures. The minister of court, Shayr Jan, will tell you what to write." Nadir ^{c}Ali promised to write this letter the next day and the Hazarah leaders asked leave to go to the quarters that had been prepared for them.

August 3: Rumors circulated today that the troops of Habib Allah had been defeated in Jalriz. Hazarah braves carried out a foray against a contingent of Habib Allah's men in Jalriz and killed eight hundred soldiers.

Also at this time, Nadir ^{c}Ali, as cunning as a fox and as villainous as a jackal, appeared at the house of Sayyid Ja^{c}far and appealed to him for advice on the letter he had promised to write. I was there and reprimanded him for the fact that he had obtained an oath of allegiance from the Hazarahs of Jaghuri. "Although you managed to do this without the application of force and without the armies of Habib Allah, you destroyed the unity of the Hazarahs and set them against each other. You performed this vile act because of your own avarice, hoping to get some kind of reward from Habib Allah. And because of this, everyone will blame the Hazarahs." Unable to find words to justify what he had done, he showed us a farman from Habib Allah that was addressed to the Pushtun, Rahim Khan Kakari.[261] It said, "All the lands of the Hazarahs, their belongings, and wealth that you seize will be yours." Then Nadir ᶜAli said, "I was forced to obtain the oath of allegiance out of fear that the Pushtuns, who believe this farman to have the force of law, would attack us. But since the dreams of Habib Allah have not been realized, the Pushtuns have not been able to unleash a religious war stretching from the [eastern] frontier of Afghanistan to Khurasan." He promised to bring me the draft copy of the letter for correction before he took it to the minister of court.

After the departure of Nadir ᶜAli, Sayyid Jaᶜfar advised me as a friend, "You're wasting your time talking like this with him. The man is very greedy and ambitious. God forbid that he should report you to Habib Allah." I was worried about this but not overly.

August 4: Nadir ᶜAli again visited Sayyid Jaᶜfar, with whom I was staying. Although he had promised to bring the draft copy of the letter, he lied. He had already written the letter to the Hazarahs as instructed by Habib Allah and the minister of court. And the Hazarah elders from Muhammad Khwajah, Jaghatu, and the environs of Ghazni, whom Nadir ᶜAli had dragged into the snares of Habib Allah and forced to come to Kabul, had signed it. Already yesterday he had dispatched the letter via the elders of the Ghazni Hazarahs—Mustawfi Sayyid Qasim Sarabi, who received the rank of "National General" (*janrāl-i kishwarī*) from Habib Allah; Shaykh Sultan ᶜAli Jaghuri; Wali Muhammad son of Baz ᶜAli Malistani; and Muhammad Nasir, who was from the Ahmadi clan that lived in Jaghuri. Glibly, Nadir ᶜAli said, "Habib Allah and the minister of court forced me to write the letter and the Hazarah elders to sign it in their presence. Then he immediately entrusted it to the four men and sent them by car to Sar-i Chashmah to pass it on to the Hazarahs."

Despite his obsequiousness, it was clear that Nadir ᶜAli himself had devised all these strategems for his own ends. He will do anything for a crust of bread and will chase after a hundred horsemen for a single qiran. He wants to turn the Hazarahs, like the Pushtuns, into unbelievers who have forsaken honor and pride.

I asked him, "Did you keep a copy of this letter?" In reply, he pulled out his original draft. Thinking he heard some note of approval in my voice, he enthused, "I first wanted to bring this draft to you and then take it to Habib Allah but the latter, not giving me the time, forced me to write it directly and then quickly sent it off. But I brought you the original draft." In this letter Nadir ᶜAli tried to instill fear in the Hazarahs by asserting the power of his tribe and of the elders who had signed the letter. He also made promises to Habib Allah. This is the text of the message:

> Hazarah brothers of Bihsud! Being your fellow tribesmen and coreligionists, we want what is best for you and would like to offer our advice. Why have you let yourselves be led astray by villains and mercenary-minded people and opposed the padishah of Islam? Because of this, you have been deprived of high posts. When the Pushtuns were in power, you were humiliated and abused. Now that we have all been freed from the cruel regime of the Pushtuns and power has passed into the hands of a padishah and sincere Muslim who speaks the same language we speak [Dari Persian], with the help of the Almighty, we will be masters of our own lands, wealth, honor, and rights of which we have been deprived for so many years. We will also get high posts and ranks. But for this, you must express your obedience and end the bloodshed and war as soon as you read this letter. Otherwise the government will send its forces, we will all be attacked, and death will surely await us.

For this letter Nadir ᶜAli was nicknamed "Nard Allah."[262]

August 6: Today the letter which that intriguer, Nadir ᶜAli, had written on behalf of the Ghazni tribes now reached the Hazarahs. After reading of the threat of an attack on them, they stopped fighting and began negotiations with Muhammad Siddiq "No-Nose," who had sent them a Koran and some sheep. In the message they sent him they suggested a meeting in some mutually acceptable place. If the government recognized the conditions set forth by the Hazarahs, they promised to fulfil any decisions on an oath of allegiance adopted in the course of the negotiations.

The cause of discord and dissension would then disappear. Thus, as a result of the treachery of Nadir ᶜAli, the Hazarahs were forced to cease hostilities against Habib Allah and agree to a truce.

Mirza Hasan ᶜAli, secretary to the governor-general, Malik Muhsin, had voluntarily gone to Bihsud[263] to receive an oath of allegiance. He was detained there even though he had brought with him an affidavit from the Hazarah elders of Bihsud and Prince Muhammad Amin attesting to his loyalty. One night, he helped a servant of his secretly climb over the walls of the fort at Bihsud and escape. This man went to Kabul to inform Malik Muhsin and arrived today. Malik Muhsin asked him, "What are the losses that both sides have sustained since the outbreak of fighting between the Hazarahs and the amir?" The servant replied, "Among the Hazarahs there have been two men killed and wounded and one taken prisoner. About thirty pieces of artillery have fallen into their hands along with a large quantity of rifles and ammunition. At the moment, the Hazarahs have ample artillery, rifles, and ammunition to continue fighting indefinitely. But now that they have received Nadir ᶜAli's letter and met with the Hazarahs of Jaghuri and other regions, they are no longer fighting."

August 8: Prince Muhammad Amin and his deputy, Khwajah Hidayat Allah, meanwhile were in a state of despair. News of the arrival of the delegation of Hazarahs from Ghazni, their letter, and the threats of Nadir ᶜAli had unnerved them. Nadir ᶜAli had warned them that if the Hazarahs of Bihsud refused to submit, he would attack at the head of a force from his own tribe and crush them. The Hazarah elders reassured both men, reminding them of the terms I had urged on them. They said, "As long as there is one Hazarah still alive, then no harm will come to you or your deputy." The prince, who considered the Hazarahs devoted to the religion and upholders of their oaths and had never heard them tell lies, was reassured.

Also today, the editor of *Ḥabīb al-Islām* published an article about Nadir ᶜAli's obtaining an oath of allegiance under the headline "Praise to the Hazarahs of Jaghuri and Malistan who have broken the Hazarah coalition against the government of Saqqa." It read,

> It has been learned that, thanks to the wisdom of the sublime and auspicious padishah, who is true to the religion, a large part of the Hazarah tribes presented an oath of allegiance with pure hearts to His Highness and

> created an auspicious opportunity for other Hazarah tribes to express their obedience. During these days, the grandson of Sardar Shayr ᶜAli Khan, the Hazarah Nadir ᶜAli, Shaykh Sultan ᶜAli, and Wali Muhammad Khan, staunch leaders of Jaghuri, Malistan, Mir Adinah, Pushtah, and Shayr Dagh, have been honored by being received by His Highness and have presented an oath of allegiance from themselves personally and on behalf of their co-tribesmen. Moreover, they have said, "The Hazarahs of Bihsud are our fellow tribesmen and coreligionists and they live the same kind of life that we do. Therefore, we beg His Highness to permit us, in the course of talks, and also as an object lesson, to direct them to the path of truth and eliminate the misunderstandings that exist. We trust that they will perceive us as fellow tribesmen and will take our advice and stop the internecine bloodshed. If they do not put an end to rebellion, then permit us by ourselves, making use of our tribal alliances, to force them to stand on the true path and to submit to your Islamic government." After hearing such avowals, His Highness expressed his satisfaction and pleasure and, having accorded to each of them royal favor and blessing, sent them off in their cars to fulfill the noble task.

On the basis of this newspaper article, the readers of this book may form for themselves some idea of the nature of people like Nadir ᶜAli Jaghuri and Riza Bakhsh, the Bihsudi collector. In the grip of insatiable greed, they threaten ruin both to the government and to their fellow tribesmen, in this world and the next. Because of Nadir ᶜAli's intrigues and conspiracies, which the newspaper article confirmed, the coalition of Hazarahs was destroyed. I pray to the Almighty to direct Nadir ᶜAli to the path of truth.

The Hazarah resistance was not quite over. In Afghan Turkistan, Hazarah settlers continued to fight although Fayz Muhammad may have somewhat overstated their effect on the government in Kabul. The first meeting at Sar-i Chashmah to negotiate an agreement between the Hazarahs of the Hazarahjat ended, according to Fayz Muhammad, in disarray when the amir's forces attempted to arrest the Hazarah negotiators but failed. But negotiations soon resumed and culminated with the arrival of a Hazarah delegation in Kabul.

The end of the Hazarah resistance was virtually simultaneous with the collapse of opposition from Tagab. Nadir, too, at this point had his hands full keeping what he hoped was his coalition from disintegrating even further. There were random raids and attacks in the Logar and points east, but the possibility of a massive two- or three-pronged coordinated attack on Kabul, which Fayz Muhammad had continually invoked as the main hope of the people of Kabul, would not now materialize. Fayz Muhammad too seems to have realized that the end had come when the Hazarahjat delegation arrived in Kabul for negotiations with the amir.

August 9: Meanwhile, the threats of Nadir ᶜAli have had no effect on some brave Hazarahs who continue their struggle against Habib Allah. They regard the Korans sent by Habib Allah and Lieutenant General "No-Nose" [Muhammad Siddiq] and the proposal of a truce as mere provocations. Tonight, from the Unay Pass, Hazarahs attacked the contingent in Sar-i Chashmah, which was under the impression that a truce had gone into effect. The Hazarahs took seven hundred prisoners, their rifles, ammunition, and six loaded field pieces, and returned home in triumph. At Habib Allah's order, four soldiers who had fled to Kabul from the battlefield were put before a firing squad.

August 11: Meanwhile, Mirza Hasan ᶜAli, secretary to Malik Muhsin, continues his subversive activities. The Hazarah leaders of Bihsud, expecting the arrival of Nadir Khan in the environs of Kabul, for a while dragged their feet on offering the oath of allegiance by using any pretext they could think of, and continued to oppose Habib Allah and conduct combat operations against his forces. But they eventually lost hope in Nadir Khan and the tribes of the Southern Province and today promised Mirza Hasan ᶜAli, the Ghazni Hazarah delegation, and Muhammad Siddiq "No-Nose" that they would come to Sar-i Chashmah for negotiations on their terms for tendering the oath of allegiance.

Mirza Hasan ᶜAli reported the Hazarahs' promise to "No-Nose" and he in turn reported to the governor of Maydan, who indicated to Malik Muhsin by telephone that he would prepare everything necessary to receive the Hazarahs. After a successful conclusion of negotiations there, they would then go on to Kabul to present their oath of allegiance.

These stories had a very depressing effect on the opponents of Habib Allah's regime, who have linked their hopes to salvation at the hands of the Hazarahs. Some of them shared their disappointment with me. But I told them, "The Hazarahs are simply acting as I advised them. As far as I know, Habib Allah will never manage to obtain an oath of allegiance from them as long as the situation of Nadir and the Pushtuns remains unclear.

If they come to Kabul then it will only be for the sake of gathering intelligence about Habib Allah's army and the number of troops stationed in the capital." This reassured them.

August 13: Nadir ᶜAli, who had obtained a farman from Habib Allah giving him the title "sardar" and who, as mentioned earlier, had promised to summon the Hazarahs to obedience, today wrote a second letter, this one to the Hazarah-migrants and residents of Darrah-i Suf (in Afghan Turkistan) who were fighting against Sayyid Husayn and the Turkmen backers of Habib Allah. Their letter was printed up and published:

> May it be known to our brothers in religion and to the esteemed Hazarah settlers living in Mazar-i Sharif: Now that the present highly respected government has consolidated its power in most of the territory of Afghanistan and all the Pushtun tribes who are like brothers to us have, with pure hearts, expressed their obedience, many tribes of the Hazarahjat have also chosen us to act on their behalf and have sent an oath of allegiance to the capital, Kabul. Some two weeks have passed since we arrived in the city and had the honor to be received by His Highness, to whom we handed our oath of allegiance. His Highness was sincerely grateful to all of us and expressed the hope that in future we would live in peace and tranquillity. It is also evident to us that you, our brothers and fellow tribesmen, who are living in that province, up to now have not been aware of how sincere the amir's feelings are and so you have not given an oath of allegiance to Sayyid Husayn. Whether from fear or because of unfounded rumors spread by self-interested people, you have held yourselves aloof. Since we and you both share the same general tribal interests and good wishes for each other, we do not want you to be subject to any distress and anxiety. As fellow tribesmen, we tell you that for the past seven months, we, the residents of the Hazarahjat, have been opposed to the current government. You all know that we fought not for the sake of the office of chief (*raʾīs*) and not because there was any ancient personal or tribal enmity between us and the present powers. Our only motive was the oath of allegiance which we had given to Aman Allah. As long as he was still on Afghan soil, we supported him. When he relinquished everything and fled abroad, the conditions that applied to us and had been set out in the former oath of allegiance, lost their authority and we no longer were obliged to anyone. It would now be very stupid to refuse to submit and make oneself miserable by one's own doing. If you think things through carefully, it will be clear to you that, thanks to the way things have turned out for His Highness, the Servant of the Religion of the Prophet of God, that is, Amir Habib Allah, from the beginning of this revolution up to now, every day brings him new

> triumphs. Every sensible person realizes that in all these activities the Almighty is supporting him. If one takes into account the will of God, it will be clear that eternal suffering will be the fate of everyone who opposes him. In this regard, we advise all our brothers to submit with pure hearts as soon as possible to the present esteemed government, to ask His Excellency, Sayyid Husayn, who possesses all the qualities of the Prophet Muhammad, to forgive your past actions and to express your readiness to serve the government. God willing, your sincere protestations will evoke the concern and esteem of the amir as well as his deputy [Sayyid Husayn]. And all of us, residents and representatives of the Hazarahjat, express the hope that His Excellency Sayyid Husayn will overlook your past actions and deal with you kindly, as befits his sublime nature. We are hopeful that our friends will follow the counsels we have addressed to them, not yield to the lies of self-interested people, nor be angry with the representatives of the current esteemed government nor discomfit either us or themselves."
> 7 Rabi^{c} al-Awwal 1348 H [August 12, 1929]

Nadir ^{c}Ali wrote this callous letter in a closed session of court (*darbār*). It was signed by himself and fifteen Hazarah leaders from Muhammad Khwajah, Jaghatu, the regions of Bayat, Fuladi, Jaghuri, Shaykh ^{c}Ali, Turkman, and Surkh-i Parsa. The other signatories were Shaykh Sultan ^{c}Ali, Wali Muhammad, Mustawfi Sayyid Qasim, Niyaz Muhammad, Haydar ^{c}Ali, Muhammad Nasir, Muhammad Baqir, Zabtu, Hasan Riza, Muhammad Husayn, ^{c}Ali Riza, Fayz Muhammad "Tubchi,"[264] Khuda Rahm, Shah Husayn, and Khayr Allah, all of whom had been lured into Habib Allah's snares through deception and summoned to Kabul where they were kept under surveillance as if they were prisoners. By order of the chief villain, this letter was copied many times over and sent by plane to Mazar-i Sharif where it was scattered from the air over the territory where Hazarah settlers live and over Darrah-i Suf where the Day Mirdad [Hazarah] tribe lives.

But a few days before this, Ghulam Nabi Khan, the son of Mingbashi Gulak, had come to Bihsud with a hundred horsemen with the aim of finding out what the situation was. He was convinced by what he saw that the residents of Bihsud were continuing the struggle against Habib Allah and from them he learned of my advice and of the Koranic verses I had cited: "And the thief, male and female: cut off the hands of both, as a recompense for what they have earned and a punishment exemplary from

God"[265]; "And whoso slays a believer wilfully, his recompense is Gehenna, therein dwelling forever, and God will be wroth with him and will curse him, and prepare for him a mighty chastisement."[266] When he left, the Hazarahs [of Turkistan] were encouraged even more and, disregarding Nadir ᶜAli's letter, cursed him and those who had signed it. Taking the ordinances of the Shariᶜah and their own conscience as their guide, they refused to submit. Their courageous actions and their refusal to offer their obedience aroused the ire of Sayyid Husayn.

August 15: In Turkistan, Hazarah settlers, armed with rifles and artillery captured from government forces, occupied positions in Darrah-i Suf, Kuh-i Shadyan, and Marmal. When news of Nadir ᶜAli's letter reached them, they were furious and launched a major assault on the Turkmen. Their leaders included the above-mentioned Ghulam Nabi, the son of Mingbashi Gulak from Darrah-i Suf; Nur Muhammad, the son of the military high commissioner, Ghulam Husayn, and a grandson of Khan Shirin Khan Jawanshir; and Major General Muhammad Iklil, the son of Muhammad Afzal Darwazi. The Turkmen—prompted by a letter from the dethroned amir of Bukhara who was in Kabul,[267] by Khalifa Qizil Ayak and his accomplices, and by the Uzbek, Mirza Qasim—gave their support to Habib Allah and took up arms against the Hazarahs. The Hazarahs killed and wounded many of the Turkmen and besieged the contingent under Sayyid Husayn that was stationed at the fort in Dih Dadi.[268] The survivors managed to save themselves by fleeing to their native steppes and deserts. Here is the sort of thing that Nadir ᶜAli's letter and the actions of the Hazarahs of Ghazni who had been seduced by Habib Allah led to. We will see to what extent Nadir ᶜAli succeeded in normalizing the situation among the Hazarahs of Bihsud and in satisfying Habib Allah.

August 17: As was reported earlier, agreement was reached for truce-talks to be held at Sar-i Chashmah between the government and the Hazarahs. The Hazarah arbabs were supposed to arrive in Sar-i Chashmah to negotiate a time limit with Lieutenant General Muhammad Siddiq "No-Nose" for the acceptance of their terms and safe passage to Kabul. Today a number of the arbabs arrived in Sar-i Chashmah, accompanied by an armed contingent of three hundred men, and met with the lieutenant general, that satan, the worst evildoer of all. After a meal followed by fruit and tea that had been sent two or three days earlier by Habib Allah and the governor-general, Malik Muhsin, Muhammad Siddiq planned to signal a bugler by a wink of the eye and he would sound a call to the sepoys who had surrounded the gathering. They were then to seize the Hazarahs. But before the signal could be passed to the bugler, who stood some distance away from the majlis, one of the Hazarahs, excusing himself to answer a call of nature, left the meeting, quickly climbed a nearby hill and fired three rifle shots in rapid succession. The sepoys meanwhile disarmed the Hazarahs who remained calmly sitting in the majlis. But then three thousand brave Hazarahs, lying in wait behind the hills, and on the alert to act if Habib Allah's soldiers tried anything against the arbabs, heard the three shots which was their signal to attack. They sprang from ambush and, with cries of "O ᶜAli, help us," fell upon the sepoys. They disarmed, captured, and led away the four hundred soldiers who had been guarding the majlis but that kafir, Muhammad Siddiq, managed to make his escape back to Kabul by car.

Given the speed with which negotiations resumed, this seems a somewhat unlikely story. It would be more credible, too, if the story did not fit so neatly into the hackneyed narrative convention of enemies meeting for a meal and reconciliation only to have one party conspire to use the occasion to capture and dispense with the other.

Also today a contingent of Hazarah horsemen, who had promised to escort Prince Muhammad Amin, his deputy Hidayat Allah, and his retainers safely through their territory, came to the prince. But he was worried about the negotiations going on between the Hazarahs and Habib Allah and was afraid of being taken hostage and so decided not to go with them. But they assured him that as long as one Hazarah remained alive, neither he nor any of his retinue would be subject to any harm from Habib Allah. The events in Sar-i Chashmah, the flight of Muhammad Siddiq to Kabul, and the readiness of the Hazarahs to conduct Prince Muhammad Amin safely across their territory to Wardak if he wished it, all these things worried Habib Allah. He now dispatched the tribal conscripts assembled in Kabul to Sar-i Chashmah by truck. This went on from evening until 2:00 a.m.

August 18: At this time, the Ismaᶜili, Sayyid Nadir Shah Kayani, joining forces with the Hazarahs of Shaykh ᶜAli, rose in opposition to Habib Allah's forces stationed in Bamyan, Ghuri and Baghlan. Sayyid Nadir

Shah blocked the government force's route north to Turkistan and Habib Allah's men were forced to retreat to Ghurband.

August 20: The Hazarahs' message to Muhammad Siddiq "No-Nose," in which they promised that their leaders would come [again] to Sar-i Chashmah to negotiate a peace with guarantees, had reassured Habib Allah. Convinced now that there would be no Hazarah offensive, he ordered nine brigades (*ghund*s) totaling twelve thousand men with artillery to prepare to move from Butkhak toward Jalalabad to suppress the insurgents there. En route, they were to send a vanguard to crush the tribes of the Eastern Province whom Hashim had united against the government of Habib Allah. Today those troops left Kabul for Jalalabad.

In a letter from Lieutenant General Muhammad Siddiq, Habib Allah was informed of the Hazarah oath of allegiance and their terms vis-à-vis the people of Sar-i Chashmah: he should free the innocent men and women taken captive there and pay 1.5 million rupees as compensation for their property losses and the burning of their forts. [Their rationale was that] as obedient subjects of the government, they had paid their "one-quarter" (*chāryakah*) taxes; during the past winter they had sent fifty Kabuli kharwars of provisions to the forces fighting against the Wardaks; and for seven months, expecting to be reimbursed, they had fed the one hundred sepoys stationed in Sar-i Chashmah to defend against Hazarah attack. In addition, the Hazarahs wanted the amir to release the relatives of the men who had come to Kabul in winter to sell a hundred kharwars of oil but whom the "Mu^{c}in al-saltanah," Hamid Allah, had had shot for no reason and whose homes he had burned. These relatives had themselves been forced to go to Kabul. There also had to be compensation for the damage caused to their forts. Then the Hazarahs would be convinced that the government had not misled them.

Muhammad Siddiq also wrote that after the release of the captives, the Hazarahs promise to come again to Sar-i Chashmah and begin to negotiate on the question of an oath of allegiance based on the conditions they had set out. If their terms are accepted and carried out, they would come to Kabul and swear their allegiance. Therefore, Muhammad Siddiq wrote, the government ought to make preparations to meet them in Sar-i Chashmah.

Habib Allah was overjoyed by Muhammad Siddiq's letter. Not for nothing was he always saying, "All the Pushtuns put together don't frighten me. If I bribe their leaders with rifles and a few rupees, I can make any Pushtun tribe submit, but if the Hazarahs oppose me and join forces with the residents of the north, then the situation becomes much more difficult. This is because it's impossible to get them to submit, either with bribes or punishments."

To provide a reception for Hazarah leaders, Habib Allah ordered that a sum of twelve thousand rupees from the treasury be sent to Sar-i Chashmah. He also ordered the tribesmen and women freed and delivered with a show of honor to Sar-i Chashmah in twenty vehicles. In conjunction with their release and dignified conveyance to Sar-i Chashmah, the residents of Kabul said to each other that evidently the Hazarahs are powerful if the tyrant Habib Allah is forced to reckon with them. If this is not the case, why doesn't he send captured Pushtuns home with comparable honors? The Hazarahs are brave, courageous, and powerful as well and it is for this reason that they display such sincere loyalty towards their imprisoned fellow tribesmen. This is what it means to be strong!

August 21: Meanwhile, Sayyid Nadir Shah Kayani, the Isma^{c}ili Hazarah sayyid from Shaykh ^{c}Ali, refused to submit to Habib Allah, and with the support of a kindred spirit, the Qizilbash Mirza Safdar ^{c}Ali, the tax collector for Ghuri and Baghlan, he incited the Hazarahs and Tajiks under his jurisdiction to fight Habib Allah. Together with Hazarah and Tajik volunteers from Qataghan, under the leadership of Sayyid Nadir Shah, they fought Habib Allah's forces, defeated them, and advanced as far as Khanabad, Andarab, and Ghurband. They closed the road between Kabul and Mazar-i Sharif to caravans and Habib Allah could do nothing but issue threatening decrees. Today, he ordered copies of one printed and dropped by plane over those areas where there was fighting. It called for an end to all opposition and for people to assert their obedience or be annihilated. But Sayyid Nadir Shah paid not the slightest attention to it and continues the fight.

August 23: This evening, one of Malik Muhsin's subordinates returned to Kabul. In early July, accompanied by Mirza Hasan ^{c}Ali, Hajji Rustam ^{c}Ali, Mulla ^{c}Iwaz ^{c}Ali, Mulla ^{c}Abd al-Wahid, and ^{c}Ali Khan the son of Aqa Khan, he had delivered a proclamation to the Hazarahjat containing threats from Habib Allah. The whole group had been detained there. Malik Muhsin's man also brought news of the submission of the Hazarahs to Habib Allah, news that pleased the father and other relatives of Mirza Hasan ᶜAli, for they thought that Habib Allah would give Mirza Hasan and them high offices for this service. Other people, disposed against Habib Allah, dismissed the news. But they are unaware that the collector, Riza Bakhsh, had already sent Habib Allah his oath of allegiance and assured him that, no matter what happened, the unity of the Hazarahs would be destroyed.

They also are unaware of another of Riza Bakhsh's ploys. After receiving the twelve thousand rupees that Habib Allah had sent for a reception for the Hazarahs of Sar-i Chashmah, General Muhammad Siddiq had placed them in a basket used for picking grapes and loaded it on a donkey. It was so heavy that the animal could hardly carry the load. He concealed the money under bunches of grapes and sent the donkey to Riza Bakhsh, who was to use it to sow discord among the Hazarahs. Now with fifteen Hazarah leaders and their retainers, twenty-five men in all, Riza Bakhsh set off for Kabul.

Today this group arrived in Sar-i Chashmah. Mirza Hasan ᶜAli, who had been of great service to Habib Allah, came as far as Sar-i Chashmah with the arbabs. He then spent the night in Takanah in the home of relatives of Sayyid Shahan Shah and the next day set off for Kabul, leaving the Hazarah leaders behind in Sar-i Chashmah.

There is more talk in Kabul about fighting between Hazarah settlers and the Turkmen occasioned by the murder of three Hazarahs. Sayyid Husayn, second in command to Habib Allah, refused to exact revenge himself for the killing of the Hazarahs but encouraged them to retaliate and so they attacked the Turkmen. This news raised to a higher pitch the indignation of those opposed to the unenlightened government of this unbeliever Habib Allah.

Also today a hundred horsemen from Khanabad and Andarab, frightened by the attacks of Sayyid Nadir Shah Kayani, arrived in Kabul. Habib Allah has promised them reinforcements.

August 24: Today at 1:00 p.m. Mirza Hasan ᶜAli arrived in Kabul and reported to the governor-general the impending arrival of the Hazarah leaders. Malik Muhsin in turn conveyed the good news and congratulations to Habib Allah, who called for a band serenade to be performed at the Harten Bridge and a parade with a band and people shouting "ya chahar yar" to march around the city in front of the cars carrying the Hazarah leaders. A group of military bandsmen set off for the Harten Bridge and there awaited the arrival of the cars with the Hazarahs. They showed up about sunset. The bandsmen then marched ahead of the cars, playing their instruments and shouting "ya chahar yar" and, until late in the evening, led the Hazarahs through every street and back alley of the city. While they were parading through the bazaar and Habib Allah's people were shouting "ya chahar yar," the Hazarah outlaw, Sayyid Ahmad, son of Muhammad Mir and grandson of Shah Nur, shouted at them, "You used to shout 'ya ᶜAli madad' ('O ᶜAli, give us help'), when you fled from the Hazarahs on the battlefield; and you forgot all about 'ya chahar yar.' So why don't you shout 'ya ᶜAli madad' now that the Hazarahs are not attacking you?" Habib Allah's supporters, wanting to appear to be good hosts, did not answer. They took their guests to the Cafe Wali[269] and fed them there. The time was already late, the shops were closed, and so the Hazarahs [living in Kabul] led to their homes the horses and servants of the Bihsudis. The Hazarahs of Kabul are basically sellers of straw and barley, bakers, watercarriers, and bearers, and so did not have the means to offer the kind of hospitality that their fellow tribesmen merited.

August 25: Today Malik Muhsin presented the group of Hazarah leaders to the chief of the evildoers. They included the Bihsud Hazarah leaders who arrived yesterday and eleven Hazarah leaders from Muhammad Khwajah in the vicinity of Ghazni, and from Jaghatu, Jaghuri, and Surkh-i Parsa who had been drawn into Habib Allah's snares by Nadir ᶜAli. The amir now got them to sign a letter that he dispatched to the Hazarahs of Bihsud, Day Zangi, Day Kundi, the settlers in Turkistan, Day Mirdad, and Darrah-i Suf requesting that they affirm their obedience to Habib Allah's government. If they did, they would all receive the title "sardar."

Although the Hazarahs fought him tenaciously, Habib Allah received the delegation with pronounced deference because he understood that their submission and alliance with the northerners would be a guarantee of his personal security. But he also admonished them for taking up arms against him. The Bihsud collector, Riza Bakhsh, who earlier had sent an oath of allegiance and felt somewhat sure of himself replied,

> We sent a letter with a promise to give an oath of allegiance. Your brother loosed the hounds of war on us and attacked Sar-i Chashmah and the Unay Pass, where loyal subjects of your government live. As a result of his attack, we thought that if we gave an oath of allegiance and expressed obedience then we would be attacked and plundered like the people of Sar-i Chashmah and Unay Pass. So we entrusted our fate to the Almighty and, in accordance with the holy Shari^{c}ah, undertook to defend ourselves and our families. Now that we have come to you we are not afraid of death, imprisonment, or punishment for insubordination because we are by no means all the Hazarahs. As every one knows, although Amir ^{c}Abd al-Rahman killed or drove into exile six hundred thousand Hazarahs and seized their cultivable lands and pastures in violation of the Shari^{c}ah, nevertheless he was unable to exterminate them. And now thousands of Hazarahs are to be found in this country and abroad. All of them are devout Muslims and proponents of Islam. Should something happen to the few people who have come to Kabul, this will have no effect on the wider community of Hazarahs.

As for the war, Habib Allah knew that his brother had started it and therefore he decided it was not worth dwelling on the past. He said that in future, the Hazarahs, who had been under the yoke of a Pushtun government and deprived of their legal rights for a very long time, ought to join forces with the Tajiks so that they would not again become slaves of the Pushtuns who always persecuted them. Later, he addressed a request to the arbabs to help him with money and three thousand fighters for the struggle with the Pushtuns. But despite the fatwa of the hazrats and pseudo-mullas declaring the Hazarahs infidels, the Hazarahs refused to fight against the Pushtuns. I convinced them that since the throne had been taken away from the Pushtuns and they were fighting Habib Allah to retrieve it, then as long as all the Pushtuns were not subjugated, the Hazarahs ought not to assign their own people to fight them.

After the audience with Habib Allah, the Hazarahs returned to the lodgings assigned to them. For a day and a night each of them had only two rupees to live on. For two or three days they were entertained as guests of the padishah. But being somewhat ignorant, they did not appreciate the respect that was shown them and did not take advantage of their position. They refused to eat alongside others in the guest house but went to the homes of their fellow clansmen, some of whom were bakers. So, in place of the pilaf which they would have been served at the guest house, they each received two rupees.

August 26: Today rumors spread through Kabul that Hazarah settlers in Turkistan had successfully attacked Mazar-i Sharif and defeated Sayyid Husayn.

August 27: Nadir ᶜAli, the son of Sultan ᶜAli and grandson of Sardar Shayr ᶜAli Khan Jaghuri, who had been given the nickname "Dog" by his fellow tribesmen,[270] was named to the post of military high commissioner of the Hazarahjat today, with the backing of the minister of court, Shayr Jan. He was unable, however, to go there since the arbabs of Bihsud did not believe he deserved the post.

August 28:[271]

Epilogue

Fayz Muhammad's work in progress ends at this point. He himself lived for another year and a half, and perhaps his death, or the fatal illness that preceded it, is signaled by the abrupt ending of his work, as if he had put his pen down one day in the midst of his revisions and was never able to pick it up again. Someday the actual journal may be discovered and we will know the rest of his account of the period.

Some seven weeks pass between the time of Fayz Muhammad's last entry and the sudden and surprising end of the reign of Habib Allah. Details of this period have been published by contemporaries, Mohammed Ali, Muhyi al-Din Anis, and Burhan al-Din Kushkaki. Mohammed Ali provides the most flourishes in his account of the Musahiban family's ousting the Tajiks and restoring Afghan hegemony over the country. But his story is chronologically imprecise, with a linear sense of progress in the narrative but no dates from which to get one's bearings. Anis and Kushkaki, on the other hand, while occasionally at variance with each other on dates and places, both cover the final weeks of Habib Allah's regime day by day and in great detail.[272] But their perspective differs from Fayz Muhammad's. They were not in Kabul and they report the march of Nadir's forces toward Kabul from the border areas to the south and east only from the Musahiban perspective. They have little to say about Habib Allah's countermeasures or what was happening elsewhere in the country, among the Hazarahs, for example, or in Afghan Turkistan.

Habib Allah's last major triumph came in taking Jalalabad early in September.[273] But trouble soon broke out in Qandahar, where opposition centered on an Achakzai leader, Mihrdil Khan.[274] The Tajik government appears to have been harassed throughout most of September, first by the Achakzai tribe and its allies and then by the populace of Qandahar itself. On or about September 1, Nadir sent his brother Hashim to Qandahar to persuade the opposition there to support the Musahiban cause. On September 23, Nadir received word that there had been a major uprising in the city in his name. It is unclear from these sources what Hashim's role was, if any, in the uprising. Habib Allah, in response to the news coming from Qandahar, had ordered all the troops at his disposal to go there. This appears to have included his field marshal, Purdil Khan.

Meantime at the end of August, Nadir had sent another brother, Shah Wali, to Dubandi, a town just north of Gardiz, to organize the tribal forces that he hoped would assemble there. Although Nadir had reached agreements with a number of tribes to support his attempt to oust Habib Allah, some of them lived on the Indian side of the border and needed British permission to cross. And the British position seems to have been to allow prime combatants (i.e. the Musahiban family) to cross only once from India, but not to allow them back into Afghanistan if, for some reason, they returned to India. Tribal groups resident on the Indian side were treated differently and efforts were made to prevent them from crossing at all into Afghanistan. This was done in the name of a policy of professed neutrality.[275] One large group, the Urakzai, which lived just over the border, was turned back when its members attempted to link up with Nadir. On the other hand, a large force of Wazir—some of whom, at least, came from the Indian side—managed to evade the British and join Nadir at ᶜAli Khayl. According to Anis, the Musahiban leader divided the Wazir into two lashkars (tribal armies), sending one to Shah Wali at Dubandi and assigning the other to a third brother, Shah Mahmud, whom he then sent toward Gardiz.

Shah Wali was at Dubandi by September 1 or 2. Within three weeks he had been joined by the Wazir force and contingents from the Masᶜud, Mangal, Ahmadzai, Jaji, and Tutakhayl tribes. His two principal commanders were Muhammad Gul Khan, who would later earn a notorious reputation for his Pushtun chauvinist policies in Afghan Turkistan, and Mawlawi Allah Nawaz Khan, a native of India who had come to Afghanistan at the age of fifteen and eventually become an Afghan citizen.

Shah Wali's force proved to be the crucial one in the final assault on Kabul. On September 28, he left Dubandi and marched north to Khushi, which he occupied on the 29th. On the 30th he sent a thousand-man force ahead to the Tangi Waghjan, the gorge on the road to the Logar Valley. His men took the gorge, surrounded the government forces there, and captured their weapons and ammunition stores. On October 3, Mawlawi Allah Nawaz led his force against the town of Muhammad Aghah, headquarters for Habib Allah's troops in the Logar and home to two brigades (ghund) at the time. After a fierce fight, he took it the same day. Kushkaki says that Habib Allah himself took part in the battle and was forced to flee back to Kabul in his car to avoid capture.[276]

On the 5th the troops under Mawlawi Allah Nawaz had pushed on to Charasya while Shah Wali reached Chihil Tan (according to Kushkaki) or Chihil Sutun (according to Anis) on the following day. The amir meanwhile consolidated his forces on the heights of Shayr Darwazah and Asmaʾi in the city and at the Bala Hisar. He set up his command post on Marinjan Hill which covered the approach to the city from the east.

On the 6th and 7th there was heavy fighting at all these points and the amir's loyalists were pushed back. On either the 6th or the 7th, the amir retreated into the Arg to make his last stand. It appears that Shah Mahmud, who had earlier been sent toward Gardiz, had instead marched north to approach Kabul from the east, through the Tangi Gharu. He arrived at this time in Kabul. At about the same time a message came from Nadir, still in ᶜAli Khayl, dividing administrative responsibilities between the two brothers. Shah Mahmud was to be in charge of civil affairs (mulkī) and Shah Wali, military (niẓāmī).

On October 9, the siege of the Arg began. Purdil, who was hurrying back from his mission to retrieve Qandahar, arrived at this point. Kushkaki has him coming to the city via Paghman and then Khayr Khanah Pass. He and Shah Wali's forces clashed at Bagh-i Buland (the present site of the Women's Park, the Bagh-i Zananah). In the fighting, which took place on the 9th, he was killed and his two-thousand-man force scattered.

Besides the amir, his brother, and other supporters, the Musahiban wives were also besieged in the Arg. According to Mohammed Ali,[277] this presented Nadir with a moral dilemma. But despite the danger to the women, he sent instructions to Shah Wali two days after the Arg was surrounded to begin bombarding it. What Anis calls a rapid-fire artillery piece was set up in the public gardens opposite the south wall of the Arg and firing commenced. In a short time, the arsenal inside the Arg exploded and the buildings inside the walls were engulfed in flames. In the confusion of the smoke and fire, Habib Allah, his brother, and other loyalists slipped out the north gate and escaped to Kuhdaman and Kuhistan.

Miraculously, the Musahiban women were rescued unharmed, but the buildings inside the Arg were heavily damaged, some sections being completely destroyed by the fire.

The capture of the Arg on October 13, 1929 marked the end of the Tajik regime, although the dénouement was yet to come. Nadir received word of the victory in ᶜAli Khayl and immediately set out for the capital, arriving in the city on the 15th. He assigned Shah Mahmud to find and bring back the deposed amir. Habib Allah meanwhile had linked up with two of his principal officials, Malik Muhsin and Shayr Jan, and for the time being had made the citadel at Jabal al-Siraj his headquarters. Sayyid Husayn, who was at Mazar-i Sharif, gathered a force on hearing the news and headed south to join Habib Allah.

Between October 15 and 22, the propaganda machinery of the Musahibans must have been operating at full capacity. A recently published document issued by the new regime warned all "Saqqawists" living in Kabul to stay in their homes and make no attempt to send information on the situation to Kuhdaman or Kuhistan nor to cause any trouble. Should they do so they would be subject to the "severest punishment."[278] The document is unsigned and undated but could only have come from this particular moment. Besides residents of Kabul who might sympathize with the ousted Tajik regime, the Tajiks of "the North" (Kuhistan and Kuhdaman) were encouraged to pressure their leaders into reaching accommodation with the new occupiers of Kabul by being warned that, as was the custom, they would be held collectively responsible for the acts of their leaders. At the same time a carrot was waved in Habib Allah's face, a promise that if he swore obedience to Nadir he would be pardoned. In that third week in October, the resolve of the Tajiks at Jabal al-Siraj apparently disintegrated. Why this happened is not clear. We do not know what effect the Kayani-led force of Shaykh ᶜAlī Hazarahs was having in the Ghurband Valley nor the extent to which the arrival of Nadir in Kabul encouraged a renewal of hostilities against the "northerners" by Hazarahs and others in the regions adjacent to Kuhistan and Kuhdaman. But it is clear that Habib Allah was now looking for a way out and so he now grasped at the straw offered to him. On the 23rd he put himself and his principal officials in the hands of Nadir's supporters and was brought to Kabul and held under guard in the Arg.[279]

But pressured by the same tribal leaders who had made his success possible, Nadir Khan (now Nadir Shah following his selection as new ruler of Afghanistan by a tribal assembly) broke his promise and withdrew the pardon. A week after these remnants of the first Tajik government of Afghanistan were brought back to Kabul, the new ruler ordered their liquidation. On November 1, late in the afternoon, Habib Allah Kalakani, the "watercarrier's boy," along with his brother Hamid Allah, Sayyid Husayn Charikari, and nine others were lined up against the west wall of the Arg and shot. Their bodies were then hung in the Chawk "as an example to others." It is probably safe to assume that Fayz Muhammad was not saddened by the news.

Notes

Introduction

1. The epithet in Persian (or Dari as the language is called in Afghanistan) is *baçça-i saqqā*, pronounced "bah-cháy-yi suc-cow."
2. See, for example, Ludwig Adamec's excellent account of the period in *Afghanistan's Foreign Affairs to the Mid-Twentieth Century* (Tucson: University of Arizona Press, 1987), Chapter 5. V. G. Korgun, *Afganistan v 20–30-e gody XX v.* (Moscow: Nauka, 1979), pp. 66–116, and Leon B. Poullada, *Reform and Rebellion in Afghanistan, 1919–1929: King Amanullah's Failure to Modernize a Tribal Society* (Ithaca: Cornell University Press, 1973), pp. 171–95, also cover the period in some detail, Korgun from contemporary Soviet and Afghan newspaper and documentary sources and Poullada from the rich documentation of British intelligence as well as Afghan governmental and individual oral accounts.
3. Muḥyi al-Dīn Anīs was in Kabul during the first two months of the siege, the period covered least thoroughly by Fayż Muḥammad. Anīs then left and spent the rest of the Saqqāwist period in the Southern Province. He published a history of the time entitled *Buḥrān wa najāt* (Kabul: Anīs, n.d.), and at the end (p. 287) he explains, "Since I was in Kabul for the first two months of the rebellion *(ightishāsh)* and then was in the Southern Province until the the beginning of the third *ḥalqah* (end of June) I can speak of events in those places, as well as the conquest of Kābul (in October), from personal experience. But for events in other provinces I have relied on information provided by people who were in those places."
4. Ibid., pp. 258–59.
5. The story that explains the Ṭālibān disaster at Mazār-i Sharīf in late May 1997 concerns Ṭālibān efforts to disarm the Hazārah residents of Sayyidābād, a district of Mazār-i Sharīf, and the fierce Hazarah resistance that led to the destruction of the Ṭālibān force. One can easily imagine, given the history of Pushtūn-Hazārah relations, that the Hazārahs of Sayyidābād expected much worse from the Ṭālibān entering their village in May than simply confiscation of their weaponry.
6. Adamec, op. cit., p. 78.
7. Mohammad Hashim Kamali, *Law in Afghanistan: A Study of the Constitutions, Matrimonial Law and the Judiciary* (Leiden: E. J. Brill, 1985), pp. 7, 102, 110, 135–36.
8. D. Balland, "Afghanistan. Political History," *Encyclopaedia Iranica* (henceforth *EIr*), ed. E. Yarshater (London and New York: Routledge and Kegan Paul, 1989), vol. 1, p. 555.
9. Most probably Fayż Muḥammad is referring here to the *niẓām-nāmah* entitled *Jazā-yi ᶜUmūmī.*
10. Fayẓ Muḥammad is certainly mistaken here. Jamāl Pāshā, a Young Turk activist and Ottoman general in Syria during the Great War, was courtmartialed for his loss of Syria and fled Istanbul for Europe in 1918. There, probably in early 1920, he offered his services to Amān Allāh. He was in Afghanistan from mid-1920 to September 1921 and was assassinated in Tbilisi by Armenian nationalists in July 1922 while returning to Afghanistan from Moscow. See D. A. Rustow, "D̲jemal Pas̲h̲a," *Encyclopaedia of Islam,* New Edition (henceforth *EI²*), ed. B. Lewis et al. (Leiden: E.J. Brill, 1978), vol. 4, pp. 531–32. Another Turk, Badri Beg, who died in Kabul in 1923, is usually credited with the authorship of the *Jazā-yi ᶜUmūmī*. (See Adamec, *Afghanistan's Foreign Affairs*, p. 86. I am grateful to Dr. May Schinasi for pointing out that the "*niẓām-nāmah*" referred to by Adamec is the *Jazā-yi ᶜUmūmī*.)
11. Fayż Muḥammad, *Kniga upominaniia o miatezhe* (Moscow: Nauka, 1988), pp. 33–34.

12. For the earlier date see A. I. Shkirando's introduction to Fayż Muhammad, op. cit., p. 12 and recently Amin H. Tarzi, "Fayz Mohammed Kateb, un historien méconnu," *Les Nouvelles d'Afghanistan* (Paris: AFRANE, 1995), no. 70, p. 14. For the later date see D. Balland, "Baçça-i ṣaqqā," *EIr*, vol. 3 (Costa Mesa: Mazda, 1988), p. 336, and ᶜAbd al-Ḥayy Ḥabībī, *Junbish-i mashrūṭiyyat dar Afghānistān* (Qum: Iḥsānī, 1993), p. 72.
13. Fayż Muḥammad, *Sirāj al-tawārīkh* (Kabul: Maṭbaᶜah-yi Ḥurūfī, 1333/1915), vol. 3, p. 588.
14. Ḥusayn Nāyil, "Pazhūhishī dar bāz namāᵓī wa bāz shināsī āṯār-i Kātib," *Kitāb* (Kabul), no. 1, 1361/1982, p. 44. The title of the collection of decrees was *Dastūr al-ᶜamal Agahī*, according to Nāyil.
15. Fayż Muhammad, *Sirāj al-tawārīkh*, p. 1107.
16. ᶜAbd al-Ḥayy Ḥabībī, op. cit., pp. 71–72.
17. A. I. Shkirando, introduction to Fayż Muḥammad, *Kniga upominaniia*, p. 15.
18. Ḥusayn Nāyil, op. cit., p. 34.
19. Volumes one and two were published in one binding in Kabul 1913. The title page of volume three bears the date 1915 but this marks only the beginning of its publication.
20. Muḥammad Ghubār, *Tārīkh-i adabiyāt-i Afghānistān* (Kabul, n.d.), p. 396.
21. V. A. Romodin, "Istochniki *Siraj al-tawarikh*," *Pis'mennye pamiatniki i problemy istorii kultury narodov Vostoka*. Kratkoe soderzhanie dokladov V godichnoi nauchnoi sessii LO IVAN, May, 1969, p. 114.
22. For example, *Sirāj al-akhbār*, Sāl-i panjum, no. 22, p. 12.
23. A. I. Shkirando, introduction to Fayż Muḥammad, *Kniga upominaniia,* p. 18. (Shkirando incorrectly converts 16 S̱awr 1299 as 5 May 1921.) He apparently took this information from Nāyil, op. cit., p. 40.
24. A. I. Shkirando, introduction to Fayż Muḥammad, *Kniga upominaniia,* p. 18. Nāyil, op. cit, pp. 41–42, quotes Ustād Shahristānī as saying that he saw a copy of the work in Fayż Muḥammad's hand in the possession of ᶜAbd al-ᶜAfw Gharqah, later Bāburī, who had taken it from the library of the Ministry of Education (*kitābkhānah-i maᶜārif*) but apparently never returned it.
25. A. I. Shkirando, introduction, p. 17.
26. Ghubār, op. cit., 396.
27. A. I. Shkirando, introduction, p. 17.
28. Ḥusayn Nāyil, op. cit., p. 30.
29. For example, three partial editions of *Sirāj al-tawārīkh* have appeared recently—one from Muᵓassasah-i taḥqīqāt wa intishārāt-i Balkh in Tehran dated 1372–73 (1993–94), another from Argān-i Sayyid Jamāl al-Dīn al-Ḥusaynī, n.p. (Qum?), winter 1372 (1993–94), and the third from the Chāpkhānah-i Ṣadr, Qum, n.d. In the introduction (p. *dah*) to the Argān-i Sayyid Jamāl al-Dīn al-Ḥusaynī edition, the editor says that in 1369 (1990–91) the manuscript copy of the full third volume came into the hands of the press and it is from that and the Kabul edition that he is publishing his version (so far only about a third of the original volume three).
30. *Who's Who*, p. 252.
31. A. I. Shkirando, introduction to Fayż Muḥammad, *Kniga upominaniia*, pp. 11–12.
32. Sayyid Mahdī Farrukh, comp. *Kursī-nishīnān-i Kābul*, ed. Muḥammad Āṣif Fikrat (Tehran: Pazhūhish wa muṭālaᶜāt-i farhangī, 1370 [1991]).
33. Ibid., pp. 252–54.
34. Tehran 1314/1936, second edition Qum, 1371/1992.
35. The original of the *tamlīk-nāmah* is probably in the National Archives. A fold in the document partly obscures the last part of Mīrzā Aḥmad ᶜAlī's name.
36. For a complete listing of his works see Ḥusayn Nāyil, op. cit.
37. *Tārīkh-i ḥukamāyi mutaqaddimīn az hubūṭ-i ḥażrat-i Ādam tā bi-wujūd-i āmadan-i ḥażrat-i ᶜĪsā* (Kabul: Maṭbaᶜ-i Wizārat-i Maᶜārif, 1 Qaws 1302 [20 November 1923]), 189 pp.
38. Ed. ᶜAzīz Allāh Raḥīmī with introduction and notes by Ḥājj Kāẓim Yazdānī (Qum, 1993). The published version represents a later revision of the work used by Mirza ᶜAbd al-Muḥammad.

39. The *Aman al-tawārīkh* has not been published. The rare books collection (Fales Library) of Bobst Library, New York University, has a manuscript copy of the seven-volume work.
40. Fayż Muḥammad, *Kniga upominaniia o miatezhe*, p. 223.
41. See p. 62.
42. My assumption throughout is that A. I. Shkirando, the Russian translator, when using the word "lzhemully" is translating the rhyming phrase "mullāyān-i kāẕibān."
43. The title "Ḥażrat of Shūr (Shor) Bāzār" was held by members of the Mujaddidī family, leaders of the Naqshbandī order in Kabul and descendants of the seventeenth century Naqshbandī thinker, Aḥmad of Sirhind. The title "ḥażrat" literally means "presence" and appears in a number of forms, including "ḥażrat-i īshān" (Their Presence) and "aᶜlāḥażrat" or "ḥażrat-i aᶜlā" (Most Sublime Presence) used as an honorific for royals and for prominent religious figures.
44. Fayż Muḥammad, *Nizhād-nāmah*, p. 57. See Adamec, *Afghanistan's Foreign Affairs*, pp. 152–53, on Lawrence's presence on the Northwest Frontier at this time.
45. Fayż Muḥammad, *Kniga upominaniia o miatezhe*, pp. 24–25.
46. Ludwig Adamec, ed., *Historical and Political Gazetteer of Afghanistan* (Graz, Austria: Akademische Druck- u. Verlagsanstalt, 1985), vol. 6 (*Kabul and Southeastern Afghanistan*) (henceforth *Gazetteer*); idem, *Historical and Political Who's Who of Afghanistan* (Graz, Austria: Akademische Druck- u. Verlagsanstalt, 1975) (henceforth *Who's Who*); and Muhammad Ḥakīm Nāhiż, *Qāmūs-i jughrāfiyāʾī Afghānistān* (Kabul: Aryānā, 1335/1956–1339/1960). Another useful source is Daniel Balland, "Bačča-ye Saqqā," *EIr*, vol. 3, pp. 336–39. In contrast, the so-called autobiography of Ḥabīb Allāh, *My Life: From Brigand to King (Autobiography of Amir Habibullah)* (London: Sampson, Low, Marston & Co., Ltd., n.d. [1936] and recently reprinted) is utterly worthless as a source for the events of the period. It appears to have been written by someone who had never set foot in Afghanistan but collected and expanded various legends concerning the Tājik leader.

Part One

47. The newspaper *Amān-i Afghān* for October 15, 1927, cited by Adamec, *Afghanistan's Foreign Affairs*, p. 113.
48. Fayż Muḥammad seems to have been uncertain about the name of Ḥabīb Allāh's father. First he calls him Hidāyat Allāh, then later Amīr Allāh. In the *Nizhād-nāmah* he calls him Amīr Allāh. Shkirando, the Russian translator, says the father's real name was Hidāyat Allāh (without giving a source) but also notes that in various places he is referred to as Amīn Allāh and Karīm Allāh. (*Kniga upominaniia,* p. 261, note 42.)
49. See Adamec, op. cit., p. 143 and note 55, citing Sayyid Qasim Rishtiya; also D. Balland, op. cit., p. 337.
50. Literally "O Four Friends," a Sunnī war-cry invoking the assistance of the first four caliphs, the legitimate successors, in Sunnī eyes, to the Prophet Muhammad as head of the Muslim community. The analogous Shīᶜī battle cry was "*yā ᶜAlī madad*" ("O ᶜAlī, help us"), or simply "*yā ᶜAlī,*" invoking the name of ᶜAlī b. Abī Ṭālib, son-in-law of the Prophet Muḥammad and, in Shīᶜī eyes, his legitimate successor.
51. On December 18, 1928, according to Adamec, op. cit., p. 143.
52. A Muḥammadzāʾī, he would have been in his early eighties by this time. He had a long record of government service under all the Amīrs from ᶜAbd al-Raḥmān on. Under Amān Allāh he was arrested and his property confiscated in 1920 but by 1922 he was back in favor and power as President of the National Assembly or National Council (*majlis-i shūrā*). He had close personal ties to the Mujaddidī family. Ḥabīb Allāh Kalakānī would put him to death. Ludwig Adamec, ed., *Who's Who of Afghanistan* (Graz, Austria: Akademische Druck- u. Verlagsanstalt, 1975) (henceforth *Who's Who*), pp. 260–61.
53. ᶜAbd al-Quddūs, the son of Sardār Sulṭān Muḥammad, and nephew of Amīr Dūst

Muḥammad Khān, was born about 1845. He went into exile with ᶜAbd al-Raḥmān Khān and after repatriation was appointed deputy governor to Muḥammad Isḥāq Khān, the governor-general of Turkistan. He later became governor-general of Maymanah. Subsequently he served as *īshīk-aqāsī* and was considered one of the most influential sardars of Afghanistan. At the outset of Amīr Ḥabīb Allāh Khān's reign, he was his right-hand man. In 1905, he was appointed prime minister, but his influence and authority gradually declined and by the summer of 1906, for all practical purposes his political career was over and ᶜAlī Aḥmad Khān and Sardār Sulaymān Khān assumed his duties. In 1916, he participated in the sessions of the Majlis-i Shūrā and called for neutrality during the First World War. In 1919, he was again named prime minister. In April 1919 he took part in the fighting on the Qandahar front but was then dismissed and his title, *ṣadr-i aᶜẓam*, became little more than symbolic. He died on March 16, 1928. (*Who's Who,* pp. 100–1.)

54. ᶜUlyā Ḥaẓrat S̱arwat al-Salṭana ("Her Most Sublime Presence, Treasure of Sovereignty"). A formidable woman, she played a prominent political role during her husband Ḥabīb Allāh's reign and after his assassination in 1919 actively worked for her son, not considered first in line, to succeed him. In 1929, she left Kabul with Amān Allāh, accompanying him first to India and then Italy. She died in Istanbul in 1965. (*Who's Who*, p. 257.)
55. A name applied both to the suburbs of Kabul to the south and west and to a village to its southwest. (*Gazetteer,* p. 130.)
56. The text of the decree is published in al-Ḥājj Nangyāl, comp., *Asnād-i tārīkhī Afghānistān* (Peshawar: Bak Agency University, n.d.), p. 19.
57. Maḥmūd Ṭarzī, a Muḥammadzāʾī, was a literary figure, politician, statesman, and advocate of modernist reforms, editor of the newspaper *Sirāj al-akhbār* during the reign of Amān Allāh's father and for a time Amān Allāh's Foreign Minister. (See *Who's Who*, pp. 185–86.)
58. ᶜAbd al-Aḥad, the son of Qāẓī Ghulām, was born about 1880. He received the title *sardār-i ᶜālī* and held the posts of *ᶜarż-begī* and governor of Qaṭaghan under Amīr Ḥabīb Allāh. He and his brother were arrested on suspicion of complicity in the assassination of Ḥabīb Allāh in 1919 but were freed. At the time of the Mangal uprising of 1924–25 he was sent to Wardak to restore order. During Amān Allāh Khān's lengthy European tour, he was governor of the Eastern Province and then was recalled and sent to Moscow to meet Amān Allāh there. During the regime of Ḥabīb Allāh Kalakānī, he backed Amān Allāh's efforts to regain the throne. In 1930 he was elected a representative to the National Council and re-elected in 1934, 1935, and 1936. (*Who's Who*, p. 93.)
59. See above, p. 37.
60. The title "sardār" was the right of members of the Muḥammadzāʾī family. Occasionally, non-Muḥammadzāʾī were accorded the honorary title "sardār-i ᶜālī," perhaps best expressed as "life sardār."
61. ᶜAbd al-Azīz was born in 1876. In 1921 he was appointed minister of court and also held the post of *īshīk-aqāsī mulkī*. In December 1921 he was appointed governor-general (*nāʾib al-ḥukūmah*) of Qandahar and in 1924–25, minister of defense. In June 1925 he became minister of internal affairs, and in November 1928 he was again appointed minister of defense. (*Who's Who*, p. 93.)
62. I.e. Wednesday night.
63. I.e. Wednesday night, January 16.
64. I.e. Thursday night.
65. I.e. Thursday night, January 17.
66. Chaman is the border town (on the Indian, now Pakistani side) on the road between Qandahār and Quetta.
67. The British ambassador, Francis Humphrys, wrote a letter in July to the British Foreign Secretary in which he places himself at the center of the negotiations that led to the transfer of power. On the basis of the letter, Adamec writes, "[he] assumed the responsibility for facilitating the transfer of power." (Adamec, op. cit., pp. 144–45.)

But there is nothing in Fayż Muḥammad's account suggesting any more of a role for the British envoy than relaying the request for airplanes for the transport of ᶜInāyat Allāh and his family out of the country. Humphrys may have feared being accused of "losing Afghanistan" and so, perhaps, justified his role in helping ᶜInayat Allāh leave by evoking the specter of the "destruction of the city and the foreign legations in it" had he not acted.

Part Two

68. *Who's Who*, pp. 124–25.
69. Arthur J. Arberry, *The Koran Interpreted* (Oxford: Oxford University Press, 1964), V:56, p. 108 (henceforth *The Koran Interpreted*).
70. This was Ṣāḥirah "Sirāj al-Banāt" ("Lamp of Daughters," after her father's style "Lamp of the Nation and the Religion"). (*Who's Who*, Table 62.)
71. Ludwig Adamec, *Afghanistan's Foreign Affairs,* p. 121.
72. Maḥmūd Khan Yāwar was a Bārakzāʾī who had served Amān Allāh in a number of roles—as aide-de-camp (whence the title Yāwar) from 1919 to 1920, governor of Kabul in 1925 and 1927, and as partner with Walter Harten on the Dār al-Amān government center. (*Who's Who*, p. 182, has him as Mahmud Jan.)
73. The terms *raīs-i aᶜlā, mukhtār-i muṭlaq,* and *raʾīs-i tanẓīmīyah* seem to be used interchangeably, although the last appears to be the official title for a person sent out to the provinces on an urgent matter for which he had been invested with full power to act. All permanent officials—governors, military commanders, finance officials—became subordinate to a *raʾīs-i tanẓīmīyah.* The term *mukhtār-i muṭlaq* appears in the Russian translation only in this one instance.
74. Samūchhā-i Mullā ᶜUmar lies at the western end of the Lataband Pass (see map) (*Gazetteer,* p. 690). Tangī Khūrd Kābul is a narrow and deep gorge (six miles long and one to two hundred yards wide) that begins about ten miles east of Kabul, about a mile and a half beyond Butkhāk on the Lataband road, and was the site of a massacre of the retreating British-Indian army in 1841. (*Gazetteer*, vol. 6, p. 432.) Chinārī is a camping place between Lataband and Tangī Khūrd Kābul. (*Gazetteer*, vol. 6, p. 139.)
75. Jagdalak lies about halfway between Kābul and Jalālābad, forty-seven miles from the former and fifty-two from the latter (*Gazetteer*, vol. 6, p. 275), at the eastern entrance of another difficult gorge, the three and one-half mile long Jagdalak or Parī Valley (Parī Darra) Gorge.
76. Gul Muḥammad, the son of Tāj Muḥammad Muḥammadzāʾī, was Afghan ambassador to India for all of Amān Allāh's ten-year reign. (*Who's Who*, p. 153.)
77. This would seem to be another name for the Pari Darra or Jagdalak Gorge.
78. ᶜAbd al-Raḥman's father was known as "Chief of the Ghilzāʾī" and had led them against the British in 1879. ᶜAbd al-Raḥman likewise had incited the Shinwārī against the British in 1919. He was rewarded with the title "Khan of the Kabul Ghilzāʾīs" but in 1929, as seen here, shifted his support to Ḥabīb Allāh. He later made his peace with the Muṣāḥibān government and died in 1936. (*Who's Who*, p. 103.)
79. The title is that of a religious figure, traditionally the official who monitored individual claims to sayyidship (direct descent from the Prophet Muhammad). It could also refer to a Sufi leader. For example, the hażrat of Chārbāgh was known as "Naqīb Ṣāḥib." Here the context clearly indicates a figure who enjoyed considerable influence among the tribal rank and file of the Eastern Province.
80. As translated from ᶜAbd al-Raḥman's *Pand-nāmah-i dunyā wa Dīn* by Sultan Mahomed Khan in *The Life of Abdur Rahman Khan*, 2 vols. (London: John Murray, 1900), vol. 1, p. 238.
81. What follows is Fayż Muḥammad's summary of the nineteen points contained in another decree issued by Habib Allah, probably in January. The undated decree is reproduced in al-Ḥājj Nangyāl, op. cit., pp. 33–34.
82. This law (*niẓām-nāmah*) was issued by Aman Allah under the title *Jazā-yi ᶜUmūmī.*

(See Leon B. Poullada, *Reform and Rebellion in Afghanistan*, p. 101.)

83. The legal doctrine followed by most of Afghanistan.
84. *The Koran Interpreted*, II:282. The Russian here actually reads "The new qāżī . . . began to process cases even if there were no great urgency when documentation was missing only relying on the Koranic injunction . . . " yet the sense of the context would appear to be that the qāżī-judge would have ignored the provision, both Koranic and according to customary usage, that called for documentation in his desire to expedite cases in order to collect bribes.
85. Another farman of the period, one which has particular resonance in the late twentieth century, was addressed to the "ᶜulamā, sayyids, shaykhs, khāns, and other subjects of the Eastern Province." It rescinded many of Amān Allāh's policies and is not mentioned by Fayż Muḥammad. It contained ten articles: 1) the abrogation of all niẓāmnāmahs issued by Amān Allāh that were deemed not in compliance with the Sharīᶜah; 2) the re-opening of all religious schools (*madāris-i ᶜulūm-i dīnī*) closed by Amān Allāh; 3) the closing of all girls' schools and all boys schools teaching the modern subjects of geography and mathematics. Boys were to study in the mosques under the authority of the mullas. However, some boys studying telegraph, aviation, and munitions would continue to do so, for these things were deemed necessary for the kingdom of Islām; 4) tax arrears dating from 1919 to the end of 1928, whether agricultural or commercial, were, with a few exceptions, forgiven; 5) the stipends for sayyids, ulama, shaykhs, hazrats and other stipendiaries set during the late Ḥabīb Allah's time but annulled by Amān Allāh were restored; 6) stipends for mosque officials that had not been paid during Amān Allāh's time would be paid by the treasury in accordance with the terms set during the late Ḥabīb Allāh's time; 7) compulsory military service as instituted by Amān Allāh was rescinded; 8) "promoting virtue and prohibiting vice" (*amr bi'l-maᶜrūf wa nahy ᶜan al-munkar*) annulled by Amān Allāh was to be restored as before; 9) permission for the Suhrawardī, Chishtī, Naqshbandī and Qādirī *ṭarīqah*-orders to give instruction, something which Amān Allāh had prohibited, was again granted; and 10) other miscellaneous fees and taxes instituted by Amān Allāh were repealed. After this itemizing, the new amir adds, "in return for these things, I expect your oaths of allegiance." (Copy of undated farman, *Iᶜlān-i sarkārī*, courtesy of Ashraf Ghani and Amin Tarzi.)
86. Burhān al-Dīn Kushkakī, *Nādir-i Afghān* (Kabul, 1310/1931), p. 365.
87. Ibid. Later on Fayż Muḥammad names Sulṭān Aḥmad Khan, the son of Colonel Shayr Aḥmad Khan, as the qalᶜah-begi but does not say when he was appointed.
88. Ibid.
89. Perhaps the author is referring to the stipend associated with the office of deputy minister (*muᶜīn-i wazīr*). Another form in which the term *muᶜīn* appears is in the title "*muᶜīn al-salṭanah*" (Supporter of the State). This was awarded to princes and others closely related to the king. Ḥamīd Allāh, younger brother of the new Amīr, took the title in 1929 and perhaps there was also a set stipend attached to it.
90. The term arbāb was particularly widespread among the Hazārahs as a title of leadership.
91. The Mastūrāt School (*maktab-i mastūrāt*) opened in Kabul in January 1921. On the school and its history see May Schinasi, "Femmes afghanes. Instruction et activité publiques pendant le règne amâniya (1919–1929)," *Annali* vol. 55, fasc. 4 (Napoli: Istituto Universitario Orientale, 1995), pp. 446–62.
92. Another name for the Harten Bridge (Pul-i Artan).
93. *The Koran Interpreted*, V:42, p. 106.
94. According to Adamec, *Afghanistan's Foreign Affairs*, p. 159, the evacuation ended a few days later; on February 24, the French, Italian, and German embassy staffs were airlifted to Peshawar, and on the 25th, thirty-nine British embassy staffers left, including the ambassador, Sir Francis Humphrys.
95. Many foreigners must have remained in Kabul during the Saqqawist nine-month rule. Fayż Muḥammad himself refers to a German adviser to Ḥabīb Allāh; Ludwig Adamec, *Afghanistan's Foreign Affairs*, pp. 169, 179, says that Leonide Stark, the

Soviet ambassador, stayed part of the period and his assistant Col. Ricks assumed his duties after he left, and Adamec quotes a German merchant, Otto Ebert, who spent the entire period in Kabul. A photograph of the reviewing stand at the Independence Day celebrations in August shows a number of men and one woman in European dress among the dignitaries seated to Ḥabīb Allah's right. Dr. Schinasi has identified them as "[Baron] von Plessen, German chargé d'affaires; Yusuf Hikmet Bey, the Turkish ambassador, Ria Hackin; and Hajeb, the Persian chargé d'affaires." (Personal communication)

96. It is not clear what the term "nāẓir" means here. In general it can be translated as "supervisor, overseer." But Fayż Muḥammad seems to have a specific office in mind here.
97. See *Gazetteer,* p. 802.
98. As noted earlier, Fayż Muḥammad had revised or was in the process of revising this part of the work into a more coherent narrative. The Russian translation provides headings (here "Baçça-i Saqqā's army is defeated at Wardak") in this section that are presumably the work of Fayż Muḥammad and part of the format for a restructured work, although without access to the Persian original it is impossible to be sure.
99. Jalrīz and Sanglākh are towns in Maydān. Jalrīz is about halfway to the Ūnay Pass from the junction with the Kābul-Ghaznī road. Sanglākh is on a spur just north of Jalrīz.
100. This Sar Buland would appear to be the "Sarboland Khan" of *Who's Who*, p. 224. He was a native of Arghandah and held governorships under ᶜAbd al-Raḥmān and Ḥabīb Allāh. His son apparently did not rate an entry in the biographies compiled by British intelligence that make up the *Who's Who*.
101. Presumably in place of Sayyid Ḥusayn Chārīkārī.
102. Also known as Doranay, it is located twenty-nine miles from Kābul on the road to Ghaznī. (*Gazetteer*, p. 165.) Dasht-i Tūp (the plain of Tūp, or Top Kalay in Pashto) is in the same general vicinity.
103. From March 30 on, Fayż Muḥammad organized the work by date rather than by topic.
104. The Wazīr and Jadrān are Pushtūn tribes. The Wardak are ethnically more problematic. Their identity at this time was mainly constructed around the claim to descent from the Prophet Muhammad rather than from affiliation to a Pushtūn ethnicity. Fayż Muḥammad himself, in his ethnography *Nizhād-nāmah-i Afghān*, classifies them as one of the groups (*firqah*) "affiliated with the Pushtūns" (*mulḥaqah bi-Afghān*). His description is worth quoting. "This group considers itself sayyids; it comprises ten tribes (*qabīlah*) of 12,500 households." Then after giving the boundaries of the region in which they live (the region known as Wardak) he continues, "The general populace are long-suffering (*zahmatkash wa mutaʾammil wa ṣubūr*) and are farmers. Karīm Khan, hoping that Amān Allāh would arrive from Qandahar on his way to Kabul, fought several heroic battles with the watercarrier's boy. Eventually he was captured and killed. Thanks to his pride and courage, the entire Wardak people enjoy a good reputation and are honored and respected by the government and given high posts." (pp. 129–30) (See also *Gazetteer*, pp. 802–3.)
105. According to British intelligence sources of the time, Beg Samand was a collection of thirteen forts about fourteen miles west of Shaykhābād. Apparently ᶜAbd al-Ghanī's was one of the thirteen. (*Gazetteer*, p. 102.)
106. Fayż Muḥammad in *Nizhād-nāmah* reports that Karīm Khān Wardak was indeed killed by Ḥabīb Allāh but does not describe the circumstances.
107. The bridge was named for Walter Harten, a German engineer who was also responsible for the construction of the Dār al-Amān government complex. In 1929 it spanned the Kābul River to the southwest of the city center.
108. See pp. 97–99.
109. Jāghūrī is a district some twenty-five miles northwest of Ghaznī. (*Gazetteer*, pp. 279–80.)
110. The location of the Majīd (Mājid? Masjid?) Pass and Shaykh Amīr are presumably somewhere in the vicinity of Ghaznī.

111. Kūh-i Asmāʾī or Asmāʾī Hill is the northernmost of the two small mountains that divide Kābul into two parts.
112. The Russian translation consistently spells this “Adgar,” which makes little sense. According to the location given in the text, Dr. Schinasi believes the tower referred to is the Red Tower of the Shahr Ara Palace. According to her, “there is an inscription carved during Amanollah’s time which tells that the palace was built ‘in commemoration’ (*yādgār*) of ᶜAbd al-Raḥman’s arrival in Kabul [in July 1880].” (Personal communication.)
113. See p. 115–16.
114. Mohammed Ali, *Progressive Afghanistan* (Lahore: Punjab Educational Electric Press, 1933), pp. 66–69.
115. See above, pp. 33–34.
116. *Who’s Who*, pp. 109–10.
117. The term is equivalent to minister plenipotentiary. Among other things, it was used for the head of an Afghan diplomatic mission, the ambassador.
118. The British records say he was sent to Chārīkār to raise recruits to help deal with the Shinwārī uprising. *Who’s Who*, p. 109. But see above, p. 34.
119. It is not clear which five branches Fayż Muḥammad had in mind. There is differing information on the branches of the Durrānī, the confederation that had produced all Afghan dynasties until 1978. According to Mounstuart Elphinstone (cited by M. E. Yapp in *The Encyclopaedia of Islam* [Leiden: E. J. Brill, 1965] New Edition [henceforth EI^2], vol. 6, p. 629), the Durrāni were divided into the Zīrak and the Panjpā. The Zīrak included the Popalzāʾī (Fūfalzāʾī), ᶜAlīkūzāʾī, and Bārakzāʾī and the Panjpā included Nūrzāʾī, ᶜAlīzāʾī, Isḥaqzāʾī, Khogānī (not Khugyānī), and Makū. The Achakzāʾī were a branch of the Bārakzāʾī and the Sadūzāʾī and Bāmīẓāʾī were branches of the Popalzāʾī. Daniel Balland, “Dorrānī,” *EIr*, vol. VII, p. 513, more or less follows this division. Louis Dupree, *Afghanistan* (Princeton: Princeton University Press, 1980), follows Olaf Caroe in dividing the Zirak into four subdivisions rather than three, adding the Achakzāʾī. But all these divisions were continually shifting as the fortunes (and numbers) of the members shifted. The five subdivisions of the Durrānī Fayż Muḥammad speaks of here may have been ones he directly associates with Qandahār in his *Nizhād-nāmah-i Afghān*, pp. 55–59. These are the Sadūzāʾī, Popalzāʾī (Fūfalzāʾī), Bārakzāʾī, ᶜAlīkūzāʾī, and Nūrzāʾī.
120. See above, pp. 52–55, for more detail on this episode.
121. According to the Russian translator, who notes, but does not correct, the error, Fayż Muḥammad repeats the date July 10 here and continues the work with the journal off by one day in its Christian date. The Muslim and Afghan calendar dates which he also gives are correct as are the weekday correspondences, allowing for the fact that as was customary in Afghanistan at the time, the day began at sundown of the preceding day on the European calendar.
122. But see below, p. 221, where the author says that ᶜAbd al-Wāsiᶜ was spared and it was the qāżī, ᶜAbd al-Shukūr, who was executed.
123. Burhān al-Dīn Kushkakī, *Nādir-i Afghān* (Kabul: Maṭbaᶜ-i Sangī, 1931), p. 370, identifies the main opposition figures as Jānbāz Khān (perhaps to be identified with Amān Allāh’s governor of Ghaznī who was ousted by Ḥabīb Allāh), Shayr Muḥammad Khān Charkhi, Mīrzā Muḥammad Nawrūz Khān (the Dār al-Amān manager), Ḥājī Muḥammad Nawwāb Khan and his sons ᶜAbd al-Jamīl Khān Kulangārī and ᶜAbd al-Ghanī Khān Surkhābī.
124. Mohammed Ali, op. cit., p. 79, has him boarding the ship Kaiser-i Hind at Nice on January 25, while *Who’s Who,* p. 198, says he left Marseilles by ship on February 8th. Kushkakī, op. cit., p. 346, also has him leaving Nice on the 25th but without indicating the means of transportation. According to May Schinasi (personal communication dated December 14, 1997), no liners left from Nice and he must have traveled from Nice (or his home in nearby Grasse) by train or car to Marseilles.
125. Sardār ᶜAbd al-ᶜAzīz, a Muḥammadzāʾi, had had several diplomatic postings abroad including Rome and Tehran. According to *Who’s Who*, p. 94, he was appointed

ambassador to Tehran in 1927 and relieved in 1928 by Amān Allāh.

126. He may have gotten only as far as India on his way to France if the information about the earlier date of Nadirīs sailing is correct.

127. According to Fayż Muḥammad's introduction to his description of the different Afghan tribes in *Nizhād-nāmah-i Afghān*, p. 52, the Afghans are subdivided into seven branches: Sarbanī, Ghurghushtī, Baytanī, Matī, Sarwānī, Gaṛrānī and Usturāni. (The variant forms given in the text here may be due to the Russian translation.) See also G. Morgenstierne, "Afghān," in *EI*[2] for more on the legendary origins of the Afghans and the lore about the various lineages (there called Sharkhbūn, Kharshbūn, Biṭan, Matī, Ghurghusht, and Kaṛrān) from Qays ᶜAbd al-Rashīd, the mythic common ancestor of the Afghan tribes.

128. Chārāsyā (Chahār Āsyāb) is the first substantial settled area in the Logar heading south from Kabul. In 1914 the area was primarily inhabited by Tājiks and Afghans (Pushtūns). (*Gazetteer*, pp. 126–27).

129. The term *ghulām* at this time meant a bondsman or male slave. The newspaper *Iṣlāḥ* (vol. 1, no. 8, 15 December 1929) reported that he arrived from Chitrāl at the age of 8, probably as a slave. British sources (*Who's Who*, p. 214) identify Panin Beg as "originally from Afghan Turkistan," not from Chitrāl. Whatever his origins, he would pay with his life for supporting Ḥabīb Allāh, being sentenced to death on December 6, 1929 (*Iṣlāḥ*, vol 1, no. 7, 8 December 1929). (For the *Iṣlāḥ* references I am grateful to Dr. Schinasi.)

130. Either the Russian translator or Fayż Muḥammad seems somewhat confused here since Tagāb and its inhabitants were fighting the forces of the amir some sixty miles away by road. The reference here may be to their unwillingness, as residents of Najrāb, Tagāb's neighbor, to go and fight the Tagābīs.

131. W.K. Fraser-Tytler, *Afghanistan* (London: Oxford University Press, 1967), p. 220. Burhān al-Dīn Kushkakī, op. cit, p. 362, says he crossed on the 19th of Ḥūt 1307/11 March 1929. Between pp. 560 and 561, Kushkakī provides a map showing Nādīr Khān's path from the time he crossed the border until October when he entered Kabul and dislodged Ḥabīb Allāh. The same map is found in Mohammed Ali, *Progressive Afghanistan* (in English), and in Anis, op. cit.

132. Kushkakī, op. cit., pp. 377–78.

133. Mohammed Ali, op. cit., pp. 106–7.

134. The first of Ramażān, the date Fayż Muḥammad gives, fell on a Monday. In naming a day, or describing the events of a day, Fayż Muḥammad often begins with the evening or night of the preceding day, i.e. the eve of the day. Here, he simply seems mistaken about the day or the date.

135. The preceding sequence of events is based on Mohammed Ali, op. cit., pp. 113–20. Fayż Muḥammad, whose information is much less coherent but might have been accurate, reports that on April 7, a force led by Nādir Khān had taken up positions on the southern approach to the Tīrah (Altamūr) Pass and, if so, had by then cut Gardīz off from Kabul.

136. Fayż Muḥammad seems to have been somewhat uncertain about the place of incarceration of the Musahiban women, placing them first in Fatḥ Muḥammad's house and then in the Mujaddidīs' custody. In the manuscript from which the Russian translator worked, the name Fatḥ Muḥammad Khān was originally written and then crossed out by Fayż Muḥammad but no other name was substituted.

137. Muḥammad Āṣif was Nādir's paternal uncle and he and his brother, Sardār Muḥammad Yūsuf (Nādir's father), were *muṣāḥibān-i khāṣṣ* ("special companions") to both Amīr Ḥabīb Allāh and Amān Allāh—hence the family name "Muṣāḥibān." (*Who's Who*, p. 123.)

138. A reference to Sardār Muḥammad Yūsuf Khān and Ahmad Shāh Khān, both being present at the place where Ḥabīb Allāh was assassinated. According to British records, Aḥmad Shāh would have been Nādir's cousin (as son of Muḥammad Āṣif), not uncle. He was commander of the guard on the night of Ḥabīb Allāh's assassination. (*Who's Who*, p. 111.) The events surrounding the assassination in February

1919 remain shrouded in mystery.
139. *The Koran Interpreted*, IV:62, p. 81.
140. Mohammed Ali, op. cit., pp. 126–30.
141. In all other references he is called "major general" (*firqamishr*) so perhaps Ḥabib Allāh promoted him.
142. The Russian translation gives the date 13 Shaᶜbān (1347)/25 January (1929), which is clearly an error, probably of Fayż Muḥammad's doing.
143. Another name for Herat Province.
144. Two neighboring districts just south of Jalālābād.
145. See above, p. 105.
146. May 19, 1929 would have been a Monday. The *khuṭba* is the homily delivered at the Friday service.
147. For a markedly different version of this letter see Mohammed Ali, op. cit., pp. 137–40. Kushkaki, op. cit., pp. 459–61 and 466–67 reproduces what he calls two replies from Nādir to Ḥabīb Allāh. The first is dated 26 S̲awr (16 May) and it calls on Ḥabīb Allāh to let a jirgah settle the question who should rule and brushes off the threat to the Muṣāḥibān women. The second, not dated, simply challenges the Amīr to stop the bloodshed and warns him that he will continue to fight for as long as he lives. It is difficult to know what to make of this. The published works that postdate Nadir's success in toppling Ḥabib Allāh are invariably worshipful in their treatment of him and the words they attribute to him are invariably kingly. On the other hand, Fayż Muḥammad's account as it comes to us through the Russian translation is unfortunately not corroborated in any way either.
148. This is probably Sardār ᶜAlī Shāh K͟hān son of Sardār Muḥammad Sulaymān Khān and grandson of Sardār Muḥammad Āṣif Khān, Nādir Khān's uncle. If so this would make them first cousins once removed rather than nephew and uncle.
149. Not detailed by the author but presumably carried by Ḥamīd Allāh on May 24.
150. Anīs, op. cit., p. 232. Mohammed Ali describes the circumstances of the Saqqāwist retaking of Gardīz but does not say when it happened.
151. This is the first time Fayż Muḥammad refers to Sarūbī as a center of Ḥabīb Allāh's pre-amirid outlaw activities.
152. The central market area of old Kabul.
153. In fact Fayż Muḥammad had not mentioned a group of forty prisoners before this.
154. This was the man General ᶜUmar Khān refused to put to death, for which he himself was killed in July. (See above, pp. 77–78.)
155. A sub-district of the province of Kabul. (*Gazetteer,* p. 158.)
156. Muḥammad Ḥakīm Nāhiż, *Qāmūs-i Jughrāfiyā-i Afghānistān*, vol. 2 (Kabul: Aryānā, 1957), p. 418.
157. This would have meant sending them to Bamyan, then south into the Hazārahjāt rather than the more direct route through the Unay Pass where resistance had yet to be overcome.
158. This is the person whom Fayż Muḥammad identifies elsewhere as "Mīrzā Muḥammad Qāsim, an Uzbek and head of a high commission" (*riyāsat-i tanẓīmīyah*).
159. This is one of Chārīkār's 70-odd villages. The *Gazetteer* (p. 131) renders the name Khwaja Siahran Aolia (i.e. Khwājah Sayyārān-i Awliyāᵓ), and says it had about three hundred households of Tājiks living there in the 1880s. Situated two and a half miles south of Chārīkār, it was noted for its *arghawān* (redbud or Judas) trees and up to the present has continued to be the site of the spring festival. (See Nāhiż, op. cit., vol. 2, p. 158.)
160. A mountain ridge with peaks in the twelve- to fourteen-thousand-foot range rises to the west of Shakar Darra (Sugar Valley). Which of these Fayż Muḥammad intended by the term "Kūh-i Katan" (other possibilities from the Russian: Kātan, Kāṭan, Kaṭān, Katan, Kaṭan, Qātan, Qāṭan, Qatān, Qatan, Qaṭan, or Qaṭān) is not known. No maps or gazetteers available to me have this name.
161. *The Koran Interpreted*, V:42, p.106.

162. Ibid., IV:95, p. 86.
163. Ibid., IV:62, p. 81.
164. Ibid., XXXIX:54, p. 477.
165. See below, p. 165.
166. See above, p. 120.
167. Ludwig Adamec, *Afghanistan's Foreign Affairs*, p. 162.
168. Ibid., p. 161.
169. See p. 153–54.
170. Fayż Muḥammad's account here differs significantly from what Ludwig Adamec has published from British archival records concerning the sequence of events relating to Ghulām Nabī's capture of Mazār-i Sharīf in April and surrender of it in June. Fayż Muḥammad has 1) an uprising by the Kuhistanis and an overthrow of Amān Allāh's governor, ᶜAbd al-ᶜAzīz Charkhi, 2) an uprising of Isḥāqzāʾī and Hazārahs against Ḥabīb Allāh's first governor, Khwājah Mīr ᶜAlam, 3) the arrival of Ghulām Nabī and his taking the city, the way prepared by the Isḥāqzāʾī-Hazārah coalition, and his ouster of ᶜAbd al-Raḥīm, a Tajik (although how ᶜAbd al-Raḥīm has gotten into the picture at this point is unclear), 4) ᶜAbd al-Raḥīm's subsequent flight to Herat where he established himself, and 5) the eventual withdrawal of Ghulām Nabī Charkhī (in June apparently) with Sayyid Ḥusayn Chārīkārī occupying Mazār-i Sharīf sometime after this. And somewhere in the midst of this is the appointment of Mīrzā Muḥammad Qāsim Uzbek as military high commissioner.

    Adamec's account puts the taking of Herat later, after Ghulām Nabī's withdrawal from Mazār-i Sharīf. In his sequence (he does not discuss the events before the end of June), 1) Ghulām Nabī takes Mazār at the end of April then abandons it in June when he hears of Amān Allāh's departure for India, 2)ᶜAbd al-Raḥīm comes on behalf of Ḥabīb Allāh and ousts Ghulam Nabī's brother, ᶜAbd al-ᶜAzīz (who has taken over from Ghulām Nabiʾ?), and 3) ᶜAbd al-Raḥīm then gradually extends his control of the north and west outward from his base in Mazār, first taking Maymanah and then Herat. Fayz Muhammad also has Sayyid Ḥusayn Chārīkārī in Mazār-i Sharīf no later than the third week in August but does not tell us when or why he came to Mazār. Fayż Muḥammad does offer a clue in his report of the arrival in Kabul on August 21 of Sayyid Ḥusayn's secretary, a man named Ghulām Qādir, whom he first says brought secret dispatches about the situation in Turkistan, deteriorating, says our author hopefully, because of the resistance being mounted by Hazarah settlers there. But later under August 26 he says that Ghulām Qādir came to Kābul to get instructions for dealing with the Russians and this, indeed, seems like a plausible reason for sending the number two man in the Tajik administration to Afghan Turkistan. The Soviets were certainly interested in the security of their southern border and, although they had not extended recognition to the Tajik regime, it seems very likely that they would have been eager to have contacts with the regime, even if unofficial.
171. Muḥammad Ibrāhīm was an uncle (mother's brother) of Amān Allāh and had held a variety of high posts, including those of *raʾīs-i tanẓīmīyah* of Turkistan and Minister of Justice. As the passage indicates, he was killed in 1929. (*Who's Who,* p. 166.)
172. Ghulām Ṣiddiq, another Charkhī brother, born in 1894, had held many posts under Amān Allāh including that of acting foreign minister (in the absence of Maḥmūd Ṭarzī in Europe in 1927) and that of foreign minister a month before Ḥabīb Allāh's rebellion. He fled with Amān Allāh to Qandahār and spent the rest of his life abroad. (*Who's Who*, pp. 151–52.) For his role in the Shinwari uprising of late 1928 see above, p. 58.
173. Muḥammad Yaᶜqūb, born in 1889, was from the Mohmand tribe. He held a number of court positions under Amān Allāh, including that of Minister of Court. Nādir Shāh did not favor him and after the latter's assassination, his family, linked by marriage to the Charkhis on whom blame for the assassination was pinned, was deported. (*Who's Who*, pp. 266–67.)
174. The minister of war, ᶜAbd al-ᶜAzīz, was a Barakzāʾī sardar who also fled with Amān

Allāh to Qandahar and then India, returning to Afghanistan after the overthrow of the Saqqāwists. (Ibid., p. 93.)

175. Maḥmūd Khān Yāwar, a Bārakzāʾī, was captured by Ḥabīb Allāh Kalakānī but released in August 1929 during the Independence Day celebrations. He worked with the German engineer Walter Harten, after whom the Harten Bridge (Pul-i Artan) in Kabul is named, on the Dār al-Amān project. (Ibid., p. 182)
176. Ḥayāt Allāh Khān, born in 1888, was the second son of Amīr Ḥabīb Allāh. He served as governor of Qataghan during his father's reign but was arrested on charges of corruption and kept under house arrest for a time. In April 1917, he was awarded the title "ᶜAżud al-Dawlah" (Right Arm of the State). He held two ministries during his brother's reign (Education and Justice) but according to British sources was a rather passive figure in Afghan politics. When the Tājiks from the north took over he offered Ḥabīb Allāh Kalakānī his support. His reward was to be executed by the Tājiks in July. His tombstone bears the date 7 Ṣafar 1348/24 Saraṭān 1308 (July 15, 1929). (See M. E. Khalīl, *Mazārāt-i Kābul*, pp. 166–67. I am grateful to Dr. Schinasi for this reference.) *Who's Who*, p. 161, incorrectly gives the date of his death as October 17, 1929.
177. The Russian translation has "tsarevich" which may be a literal rendition of "shāhzādah" or "sulṭānzādah." I have not been able to identify this person, who, judging by his name, is certainly not a Muḥammadzāʾi and probably not even an Afghan (Pushtūn).
178. The very smallest unit of Kabul weight is the *nukhūd*: 24 *nukhūd* = 1 *misqāl*; 24 *misqāl* = 1 *khurd*; 4 *khurd* = 1 *pāw*; 4 *pāw* = 1 *chārak* (*chahār yak*); 4 *chārak* = 1 *sīr*; 8 *sīr* = 1 *man*; 10 *man* = one Kabuli *kharwār*. The *paw* is roughly a pound avoirdupois.
179. Fayż Muḥammad either meant one and a quarter *pāw* of beef with bone or he intended that the weight should be 144 *misqāl* for one and a half *pāw*. But then the phrase "two-thirds of the meat" does not exactly add up either.
180. Later, under the events of April 21, Fayż Muḥammad says that Maḥmūd Khān Yāwar was sentenced to hang but bought himself a pardon for a hundred thousand rupees. (Fayż Muḥammad, *Kniga upominaniia*, p. 98.)
181. The title means "reader, reciter" of the Qurʾān and signifies expertise in one or all of the approved canonical readings of the sacred text.
182. See above, p. 59.
183. Fayż Muḥammad is referring to ᶜAbd al-Raḥmān's war of 1891–93 against the Hazarahs and the evidence of widespread sexual assaults on Hazarah women as well as the fact that Ḥabīb Allāh had at least twelve Hazarah concubines in his harem, some of whom may have been spoils of that war. (*Who's Who*, Tables 64–68.)
184. See p. 98.
185. The shrine, situated on the east slope of the Kuh-i Shayr Darwāzāh in the center of Kābul, was renovated by the first Amīr Ḥabīb Allāh in 1905 and was the Kabul locale for celebrating the spring Redbud Festival. See Nancy Hatch Wolfe [Dupree], *An Historical Guide to Kabul* (Kabul: The Afghan Tourist Organization, 1965), p. 126.
186. The village lies six miles west of Kabul in the district of Paghmān. (*Gazetteer*, p. 137.)
187. The Russian translation is unclear although the issue itself should be fairly straightforward. The crescent or new moon signaling the beginning of the month Ẕū'l-Ḥijjaḥ would presumably have been sighted some eight or nine days earlier. The references to Friday and Saturday would logically therefore be to the preceding week when one or the other would have had to be the first day of the month (when the moon should have been sighted or if not actually sighted presumed to be sighted after the passage of the requisite number of days in the preceding month).
188. The Day of ᶜArafāt refers to the great gathering of pilgrims that takes place in the plain of ᶜArafāt outside Mecca at which specific ceremonies of the hajj (pilgrimage) are performed.
189. By "Foucher François" Fayż Muḥammad probably meant "Foucher, the Frenchman"

(Français), i.e. A. Foucher, the first head of the Délégation Archéologique en Afghanistan (DAFA) and author of a two-volume study of the Hellenic legacy there. The other archaeologist he mentions is Jules Barthoux, who published two volumes on the excavations at Hadda.

190. A deputy or regent, in this context.
191. The context suggests either the Karkchah ridge between Gandamak and Butkhāk, "the last and highest of the [Safīd Kūh] ridges which are crossed on the road to Kabul from Jalalabad" (*Gazetteer*, p. 399), or the Quruq Mountains southwest of Kabul.
192. *The Koran Interpreted*, VI:164, p. 142.
193. See above, pp. 134–35.
194. Shaᶜrbāf means weaver and his son's nickname means "the man who narrates the story of Imām Ḥusaynīs martyrdom at Karbalā like a nightingale."
195. Presumably Fayż Muḥammad means here that they would propose to the amir names of likely candidates for these posts in the Hazārahjāt.
196. *The Koran Interpreted*, LV:60, p. 559.

Part Three

197. For example, Mohammed Ali, op. cit, pp. 66, 91, allots exactly two sentences to their part in the resistance to Ḥabīb Allāh. Muḥyi al-Dīn Anīs, *Buḥrān wa nijāt,* pp. 258–59, has a chapter entitled "Hazārah" but in its two pages gives only the sketchiest information about their activities.
198. Shayr Ahmad (Sher Ahmad), a Muḥammadzāʾī, was appointed President of the National Council (*shūrā-yi millī*) in 1924, at the age of 39. In 1928 he was named Prime Minister. He proved to be a deft politican. He survived Amān Allāh's overthrow and served as an advisor to Ḥabīb Allāh, and later survived Ḥabīb Allāh's downfall and became a high official in Nādir Shāh's government. (*Who's Who*, pp. 241–42.)
199. Mullā Mīr Aqā, a Qizilbāsh from Kābul, will appear again as a member of the delegation on which Fayż Muḥammad himself served. On the basis of the title "mīrzā" and the circumstances, it is highly likely that Muḥammad Ismāᶜīl was also a Qizilbāsh, and he may be the same Muḥammad Ismaᶜīl whose house was torn apart by Ḥabīb Allāh's men in search of money. (See above, p. 155.)
200. In fact this delegation would never be sent.
201. There are two towns called Sar-i Chashmah, one 8.5 miles east of the Unay Pass and the other in Bihsūd, on the west side of the pass. (*Gazetteer*, pp. 701–2.) There is also a valley called Sar-i Chashmah, which lies east of the Unay Pass. The reference here is to the valley.
202. In the Russian translation Aḥmad ᶜAlī is called the son of Sardār ᶜAbd Allāh Khān Tūkhī. I have inserted the 'and' that seems to be required. First, the Tūkhī are Pushtūns, not Hazārahs (Fayż Muḥammad himself was well aware of that fact; see his *Nizhād-nāmah*, p. 98). Second, when the author referred to Aḥmad ᶜAlī earlier (see above, p. 160) he had simply called him a Hazārah from Day Mīrdād. As the passage indicates, ᶜAṭā Muḥammad was also a son of Sardār ᶜAbd Allāh Khān, and while both are mentioned in *Who's Who* (pp. 124–25), there is no indication there of who the second brother, hanged here, might have been.
203. See above, pp. 155–56.
204. *Who's Who*, p. 110.
205. One of the sons is Prince Muḥammad Amīn. Fayż Muḥammad does not mention the other.
206. It is not clear exactly how many men were official members of the delegation. At one point Fayż Muḥammad seems to indicate the delegation numbered ten when he says that Nūr al-Dīn invited the seven Qizilbāsh members who would be in the delegation to his house on June 2. If Nūr al-Dīn is the eighth, and the Tājik "minder" Muḥammad Zaman from Parwān is number nine, then Fayż Muḥammad would have

been the tenth. In the course of his account he does name ten (besides himself, Nūr al-Dīn, and Muḥammad Zamān): Mir Aqā, Muḥammad Mahdī Afshārī, Muḥammad ᶜAlī (nephew of Khānshirīn Khān Jawānshīr), Ḥājjī Muḥammad Yaᶜqūb Khān, Colonel Ghulām Nabī son of Ghulām Riżā, Mullā (Khalīfah) Ghulām Ḥasan, and Mīrza Muḥammad Qāsim. In addition, the delegation took along a group of nine Hazārah schoolboys returning home from Kābul.

207. According to the genealogical charts compiled by Ludwig Adamec as an appendix to *Who's Who*, Muḥammad Amīn was a half brother to Amān Allāh and the son of one of Ḥabīb Allāh's concubines, an unnnamed Hazārah woman. See Table 68.

208. These are the quarters and suburbs of Kābul in which the Twelver Shīᶜite population, both Hazārah and Qizilbāsh, were concentrated.

209. Between 1921 and 1928 he held the governorships of Ghazni, the Eastern Province, Afghan Turkistan, and Qandahar. During the reign of the first Ḥabīb Allāh he had been governor of the Hazārahjāt, which helps explain why Amān Allah sent him there to rally support. (See *Who's Who*, p. 98.) Further on he is described by Fayż Muḥammad as the brother of Mullā ᶜAbd al-Wasiᶜ, who was arrested with ᶜAli Aḥmad Lūynāb at Qandahār and (supposedly) executed in Kabul.

210. *The Koran Interpreted*, XXV:72, p. 368.

211. This sister was Rāziya, known as "Nūr-i Sirāj." She married Muḥammad Ḥasan, a grandson of Amīr ᶜAbd al-Raḥman. (See *Who's Who*, "Genealogies of Afghan Families," Tables 54, 62.)

212. The feast of the 10th of Muḥarram (which would occur June 18) is celebrated by Twelver Shīᶜites as a day of mourning for Imām Ḥusayn (the son of the first imām, ᶜAlī b. Abī Ṭālib), who was slain at Karbalāʾ, Iraq, in 680 C.E. Although the Russian here reads "nephew" (plemiannik) of the Prophet, neither figure was related to the Prophet as a nephew. Ḥusayn was the Prophet's grandson and ᶜAlī b. Abī Ṭālib was both son-in-law and cousin to the Prophet.

213. A building or room for celebrating the mourning ceremonies called *taᶜziyah.*

214. The recitation of the sufferings and martyrdom of Imām Ḥusayn performed during the ᶜAshūrā (Feast of the Atonement) holiday.

215. In Twelver Shīᶜism, "mujtahid" is the generic title for a scholar widely respected for his knowledge of the Koranic sciences.

216. A canonical tax of 20% nominally due to the leader of the community.

217. Another name for a ḥusayniyah.

218. Cf. p. 186, where Fayż Muḥammad names Mīrzā Ghulām Nabī as tax collector (*maʾmūr-i māliyah*) of Behsūd. Perhaps we should understand that Muḥammad Isḥāq had formerly been tax collector and at this time was governor (*ḥākim*).

219. The *taḥṣīldār* was a district revenue officer apparently subordinate to the *maʾmūr-i māliyah*. In ᶜAbd al-Raḥman's time, there was supposed to be one *taḥṣīldār* appointed for every hundred thousand rupees of assessed revenues. (See Hasan Kawun Kakar, *Government and Society in Afghanistan: The Reign of Amir ᶜAbd al-Rahman Khan* [Austin: University of Texas Press, 1979], p 79.)

220. See p. 183, where Muḥammad Ishāq appears to be given this title.

221. A villain in the story of Imam Ḥusayn's martyrdom.

222. The city in Iraq near which Ḥusayn was martyred.

223. In the martyrdom stories, Shimr was the man who actually killed Ḥusayn. His name is synonymous with cruelty and inhumanity.

224. This may have been the same man whose son was arrested in Kābul. (See above, p. 161.)

225. Dakka is a village in the Shakar Darrah district of Kuhdaman. (*Gazetteer*, p. 145.)

226. A region near Samangan and usually considered part of Mazar-i Sharif (Turkistan) province. (*Gazetteer*, vol. 4, pp. 179–92.)

227. From the context, the shrine must have been located somewhere in the Sar-i Chashmah region.

228. I have not been able to locate a village by this name near Jawqul. On Map 9-C in *Gazetteer* (vol. 6), however, there is a Badragha (near Jawqul) which would have

been on an alternate route of retreat for Hamid Allah.

229. This is a transliteration from the Russian. The actual make of bicycle is unknown.

230. See below, pp. 259, 261.

231. This is one of several cases in which Fayż Muḥammad confuses the identities of people he talks about. Earlier (see above, pp. 77–78) he recounts first the beating and imprisonment and then the crucifixion on May 14 of General ᶜUmar Khān the son of Zayn al-ᶜĀbidīn Khān Dāʾūdzāʾī, apparently this same person.

232. A son of Amīr Ḥabīb Allāh, the son of Amīr ᶜAbd al-Raḥman by Shukufa (Shikūfah?) a Nuristāni consort. (See *Who's Who*, Table 66.)

233. See above, pp. 84–85.

234. This is again a case of Fayż Muḥammad (or the Russian translator) providing directly contrary information. Above (p. 84), he says that Mulla, or Mawlawi, ᶜAbd al-Wāsiᶜ was strapped to the muzzle of a cannon and blown to bits at the same time as ᶜAlī Aḥmad Lūynāb was put to death.

235. Shāh Maḥmūd Sadūzāʾī reigned twice in Kābul, from 1800 to 1803, then from 1809 to 1818. (See C. E. Bosworth, *The Islamic Dynasties* [Edinburgh: University of Edinburgh Press, 1967], p. 214.) It is not clear what events or circumstances Fayż Muḥammad alludes to here by invoking Shāh Maḥmūd's name.

236. See above, p. 161.

237. Ḥayāt Allāh was a son of Amīr Ḥabīb Allāh by "Sandal, a Chitrālī consort." (See *Who's Who*, Table 65.)

238. Nāṣir al-Dīn Shāh's forces captured Herat in October 1856 but were forced to relinquish it under the terms of the Anglo-Persian treaty of 1857 negotiated in Paris. During the period of Qājār dominion, the governor of the city was Sulṭān Murād Mīrzā, "Ḥusām al-Salṭanah." With the withdrawal of Ḥusām al-Salṭanah and his force, the terms of the treaty, according to Muḥammad Yūsuf Riyāżī, were that the shāh could appoint as governor one of the Afghan Durrānī sardārs resident in Tehran and so he named Sulṭān Aḥmad Khan, known as "Sultān Khān-i Afghān," son of Muḥammad ᶜAẓīm Khān, older brother of the Afghan Amīr Dūst Muḥammad Khān. (See Muḥammad Yūsuf "Riyāʾzī," *ᶜAyn al-waqāʾiᶜ* [Tehran, 1324/1906], p. 130.) It is Sulṭān Aḥmad Khān that Fayż Muḥammad is referring to here as Sardār Sulṭān Khān.

Part Four

239. The son of Khwājah Jān Ṣāḥibzādah, he had been military governor of the Eastern Province during the last two years of Amān Allāh's reign, then went over to Ḥabīb Allāh. (Information from Sayyid Qasim Reshtiya provided through a personal communication from May Schinasi.) Fayż Muḥammad here gives him the rank "ghundmishr" (brigadier general) but on every other mention of his name he calls him "firqamishr" (major general).

240. The wife's name, according to *Who's Who*, Table 65, was Maᶜṣūmah Rafīq. Muḥammad ᶜAlī was a half-brother of Amān Allāh and the son of a Shighnānī concubine.

241. According to *Who's Who*, p. 103, he was a Jabbār Khayl Ghilzāʾī, a supporter of Ḥabīb Allāh Kalakānī and a man with influence among the Shinwārī. The British understood the Jabbār Khayl to be a branch of the Ghilzāʾī found mainly in the Laghmān Valley. (See *Gazetteer*, pp. 270–72.)

242. This Chārbāgh is apparently in Jalālābād. The *ḥażrat* was a mulla, related to the Mujaddidī family of Shūr Bāzār in Kābul, and was an important part of the mulla network that backed the fall of Amān Allāh and the coup of Ḥabīb Allāh Kalākānī. (*Who's Who*, p. 161.)

243. Alternatively Hindaki. The Russian transliteration of the Persian original admits of either reading. Nancy Hatch Dupree, "Çehel Sotūn, Kabul," *EIr*, vol. 5, p. 115, gives other variants of the name and provides a photograph of the palace, which was situated about six miles south of the center of the city.

244. Perhaps the best known of this group, Naranjan Dās took part on the Afghan side in the Rawalpindi Peace Conference of 1919 at which Afghanistan gained its formal independence. He was also a member of the Afghan delegation to the Mussoorie Conference of 1920, called to settle the final terms for the relations between Afghanistan and Britain. Born in Kabul in 1853, his father and grandfather before him had worked for the Afghan government. He was a trusted civil servant under Amīrs Ḥabīb Allāh and Amān Allāh and eventually rose to the top financial position in the government of Comptroller General (*mustawfī al-mamālik*). (*Who's Who,* p. 207.)
245. As it stands in its Russian translation this sentence is somewhat unclear. Since these are the words of Ḥabīb Allāh, perhaps the "great leader" referred to is the Prophet Muḥammad.
246. The Afghāni, still called a "Kabuli rupee" at this time, was divided into 100 parts (*fals*, *pūl*) and a *qirān* was fifty pul. (Mohammed Ali, *A New Guide to Afghanistan* [Kabul, 1958], p. 280.)
247. Bībi Māhrū, a village at the time, is presently incorporated within the city limits of Kābul itself. It stands on the east side of the city on the road to the new airport.
248. This was the third son of Amīr ᶜAbd al-Raḥmān Khān. He was forty-three years old at this time and had been arrested in January by Ḥabīb Allāh.
249. This was the power station built under the supervision of an American engineer, A. C. Jewett, for Amīr Ḥabīb Allāh, the son of ᶜAbd al-Raḥmān. (Louis Dupree, *Afghanistan* [Princeton: Princeton University Press, 1980], p. 439.)
250. This was Fayż Muḥammad Zakariyā son of Sardār Gul Muḥammad Khān. (*Who's Who*, p. 135).)
251. *Gazetteer*, p. 794.
252. The Koran was used for its intercessory and protective powers, either as a signal of surrender or of a willingness to negotiate.
253. Is this the same "son of Shāh Nūr" who earlier (see above, p. 162) had helped Kākā Muḥsin, Ḥabīb Allāh's governor for the Hazarahjāt, make his way safely back to Kabul? If so, it is not clear why his having stayed the night at Sayyid Abū'l-Qāsim's fort would have given rise to such anger on the amir's part. Below, p. 269, another (?) member of this outlaw family is referred to, Sayyid Aḥmad son of Mīr Muḥammad and grandson of Shāh Nūr, also placed in an anti-Sunnī, anti-government context.
254. Abū Ḥanīfah (d. 767) was the eponymous founder of the Ḥanafī legal school, the legal school of the Sunnis of Afghanistan. He is also known by his given name, Nuᶜmān b. S̱ābit.
255. An authoritative twelfth century Ḥanafī-Sunnī legal manual written by Burhān al-Dīn Marghīnānī as a commentary on another work of his. It was probably the most important legal manual for Ḥanafī Muslims in Central Asia and India and, during the colonial period, was translated into English for British magistrates in India.
256. A town just on the Indian (Pakistani) side of the border in the Kurram Valley.
257. This man should not be confused with Major General (*firqamishr)* Muḥammad Ṣiddīq nor with another similarly named figure with a nasal nickname, Ghulām Ṣiddīq "Manqa" (variant of *minqār*, beak?).
258. Shkirando, the Russian translator, treated the word "Farrāsh" as a proper name but it is possible that Fayż Muḥammad was referring to the office or occupation (custodian) of the Shīᶜites referred to here. (Dr. S. A. Mousavi has informed me that the term would have been reserved for the custodian of a ḥusaynīyah.) Afshar, along with Wazirabad, was one of the best-known Shiᶜite villages of the Kabul suburbs, along with Wazīrābād.
259. A district of Ghaznī province, lying southwest of the city of Ghaznī just beyond the district of Qarābāgh, Fayż Muḥammad's native region.
260. According to *Who's Who*, Table 66, this was a Hazārah *kanīzak* (concubine, consort) named Ḥakīmah.
261. See above, p. 218.

262. A play on the name "nādir" (meaning "rare, unique") by transposing the consonants. In a footnote, the Russian translator says the term is a vulgarity, equivalent in meaning to the Russian "potaskun" (pimp) or "zhulik" (swindler). Perhaps the reading should be "Narād Allāh" or "Narrād Allāh." See ᶜAbd Allāh "Afghānī Nawīs," *Lughat-i ᶜāmyānah-i fārsī Afghānistān* (Kabul: Dawlati Matbaᶜah, 1961), for *narād* meaning a low-life (*rind*).
263. See above, p. 215.
264. The nickname *tūbchī/tūpchī* ("gunner") probably derives from his military service in the artillery.
265. *The Koran Interpreted,* V:42, p. 106.
266. *The Koran Interpreted,* IV:95, p. 86.
267. Sayyid Amīr ᶜĀlim Khān, the last Manghit ruler of Bukhara, had arrived as a refugee in Kabul in the spring of 1921 after the invasion of the amirate by Soviet forces. (See Seymour Becker, *Russia's Protectorates in Central Asia: Bukhara and Khiva, 1865–1924* [Cambridge, Mass.: Harvard University Press, 1968], pp. 303–5.)
268. A garrison village midway between the site of ancient Balkh and Mazār-i Sharīf.
269. The Cafe Wali was a fashionable place on the corner where the Kabul Hotel more recently stood. For a photo of it as it appeared in 1932, see *Salnāmah-i Kābul* (Kabul: Anjuman-i Adabī), facing p. 414.
270. Fayż Muḥammad seems to have forgotten the earlier nickname. Clearly what he seems to have been trying to communicate here was his own great distaste for Nadir ᶜAli.
271. The memoir, *Kitāb-i tazakkur-i inqilāb,* ends at this point, with only the date written down.

Epilogue

272. See Anīs, op. cit, pp. 264–86; Kushkakī, op. cit, pp. 535–63.
273. Adamec, *Afghanistan's Foreign Affairs,* p. 172.
274. Mohammed Ali, *Progressive Afghanistan,* p. 132.
275. According to a later British ambassador in Afghanistan, W. K. Fraser-Tytler, the British government, although officially neutral, was very concerned about the political vacuum they perceived Afghanistan to be and "made up a set of rules to govern the situation. It was unneutral to refuse an Afghan entry into Afghanistan, but once he was in he became a contestant, and it would be unneutral to allow him to recross the border, seeking a brief asylum before plunging again into the fray. And so in a mixture of the rules of cricket and football it was ordained that a player might go on the field once, and play for the crown. But if he was forced into touch, and recrossed the line, whether voluntarily or not, he was 'out' and the referee would not let him back into the game." (W. K. Fraser-Tytler, *Afghanistan,* p. 221.)
276. Kushkakī, op. cit., p. 549.
277. Mohammed Ali, op. cit.
278. Recently published in Ḥājī Nangyāl, comp., *Asnād-i tārīkhī Afghānistan* (Peshawar: Bak Agency University, 1366/1989), p. 37.
279. D. Balland, "Baçça-i Saqqā," *EIr,* vol. 3, p. 338.

Glossary

Government offices, ranks, and official terms

ᶜalāqahdār—Administrator of a provincial district (*ᶜalāqah*).
amīn-i niẓām—Army paymaster.
Amīr—The Afghan sovereign.
arbāb—Headman (a term widely used in the Hazārahjāt).
ᶜarżbegī—Usher, official who receives complaints and petitions at the Ministry of Court.
bandardār—Officer in charge of a customs checkpoint.
birgid-i lashkarī wa kishwārī—"Brigadier of the Army and the Country."
dafᶜahdār—A sergeant in the cavalry.
fawj—Regiment.
fawj-i piyāda—Infantry regiment.
firqamishr—Major General.
ghund—Brigade.
ghundmishr—Brigadier General.
ḥākim—Governor.
ḥawālahdār—Infantry sergeant.
ḥukūmat-i aᶜlā—A province of the second rank (below *wilāyah*).Included Eastern, Southern, Farah and Maymanah Provinces.
idārah-i żabṭ-i aḥwālāt—Intelligence Directorate.
īshīk-aqāsī—Chamberlain.
īshīk-aqāsī mulkī—Chamberlain (civil).
janrāl-i kishwārī—"National General."
janrāl-i tūp khānah—General of Artillery.
kadkhudā—Elder, headman of a village.
kalāntar—Headman of a city quarter or village.
karnayl—Colonel.
kumandān-i kutwālī (qūmandān-i kutwālī)—Commandant of Police.
maʾmūr-i māliyah—Head of provincial tax collection.
manṣabdārā-i niẓāmī—military officer.
mīrākhūr—Chief Equerry.
mudīr—director.
mudīr-i gumruk-i ᶜumumī—Director of Customs.
mudīr-i māliyāt—Director of Taxation.
muᶜīn—Deputy Minister.
muᶜīn al-salṭanah—("Helper of the State," i.e. Deputy Regent) Title awarded to Ḥabīb Allāh's brother, Ḥamid Allāh.

nāʾib al-ḥukūmah—Governor of one of the *ḥukūmāt-i aʿlā.*
nāʾib al-salṭanah—Vice Regent. A title held by Sayyid Ḥusayn Chārīkārī.
nāʾib sipāhsālār—Lieutenant General.
nāʾib sālār-i lashkarī wa kishwārī—"Lieutenant General of the Army and the Country."
nāẓir—Superintendent, overseer.
niẓām-i Harātī—Herat Troop.
qalʿah-begī—Commander of the Citadel or Arg (the residence of the amir in Kabul).
qarāwul—Cavalry scout.
qāżī—Magistrate, judge in a *sharʿī* court (*maḥkamah*).
qāżī al-qużāt—Chief Magistrate.
raʾīs—Headman, chief.
raʾīs-i tanẓīmiyyah—A minister plenipotentiary, high commissioner, usually someone sent from Kabul to deal with a specific problem in the provinces. Provincial officials were answerable to a *raʾīs-i tanẓīmiyyah.*
raʾīs-i aʿlā (wa mukhtār-i muṭlaq)—Another name for the *raʾīs-i tanẓīmiyyah.*
raʾīs-i baladīyah—Mayor.
ṣad-bāshī—Centurion, captain.
ṣadr-i aʿẓam—Prime Minister.
sardār—Chief, headman, the title carried by Muḥammadzāʾī males.
sardār-i ālī (*aʿlā*)—Life Sardar.
sarhang—Colonel.
sipāhi—Sepoy, soldier.
sipāhsālār—General; Field Marshal.
taḥṣīldār—Revenue officer, tax collector.
wakīl—Agent, attorney.
wazīr-i dākhilīyah—Minister of the Interior.
wazīr-i jang—Minister of War.
wazir-i mukhtar—Minister without Portfolio.
yāwar—Aide-de-camp.

Religious titles and terms

Ahl-i Qiblah—"People of the Qiblah," those who face Mecca (the qiblah direction) when praying, i.e. Muslims.
ʿālim (sing. of *ʿulamāʾ*)—A religious scholar, theologian.
ʿĀshūrā—The 10th of Muḥarram, the Feast of Atonement and the date on which Ḥusayn the son of ʿAlīand grandson of the Prophet Muḥammad, was killed at Karbalāʾ.
fatwā—A religious decree or opinion on a point of law.

ghāzī—Defender of Islam, holy warrior.

ḥajj—The pilgrimage to Mecca. One of the five obligations of every Muslim. It consists of a number of rituals performed at and near Mecca on the ninth day of Z̲ūīl-Ḥijja, the last month of the Muslim year.

ḥājjī—A person who has made the pilgrimage to Mecca and performed the prescribed rituals on the ninth of the month of Z̲uīl-Ḥijjah.

ḥaẓrat— "Presence," a term of respect for the most revered of religious personages.

ḥusaynīyah—Building in which the Shīʿī ceremonies of mourning (the *rawzah-khwānī*) for the death of Ḥusayn are held.

ʿĪd al-Aẓḥā (ʿĪd-i Qurbān)—Festival of the Sacrifice celebrating Abraham's willingness to sacrifice Ismāʿīl. It occurs on the 10th of Z̲ūīl-Ḥijja and marks the end of the ḥajj-pilgrimage.

imām—Worship leader at a mosque.

jihād—A struggle in defense of Islām.

kāfir—An unbeliever.

karbalāʾī—A Shīʿite who has made pilgrimage to the shrines of ʿAlī and Ḥusayn in Karbalāʾ and Najaf in ʿIraq.

khums—A canonical tax of 1/5th due the ruler.

khutbah—Invocation for the ruler in the Friday sermon.

khwājah—Often used for a member of the Naqshbandī Ṣūfī order.

mawlawī—Teacher, scholar of the religious sciences, a general term of respect.

mujtahid—The Shīʿī term for a religious scholar.

mullā—A variant form of mawlawi used especially for local religious leaders.

naqīb—A religious title connected with Naqshbandi Ṣūfism.Its precise meaning in 1929, other than as a title of respect, is unclear.

rawżah-khwānī—The recitation of the story of Ḥusaynīs death at Karbalāʾ in 680.

sayyid—A person who can prove descent from the Prophet Muḥammad (d. 632 C.E.).

shaykh—A title of respect for a Ṣūfī leader or head of a shrine family.

takfīr—Declaring someone an unbeliever and therefore removing legal protections of life and property.

yā chahār yār—"O Four Friends!" The Sunnī battlecry invoking the first four caliphs (successors) of the Prophet Muḥammad—Abū Bakr, ʿUmar b. al-Khaṭṭāb, ʿUs̲mān b. ʿAffān, and ʿAlī b. Abī Ṭālib.

yā ʿAlī madad—"O, ʿAlī help us!" The Shīʿite battlecry invoking the name of the first rightful successor to the Prophet Muḥammad, ʿAlī b. Abī Ṭālib, in the (Imāmī, Twelver) Shīʿite view.

zakāt—Alms-tax on income and wealth which theoretically goes for the needs of the poor. One of the five obligations of every Muslim.

zuwwār (sing. *zāʾir*)—Pilgrims, generally for pilgrimages other than the hajj.

Weights, Measures, Units of Currency

ᶜabbāsī—A silver coin.
chāryak (chahāryak)—A unit of weight equal to four *pāw*. Four *chāryak* equal one *sīr* (seer).
crore—Ten million.
fils—One-hundredth of a rupee.
gaz—Unit of length; a pace. There were many different *gaz* measures ranging from 0.6 to slightly over one meter.
kharwār—Unit of weight (literally "donkey-load") roughly equivalent to one-half metric ton.
khūrd—Unit of weight. Four *khūrd* in a *pāw*.
kurūh—Unit of distance equal to 4,000 *gaz*.
lak—100,000 (a unit for counting money).
mīrzā—A title, sometimes indicating a scribal occupation.
mis̱qāl—Unit of weight. 96 *mis̱qāls* in a *pāw*.
pāw—Unit of weight. Four *pāw* in a *chāryak*.
paysā—Pice, equivalent to *fils*.
qirān—50 *fils* or 1/2 a rupee.
rūpiyah (rupee)—The Kābulī rupee was the unit of account. According to MacMunn, the rate of exchange in 1929 was twenty rupees to the pound sterling.
sīr (seer)—A unit of weight. 80 seer equal one *kharwār*.

Miscellaneous

amān-i jān—Guarantee of safe passage, personal safety.
chārpāʾī (charpoy)—A bed. (Literally, "four-legs.")
chūkha—A man's long-sleeved outer garment or cloak.
dasht—Desert, waste ground.
dih—Village.
farmān—Royal decree.
gādī—Horse-drawn buggy.
kūh—Mountain.
kūtal—Mountain pass.
lūyah jirga—National assembly of tribal leaders.
majlis—Session, assembly.
manzil—A stage, stopping-place.
qalᶜah—Fort.
shūrā—Council.
tang(ī)—A gorge, defile.

Bibliography of Works Consulted

Adamec, Ludwig, *Afghanistan's Foreign Affairs to the Mid-Twentieth Century* (Tucson: University of Arizona Press, 1987).

———, ed., *Historical and Political Gazetteer of Afghanistan* (Graz, Austria: Akademische Druck- u. Verlagsanstalt, 1985), vol. 6 (*Kabul and Southeastern Afghanistan*).

———, ed., *Historical and Political Who's Who of Afghanistan* (Graz, Austria: Akademische Druck- u. Verlagsanstalt, 1975).

"Afghānī Nawīs," ᶜAbd Allāh, *Lughat-i ᶜāmyānah-i fārsī Afghānistān* (Kabul: Dawlati Matbaᶜah, 1961).

Ali, Mohammed, *Progressive Afghanistan* (Lahore: Punjab Educational Electric Press, 1933).

———, *A New Guide to Afghanistan* (Kabul, 1958).

Anīs, Muḥyi al-Dīn, *Buḥrān wa najāt* (Kabul: Anīs, n.d.).

Arberry, Arthur J., *The Koran Interpreted* (Oxford: Oxford University Press, 1964).

Balland, D., "Afghanistan. Political History," *Encyclopaedia Iranica*, ed. E. Yarshater (London and New York: Routledge and Kegan Paul, 1989), vol. 1, p. 555.

———, "Baçça-i ṣaqqā," *Encyclopaedia Iranica*, vol. 3 (Costa Mesa: Mazda, 1988), p. 336.

———, "Dorrānī," *Encyclopaedia Iranica*, vol. 7, p. 513.

Bosworth, C. E., *The Islamic Dynasties* (Edinburgh: University of Edinburgh Press, 1967).

Dupree, Louis, *Afghanistan* (Princeton: Princeton University Press, 1980).

Farhang, Mīr Muḥammad Ṣiddīq, *Afghānistān dar panj qarn-i akhīr* (Qum: Muᵓassasah-yi Maṭbūᶜātī Ismāᶜīliyān, 1371/1992), vol. 1, part 2.

Fayż Muḥammad, *Kniga upominaniia o miatezhe* (Moscow: Nauka, 1988).

———, *Sirāj al-tawārīkh* (Kabul: Maṭbaᶜah-yi Ḥurufī, 1333/1915), vol. 3. (Other partial editions of vol. 3: Tehran: Muᵓassasah-i taqīqāt wa intishārāt-i Balkh, 1372–73 (1993–94), Qum?: Argān-i Sayyid Jamāl al-Dīn al-Ḥusaynī, 1372 (1993–94), and Qum: Chāpkhānah-i Ṣadr, n.d.)

———, *Nizhād-nāmah-i Afghān*, ed.ᶜAzīz Allāh Raḥīmī (introduction and notes by Ḥājj Kāẓim Yazdānī, Qum, 1993).

Fraser-Tytler, W.K., *Afghanistan* (London: Oxford University Press, 1967).

Ghubār, Mīr Ghulām Muḥammad, *Afghanistan dar masīr-i tārīkh* (Kābul: Maṭbaᶜah-yi Dawlatī, 1346/1967), vol. 1.

———, *Tārīkh-i adabiyāt-i Afghānistān* (Kabul, n.d.)

Ḥabīb Allāh, *My Life: From Brigand to King (Autobiography of Amir Habibullah)* (London: Sampson, Low, Marston & Co., Ltd., n.d. [1936]).

Ḥabībī, ᶜAbd al-Ḥayy, *Junbish-i mashrūṭiyyat dar Afghānistān* (Qum: Iḥsānī, 1993).

Kakar, Hasan Kawun, *Government and Society in Afghanistan: The Reign of Amir ᶜAbd al-Rahman Khan* (Austin: University of Texas Press, 1979).

Kamali, Mohammad Hashim, *Law in Afghanistan: A Study of the Constitutions, Matrimonial Law and the Judiciary* (Leiden: E. J. Brill, 1985).

Khan, Sultan Mahomed, *The Life of Abdur Rahman Khan* (London: John Murray, 1900), 2 vols.

Korgun, V. G., *Afganistan v 20–30-e gody XX v.* (Moscow: Nauka, 1979).

Kushkakī, Burhān al-Dīn, *Nādir-i Afghān* (Kabul, 1310/1931).

MacMunn, Lt. General Sir George, *Afghanistan from Darius to Amanullah* (London: G. Bell and Sons, 1929).

Morgenstierne, G., "Afghān," *Encyclopaedia of Islam*, New Edition, ed. B. Lewis et al. (Leiden: E.J. Brill, 1960), vol. 1.

Mousavi, S. A., *The Hazaras of Afghanistan* (New York: St. Martin's Press, 1997).

Nāhiż, Muhammad Ḥakīm, *Qāmūs-i jughrāfiyāʾī Afghānistān* (Kabul: Aryānā, 1335/1956–1339/1960), 4 vols.

Nangyāl, al-Ḥājj, comp., *Asnād-i tārīkhī Afghānistān* (Peshawar: Bak Agency University, n.d.).

Nāyil, Ḥusayn, "Pazhūhishī dar bāz namāʾī wa bāz shināsī āsār-i Kātib," *Kitāb* (Kabul), no. 1, 1361/1982.

Olesen, Asta, *Islam and Politics in Afghanistan* (Richmond, Surrey: Curzon Press, 1995).

Poullada, Leon B., *Reform and Rebellion in Afghanistan, 1919–1929: King Amanullah's Failure to Modernize a Tribal Society* (Ithaca: Cornell University Press, 1973).

"Riyāʾẓī," Muḥammad Yūsuf, *ᶜAyn al-waqāʾiᶜ* (Tehran, 1324/1906).

Romodin, V. A., "Istochniki *Siraj al-tawarikh,*" *Pisīmennye pamiatniki i problemy istorii kultury narodov Vostoka*. Kratkoe soderzhanie dokladov V godichnoi nauchnoi sessii LO IVAN, May, 1969.

Rustow, D. A., "Djemal Pasha," *Encyclopaedia of Islam,* New Edition, ed. B. Lewis et al. (Leiden: E.J. Brill, 1978), vol. 4, pp. 531–32.

Schinasi, May, "Femmes afghanes. Instruction et activité publiques pendant le règne amâniya (1919–1929)," *Annali* vol. 55, fasc. 4 (Napoli: Istituto Universitario Orientale, 1995), pp. 446–62.

Tarzi, Amin H., "Fayz Mohammed Kateb, un historien méconnu," *Les Nouvelles d'Afghanistan* (Paris: AFRANE, 1995), no. 70, p. 14.

Wolfe [Dupree], Nancy Hatch, *An Historical Guide to Kabul* (Kabul: The Afghan Tourist Organization, 1965).

Yapp, M. E., "Durrānī," *The Encyclopaedia of Islam* (Leiden: E. J. Brill, 1965), vol. 6.

Index

Abbreviations: Gh. = Ghulām; K. = Khān, M. = Muḥammad; Q. = Qalᶜah-i; S. = Sardār; Sh. = shaykh; b. = brother of; m. = mother of; s. = son of; Haz. = Hazārah; Qiz. = Qizilbāsh